ORESTEIA

AESCHYLUS lived from about 525 BC to 456. Throughout these years there was constant political upheaval in his home city of Athens as well as the threat to all of Greece from Persian invasions in 490 and 480. Aeschylus took part in the fighting and celebrated the final Greek victory in his *Persians* of 472, a uniquely surviving 'historical tragedy'.

Aeschylus competed in the annual dramatic festivals at Athens from about 500 until his death; in this time he wrote, and often produced, about eighty plays, three-quarters of them tragedies, for which he often won the tragedians' prize and which brought him wide fame in the Greek world. Only seven tragedies survive complete; one of these, *Prometheus Bound*, is generally deemed inauthentic. Of the six certain plays, three now stand alone: *Persians*; *Seven against Thebes* (467), the last play of an original thematic trilogy upon the extinction of the royal line of Thebes (the Oedipus-story); and *Suppliant Women* (late 460s), probably the middle play of a trilogy handling dynastic conflict. The other three plays are those of the *Oresteia* (458), the only trilogy to survive from Greek Tragedy, which has been regarded since antiquity as one of its greatest monuments and is the culmination of Aeschylus' dramatic and poetic achievement.

CHRISTOPHER COLLARD was Professor of Classics at the University of Wales, Swansea from 1975 until his retirement in 1996.

OXFORD WORLD'S CLASSICS

*For over 100 years Oxford World's Classics have brought
readers closer to the world's great literature. Now with over 700
titles—from the 4,000-year-old myths of Mesopotamia to the
twentieth century's greatest novels—the series makes available
lesser-known as well as celebrated writing.*

*The pocket-sized hardbacks of the early years contained
introductions by Virginia Woolf, T. S. Eliot, Graham Greene,
and other literary figures which enriched the experience of reading.
Today the series is recognized for its fine scholarship and
reliability in texts that span world literature, drama and poetry,
religion, philosophy and politics. Each edition includes perceptive
commentary and essential background information to meet the
changing needs of readers.*

OXFORD WORLD'S CLASSICS

AESCHYLUS

Oresteia

Translated with an Introduction and Notes by
CHRISTOPHER COLLARD

OXFORD
UNIVERSITY PRESS

OXFORD

UNIVERSITY PRESS

Great Clarendon Street, Oxford OX2 6DP

Oxford University Press is a department of the University of Oxford.
It furthers the University's objective of excellence in research, scholarship,
and education by publishing worldwide in

Oxford New York

Auckland Bangkok Buenos Aires Cape Town Chennai
Dar es Salaam Delhi Hong Kong Istanbul Karachi Kolkata
Kuala Lumpur Madrid Melbourne Mexico City Mumbai Nairobi
São Paulo Shanghai Taipei Tokyo Toronto

Oxford is a registered trade mark of Oxford University Press
in the UK and in certain other countries

Published in the United States
by Oxford University Press Inc., New York

British Library Cataloguing in Publication Data

Data available

Library of Congress Cataloging in Publication Data

Data applied for

ISBN 978-0-19-953781-5

6

Printed in Great Britain by
Clays Ltd, St Ives plc

Preface and Acknowledgements

THE three plays of the *Oresteia* are continuous in plot and closely interconnected; they are the only trilogy which survives from Greek Tragedy. The text is so rich in every way that the *Oresteia* has excited the most detailed technical commentaries and the most profuse critical discussion of any work of its kind from Classical antiquity, more even than Sophocles' *Oedipus the King*; its stature as dramatic poetry is comparable for example with that of *Hamlet* or *Faust*.

All these qualities dictate the character of this volume, in particular Explanatory Notes much fuller than are usual in this Series. I have been as factual and objective in these as I can. From a strong belief that the *Oresteia* should in the first instance be interpreted from within itself, I have provided a large number of cross-references to the play-texts; I hope that readers will be able to let their eyes slide past them if they wish, particularly in the Introduction itself. I have wished not to slant either Introduction or Notes towards any one critical approach; instead, the Introduction offers a selection of references to secondary literature given in the Bibliography and Further Reading; many of the works listed there orientate readers among both older and newer interpretations. Because of the trilogy's complexity I also preface the Introduction with a detailed summary of the stage-action.

I thank Hilary O'Shea of Oxford University Press for the initial idea of attempting this high peak of world drama, as astonishing to me as it was irresistible. She and her colleague Judith Luna combined patience with goodwill during my slow climb.

I am grateful to the Principal and Fellows of St Hilda's College for generously accommodating me in the room where I did most of the work when I was not diverted by its wonderful view of the Oxford skyline.

My very warm thanks for reading parts of the Translation and

Notes in differing stages of draft go to Ruth Bardel, Shirley
Barlow, Cecilia Hewett, Bill Race, and Chris Stray, and for
reading all of them to James Diggle and James Morwood. The
Introduction was beneficially read by Doreen Innes, †Kevin Lee,
and James Morwood. The help and encouragement which I had
from all these readers were very great. They persuaded or
enabled me to rethink and to rephrase, and offered many
suggestions. Brian Taylor most kindly read a proof. Jean gave
a wife's loving support—and also improved parts of the translation.

Oxford 2001   Christopher Collard

Contents

Abbreviations: Play-Titles and Works Frequently Cited

Ag.	*Agamemnon*
LB	*Libation Bearers* (Greek *Khoephoroi*, Latin *Choephori*)
Eum.	*Eumenides*
Seven	*Seven against Thebes* (Greek *Hepta epi Thebas*, Latin *Septem contra Thebas*)
Suppliants	*Suppliant Women* (Greek *Hiketides*, Latin *Supplices Mulieres*)

The titles of *Persians* (Greek *Persai*, Latin *Persae*), *Prometheus Bound* (disputably authentic) and fragmentary plays are not abbreviated.

CCGT	P. E. Easterling (ed.), *The Cambridge Companion to Greek Tragedy*, 1997
CHGL	P. E. Easterling and B. M. W. Knox (eds.), *Cambridge History of Classical Literature, I: Greek Literature*, 1985
Csapo-Slater	E. Csapo and W. J. Slater, *The Context of Ancient Drama*, 1993
Rosenmeyer, *AA*	T. G. Rosenmeyer, *The Art of Aeschylus*, 1982
Sommerstein, *AT*	A. H. Sommerstein, *Aeschylean Tragedy*, 1996
Taplin, *Stagecraft*	O. P. Taplin, *The Stagecraft of Aeschylus*, 1977

Summary of the Stage-Action

AGAMEMNON

THE play is set before the palace at Argos of King Agamemnon. For ten years he has been leading the Greek forces besieging Troy. We learn as the play unfolds that Clytemnestra his wife has betrayed him by adultery during his long absence; with her lover Aegisthus she has usurped his power and now plots his murder.

In the play's prologue a Watchman receives a night-beacon signal that Troy has fallen. Agamemnon's return can now be expected; later it is confirmed as imminent by a Herald. The Chorus of elderly Argives still faithful to Agamemnon fear what Clytemnestra may intend against him. In their opening lyrics they review his family's ominous history, a past which adds to their fear for him now: Paris of Troy did wrong against Greece in abducting Helen, wife of Agamemnon's brother Menelaus; he was Menelaus' guest at the time, and thereby offended the supreme god Zeus, who oversees the laws of hospitality. Agamemnon has now punished Troy with Zeus' aid, yet he had also to sacrifice his own daughter Iphigenia in order to placate another god's opposition, that of Artemis. For this crime, both involuntary and voluntary, he must pay, the Chorus imply, just as Troy inescapably paid for the sin of Paris, and pay with his own life. Clytemnestra's long-established dominance cows the Chorus, however, and they lose all courage either to thwart her suspected intentions or to warn Agamemnon explicitly against her hypocritical welcome.

After the Herald confirms the victory at Troy, and its cost in suffering, Agamemnon enters royally in a chariot which carries also the Trojan princess and prophetess Cassandra, a spoil of war and now his bedmate. His reunion with his wife is chilling: he is detached, she is fulsome. Then, in a starkly brief conflict of wills, Clytemnestra overrides his moral discomfiture and induces him to enter the palace, treading ominously over sumptuous and

purple fabrics which she spreads in his path. Cassandra is silent
throughout this dangerous scene; she also silently defies Clytemnestra's command to go in herself, and the queen retires baffled.
Cassandra does enter, but first she breaks into riddling prophecy
of her own and Agamemnon's murder once they pass the palace-
door. Despite the doom set on her by the god Apollo that her
prophecies should never be believed, she appals but convinces
the Chorus with accurate visions of the ancient and hideous
bloodshed in the palace, the children of Thyestes slaughtered by
his brother Atreus, Agamemnon's father, and then served to
Thyestes as meat. There is now a demon of bloody vengeance, a
Fury, in the house which will strike Agamemnon down;
Clytemnestra's lover Aegisthus, who is Thyestes' son, shares
her murder-plot against Agamemnon as a way of avenging his
father. At the prospect of further blood and horror the Chorus
are stirred to renewed opposition, but they cannot prevent the
two murders inside the palace.

Clytemnestra displays the bodies, covered by robing in which
she trapped Agamemnon during his bath before killing him. Her
long and loud triumph over the bodies—she has punished
Agamemnon for the sacrifice of their daughter Iphigenia, and
to have killed his bedmate Cassandra adds to her relish—
dwindles when the Chorus forecast that the family demon will
claim her life too. She is joined on stage by the preening but
weak Aegisthus, and the Chorus start to offer resistance: they
warn that Agamemnon's son Orestes will come home from exile
for vengeance upon both. The murderous pair assert a thin
confidence, and the play ends in uneasy tension, foreshadowing
further tragedy.

LIBATION BEARERS

The second play is again set at the palace, but some long time
later. It begins with Orestes' return to avenge his father; his
friend Pylades is with him. He lays a devotional lock of hair on
Agamemnon's tomb; then, unseen, he watches his sister Electra
and the sympathetic Chorus of her slave-women bearing libations to the tomb from Clytemnestra; she has sent these gifts to
avert a dream figuring her son's vengeance. Electra and the
bearers, however, offer the libations with a prayer that Agamem-

non will instead assist his son from beyond the grave. When Electra finds the lock of hair, Orestes reveals himself and describes the god Apollo's oracular command that he shall avenge his father upon his mother. Then, by singing together a great Incantation for Agamemnon's help, his sister and the Chorus join him in nerving himself to the matricide. Orestes is encouraged by the details of Clytemnestra's dream: she gave birth to a snake which then drew blood from her breast—just as Orestes intends to draw it, the child she bore and suckled. He will trick his way into the palace; Electra's part is merely to keep watch and warn, and she goes inside, not to be seen again.

The vengeance begins. Unrecognized in his guise as a traveller, Orestes deceives Clytemnestra into offering hospitality by falsely reporting his own death; the deception allays the fears caused by her dream. Orestes' old Nurse trusts the news too; she laments her lost darling and so is credibly persuaded by the Chorus to modify the message she carries from Clytemnestra to Aegisthus: he is to come to the palace, to hear the comforting report confirmed in detail, but without his guards. He arrives and is summarily killed inside; Clytemnestra and then Orestes come out and he confronts her with dripping sword. He has a crisis of sudden hesitation, but the long-silent Pylades in his only spoken words reminds him of Apollo's command. Orestes drives his mother in to be killed but, ominously, her last words warn him of inevitable persecution by her Fury-hounds.

In a scene which mirrors Clytemnestra's own display of the murdered Agamemnon and Cassandra, Orestes is shown standing triumphant over the bodies of his mother and Aegisthus; and they are covered by the same robing. The triumph is again brief, however: Orestes is already slipping into madness, the symptom of endless torment by his mother's Furies, and amid hallucinations of their grim presence he rushes away to refuge in Apollo's temple at Delphi.

EUMENIDES

The final play begins at Delphi, in front of the temple, the seat of Apollo's ancient oracle. His Prophetess makes a terrified discovery: the Furies are within the temple, asleep but surrounding Orestes. While they still sleep, Apollo himself brings Orestes outside and orders him to seek sanctuary in the goddess Athena's temple at Athens; he will present Orestes' case there and win a judgement freeing him from the Furies. After Orestes leaves, Clytemnestra's ghost appears; she wakes the Furies and accuses them of idleness in hounding her matricidal son; they regroup (forming the play's 'chorus'), sing of their renewed determination against Orestes, and argue Clytemnestra's cause against Apollo before pursuing Orestes to Athens.

The scene changes to the Athenian Acropolis, where Orestes formally supplicates the absent Athena's protection before the Furies again close round him, this time with a harsh binding-song. Athena appears, and learns the identities and claims of her suppliant and his persecutors. She announces that the matricide is too large an issue even for her to decide, and that she will refer it for judgement by her Athenian citizens, in a jury-court which she will institute especially but which is to serve the city for ever. The Furies sing of their alarm that Orestes might escape their own ancient and unquestioned justice through this unheard-of process. A crowded and powerful scene, to be imagined now on the Areopagus-hill near the Acropolis, begins the trial: Athena presides over citizen jurors; the Furies are one party-at-law, Orestes the other, and they have an initial altercation—but Orestes is then joined by Apollo, who takes over his case. Athena again ordains that her new court on the Areopagus shall last for all time, a precedent and model for civic justice. After the jurors' votes are cast, she announces that she will vote for Orestes and that he shall go free if the tallies are equal. They prove to be so; Orestes rejoices, promises his own and his city Argos' eternal gratitude and alliance with Athens, and leaves for home.

The Furies must now abandon their persecution of Orestes; they remain where they are, however, angry and vindictive towards Athens, but the goddess gradually conciliates them. She promises them a permanent cult and underground home near the Areopagus; they shall remain dread but respected powers, deterring fratricidal and civic conflict but also securing fertility of land and body for her law-abiding people. Play and trilogy end with celebratory processions, as the Furies begin the role at Athens in which they will become known as the Eumenides, the 'Kindly Ones'.

Introduction

1. AESCHYLUS AND THE *ORESTEIA*

THE immediate emotional responses of Aeschylus' original theatre audience might have differed little from ours: tense expectation; quick surrender to the drama's inevitable momentum, once the Watchman's prologue foreshadows Agamemnon's return and Clytemnestra's plans against him; enthralment to the vivid and often majestic poetry. In some important respects, however, his audience entered the theatre with a quite different preparedness. The evidence we have is that until a generation or so after Aeschylus' death in 456 BC, all plays produced in the great city-festivals at Athens were not just first but also sole performances. Hardly any spectator, and probably not even all the performers, would have had access to a written play-text, either before or even after the production; but many of the audience would have known the play-titles in advance and some would have seen 'trailers'; they could therefore make a good guess at the content. Expectation of the plot, from a familiar myth (see §2.1 below), brought some degree of emotional anticipation as well; but each fresh dramatization nevertheless invited variations in detail and emphasis, with continuing scope for surprises to both emotions and intellect. The *Oresteia* had many such effects, like the confrontation of Agamemnon and Clytemnestra, Orestes' sudden hesitation before the matricide, the casting of the Furies as play-characters, the move of scene to Athens, and the argumentation of the jury-trial.

Next, attendance of the modern theatre is a deliberate, paying choice by individuals, who can select from a variety of plays and dates; but Aeschylus' audience gathered in huge numbers for open-air performance as part of annual religious and civic festivals, of which the most important for Tragedy was the Great or City Dionysia: the god Dionysus was honoured with music, dance and poetic drama and song, and poetry. The celebration was strongly formalized, and much was traditional; it was 'political', in the Greek sense that it demonstrated the communal values of the *polis*; and the audience fully represented those who voted citizens into political office and took political decisions. Through the middle of the fifth century the Great Dionysia came increasingly to focus and display the ethos of a proudly democratic but frequently self-questioning city. Some parts of the festival programme, like the theatre-parades of war-orphans and, later on, of the annual money-tribute from Athens' allies, registered in the most public and effective way the costs and gains of the city's international prominence; the performances themselves proved the riches of its artistic superiority; the poets and performers competed for 'victory' and 'rank' in public esteem.[1]

The tragic poets found ways to link the commonest theme of myth, family-lines and their preservation, with the 'political' phenomena of contemporary Athens. The mythic families and particularly their male heads provided parallels and scene for the real-life city's chief concerns, stability and morality in all its conduct, in the home and in public decisions. All six of Aeschylus' certainly authentic tragedies portray the dangerous burdens of leadership: the disastrous ambition of kings in *Persians* (this is the only surviving 'historical' Greek tragedy); inexorable dynastic conflict in *Seven*; the imperatives of maintaining a royal blood-line in *Suppliants*—and all of these issues in the *Oresteia*. Yet *Eumenides* shows something greater still, of intensely Athenian significance. Here, a mythic family's internal conflicts, which both uphold and threaten the gods' own justice, are resolved by gods and men together, in Orestes' jury-trial, not through divine will alone. Aeschylus offers this unprecedented means of resolution as a founding emblem of Athens' moral and political ethos, the rule of communal law which had been first securely established only in very recent years. He persuaded his original audience that the stage-jurors were their own historical

---

[1] The 'civic ideology' manifested in the Dionysiac festival is emphasized in much recent writing: see especially the various papers in Winkler and Zeitlin and Goldhill and Osborne in Bibliography §5; and P. Cartledge, S. Goldhill, and P. E. Easterling in *CCGT* 3–68, three chapters pursuing the topics of my paragraph; also, E. Hall, pp. 93–126 of the same volume, contributes a 'sociology' of tragedy at Athens; see most recently the exchanges between J. Griffin, R. Seaford, and S. Goldhill (1998–2000), also in Bibliography §5. The documentary evidence is given by Csapo–Slater, 17–18.

forebears: they should see themselves in their image, Athenians assembled under a god within the play for the great purpose of civic justice, even as they had themselves assembled in the theatre for a great religious and civic occasion. Many of the audience served as jurors in the Athenian courts; some of them would belong to the very court of the Areopagus-Council which the city's patron-goddess Athena sets up in the play's mythic setting but which is to last for all time (*Eum.* 484, 683–4). The innovation is seized upon by the Furies as dangerous to their age-old prerogatives; contemporary members of the Council would be brought to reflect hard upon recent reforms to their own powers (see below).

There is nevertheless a long-standing argument, whether and how much the tragic poets played to their audience in 'political' terms; for comedy had a place in the same festivals and in the fifth century often became a drama of political satire and travesty. If the tragedians drew upon native Athenian myths, especially those which featured the city's past as springboard for its present democracy or its professedly altruistic role in wider Greece, were they merely aiming for applause and victory in the dramatic competition? Were they simultaneously encouraging communal pride? Or were they disinterestedly inviting their fellow citizens to examine current but timeless issues against a mythic precedent? In the half century after Aeschylus' death one poet at least used myth more actively in these last two ways— Euripides. His plays, which survive in greater number than those of Aeschylus and Sophocles, afford good evidence (and are supported by his fragmentary plays, also the most numerous); no plausible case has been made for any overt, let alone sustained, political purpose in Sophocles, despite his prominence in public life, even if he regularly touches upon topics of moral, social, or 'political' importance.[2]

Half of Aeschylus' surviving plays have a direct Athenian

---

[2] Two plays of Euripides in particular, *Children of Heracles* and *Suppliant Women*, invite the audience to examine issues both internal to Athens and timelessly universal, and this around 430 BC, a period in which Athens' domestic constitution and her policies towards both allies and opponents were under strain, in the first phase of the great Peloponnesian War recorded by Thucydides. In many plays Euripides accommodates within the mythic setting quite large-scale and probing debate in contemporary rhetorical mode upon such issues as women's experience and role (e.g. *Medea*), power-politics (e.g. *Phoenician Women*), and political expedience (e.g. *Hecuba, Trojan Women*).

bearing. The 'historical' *Persians* gives a measured prominence to Athens' part in the Greek victory at Salamis in 480 BC. In *Suppliants* the surprising 'democratic' decision-making of mythic royal Argos seems to resemble that of the kingly but proto-democratic Athens so attractive to Euripides in his much later *Suppliant Women*. It seems to reflect, if not actually to commend, the correctness of having such an Argos as an ally for Athens in the years of its production, the 460s; with easy naturalness too the poet moves his contemporary world into the mythic one, bringing life to both.[3] *Eumenides*, however, is distinctive in all surviving Greek Tragedy for the 'relevance' of its Athenian episodes to what we know of contemporary political developments. It is however very difficult to judge whether Aeschylus' purpose is programmatic or biased in any one direction. The temptation to think this is perhaps increased by the sharp break between the first two plays of the trilogy and the third—the shift from Argos, where the stage is peopled throughout by mortal and very apprehensive persons, to Delphi and then Athens where Orestes is the only mortal speaking among gods; yet in Athens he is saved through a judicial mechanism, instituted by god but dependent upon living men, which was not only extant in real life but a focus of recent reform.

The principal considerations are these. A few years before the *Oresteia*'s first production in 458 BC, Ephialtes and the much younger Pericles began to establish more democratic institutions in Athens. By 462 or 461 they had curtailed the powers of the Council of the Areopagus. In the misty past this was apparently a consultative body of nobles; later it became a conservative, almost oligarchic, college of former office-holders and magistrates which perpetuated a second, acquired role of overseeing the constitution; so it was *de facto* a powerful but not all-powerful source of political influence or initiative. Earlier democratization, while Aeschylus was young, had in fact started the Council's decline, not least through changed electoral processes dependent largely upon lot rather than voting. Yet one of its earliest temporal powers survived, its judicial authority in cases of homicide, above all family murder. So Aeschylus may have

---

[3] Good reviews of Aeschylus' 'politics' are offered by Macleod (Bibliography §7), 20–40 and Sommerstein, *AT* 393–421; for the issues both timeless and immediate raised by his plays see *AT* 423–43.

been endorsing its new if limited status when he shows Athena,
the city's patron-goddess, as its foundress in precisely that
function, and in some sense he comforts the aristocratic interest
with which it continued to be associated, for he reinforces its link
with the deterrence of anarchy and despotism (*Eum.* 696–8), a
general role already claimed by the Furies and now to be taken
in Athens itself (517–21, 976–83, etc.).[4] Another of Ephialtes'
policies was to shift long-standing aristocratic support at Athens
away from conservative Sparta towards Argos. When Argive
Orestes and then his protector the god Apollo promise future
alliance between the two cities, if he is saved in Athens
(*Eum.* 289–91, 667–73), and Orestes then confirms it (762–6),
is Aeschylus merely anchoring a real and recently accomplished
treaty in mythic precedent, or is he lending his poetic support to
its desirable adoption? In the dramaturgy Athena on Athens'
behalf prudentially accepts Argos as ally because Orestes, its new
king, is now freed of the moral taint endangering his royal house
(474, cf. 798–9). Further, as Athena accepts Argos in a
rehabilitated Orestes, so she also welcomes the Furies to their
permanent cult in the city, as her fellow-residents (833, 855–6,
etc.; the Furies agree at 916, 1018).[5] She persuades them to
continue their age-old deterrence of all wrong, especially of the
murder which is most destructive of civic and political stability,
the killing of kin (517–37 and 976–83 again; also 858–66, 956).
They are to be guardians and guarantors of the communal
prosperity which goes with communal morality (902–10 etc.,
984–95); their role will again be in parallel with the human
Council.

For the original audience contemporary political circumstances therefore made the ending of the *Oresteia* specially
significant; and the whole trilogy's mythic grandeur would

[4] For a recent and judicious assessment of the political counterbalances in *Eumenides*,
and the conclusion that they reveal no particular attitude in Aeschylus, see Pelling,
Bibliography §5 (2000), 164–88, at 167–77. Most recent writers take a similar position,
e.g. Conacher (1987), 197–206, in Bibliography §3.2, Podlecki (1999) in §6.1, Bowie
(1993) in §7, and Sidwell (1996) in §8.3; Macleod (previous note) and Sommerstein, *AT*
392–403, 413–21, esp. 402, see quite positive support of the democracy. In general, cf.
also Wilson, Bibliography, §5, (2000), 117–20.

[5] For the Furies/Erinyes and their cult on the Areopagus at Athens as the 'Semnai' or
'Awesome Ones' see Sommerstein, *Eumenides* (1989), 10 (Bibliography §3.2). R. Parker,
Athenian Religious History (1996), 130, describes the Areopagus as 'a kind of citadel of
reverent fear'.

have increased its impact. Not only did it win Aeschylus the tragedians' prize for the year, but it achieved lasting fame. We find widespread echoes and apparent reflection of the trilogy in Sophocles' and Euripides' Electra-plays, both of which dramatize the vengeful killings of Clytemnestra and Aegisthus differently, and to a smaller extent in Euripides' *Iphigenia in Tauris*, which develops Orestes' story after the matricide very differently from that in *Eumenides* (cf. also §2.1 below, on the vase-paintings). It quickly became part of Athens' conscious heritage; it seems to have had the exceptional honour of being revived in the theatre during the final years of the fifth-century Athenian democracy, and there were revivals in the fourth century. Most importantly, the three plays eventually entered later antiquity's select corpus of Greek Tragedy for literary education. They became primarily texts for reading, an uncertain destiny from which only good fortune preserved them to our own day, and from which only our own day has restored them to the stage (see §4 below).[6]

2. A VIEW OF THE *ORESTEIA*

2.1. The dramatic ideas and their sources

Many of Aeschylus' plays dramatize mythic incidents for which Homer is the earliest evidence.[7] The *Odyssey* in a few places recounts the death of Agamemnon and the vengeance of Orestes upon both Aegisthus and Clytemnestra, sometimes with slight variation or addition. Many of these Homeric details were perhaps developed before Aeschylus by other poets now lost, especially the lyric poet Stesichorus in the generation before him: an ancient commentator records that this poet 'used narratives and most of the other poets used his material; for after Homer and Hesiod they agree above all with Stesichorus'; his own *Oresteia* was a lyric narrative, but only a few lines or words survive.

Aeschylus may have drawn upon, or modified, Homer for

---

[6] Revivals: Csapo–Slater, 12; later performances: Easterling *CCGT* 213; educational curriculum, ibid. 225. For Aeschylus' manuscript history see 'Note on the Text' below.

[7] See Sommerstein, *AT*, ch. 10, 'Slices from Homeric feasts'—a title allegedly reflecting Aeschylus' own description of his indebtedness. Full recent documentation of mythic sources in T. Gantz, *Early Greek Myth* (1993).

some important ideas, in particular the continuous theme of sin committed despite divine forewarning and inevitable punishment by the gods: Homer exemplifies this right at the start of the *Odyssey*, in the case of Aegisthus determinedly killing Agamemnon (Book 1.35–43). Homeric origin or influence may lie behind the following elements:

In *Agamemnon*: Agamemnon is a victim of Helen's and Clytemnestra's wickedness, a sign of Zeus' hostility to him, *Od.* 11.435–9 (reflected throughout the play but especially in 1448–68, 1481–1503, 1541–6 once Cassandra has prophesied at 1223–38, 1245–52). Despite Agamemnon's good qualities, he is victim also of a fate from which the gods cannot save him, *Od.* 3.234–8 (cf. e.g. *Ag.* 1335–42 and 1560–4). The spy set (by Aegisthus) to watch for Agamemnon's return (*Od.* 4.524–9) becomes Clytemnestra's Watchman, giving her time to prepare her plot (*Ag.* 1–11, 34–9; cf. 1374–8)—but the plot in Homer is largely Aegisthus': 1.300, 4.525–31, (at a banquet) 11.410. Agamemnon brings Trojan Cassandra with him, and she becomes the pitiable victim of Clytemnestra, *Od.* 11.421–3 (cf. *Ag.* 1069–71, 1295–9, 1438–47).

In *Libation Bearers*: Clytemnestra refuses Agamemnon a proper funeral, prompting his children's even more bitter anger, 429–50, cf. 87–99, *Ag.* 1543–6: at *Od.* 11.424–6 she would not even close his eyes in death. Aegisthus' suppression of Agamemnon's former subjects (*Od.* 3.304–5) is a further cause of Orestes' anger, *LB* 302–5, 974.

In both *Libation Bearers* and *Eumenides*: Orestes returns from abroad for revenge, but in Homer he returns from Athens, *Od.* 3.306–8.[8] This tiny detail may have prompted Aeschylus to elaborate the trial-scene there—indeed an ancient 'introduction' to *Eumenides* states that it is found in no other poet (see the start of the Explanatory Notes to the play).

As to Stesichorus, Aeschylus appears indebted for Orestes' lock of hair (Fragment 217: *LB* 6–7, 168 ff.), Clytemnestra's nightmare of the bloody snake (Fragment 219: *LB* 523 ff., cf. 32–3) and perhaps Orestes' nurse (Fragment 218: *LB* 731 ff.)— but this figure is developed by Pindar in *Pythian* 11.17 ff., a lyric

---

[8] The ultimate model for an avenger returning in disguise (Orestes in *Libation Bearers*) is Odysseus himself. This plot-line is quite common in Tragedy: see Burnett (1998), Bibliography §5.

poem a little earlier than the *Oresteia*; Aeschylus may have found
a model in Odysseus' old nurse Eurycleia at *Od.* 19.353 ff., 471–
2 for the fond recollections at *LB* 749–62.

Vase-paintings certainly datable before the *Oresteia*'s first
production in 458 BC are not numerous, some of them may
reflect elements from earlier but now lost poets and appear only
by the accident of survival to have given this or that idea to
Aeschylus. Most suggestive is an Attic red-figure wine-bowl of
about 470 BC which shows Agamemnon killed while trapped in a
filmy, web-like garment—a device both literal and metaphorical
of which Aeschylus makes much (alluded to first at *Ag.* 1115–16
and 1128, on which see the Notes; cf. p. lv below). A number of
vases depicting Orestes and Electra at their father's tomb, or
Orestes with the Furies, date from the mid-fifth century but
cannot confidently be set earlier than the trilogy; again, they may
as much reflect well-known versions previous to Aeschylus as
show direct debt to the *Oresteia*, but the sudden rise of interest in
the myth suggests that the trilogy had a lasting impact.[9]

Aeschylus makes hardly any use of crimes in Atreus' family
earlier than his own against his brother Thyestes; or of their
tragic reverberations attested elsewhere in myth (but not in
Homer), even though these might further have darkened the
background of doom. The crimes were those of Tantalus,
founder of the family, who in some versions offended the gods
by serving them the flesh of his own son Pelops to eat (a
preliminary 'doublet' of Atreus' crime), and of Pelops himself,
restored to life by the gods, whose betrayal of his benefactor
Myrtilus provoked an initial curse upon the family; and he
merely alludes to the issues between the brothers Atreus and
Thyestes, the kingship (*Ag.* 1585) and Thyestes' adultery
(*Ag.* 1193), without mentioning the golden ram which was the
royal symbol. Instead, and possibly original to Aeschylus, the
weight is laid upon Thyestes' curse, bringing a demon to destroy
the family in tandem with the gods' inevitable punishment of sin.
Aeschylus replaces Thyestes' son Aegisthus with Clytemnestra as

---

[9] A handy summary in T. H. Carpenter, *Art and Myth in Ancient Greece* (1991), 236–7;
cf. esp. Trendall and Webster in Bibliography §6.4, III.1.1–12 and Plates, pp. 41–9, and
Prag in Bibliography §7 (who discusses the wine-bowl of 470 BC on pp. 3–4, with Plates
3–4; cf. Carpenter, Pl.351; Trendall and Webster omit it). Also: *Lexicon Iconographicum
Mythologiae Graecae* VII.1 (1994), 68–70 and Plates.

the more powerful plotter against Agamemnon (altering Homer, above—but see Aegisthus' boasts at *Ag.* 1604–9); in this he is calculatedly increasing Clytemnestra's stature as mental and physical antagonist to father and son (§2.2 below, on 'The characters'). Unique to Aeschylus is the intricate combination of Agamemnon's murder with his Zeus-assigned role against Troy (§2.3 below, at the start), especially the sacrifice at Aulis:[10] it is his brother Menelaus who is the injured party, but Aeschylus associates Agamemnon more closely with his brother's case by housing them both in one palace at Argos (*Ag.* 400 etc.) and abandoning Menelaus' traditional home at Sparta. Original too are the dramatic prominence of Cassandra (strongly developing her mere mention at *Od.* 11.421–3: above), and almost the whole plot of *Eumenides*, especially the Furies as stage-figures, the jury-trial at Athens and its connection with real-life institutions (end of §1 above). Aeschylus concentrates the crimes within the three generations of Atreus, Agamemnon, and Orestes, and gives depth to the chief characters, so as to allow himself intensive moral and theological commentary.

2.2. The dramatic design and the characters

The dramatic design. The *Oresteia* begins 'in the middle of things', with the family's story well advanced: a further danger for its current head is imminent, Clytemnestra's plot against Agamemnon. Aeschylus creates instant tension very well, with the abrupt beginning of the Watchman on the roof; he ensures that his audience can appreciate every immediate or pending circumstance in relation to its cause, whether recent or old. The first play particularly, and less often the second, narrate and examine the grim background to the new danger, and anxiously project its consequences. They constantly draw out the unchanging moral and theological issues which underlie the family's history, including its involvement with Troy's punishment; the family, like Troy, must learn the hard lesson of Zeus' inevitable justice, a

---

[10] On the other hand, Aeschylus gives no explanation why or how Iphigenia was at Aulis, for he passes over Stesichorus' story (Fragment 217) that Agamemnon summoned her ostensibly to marry Achilles (a motif taken over strongly by Euripides for his tragedy *Iphigenia in Aulis*); but at *Ag.* 1524 Clytemnestra may allude to this deception with 'did he not also bring ruin on the house through treachery?' Aeschylus has unsurprisingly made use of Pindar's explanation why Clytemnestra was so bitter against Agamemnon, the killing of their daughter (*Pythian* 11.17 ff.): *Ag.* 1415–18, 1525–6.

truth stated bleakly at the start ('Suffer and learn', *Ag.* 177: §2.3 below, at the start). Retrospection and fresh consideration keep the successive disasters anchored in their first causes, the crimes of Agamemnon's father Atreus and of Trojan Paris.

The structure of the trilogy forces this continuity upon us. The first two plays are loosely similar in plot; both end with revenge-killings which portend only further, inescapable death. Other motifs repeated from *Agamemnon* into *Libation Bearers* help the sense of inevitable momentum towards disaster. In the first play, the victims, Agamemnon and Cassandra, come home from abroad, amid ominous anxieties from those faithful to the king, principally the Chorus. The victims enter the palace with misgivings or helpless dread, and are netted like prey in Clytemnestra's and Aegisthus' revenge-plot. Their bodies, so triumphantly exposed by Clytemnestra, signal mutely that Orestes will return to take his own revenge, in fresh, inexorable justice, as Cassandra prophesies (*Ag.* 1280–4) and as the Chorus warn Clytemnestra (1507–8). In the second play, he indeed returns from abroad; he tricks his way into the palace, luring Aegisthus into it unguarded, approximately as Agamemnon was lured inside when off his guard, and after him Cassandra; and then Orestes kills him inside before driving his mother in to die near him. The exposure of the two bodies again forebodes the terrible consequence, the threat of retribution upon Orestes; it is at once made real in the closing scene when the hideous Furies appear to him.

Critics emphasize the identical importance of the two plays' setting: the palace-front, especially its door as the theatrical and metaphorical focus of the action. Control of the door is control of the palace, of the kingdom and its riches, and of the family (compare Francis Bacon's *Triptych*, §4 below). Agamemnon enters the palace on Clytemnestra's terms before she dispossesses him of it, to share it with Aegisthus, even if insecurely; Orestes enters the palace to dispossess them of it and to regain his patrimony—only to be forced to flee at once by the Furies, in the likelihood of its irrevocable loss to his family.[11] The murder-

---

[11] For the door's importance, see in *Agamemnon* also 518–23, the Herald greeting his home; 851–4, Agamemnon's homecoming, with emphasis on royal success, followed by looming disaster in the successive door-scenes involving himself 904–74 and then Cassandra 1035–1330; in *Libation Bearers* the potent door-scenes are 653–718 (Orestes), 838–54 (Aegisthus), 885–930 (Clytemnestra).

victims of both plays are exposed through this all-important doorway,

These first two plays, however, also differ importantly. *Agamemnon* is greatly longer than *Libation Bearers* (which is of a length with *Eumenides*), because it contains much evocative narration of the past; and it analyses mentality and events not just at Argos before, during, and after the victorious campaign against Troy, but significantly at Troy itself. Trojan Paris' abduction of the willing Helen brought on disaster as inevitably as Atreus' crime against Thyestes brought on the intense sequence of deaths within his family, those of Agamemnon's daughter Iphigenia and then of the father, the mother, and potentially the son. This sequence, either narrated or dramatized, begins at the start of the first play and drives forward into the third. The family's role in punishing Troy is almost forgotten after Cassandra's death, as *Agamemnon* nears its end; so too the slaughter of Thyestes' children after its end, for his vengeful son Aegisthus figures in *Libation Bearers* only as the objective of Orestes' sword (571–84, 989–90), and he is killed before Clytemnestra's more important death, at the end of the second play. Aeschylus' design is to concentrate upon Orestes as a matricide. The vivid theatre of his revenge creates an urgent excitement immediately matched at the start of the third play.

Eumenides otherwise makes a sharp break, however. It brings rescue for Orestes in a resolution of the trilogy's tragic dilemmas which may seem equivocal (p. xxxv below), an effect increased by calculated management in the theatre. All this third play's action and on-stage effects are different from those of the first two. The setting changes from the family palace at Argos. More importantly, rescue and resolution are enacted in two seats of gods, Apollo's temple at Delphi and Athena's own city of Athens—the city of the audience. The play is still one of intended retaliation, but now it is of constantly visible persecution, of a single mortal man by supernatural powers. The hideous Furies besiege and pursue a refugee Orestes dependent upon Apollo's protection and Athena's merciful justice. The end of their persecution is heralded when the scene within the play changes from Delphi to Athens. Orestes' acquittal in the jury-trial ends the family's tragedy, but comes as early as two-thirds into this final play, only to lead to a different danger, this time to

Athens itself, from the Furies, resentful of their victim's escape. Their conciliation by Athena is a triumph of Athenian virtues and persuasion, and the trilogy celebrates it with concluding colourful processions. This double resolution achieves a specifically local closure for a timeless, universal conflict of rights.

The whole is an effective design for a trilogy, two similarly plotted plays leading to a very different third; it may have been unique in this regard. Other Aeschylean trilogies appear to have accumulated weight and meaning through simple progression, even if, as in the *Oresteia*, their individual plays spread the events through successive generations.[12]

The characters. The nature and depth of characterization in Greek Tragedy have long been disputed. Most critics now tend to accept Aristotle's insistence in his *Poetics* (ch. 6) that plot is the supremely important element of drama; and they judge characterization chiefly according to the success with which words express thoughts and thereby explain or move the action credibly forward.[13] This does not mean that characters are mostly two-dimensional, for some break out strongly from the plot and assume individuality. Furthermore, despite the divine and supernatural powers which seem to drive the trilogy forward, often impelling men irresistibly into wrong, the main characters' motives and behaviour are presented quite fully; and they are kept realistically human throughout.

Clytemnestra's revenge springs from naturally strong anger over her daughter's death (*Ag.* 1417 ff., 1432, 1525 ff.); she glosses over her adultery with Aegisthus as best she can in

---

[12] The most securely reconstructed is that upon the Oedipus-myth, comprising the lost *Laius* and *Oedipus* and as its third play the extant *Seven,* comparable with the later *Oresteia* in portraying the extinction (but there final) of one family through inherited criminality. The course of the Danaid-trilogy is less certain: probably the lost *Egyptians* came first, the extant *Suppliants* second, and the very fragmentary *Daughters of Danaus* last: in this family history, predetermined like the Atreus and Oedipus stories and early disclosed by an oracle, Aeschylus made tragedy from personal and political motives attending marriage (see especially Sommerstein, *AT* 141–52; for a complete survey of what is known about other trilogies, see his pp. 53–68 and West, *Studies in Aeschylus* (Bibliography §2), 3–72).

[13] For this whole topic of characterization see especially Goldhill in *Reading Greek Tragedy*, (Bibliography §5), 169–74 and in *CCGT* 340–3 'psychoanalysis and Greek Tragedy', in both places with excellent bibliography. For general discussion of Aeschylean characters see e.g. Rosenmeyer, *AA* 211–56 and especially Dawe, Easterling, and Goldhill in Bibliography §6.3. There is an excellent summary appreciation of Aeschylus' minor characters by Winnington-Ingram in *CHGL* 291.

front of the Chorus (1435 ff.)—as later she does in front of Orestes (*LB* 893, 917 ff.); but her unfeminine domination makes her a dramatic figure of singular power (Explanatory Notes on e.g. *Ag.* 489, *LB* 154), one towards whom an audience's feelings shift constantly. Scholars argue whether Aeschylus is mounting an early and deliberate 'feminist' platform with this Clytemnestra, who is pointedly signalled at once as usurping the male role and 'whose heart in its hope plans like a man' (*Ag.* 11; her unconformity is soon repeated, at 348, 485–7, and later at e.g. *LB* 626–30); but it seems unnecessary to think of her as more than a playwright's imaginative construction for the sake of his drama.[14] Clytemnestra in the *Oresteia* is the principal antagonist to the males of the family into which she has married; as adulterous wife and vengeful mother, and victim of her own vengeful son, she is the embodiment of the woman's interest, but increasingly also the instrument of the retributive family-demon and of the female Furies. She becomes a monstrous figure in Orestes' imagination as he stands over her corpse (*LB* 994–6), and she resembles the Furies herself in rampant hostility when as a *revenante* she harries them into fresh pursuit of him (*Eum.* 94–139). It is therefore a striking feature of *Agamemnon* that her domination of the male Chorus and her husband ends with defeat by another woman, the stubborn (and god-possessed) Cassandra (*Ag.* 1068); this, and her consequent moral submission to the newly assertive Chorus, forebode her inevitable defeat when in the conflicts of *Eumenides* the Furies argue her female and maternal role as a test-case; she and they are overcome not just by a male jury but by the motherless Athena.

Of the other female characters, only Cassandra requires comment—for Electra moves simply from doubt and diffidence to fervent optimism; the Nurse is primarily functional, an

[14] The most level-headed discussion of this issue remains Winnington-Ingram's, Bibliography §6.1 (1983), 101–31; see also Conacher, Bibliography §3.2 (1987), and Sommerstein, *AT* 255–73. For 'gender-politics' in Tragedy see Cartledge, *CCGT* 26–31, Hall, ibid. 103–10 (Clytemnestra on 107–8) and Goldhill, ibid. 344–5; Wilson (Bibliography §5), 130–2. Greek myth had many resourceful, dangerous, and retaliatory women whose fortunes were the field of violent emotions and deeds (*LB* 594–638 set Clytemnestra alongside some of them). In this same Atreid-myth Sophocles and Euripides made Orestes' sister Electra their title-character in the revenge-story, but her role in Aeschylus is small in extent if large in evoking sympathy. The two bigger Electras and for example Sophocles' Antigone and Euripides' Medea or Phaedra show what was possible in the dramatic generation after Aeschylus.

accomplice unawares in the deception of Aegisthus, even if her cameo-scene creates both tension and emotion; Apollo's Prophetess has only an expository and theatrical part. Cassandra, in contrast, makes her first strong appearance here in surviving literature, almost schizoid (we might say) as she alternates between pathetic victim and manically assertive seer; this characterization later became stereotypical, prominently in Euripides' *Trojan Women*. Cassandra has important functions: she is the only Trojan survivor in the play and confirms her city's punishment for wrongdoing as inevitable (1156–7, 1167–71, 1286–8); so she corroborates the Chorus's emphasis on this moral doctrine in the case of both Troy and the family; her enigmatic visions of past and future vividly supplement those of the choral odes, which are often cast with didactic clarity; not least, she delivers Clytemnestra her first defeat.

Of the male figures, the Watchman and Herald in *Agamemnon* and Aegisthus' servant in *Libation Bearers* say what may be expected in the plot, but Aeschylus differentiates their almost selfish preoccupations just enough to colour the emotional ambience. Pylades is in *Libation Bearers* solely for his three lines which brace Orestes at the crisis: they point to Apollo, who, like the goddess Athena and her opponents the Furies in *Eumenides*, is not characterized but presented in his essential mythic and religious image; in the trial-scene all three are largely mouthpieces of argument, but Athena afterwards develops a strongly Athenian partiality. Aegisthus is scarcely more than one-dimensional in his two brief appearances (*Ag.* 1577–1673, *LB* 838–54); Cassandra (*Ag.* 1224–5, 1258–9) and the Chorus (intermittently in *Ag.* 1612–71) tell the audience, or say to his face, as much as he reveals of himself, for Aeschylus gives him language of superb economy to suggest his emptiness (Explanatory Notes on *Ag.* 1628–32 and *LB* 838): he is cowardly, sly, weak, and full of noisy threats—a typical 'tyrant figure' in embryo. He has his place, however, because of his father's suffering and curse (*Ag.* 1583–1602), because he provides the means for Clytemnestra's aggrandizement (1435–6), and because his weak and adulterous person throws more shadows on her judgement; he is a foil to her, and a first but necessary victim of the revenge.

Agamemnon is handled with economy and skill by Aeschylus:

his important entry is anticipated and deferred as those of few other heroes in Greek Tragedy. Heracles in the name-play by Euripides and Sophocles' Philoctetes come to mind, but they dominate their plays; Agamemnon has only one episode, and it is with his wife. We may ask if Aeschylus has done enough to meet our anticipations of him from the hopes of the Watchman and Herald, and from the Chorus's narratives and reflections. He was shown there guided by his duty as commander against Troy and must deal with instinctive revulsion from his daughter's sacrifice. On his return to Argos he is pre-eminently the gods' victorious agent but he must fence with a manipulative wife who overcomes him by exploiting precisely his ambivalent consciousness of that role (*Ag.* 810–29, 851–4, 916–49). So, when he speaks at last to reveal his character, Aeschylus makes him lose no less credibly to Clytemnestra than he was overwhelmed at Aulis. Moreover, like his son Orestes, he has less an independent personality and will than a mindset almost entirely controlled by what he perceives of his duty and fate. The son is not drawn as fully as his father, not least because Aeschylus both foretells his revenge (first through Cassandra) and first shows him to us when he is already about it (*LB* 1–3a, 18–19). Only then do we hear him talk of his motives of filial and brotherly duty, but also of the material need to regain his inheritance; he is credible in his resolve, and no less so when he falters suddenly before the matricide (*LB* 899) or doubts Apollo's guarantees (1057, *Eum.* 85–7, 609 ff.). Father and son are set almost exactly in parallel, moreover, in their moments of supreme decision. Agamemnon's is narrated, except for his live words when he falters before his daughter's sacrifice ('Fate will be heavy if I do not obey, heavy as well if I hew my child', *Ag.* 206–8); he makes his decision upon clear warning from the seer Calchas (*Ag.* 198–204), in the urgent presence of military comrades (212–13, 226–7), from obedience to Zeus' justice (250)—and amid the ruinous derangement which seizes him (219–23). Orestes' frozen moment is vividly enacted, however, as the supremely tense crisis of the whole trilogy; and it is broken when his comrade Pylades insists, like Calchas (*Ag.* 144, 158), on the irresistible command of heaven, which Orestes had sworn to obey (*LB* 900–2).

2.3. Issues and meanings

'What is there in things here which god has not ordained?'

(*Ag.* 1488)

The first Greek word spoken in the *Oresteia* is 'gods': the Watchman asks them to release him from his misery (*Ag.* 1). All three plays begin with prayers. In the last words of the trilogy Athenian temple-girls sing of a joyful outcome accomplished by the supreme god, all-seeing Zeus, together with Fate (*Eum.* 1045–6). There is constant emphasis on Zeus who in his wisdom sees and accomplishes all; a particularly important place is *Ag.* 1485–7, with its despair at the demon which afflicts Atreus' house 'through Zeus, the all-causing, the all-doing'. He controls the visible and living world, but has power in the underworld too (*LB* 382–5, cf. 1–2). In *Eumenides* the god Apollo states that his oracles are always and only the words of Zeus himself (616–21), so that his direction of Orestes has been implicitly Zeus' own; similarly the outcome for both Orestes and the Furies is managed by Zeus' daughter Athena.

Zeus' will for the world, as ruler of the gods, is expressed most commonly in his role as guarantor of 'justice' (Greek *dikê*). Through it, he determines men's lives, often simultaneously with Fate: what they are born to, what they perceive of their destiny, what they do from that perception, and what consequences their actions bring. Zeus ensures cosmic order. In human terms this is moral order, a system of balance; if it is upset, it is restored, sooner or later; everything moves towards a just end: *Ag.* 782 'she [Justice] directs all things to their ending', cf. 67–8 'Things are now as they are; they will be fulfilled in what is fated'; the Furies acknowledge the same, *Eum.* 544 'an end is appointed and waits'. Confident of this 'justice', the avengers of Agamemnon constantly appeal to the gods to be their allies and watch over their cause.

Aeschylus often presents justice as an independent, personified power, sometimes associated with Fate (*Ag.* 1535–6, *LB* 646–8) and even as Zeus' own daughter (*LB* 949). It is a complex theology, and it makes a hard world for Aeschylus' characters, who must find their way to comprehension and acceptance through suffering, whether for their own or for others' wrongdoing. Aeschylus carefully sets this theology out, early in the trilogy, at *Ag.* 177–8 'Suffer and learn', part of the 'Hymn to Zeus' which expounds his supreme power and wisdom (160–83). It is one of the longest such statements in the whole trilogy, and deliberately placed halfway through the evocative narration of Agamemnon's dilemma at Aulis: *Ag.* 206–8 'Fate will be heavy if I do not obey, heavy as well if I hew my child, my house's own darling'; his dilemma is fated (157), his decision a compulsion (218). Aeschylus enlarges regularly upon this cardinal premiss of inevitable and hard justice (*Ag.* 250, 533, 1527, 1563–4, *LB* 313, 1009, *Eum.* 520–1).[15]

Men perceive the gods' will and the nature of their justice in a number of ways. They take the lessons of the mythic past, for example when Orestes hears the Chorus set out analogies for Clytemnestra's doomed assault upon her own family (*LB* 602–38). Troy's punishment becomes the paradigm, with implications for the Atreid royal family which executes the justice under Zeus (the Chorus throughout *Agamemnon*, for example at 355–84; Trojan Cassandra at 1287–9). Most tellingly, amid tragic helplessness, men are given intimation of their inevitable future—in dreams (Clytemnestra's snake-son at *LB* 523 ff., 928–9); in visions (Cassandra's kaleidoscopic imaginings, *Ag.* 1072 ff.; Orestes' half-hallucinatory sight of the Furies confirms his mother's threat of them, *LB* 1048 ff.); in prophecies (from Calchas for Agamemnon at *Ag.* 122 ff. and, though heard only by the Chorus, from Cassandra for herself, Agamemnon, Clytemnestra, Aegisthus, and Orestes throughout 1072–1330); and in oracles or other instructions from the gods (Zeus sends Agamemnon and Menelaus against Troy, *Ag.* 60–2, cf. 41–3, but his method of command is not stated; Apollo's Delphic oracle directs Orestes' matricide, *LB* 269 ff., 558–9, 900–2, etc., but will also assure his salvation, 1030–9, cf. *Eum.* 64 ff.). Lastly, Thyestes' ancient curse upon the family lurks in the awareness of the Chorus (*Ag.* 150–5 and 990–7) before it is first mentioned explicitly (1398—by Clytemnestra, as she begins to sense its danger). Aeschylus puts that first early allusion just after Artemis' hostility to Zeus' omen brings the delaying winds to

---

[15] Almost all the discussions of Aeschylus and the *Oresteia* listed in the Bibliography §§6.1, 7, and 8.1, 8.2, and 8.3 deal with Aeschylus' 'gods' and 'world-view'. Rosenmeyer, *AA* 259–83 and Sommerstein, *AT* 355–91 are particularly well documented.

Aulis. Its suddenness and inexplicability—unless we attribute it
to her protection of wild creatures (Explanatory Notes to *Ag.* 55,
140–5)—suit the harshness of Agamemnon's dilemma whether
to sacrifice his daughter and placate the goddess or to abandon
Zeus' justice upon Troy (*Ag.* 206–17); but in deciding for the
former he only brings the same justice inevitably upon himself
(Clytemnestra at 1432–3, 1525–9).

So the tragic sufferers of the *Oresteia* either hope or fear as
understanding of what must happen grows or is forced upon
them. Agamemnon steels himself to the unholy sacrifice, his
mind deranged in the decision; he is edgy when he comes home
victorious from Troy, as if apprehensive, although neither Clytemnestra nor the Chorus makes clear allusion to Iphigenia in his
hearing (but the audience is now used to the Chorus's anxiety that
he must pay for his actions, however inescapable: *Ag.* 150 ff.
again, 250 ff., 461 ff.—or for his father's, by implication: 763 ff.).
Clytemnestra's triumph soon becomes defensive when the
Chorus hint to her Orestes' inevitable retaliation (*Ag.* 1429–30).
Aegisthus relishes a just vengeance upon Agamemnon for his
father Thyestes, but immediately falters in face of the Chorus's
predictions that he will face justice himself (*Ag.* 1615 ff.; his
anxiety reappears at *LB* 841 ff.). If the revenge by Clytemnestra
and Aegisthus has largely human motivation, they are helpless
victims but also agents of the remorseless justice which pursues
the family's male line. Clytemnestra must recognize that she too
will pay for her crime (*Ag.* 1409–11 etc.). Aegisthus will suffer
incidentally to the matricide, but it will be punishment both for
sharing Agamemnon's murder (*LB* 974) and for his adultery
with Clytemnestra (*LB* 990). Orestes' own vengeance is driven
by Apollo's assertion of its justice, but he must anticipate
supernatural persecution both if he fails and if he succeeds
(below). First Agamemnon and then Orestes are directed by
prophetic instruction to criminal killings which are both voluntary and involuntary. Only by sacrificing his daughter will
Agamemnon punish Paris, and Troy in Paris; he acts both as
the cuckolded Menelaus' brother (*Ag.* 40–4, 822–3) and as
Zeus' appointed agent of justice (*Ag.* 60–2, 523–6). Orestes is
certain to avenge his father (*Ag.* 1280–5, 1507–8), from duty and
desire (*LB* 299 ff., 435 ff. etc.) and at the command of Apollo
under Zeus (LB 269 ff., *Eum.* 616–21), to whom Orestes himself

constantly prays (*LB* 18–19, 244–6, 382, etc.). Throughout the trilogy Aeschylus presents actions and retaliations as equivocal or contradictory in their justice: Agamemnon, Clytemnestra, Aegisthus, and Orestes all deserve punishment, but have plausible or justifiable motives. The crudest expressions of this paradox come in Orestes' words at *LB* 461, 'War will meet war, and justice meet justice', and in the Furies' at *Eum.* 491–2, 'if a justice which is harm to justice shall prevail'. It is the hard tragedy of Agamemnon and Orestes that they have no escape from actions which are simultaneously their own decisions. Their line is destined for ruin, *Ag.* 1565–6 'What is there to expel the curse and its stock from the house: the family is glued fast to ruin'—until a different escape, in Orestes' jury-trial, restores his house (*Eum.* 752–61).

Punishment for wrongdoing is not always immediate or soon; it may be late but it always comes, for Trojan Paris (*Ag.* 58–71, 701–3) as well as for Atreus' house (*Ag.* 154–5, 1563–4, *LB* 61–5, 326, 383, 464). Upon Agamemnon this justice for his father's wrong works with particular harshness, but Aeschylus complicates the cause and nature of his own guilt. At the moment of his dilemma, Agamemnon is overtaken by a blind madness which drives him to the act (*Ag.* 218–23): it is later made explicit as the power of Atê, personified self-destruction, the uncontrollable impulse to criminal violence.[16] This destructive madness is evoked in language similar to that which describes Helen's destructive behaviour (*Ag.* 1455–61) and the Furies' persecution of their 'just' victims, the derangement which they bring upon Orestes (*Eum.* 328–33 = 341–6, cf. *LB* 288, 1023–4). At the same time, Aeschylus gradually reveals the ambiguous criminals Agamemnon and Orestes, and indeed Clytemnestra, as driven towards 'just punishment' by half-abstract forces or supernatural powers. Most chilling is a family-demon, a spirit haunting the house since Atreus' crime (*Ag.* 1468–84, 1501, 1508, 1569, cf. 768). The demon enacts the curse pronounced by Thyestes for the house's extinction (*Ag.* 1600–2). Again, personification

---

[16] Personified Atê in the self-destructive family, *Ag.* 769–71, 1433, *LB* 467, associated with Orestes' potential destruction, 1076—where it is pointedly the final word of the play—, cf. (not personified) *Ag.* 1192, 1283, 1483, *LB* 830; (personified) in Paris and Troy, *Ag.* 386, 735, 819. The idea of '*atê*' is found first in Homer's *Iliad*, most notably when Agamemnon attributes his disastrous handling of Achilles to it, as sent by Zeus, Books 2.111 and 19.88.

occurs (Curse, Greek *Ara*): Clytemnestra recognizes its working
(*LB* 692, cf. *Ag.* 1398); one of the Furies' names for themselves is
'Curses' (*Eum.* 417). Conversely, Orestes appeals to the Curses of
the dead to aid his own revenge (*LB* 406). The demon appears
allusively as personified Wrath at *Ag.* 155; its malign quality is
often described as 'rancour', a vindictive anger driving not only
the persons (Explanatory Note to *LB* 33) but particularly the
Furies (*Eum.* 220, 840, 900, etc.); it too is personified (*LB* 1025).

The family's wrongdoing and ruin are caused in part by Strife
(Greek *Eris*, another personification), and punishment comes
through it (*LB* 474). Atreus quarrelled with his brother (*Ag.* 1565,
cf. Cassandra at 1117, 1192–3); at *Ag.* 1461 the family's ruin is
ambiguously associated with Strife over Helen and Troy and at
697 Strife destroys Troy itself. There is War too, the Greek god
Ares, who naturally joins the conflict at Troy (*Ag.* 438, 642) but
also drives the family bloodshed (*Ag.* 1511, *Eum.* 355); at *LB* 461
(quoted above) Aeschylus describes justice and war in conflict
from both sides of the family.

Most of these half-abstract forces may operate through or
simultaneously with the supernatural and underworld Furies
(Greek *Erinues*);[17] they share a fluid or overlapping terminology.
As the trilogy progresses, the demonic Furies become ever more
active, regularly hinted at and feared by the Chorus (*Ag.* 461 ff.,
769 ff.) and then expressly made the cause of all the house's fresh
and potentially endless horrors (Chorus at *Ag.* 990 ff., 1119,
1468 ff., Cassandra at 1186 ff.). First their influence is behind
Agamemnon's killing of Iphigenia (allusively in Wrath punishing
the death of Thyestes' children killed by Agamemnon's father
Atreus at *Ag.* 150–5, Clytemnestra explicitly at 1432–3, cf.
1500–4). Then Clytemnestra herself is at certain risk from the
family demon of revenge, so that she must try to placate it
(*Ag.* 1568–76) as well as allay the murdered Agamemnon's
angry resolve to help his son's revenge (*Ag.* 1545–6, *LB* 44–7,

---

[17] The name *Erinues* is of disputed etymology; its singular *Erinus* applied originally to a
haunting, maddening goddess of punishment, and later particularly of vengeance for men
improperly killed, above all by kin. These Furies carried out curses pronounced by
parents, and are much more frequent in the *Oresteia*, e.g. *Ag.* 1190, *Eum.* 261–72. The
name nevertheless appears in the *Oresteia* first as a generally punitive power, embodied in
Agamemnon and Menelaus against Troy, *Ag.* 59; later, 743. For the Furies' variant
names see the note to *Eum.* 1041. Aeschylus does not number them; in later mythology
they are three.

etc.). Lastly Orestes risks their persecution on his father's side if he fails in the matricide (*LB* 273–83, 925) and on his mother's if he succeeds (*LB* 924, 1017, 1054; *Eum.* 465–7 etc.). Attribution of cause comes full circle for all these punitive or retributive powers. As Justice and Fate work either with gods or separately from them, so the Furies can lay claim to their support as well (Justice, *Eum.* 491–2, 508–65, 785–815, etc.; Fate, *Eum.* 335— to which the Furies are even approximated at *LB* 306, or related by birth, *Eum.* 961).

The gods' justice and the supernatural powers threaten to extinguish the Atreid line: but the matricide committed by its last male, Orestes, was at Apollo's command, and the god promised him freedom from guilt or harm (*LB* 1030–2, cf. *LB* 830 and perhaps 836–7 (the text is conjectural), *Eum.* 579–80) and release from misery (*Eum.* 83, cf. *LB* 1059–60). Aeschylus resolves this apparent contradiction, and dramatic impasse, in a daring way—one which tries to maintain the principle of unfailing punishment for wrong, but rescues the ambiguously criminal Orestes. Apollo's command is revealed also as Zeus' own will (above, but note the Chorus's earlier prayers to Zeus at *LB* 783–92, 855–8). Orestes' salvation comes when in the divided jury-court verdict at Athens, the presiding goddess Athena sides with her own father Zeus and casts her vote in his favour (*Eum.* 735).[18]

Many readers of the *Oresteia* find the mechanism of Orestes' acquittal unconvincing, especially the argumentation of Apollo against the Furies, and the position taken by Athena; the Note to *Eum.* 198–234 traces much of the rhetorical structure. Since Apollo voices the will of Zeus, he is confident from the start that in sending Orestes to Athens he will save him through arguing his case (*Eum.* 81–3), and that Athena will ensure the outcome (299–301); but the Furies assert they will prevent this. The sense of god-directed finality comes in part from manipulative theatre. Athena's role is carefully prepared from the prologue onward, before she enters at 397: the Prophetess at Delphi dwells on Athens at 10–14 and on Athena herself at 21; then come Apollo's and Orestes' expectations from her at 79–80, 235–6, 287–98. Apart from Orestes, and briefly the Prophetess at

---

[18] For the voting see the Explanatory Note and for the special meaning of these scenes to Aeschylus' Athenian contemporaries §1 above.

Delphi and Athena's temple-girls, the speaking characters of
Eumenides are all themselves gods or supernatural powers. The
mortal Orestes is theatrically isolated among them; when he
falters in his own defence (609–13), Apollo takes it over and he
speaks again only after the voting (744, 746, 754–77); then he
leaves. The Athenian jurors do not speak; their significance lies
wholly in their visible fact, part of a judgement too heavy for god
alone (Athena at 470–2). Clytemnestra's ghost drives the Furies
on; her dominance in *Agamemnon* and *Libation Bearers* is recalled
through this theatrical stroke, so that the claims of wife and
mother may be vivid in the ensuing trial. The Furies rest their
case against Orestes on their immemorial privilege, and as
underworld powers (71–2, 385–8, etc.) they represent their
own mother Night (321, 416, etc.) and so all mothers' rights
(209–10, 607–8, 624). Against the claim for the female and the
mother, Apollo counter-asserts the superiority of the male king
which derives from Zeus' own everlasting kingship (*Eum.* 625 ff.).
He stresses the outrage to Orestes' kingly father when murdered
by his treacherous wife (631–7); it is the culmination of many
emphatic references to his stature from the beginning of the
trilogy (see the Notes to *Ag.* 1226 and *LB* 723–4), so that Orestes
as Agamemnon's son has implicitly the same higher claim.
Finally Apollo instances the superiority of the generative male
sex (658–61) from Athena herself, daughter of Zeus but borne
by no mother (662–6)—all of which Athena accepts in revealing
her preference for Orestes (735–41). These arguments seem
tendentious to us, but were not unparalleled in contemporary
thought.[19]

Another tempting inference, that Aeschylus rescues Orestes
by having Zeus relent from his previously inflexible justice, is
balanced by the maintenance of the Furies' deterrent role: when
Athena conciliates them, she enacts also the will of Zeus for them
(*Eum.* 826, 850, 974), and the Furies accept their new place in
Zeus' prized city (917–20, 1001–2). There is correspondence
between what the Furies, before and after their 'defeat', claim as

---

[19] Sommerstein, *Eumenides* (1990), note on lines 657–66, suggests that the idea that
'the father's seed simply develops within the female's womb', not rare in the fifth century
and frequent after Aristotle in the fourth, may go back to the early fifth century scientific
speculator Anaxagoras. a little before the date of the *Oresteia*; the idea is associated also
with the earlier Pythagoras.

their privileges, and what Athena proposes as the function of her new and lasting Council of the Areopagus; supernatural matches human guardianship of civic order and prosperity. The Furies name fear and dread as deterrents of wrongdoing and injustice (*Eum.* 517–40), prosperity, civic order, moderation, and piety will result (526–49, 921–48, 956–67), and above all harmony rather than interfamilial strife and bloodshed (976–87). Athena foretells that fear and reverence for her Council will prevent injustice (690–2, 696–706); she confirms that the Furies through men's fearful respect (833, 990) of their powers both to destroy and to benefit (951–5) will bring all the promised good things, including fertility of man, beast, and soil (902–10, 990–1, cf. the Furies themselves in 921–48).

Athena's conciliation of the Furies is the culmination of a theme inevitably prominent in a trilogy which progresses through so many doubting or combative scenes: gods no less than men depend upon persuasion.[20] Like other abstractions, in important contexts persuasion is given emphasis through personification (*LB* 726, *Eum.* 885, 970; at *Ag.* 386 it is the accomplice of Atê, 'Ruin'). *Agamemnon* from the start shows Clytemnestra winning the reluctant credence of the Chorus that the beacon-message is true (87, 268 ff., 352–3, 475–87, etc.). Her persuasiveness establishes her dominance over them, especially when the Herald confirms Troy's fall (583). She is therefore credibly forceful in subduing her returning husband (942–4, 956). The Chorus nevertheless remain suspicious of her hypocrisy (982); and she signally fails to persuade, let alone to overcome, the captive Cassandra (1049–54—the word 'obey' appears three times in the single verse 1049). Aeschylus perhaps intends us to see the Chorus affected by Cassandra's resistance. They are forced to trust her prophecies for the house (1213, 1244) because she re-creates its past as persuasively as they did Aulis for themselves (105–6)—all this while Cassandra herself relates how Apollo denied her credibility as a seer (1212, 1239). In *Libation Bearers* Electra's slavewomen credibly direct her graveside prayers; in turn she half-convinces them that the

---

[20] The line-references in this paragraph are almost all to places where the word-root 'persuade' and its cognates, or closely related ideas of credence, trust, or obedience, stand in the Greek. R. Buxton, *Persuasion in Greek Tragedy* (1982), 105–14, gives an excellent appreciation of 'persuasion' in the trilogy.

lock of hair can be only from Orestes, before he himself appears and persuades her of his identity as her ever-faithful brother (243). He reveals Apollo's oracle, which he must believe and trust (297–8). Then in the great antiphonal lament (315–475) all three singing voices invoke Agamemnon's help from the grave, before imploring it in speech (479–509). Success in Orestes' plan to deceive Clytemnestra into giving him hospitality must still depend upon speech—or opportune silence (552–3, 555, 581–2)—because it involves a false but credible story (674–88, cf. 563–4); and then the Chorus persuade the Nurse to lend help unawares (720 ff.); Persuasion the goddess is invoked at 726, and the Nurse is persuaded at 781. In *Eumenides* the theme of persuasion runs through almost the entire play. Apollo gives an initial promise of its effectiveness at Athens (81–2; he admits that he 'persuaded' Orestes to kill his mother, 84). Clytemnestra's forceful words reinvigorate the Furies (135–6, 155–8). Orestes' trial relies on its success in the theatre for its reflection of contemporary law-court procedures and language (for example, 582–4; see the Notes to *LB* 980 and *Eum.* 81–3, 637–8). The Furies are inexorable towards men (384), but when Athena dissuades them from resentment (794, 829, 900) she puts her trust in Zeus, the patron-god of public assemblies and argument (973, cf. 826), and thanks the goddess Persuasion herself (885, 970). Lastly, the Furies are 'to find a path for their tongues to be kind' (988).

> '"The doer suffers"; that is fixed law.' (*Ag.* 1564)

While Zeus' control of justice is supreme, and other gods or powers influence men's lives strongly, there is wide room for human responsibility.

The inevitable punishment of excess is frequently stated. The insolent abuse of wealth characterizes such conduct, especially when it stems from insatiety and the wrongful pursuit of yet more possessions (*Ag.* 382, 750–80, 1001–3, 1331, *Eum.* 540–3). Such insolence generates impiety towards god and it is self-perpetuating, it 'breeds' (*Ag.* 758–72, *Eum.* 534). It is incorrect to think that the gods are indifferent to these excesses (*Ag.* 369–73, 396–8, 1168–70, *Eum.* 560). Wealth, however, does not of itself predetermine ruin, for men can maintain their prosperity if they do not abuse it: Aeschylus is careful to say this (*Ag.* 378–80,

761–2, 1008–13, *Eum.* 535–52). Athens avoids insatiety (*Eum.* 1000) even before the Furies settle there with a role to deter excess and wrongdoing.

The Trojans' cardinal sin was indeed abuse of their riches: that led to insolence and impiety (*Ag.* 367 84), and Paris' abduction of a host's wife precipitated punishment from both god (Zeus, *Ag.* 60–2, 355–66, etc.) and man (Agamemnon, *Ag.* 524–37 etc.). The lesson of Troy's ruin is made large throughout *Agamemnon*, but does Atreus' house suffer for the same original offence, abuse of wealth? Only by implication, if at all, as the two histories are constantly interwoven. Thyestes disputed Atreus' rule and cuckolded him (*Ag.* 1582–5, cf. 1191–3), and Atreus took his vile revenge (1502–3, 1590–9); but Aeschylus nowhere attributes these acts to wealth alone. Rather, these original crimes in the family led no less inevitably to punishment than had Troy's; they are parallel but different cases (*LB* 935–52). Indeed, Atreus' descendants Orestes and Electra must restore the family-line to the palace (*LB* 262–3, 503–9, etc.) in order to enjoy its material inheritance (*LB* 237, 480, 486, etc.).

Helen's crime, so destructive in its consequence (*Ag.* 406, 690, 745, 1456–7, etc.), was easy capitulation not just to Paris' charms (*Ag.* 407) but to Troy's wealth, which she then seductively adorned (*Ag.* 741–3). On the other hand Agamemnon's power and wealth were the lure for both Aegisthus and Clytemnestra (*Ag.* 350, 1638–9, 1673, *LB* 136–7, 975, etc.), just as Aegisthus' father Thyestes had disputed them with Atreus. Clytemnestra insists to Agamemnon that his house's riches are assured and inexhaustible (*Ag.* 961–3), even though she is later brought by the Chorus to profess herself content with just a portion of them (1575). In their aspiration both she and Aegisthus were extreme, destroying themselves, whatever their justification for revenge upon Agamemnon (below). So, just as excess brought Troy to impiety, Clytemnestra is 'godless' when she kills him (*LB* 46, 191, 525, cf. *Ag.* 1493 = 1517); and the same adjective describes Atreus' slaughter of Thyestes' children (*Ag.* 1590, cf. 1087–90), in order to register the enormity of this original crime (*Ag.* 1598), like Troy's an offence to god and man. Further, Aegisthus and Clytemnestra oppressed the murdered king's subjects (*LB* 302–4, 973, 1046), after their rule had been feared as tyrannous (Ag.1355, 1365, 1633).

Agamemnon's involvement with Troy endangered his whole house. A note of warning comes first from the Watchman (*Ag.* 19–20, 37–8) and later from the Chorus (799–807); and there is resentment among the Argive people for lost lives (445–74, cf. 346–7). Iphigenia's death leads to Agamemnon's own, punishment for his father Atreus' crime (Ag.154–5). Orestes' retaliatory matricide threatens extinction for the line, in accord with Thyestes' curse; as descendants, father and son must pay for their forefathers' sins (*Ag.* 1186–97; 1338–40, cf. *LB* 1018–19; *Ag.*1581–2, cf. *Eum.* 496–8, 934–5).

Zeus' ultimate justice may be unpredictable in its working, for example when Artemis' hostility at Aulis sets Agamemnon's death into motion (above). Men, however, seek their own justice through straight retaliation, dealing like for like—indeed as Artemis demands a maiden girl's life in payment for the hare and its unborn young (*Ag.* 144, 215, 229). The Chorus warn Clytemnestra that she must pay for striking Agamemnon down by being struck herself (*Ag.* 1429–30), a wording taken up particularly in *Libation Bearers* at 312, 'In return for bloody blow, let bloody blow repay' (cf. 398, 400–2). Orestes has overwhelming reasons of his own to avenge his father and to take life for life (927), but it is also Apollo's command that he should kill the killers in return (273–4) and by the same means, trickery (556–9, cf. 888). Such exact requital upon an enemy was unquestioned (*Ag.* 1374, *LB* 121–3, 309). Yet while revenge must be attempted, its futility is implicit: blood once shed can never be restored, *Ag.* 1018–19 'Once a man's blood has fallen on the ground in front of him, black and fatal, who shall call it up again by incantation?' (cf. *LB* 47, *Eum.* 261–3, 647–9). The Furies hunt upon the scent of shed blood in order to drink it from the killer (*Eum.* 264, 305, etc.); in their remorseless, immemorial, and so-far unchallenged persecution they do only what revengeful men have also done. The Athenian jury-court's divided verdict under the goddess's wise direction, and then her conciliation of the Furies, suggest that a better justice can be found than automatic vengeance; better still, the feuding which leads to it should be avoided. By the time of the *Oresteia* the Athenians had in fact already been slowly ameliorating for some time the private blood-justice sanctioned under law since about 600 BC.

Revenge is productive by itself as a tragic theme (§2.1 above). When executed upon blood-kin it is contentious; this is the prime issue in Orestes' trial. The Furies argue that Clytemnestra was not Agamemnon's blood-relative (*Eum.* 212, 605—the Chorus at *Ag.* 1508–12 state that she was, but that Orestes was hers (*Eum.* 607–8, 624, 653—as Orestes himself says at *LB* 1038). The fact underlies Orestes' crisis in killing his mother in revenge at *LB* 896–9, just as it underlies Agamemnon's in killing his daughter at *Ag.* 215. In the *Oresteia* revenge accordingly gains extraordinary power because it breaks this first of two fundamental human controls; the other is the law of hospitality.

The first control is violated by all the family-killings, not only those of revenge upon kin. Aeschylus regularly marks both offenders and victims with the Greek term *philos*, as either adjective or noun (or in verbal *philein*), connoting variously the obligations of kinship, marriage, affection, and friendship.[21] At the same time the word occurs naturally enough in relation to (to give only a few examples): Iphigenia's death at her father's hands *Ag.* 245; Clytemnestra's hospitable welcome of her husband at *Ag.* 905 and his death at her hands at *LB* 89; Aegisthus as Clytemnestra's *philos*, *Ag.* 1654, *LB* 717; Orestes' obligation to his father, *LB* 794, 1051; his mother's abandonment of her proper feelings *LB* 234, 993, etc., and her own and the Furies' similar complaint about him, *Eum.* 100, 608; his obligations to his sister at *LB* 219 and Agamemnon's to her at 496. The moral ambiguities are readily exploited for irony throughout the scene *LB* 668–718 when Clytemnestra offers hospitality to the disguised Orestes, believing him dead; she calls him her *philos*, 708.

Hospitality as a social mechanism is no less authoritative; its abuse brings disaster (the Furies too punish it as an extreme sin, *Eum.* 270, 547–8).[22] Paris as guest offended its rules when he

---

[21] The word *philos* translates into English as 'friend(ly), comrade(ly), dear, close(st), kin'. Its range is studied by E. Belfiore, *Murder Among Friends: Violations of* philia *in Greek Tragedy* (2000), with definitions especially on pp. 19–20.

[22] The principal Greek word is *xenos*, both noun and adjective, meaning both 'guest' and 'host'—but these senses develop from the original 'stranger', as does 'ally'; and host and guest often became *philoi*, accepting deeper obligations. On this concept too see Belfiore (previous note), 7–8. There is a classic discussion of supplication as moral and social mechanism by J. Gould, *Journal of Hellenic Studies* 93 (1973), 79–103, reprinted in his *Myth, Ritual, Memory and Exchange* (2001), 22–77.

seduced Helen from Menelaus' table (*Ag.* 399–402). This is the chief instance in the trilogy, but Agamemnon insults his own house when he hopes that Cassandra, his captive and now his bedmate, will be welcomed as stranger and guest (*Ag.* 950 ff.; compare Heracles and Iole in Sophocles, *Women of Trachis* 370 ff.); but she shies from entering as a stranger a house so full of death (1320 etc.): here too is irony. Clytemnestra abuses the bath customary for all homecomers and guests, in order to strike down her husband in it (*Ag.* 1128 etc.) and offers the unrecognized Orestes a similar bath (*LB* 670). Orestes has used a stranger's presumptive right to hospitality to gain entry to the palace; he names Aegisthus pre-emptively as likely to fail in a host's duty (*LB* 565 ff.), but Clytemnestra honours it (668–73) before the false news of Orestes' death makes her disguise her joy beneath a mourning face (737–41). Atreus destroyed his brother Thyestes while he was both suppliant and guest—even if polluted (*Ag.* 1588–90). Orestes' long exile while the Furies pursue him brings him hospitality—and purification—in many men's houses (*Eum.* 238–9, 285), so that Athena accepts him in supplication as a blameless stranger (441, 473–5). Apollo had warned him of rejection by all hosts after the matricide (*LB* 291 ff.) but takes him as his own suppliant (*Eum.* 91–2, 205, etc.); he cautions the Furies against Zeus if they violate such divine protection (92–3, 233–4; we have heard Clytemnestra urge them on with 119 'Suppliants are no friends of mine').

In conclusion: *Eumenides* transforms the tragic inevitabilities of *Agamemnon* and *Libation Bearers* into confident hope. The restoration of Agamemnon's house may be seen as the issue of the trilogy most likely to engross Aeschylus' original audience; the family's collapse into disorder and potential extinction is a terrifying example in a society whose communal well-being was founded upon stable households. The house's history and its involvement with Troy provide lessons about excess and impiety, and prove the need for restraint and reverence, which Athena will have the reconciled Furies guarantee in the city-state itself. Orestes is saved by the jury-verdict which both upholds his vengeance and recognizes the case against him; under the same moral laws, henceforth to be protected by the new civic justice

which Athena institutes, her city will be kept secure and strong—
the Athens of the spectators.

7.4. The plays in Aeschylus' theatre

It became regular in Aeschylus' later lifetime for tragic poets
competing at the Great Dionysiac festival to present a tetralogy in
a single day—that is, three tragedies and a concluding satyr-play
(a much shorter piece, a burlesque of myth in which the chorus
always comprised satyrs, half-human, rebellious, and drunkenly
excitable followers of the god Dionysus). We do not know if
Aeschylus was the first dramatist to exploit this compressed
timetable by basing all three tragedies, let alone a complete
tetralogy, upon a single myth, but he perfected this approach;
the satyr-play following the *Oresteia* was the *Proteus,* which
developed another well-known incident of the Greeks' return
from Troy. The *Oresteia* was designed and performed as a
continuum; and we must imagine it accordingly, if we are to
perceive its theatrical momentum.[23]

The performance-space of the Theatre of Dionysus at Athens
was large; it had two parts which in Aeschylus' day were
becoming conceptually separate but were probably still on one
level and flowed easily into each other, giving mutual access. The
first was an area enclosed on three sides by terraced seating, the
orkhêstra. The name means roughly 'dance-place', and the area
was created originally for any performance of song, danced or
stationary; in tragedy it was already on the way to becoming a
preserve of the chorus. At its centre was a small permanent altar
to Dionysus, which perhaps served to represent Agamemnon's
tomb in *Libation Bearers* (see Note to line 1) and Orestes' refuge
by Athena's statue in *Eumenides,* round which the Furies dance.

---

[23] For satyr-drama see Easterling, *CCGT* 37–44; R. Seaford, *Euripides: Cyclops* (1984),
1–48; less well Sutton, *CHGL* 346–54.

The plot of *Proteus* can be guessed; Aeschylus would have based it on the episode at
Homer, *Odyssey* 4.351 ff. Its heart was an encounter and struggle between Menelaus on
his storm-battered voyage home from Troy, and Proteus, 'The Old Man of the Sea'.
Proteus had foreknowledge; Menelaus was probably assisted by the satyr-chorus in
trapping him and learning about his eventual return home. The enquiries which the
Chorus of *Ag.* make of the Herald about Menelaus (671 ff., esp. 674–9), and
Agamemnon's mention of Odysseus as unsafe on his home-voyage too (841–4; cf. *LB*
1041b), are pointers-forward to the satyr-play's content for the audience (if they did not
already guess it from the title). Outline reconstructions by Sommerstein, *AT* 189–90 and
M. L. Cunningham, *Liverpool Classical Monthly,* 19 (1994 [1996]), 67–8.

There was access to the *orkhêstra* from both sides, between the outer ends of the seating and the second area. This was a long rectangular space used mostly by the individual actors but sometimes also by the chorus, especially when it had an active role in the plot and dialogue (in *Eumenides* above all). In part terraced out towards the rear, it may at first have had no 'backdrop', the spectators looking across it and above the naturally falling ground behind; but by the date of the *Oresteia*, it was confined at the back by a wooden structure faced with canvas, the *skênê* (in modern terms, the 'scene' or 'stage-area'; in later antiquity a raised stage developed upon this part-terrace, although its beginning cannot be certainly dated). The structure served, as the play-text tells us, as house-front (*Ag.* 3, *LB* 653) or temple-front (*Eum.* 3–4, 242) or as background for any outdoor location (*LB* 4, *Eum.* 685): so changes of scene could readily be made, indicated or implied by the dramatic text.[24] There was a two-leaved central door, opening outwards, through which any of the performers might come and go, including the chorus (*Eum.* 1–142);[25] and the structure was strong enough to support actors 'on the roof' (for example the Watchman at *Ag.* 1). Stage-properties were temporary and costume was enhanced or varied for special effect; their use and actors' movements are inferred from the play-text to give the 'stage-directions' inserted in the Translation.[26]

This plain theatre could achieve some striking physical effects, like Agamemnon's chariot (*Ag.* 783 ff., almost certainly drawn by live animals), the brilliant spreads of purple fabric on which he is made to walk (*Ag.* 909–10), or the final procession of *Eumenides* which heralds the harmonious incorporation of the Furies into Athenian public religion. Other effects were ordinary enough but nevertheless gave focus to a dramatic moment and its meaning, such as the removal of Agamemnon's boots before

---

[24] Specific changes, like that from Delphi to Athens at *Eum.* 234, are rare in surviving Tragedy; less definite changes happen occasionally, but nowhere have such significance as those at *LB* 584 (Note) and *Eum.* 566 (Notes to 235 and 490–565). For the so-called 'unity of place' see Taplin, *Stagecraft*, 103–7.

[25] Debate continues whether there were two or even three separate doors as early as Aeschylus' time; some scholars think that the scene *LB* 875–91 plays more easily with two, Orestes and Clytemnestra entering separately.

[26] See e.g. the Notes to *Eum.* 41–5, 777. At *Eum.* 117–29 a few stage-directions apparently from late antiquity survive in the Greek manuscripts.

he treads the fabrics (*Ag.* 944–5, 955–63), Cassandra's prophetic emblems which she wrenches off when she realizes that Apollo has abandoned her (*Ag.* 1269–70), Orestes' matricidal sword (*LB* 904), Clytemnestra's ghost unexpectedly appearing to harry the Furies (*Eum.* 94),[27] or the voting-urns in Orestes' trial (*Eum.* 748). A further stage-effect was perhaps developed in Aeschylus' time, a wheeled platform which was pushed out through the central door to expose static indoor-scenes (Greek *ekkyklêma*, 'a thing for wheeling out'); it became as unremarkable a resource as curtains or stage-lighting in modern theatres, although Aristophanes towards the end of the fifth century mocked Euripides for his too frequent use of it. Most scholars assume that it was employed for the display of the bodies at the ends of both *Agamemnon* and *Libation Bearers* and of the Furies asleep surrounding Orestes at the start of *Eumenides*; this seems a little more likely than merely mounting the tableaux behind the door, which would leave many spectators with an inadequate view of them when it opened. Whatever the means, the full power of the matching scenes could only have been achieved by giving them maximal and equal visibility.[28]

The constant significance of the palace-door and its control in *Agamemnon* and *Libation Bearers* has already been noted (§2.2 above); visual effects compound it. The foreboding Watchman (*Ag.* 1–39) begins the trilogy's long sequence of marking dangerous returns and entries to this door; his position on the roof is a surprise, as is the timing of it at night as he waits for the beacon-signal; both help register Agamemnon's expected return as momentous. When he eventually comes (810), his chariot itself is visibly doom-laden, for it bears as spoil of war the bizarre

---

[27] Ghosts are not rare in Greek Tragedy. Aeschylus has Darius appear above his tomb to explain the defeat which is otherwise incomprehensible to the living Persians, *Persians* 681–842 (by far the longest ghost-scene in Tragedy) and Odysseus raises the ghost of the seer Tiresias in the lost *Psychagogi* ('Soul- or Ghost-raisers'). Sophocles began his lost *Polyxena* and Euripides his extant *Hecuba* with prophetic ghosts.

[28] See also the Notes to *Ag.* 1372 and *Eum.* 85–7; Taplin, *Stagecraft*, 325–7, wonders whether stage-hands may have brought on the components of the tableaux, including the 'bodies', and assembled them in full view.

For clear descriptions and illustrations of the theatre in Aeschylus' time and immediately after, see e.g. Green (1994), Green and Handley (1995), and Wiles (1997 and 2000) from the Bibliography §§5 and 6.4. The *mêkhanê* or 'crane' is sometimes posited for Athena's aerial entry at *Eum.* 397: see the Note. General discussions of Aeschylus' handling of his theatre in e.g. Rosenmeyer, *AA* 45–74, Sommerstein, *AT* 217–41, and above all Taplin, *Stagecraft*.

and ominous figure of Cassandra; the explosive breaking of her long, immobile, and teasing silence gives even greater impact to her terror of the palace door and the grim history it hides. *Libation Bearers* has the even more effective silence of Orestes' companion Pylades from the play's start until his few crucial words brace Orestes to the matricide (899–903); then he must drive his mother inside the door. Lastly, the door's importance is further emphasized by the successive displays through it of the murder-victims who have failed to keep its control (above).

The performers available for the *Oresteia*, all male, were three speaking actors and a chorus of twelve dance-singers; its leader might also speak solo (for example *LB* 931–4; see also below on *Eumenides*) or join in spoken or sung exchanges (for example *Ag.* 263–80, 615–35 spoken; 1407–1566 both spoken and sung). Uniquely in surviving Tragedy, and with striking effect, all twelve members speak individually at *Ag.* 1348–71 (see the Note). These performers were supplemented occasionally by mute persons, to any number, and by a secondary and minor chorus (*Eum.* 1032–47).[29] Much of *Agamemnon* uses just one speaking actor on stage with the chorus, as Clytemnestra gradually reveals her nature and thinking (264–354, 1372–1576; cf. her monologue at 587–614). Aeschylus supplements the Chorus's imaginative re-creation of events at Aulis and Troy by having the single voices of the Herald (503–680) and later Cassandra (1072–1330) recount their live experience; in this way he sets out the deeper background to the king's return. The episode 810–974 is the single confrontation of Clytemnestra and Agamemnon; it throws its whole light on these two figures (who nevertheless speak directly to each other only during 914–57), but requires the third speaking actor for Cassandra, silent until they have left. Almost all of *Libation Bearers* requires three speaking actors on stage together, including the long-silent Pylades (above). *Eumenides* throughout has the largest number of performers: for the jury-trial (566–777) it not only needs the three speaking actors playing Orestes, Athena, and Apollo but also has the longest speaking role for the chorus in all surviving Tragedy, turning its leader effectively

---

[29] For mute extras in the *Oresteia* see the notes to *LB* 973 and *Eum.* 1004–5. For speculation whether a fourth speaking actor was required for *LB* 875–91, the brief scene with Aegisthus' house-slave, see the note to 886.

into a fourth actor; he has considerable speech also during
179–306, 397–435 and 881–915.

The positioning of the play-characters and their movements
are well calculated. Not only Cassandra and Pylades create
potent tension from long silence. at the start of *Libation Bearers*
Orestes and Pylades quickly move aside and remain silent and
still (Note to 21), notionally unseen while they overhear Electra
and the chorus turn Clytemnestra's placatory offerings at
Agamemnon's tomb against her; in this way Orestes learns
that there is already much within the palace to encourage his
vengeance, especially Clytemnestra's dream; only afterwards
does he reveal himself as the answer to Electra's desperate
hopes. The first two plays end with confrontations: in *Agamemnon*
verbal antagonism nears physical violence (1649 ff.), in *Libation
Bearers* Orestes in his hallucination is faced with the terrifying
Furies, invisible to the spectators (1048); their full horror is
shown soon afterwards, at the start of *Eumenides*.[30] The third play
is more active still. Frequent entries and exits in the initial scene
at Delphi convey restless pressures (1–234: there are over ten
movements, mostly from and through the temple-door). Orestes
is literally besieged by the Furies there, and figuratively later
when they reach Athens and dance their binding-song round
him as he clings to Athena's statue (259 etc.). The warrior-
goddess Athena in her majestic and iconic costume dominates
the trial-scene, which she peoples with her Athenian jurors; and
the trilogy ends in splendour when she conducts the Furies to
their cult-site in torch-lit procession with the aid of the secondary
chorus (above).

The chorus is deployed suggestively as a group helping to
support—or representing—one side in each play's conflict. In
Agamemnon the loyal retainers of the king throng before the
palace-door, agonizing helplessly while the king is killed inside
(1343–71), but regroup to defy his killers at the end (1650). In

---

[30] Some critics think they were visible at the end of *LB*, from 1048 to 1060; Wiles,
Bibliography §5 (1997), 82–6, plots possible stage-movements for the trilogy, suggesting
that the deranged Orestes mistakes the black-clad chorus for the Furies. A no doubt
exaggerated anecdote told how children in the audience were terrified by the Furies'
ghastly appearance in *Eum.*, and pregnant women miscarried: so the ancient *Life of
Aeschylus* 9, cf. Taplin, *Stagecraft*, 372; Csapo–Slater, 14. This anecdote may have
originated in a popular revival of the play in much later antiquity, possibly outside
Athens.

Libation Bearers the Chorus of women join Electra and Orestes in the great tripartite lament over the king's tomb which drives the vengeance on (308–475). In *Eumenides* the Chorus has a role greater than in any other surviving Greek tragedy, for it comprises the Furies themselves, singing, dancing, and arguing their relentless persecution of Orestes until persuaded into benevolent reconciliation by Athena.

3. DRAMATIC FORM AND LANGUAGE IN AESCHYLUS

3.1. *Dramatic form in general*

A Greek tragedy moves forward in spoken episodes (serving rather like play-acts) alternating with lyric song or chant; this general shape permitted great variety of form, length, and particularly emotional effect within its components. Episodes, including the prologue-scene and final movement, range in number from five to seven. They can be very brief, with no more than a single scene or speech from one character (as in the prologues of *Agamemnon* and *Libation Bearers*), or comprise a number of scenes, which may be thought of as bounded by entries or exits (for example the trial-scene *Eum.* 566–777 has entries at 566 and 574 and exits at 730 and 777). Episodes may be interrupted and coloured by brief lyric or chanted verses (for example *LB* 152–63, 719–29). All these variations are in themselves a means of dramatic expression, indicating moments of realization, or crisis, marking significant developments or conveying shifts of feeling.

Plot and action advance for the most part in the spoken episodes, in which individual characters converse with one another or with the chorus, or use monologue. In the three plays certainly by Aeschylus which are earlier than the *Oresteia* (*Persians*, *Seven*, and *Suppliants*), there are never more than two characters speaking together, and two actors can perform all the character-parts. In these plays variety and forward movement in the action may consequently seem more limited, but the formal spareness usually shapes an individual's progress with great concentration (cf. §2.4 above). The direct involvement of the chorus, and usually its share of the whole text, are also greater than in the later plays (*Eumenides* excepted). On the other hand three actors are required for some episodes in all three plays of the *Oresteia* (§2.4 above, at end) although it is only slightly later than *Suppliants*. The action is generally busier and more complex, especially in *Libation Bearers* and *Eumenides*; longer scenes reveal or develop attitude and action through interaction; there are more long speeches. At the end of Aeschylus' career, the *Oresteia* demonstrates the whole range of his dramatic form and technique.

In the major sung or chanted parts Aeschylus' chorus is heavily dominant, singing and dancing on its own or exchanging song, chant, or speech with one of more of the characters. These major lyric parts never exceed six in number (in *Agamemnon*, for instance); and the purely choral songs vary in number and length (three or four are usual, as in all three plays of the *Oresteia*). Both song and chant may voice the specially strong emotions of those affected, at first or second hand, immediate or prospective; and in this latter respect they often point the action forward, even anticipating its next crisis (for example at *LB* 827–30 the Chorus foresee Orestes' need to resist his mother's plea for her life, 896–8, 908–9). The functions of these lyric parts are discussed in more detail in §3.3 below.[31]

3.2. Speech and spoken dialogue

The dramatic episodes appear dominated by long speeches. Often just one character of the two or three on stage speaks at length while the others and the chorus are silent or respond only briefly or with a comparably long speech. True and progressive exchanges are usually between two persons at a time; when a third joins in, one of the other two falls silent (for example Orestes throughout *Eum.* 614–743, in the trial-scene, once Apollo takes over his defence). Long speeches, particularly monologue, often introduce new information to which the chorus or other characters react. They may be narratives like Clytemnestra's imaginative beacon-speech at *Ag.* 281–316, or emotional revelations such as when Orestes describes Apollo's command at *LB* 269–305. They are typical of all drama in tracing the formulation or change of thought, particularly in

---

[31] P. E. Easterling, *CCGT* 151–65 gives an excellent general account of the resources, forms, and modes which Greek Tragedy employs. For a full review see M. Heath, *The Poetics of Greek Tragedy* (1987).

preparation for action, for example when Orestes unfolds his plan at *LB* 554–84.

Dialogue varies much in its length and intensity. It consists mostly of shifting exchanges between two voices, with irregular short speeches, for example at *LB* 668–718 when Orestes in disguise tricks Clytemnestra into hospitality. *Eumenides* has some of the freest and most realistic spoken drama, especially in the episodes 397–488 between Athena, Furies, and Orestes, and the trial-scene 566–777. There may be spans of line-by-line exchange (stichomythia) interrupting or developing longer speeches, for example when Clytemnestra at *Ag.* 931–44 browbeats Agamemnon into entering the palace over the fabrics. In its concentrated regularity, stichomythia is peculiarly apt for any intense or pacy exchange, for example interrogation at *Ag.* 538–51; information at *LB* 164–82; persuasion at *LB* 108–23; argument at *Eum.* 201–12; confrontation at *LB* 908–30. An exchange of two lines at a time (distichomythia) seems even more deliberately formal, and is rare; for example at *LB* 1051–64 the Chorus try to reassure Orestes as the Furies begin to derange him; at *Eum.* 711–33 the structure measures out the casting of the jurors' votes.

Important dramatic encounters combine more than one form of speech: the heavily charged single confrontation of Clytemnestra and Agamemnon at *Ag.* 810–974 moves through monologues from both into brief stichomythia (above) before ending with a long speech from Agamemnon and a closing monologue from Clytemnestra. In *LB* 164–305 Electra's discovery of Orestes' lock of hair excites dialogue with the Chorus in stichomythia and then her long speech before Orestes reveals himself; their joyful reunion follows in stichomythia and a long speech from both; then Orestes in two long speeches appeals for Zeus' help and describes Apollo's inescapable oracle; this is climax enough to an already long episode, but emotional momentum is maintained by the ensuing three-voice lyric invocation of the dead Agamemnon himself over his tomb (306–475).[32]

The verse line of speech in Greek Tragedy is the iambic trimeter, described by Aristotle, *Poetics*, chs. 4 and 22 and *Rhetoric*, Book 3, ch. 8 as closest to the rhythm of everyday

---

[32] For speeches and dialogue in Aeschylus see especially Rosenmeyer, *AA* 188–210, esp. 201–5.

speech. Its general character is the alternation of 'long' (or 'heavy') and 'short' (or 'light') syllables, quantitative rather than dynamic or 'stressed'; but this pattern has some flexibility. 'Trimeter' denotes a verse of three *metra* or 'measures'; the iambic *metron* consists of a variable syllable preceding a group comprising 'long-short-long'. When such a group is followed by a variable syllable, it makes a trochaic *metron*; and trochaic tetrameters ('four-measures') are used occasionally for speech by Aeschylus, for example at *Ag.* 1348–71 and 1649–73, scenes of excitement. This trochaic rhythm gave the impression of quicker movement (Aristotle, *Poetics*, chs. 4 and 24; *troch-* is from the Greek word for 'run').

3.3. Choral song and lyric dialogue

General. Lyric is most commonly sung and danced by the chorus in 'odes'. They are arranged in pairs of metrically equivalent or 'responding' stanzas called *strophe* and *antistrophe*. We assume that the musical accompaniment, played on a pipe, similarly 'responded'. Rhythmic variety within stanzas is very great, often appearing subtle and delicate, but we lack almost all information about how to relate any particular metre or variation to mood. Almost all stanzas are self-contained in sense and syntax, however, each moving to fresh illustrative matter or a new topic. Paired stanzas, especially in Aeschylus, nevertheless sometimes have individual words, phrases, sounds, and ideas also 'responding' exactly or approximately. The phenomenon (which transfers with difficulty into English) originated in hymnic and sacral ritual and creates solemnity or a marked emphasis; final lines can be repeated at an interval, giving the effect of a refrain, for example at the end of successive stanzas at *Ag.* 121, 139, and 159, and sometimes even whole stanzas are repeated, as in the Furies' persistent anger at *Eum.* 778–93 = 808–23.

Lyric may also be sung antiphonally, in 'dialogue', between the chorus and one or more play-characters. It may be part of an alternating exchange with a speaking voice, for example between the angry Furies and a placatory Athena at *Eum.* 778–880, or with a chanting one, as when these parties unite in glad anticipation at 927–87: the effect is often to contrast an impassioned with a more deliberate and measured utterance.

Other lyric may appear as a simple sequence of verses with varying rhythm; the best example is *Eum.* 255–75 where the Furies harry Orestes with bloodthirsty threats. Lyric may also be chanted by the chorus, in regular anapaestic rhythm to accompany its pacing steps, especially at first entry as at *Ag.* 40–103, or irregularly at an emotional crisis, like that immediately before the king's murder at *Ag.* 1331–42.[33]

Lyric in the Oresteia. Aeschylus' long choral odes are richly suggestive and emotive; this quality once earned his plays the description 'lyric tragedy'. He uses lyric to depict and examine background and to link it with the immediate drama, by drawing universal from particular meaning, so that the chorus 'ruminates' or 'sermonizes', for example on abuse of prosperity at *Ag.* 750 ff. and 1001 ff. or on the need for civic justice and order at *Eum.* 517 ff. The chorus voices as it were the view of the ordinary man, 'public opinion', how the community responds when its interests are in question (see also end of §2.4 above). The poet offers a kind of running commentary on the action, as he encourages the audience how to understand and react with feeling to his own interpretation of the myth.

In these ways lyric mood prepares or completes the impact of a spoken episode, and an ode or shared sequence often points characters and action forward. The first broad movement of *Agamemnon* is a fine example (1–809), where long choral odes not only establish a deep historical, moral, and theological perspective upon Agamemnon's involvement with Troy, but also set out the danger from his absence and trace the establishment of Clytemnestra's dominance in his palace. The single confrontation of husband and wife on stage, a spoken scene, has thus a sudden and terrible intensity (810–974), after which the Chorus mark their extreme anxiety for him with another

---

[33] Note on this section. 'Odes': the Greek word is *ôidai* 'songs', but the odes of Tragedy have the technical name *stasima*, 'things [performed] in [their] station', in the *orkhêstra*. Single stanzas are sometimes attached to a pair of stanzas ('epodes'; or 'ephymnia', a form of refrain), or they stand between pairs ('mesodes'). The ancient evidence upon all these lyric matters is collected by Csapo–Slater, 289–326. The translation signals corresponding stanzas with Str(ophe) and Ant(istrophe) in the margin. Many partial and sacral responsions, word for word or in rhyme or assonance, are mentioned in the Explanatory Notes, e.g. to *Ag.* 452–5, 1541, *LB* 326–8, 935 ff. = 946 ff.

For lyric and the chorus in Aeschylus see Rosenmeyer, *AA* 145–87. Sommerstein, *AT* 206–17 offers a 'musical analysis' of *Agamemnon*.

brooding ode (975–1035). In the remainder of the play lyric is used in two extended antiphonal sequences. Both convey increasing danger and passion as they shift from an exchange of song with speech to wholly lyric exchange: Cassandra frightens the Chorus with her visions, 1072–1177, including the murder of Agamemnon which follows; the Chorus compel Clytemnestra to foresee the danger from her triumph, 1407–1576.

Libation Bearers has an altered lyric quality and sequence, suiting a plot and characters with different preoccupations; and the play, unlike *Agamemnon*, needs little exposition of background. The general tone moves from lamentation through increasing confidence to triumphant vengeance; the transition is as marked in the lyrics, both formal and irregular, as in the spoken scenes. The opening choral procession with the gifts (22–83) and the lyric exhortations over Agamemnon's tomb (Chorus alone at 152–63, three lyric voices in antiphony at 306–475) give way to purely choral odes anticipating the morally justified revenge (585–652, 783–837) and finally its joyful achievement (935–71).

Eumenides differs again: now the Chorus is the protagonist of the play, prepared from the beginning for a definitive confrontation and outcome. The Furies not only chant, sing, and dance throughout, retaining most of a chorus's regular functions of evocative commentary, but they also engage in protracted spoken argument with Apollo and Orestes, in Athena's presence; in the voice of their leader they take the place effectively of a fourth speaking actor (§2.2 above). They sing and dance to exhort themselves (142–77), to 'bind' Orestes (255–75; 308–96, including their brief speech at 299–307), and to reassert their prerogatives (490–565). After the long trial-scenes Athena reconciles them to a transformed role in a sequence which alternates their angry sung dance with her spoken persuasion (788–1022, analysed in the Explanatory Note to 778–1047). Much of the Furies' lyric in the play has a sacral tone, including many repetitions, as they describe their ancient, ritual privileges. At the end Aeschylus introduces a secondary chorus to sing the processional hymn with which the Furies are escorted to their new home (1033–47).

3.4. Language and imagery

The 'Note on the Text, Translation, and Explanatory Notes' describes the great difficulty of translating Aeschylus' poetry, because of its profuse verbal effects. Language and imagery require sustained concentration from a modern audience or reader. We have only a few hints how the ancients themselves responded. Aristophanes' comedy *Frogs*, performed in 405 BC, some fifty years after Aeschylus' death, evokes the lasting impression made by his language, especially in this trilogy: comic exaggeration represents his diction as distinctively sonorous, especially in his lyrics, and as not readily intelligible to the ordinary man in the audience. Much later ancient writers who describe Aeschylus' style as direct, heroic, and full of sound are rhetoricians and literary educators, not theatre-goers, and they mix admiration with reservations about what taste in their own day perceived as lack of discipline or refinement.[34]

Simplicity and concision contrast with lengthy mixing of ideas, images, and clauses; and their sometimes extraordinary compression makes them densely suggestive. Then there are the deliberate effects of sound particularly noticed by the ancients, which are often enhanced by the deft juxtaposition or interlacing of words which characterizes the high style in an inflected language like Greek. In support is a vocabulary of the widest provenance. Aeschylus uses, echoes, and imitates words and formations from his predecessors in epic and lyric poetry, Homer above all. His own inventiveness appears to have been remarkable, in all registers of diction; his plays are crowded with rare or compound words which occur nowhere else, or only where they are obviously imitated by later poets. Because his tragic poetry is the earliest which survives, except in minute scraps, we cannot measure his debt to earlier dramatic poets; but it is clear that he was a great shaper of his art and its diction, with a stature like

[34] Aristophanes, *Frogs* 923–6, cf. 833–4, 902–4, 1016–18, 1060, 1261–97, 1365–7. Even if comic distortion is here in play, the difficulty of comprehension was presumably real enough. These passages support other evidence that the *Oresteia* was revived for performance before the fifth century was out (see end of §1 above). Among other writers these stand out: the Greek critic Dionysius of Halicarnassus (late 1st cent. BC), *On the Arrangement of Words* 22; the Roman rhetorician Quintilian (1st cent AD), *The Institution of Oratory* 10.66; and his near-contemporary the Greek intellectual Dio Chrysostom, *Oration* 52. These and the Aristophanes passages are handily available in translation in D. A. Russell and M. Winterbottom, *Ancient Literary Criticism* (1972).

that of Shakespeare in English literature. As a poet with words he is grand, magisterial, craggy, sonorous, colourful, brilliant; but he is also delicate, natural, everyday—at times so everyday that the mere contrast with the richer styles can make him seem almost pedestrian or colloquial.

This variety is purposeful; it brings the characters instantly alive. Many speeches, both long and short, are plausibly individualized to match the dramatic moment; their syntax is broken or irregular, to reflect strong emotions—for example the Herald's account of his hardships at *Ag.* 551–83 or the distress of Orestes' old Nurse at *LB* 734–65; Aegisthus' weak blustering is superbly caught in a few lines, *Ag.* 1617 ff., *LB* 838 ff. The long speeches of Clytemnestra and Cassandra in *Agamemnon* almost compete in the crowded riches of their language, especially when the first describes her beacon-chain (281–316) or offers her husband a fulsome welcome (855–913) and the second evokes the old and new horrors of the palace (1178–97, 1215–41). On the smallest scale too, Aeschylus has a habit of employing proverbs or axioms, often phrased colloquially, to suggest pressure or stress, for example in the Chorus at *Ag.* 251–5, Aegisthus at 1623–4, and Orestes at *LB* 521.

The *Oresteia* is as rich in poetic images as in those for the eye; they work vividly to deepen the impact of its ideas, and they survive translation very well. There are many metaphors and figures which run through all the plays and assist dramatic continuity. Particularly noticeable is imagery from hunting, whether of pursuit and capture or of netting and snaring. Hunters' pursuit most aptly pictures the Furies' keen-scented persecution of their quarry, and the image dominates *Eumenides* after lines 111–13, once Clytemnestra's ghost has stirred them to fresh activity. It develops from and works together with 'netting' when Clytemnestra traps Agamemnon in the robing (*Ag.* 1115–16, 1375–6, 1382, etc., *LB* 999–1000, *Eum.* 460–1, 634–5) which subsequently becomes the Furies' snare for the whole family (*Ag.* 1580; cf. too Cassandra 'caught' at 1048 and her detection of the 'scent' at 1185); later, Orestes similarly envelops the dead Clytemnestra and Aegisthus (*LB* 981–4, 1010–15). The hunting-imagery for the family's persecutions interacts with Agamemnon's tracking-down and capture of Troy (*Ag.* 694) and the omen of Zeus' eagles capturing and

tearing the hare (114–19 etc.) before Zeus casts his net over
Troy (358–60).

Zeus' remorseless justice against that city speaks out in overt
imagery from the law-court (we first encounter Agamemnon and
Menelaus as the 'plaintiffs' against Troy, *Ag.* 40; cf. 451, 810–
17, 831, etc.); Justice herself is frequently personified (§2.3
above). This legal language is used by the successive killers for
self-justification: Clytemnestra (*Ag.* 1396, 1431, etc.), Aegisthus
(1577, 1604, 1611), and Orestes (*LB* 244, 461, 497, etc.). At
LB 980 ff. a flurry of legal images anticipates the trial-scene in
Eumenides. Both Electra (*LB* 120, 144, 148, etc., 398) and her
women use the imagery also (311); they transfer the 'plaintiff'
imagery of Agamemnon against Troy to those seeking to avenge
him (330). Then the Furies adopt the language too, as they
pursue their own 'justice' (*Eum.* 154, 260, etc.) before both
metaphor and literal meaning find sustained expression in the
trial. The whole effect helps make the constantly ambiguous
issues of the trilogy readily accessible to the regular experience of
Aeschylus' audience as jurors (§1 above).

Equally telling, but in evocative finality, is imagery from
sacrifice: death or destruction, whether of persons, animals, or
things, is regularly presented through this metaphor. The image
is literal in the death of Iphigenia (*Ag.* 223–40, 1417, *LB* 255),
but even there the stronger association is with the predestined
and ritualized killing which corrupts the family (*Ag.* 151–5,
209–15: 'lawless', it is called, 151). The image is properly
applied, in that any sacrifice acknowledges a god's demand,
but in its misapplication it registers the hideous abnormality of
her death. Even the encouraging omen of the eagles devouring
the hare is subsequently invaded by this sinister term, when
Artemis takes offence, *Ag.* 137. The image continues in the
murders of Agamemnon and Cassandra (1056–7, 1118, 1277–8,
1409, etc.), in Orestes' matricide (*LB* 904, *Eum.* 102), and in the
Furies' pursuit of him as their destined 'sacrifice' (304–5, 328 =
341, etc.). As 'hunting' and 'justice' link family and Troy on the
inevitable path to punishment, so does 'sacrifice', after the 'first
rites' of the city's destruction are enacted at Aulis (*Ag.* 65, cf.
Troy at 720, 735, etc.).

Further repeated images contribute significantly to Aeschylus'
picture of a family which is in hereditary disorder and must learn

from its suffering in order to win back moral health and stability. Medicine is naturally prominent in colouring this attempt; it is a very common metaphor in any case, and appears as early as *Ag.* 17; see also especially *LB* 471, 539, *Eum.* 503–7. Orestes' fight for vengeance is frequently compared with wrestling in an image which also pervades the trilogy, appearing first as the Greeks' struggle against Trojan wrongdoing (*Ag.* 63, *LB* 339, etc.). Wrongdoing itself 'breeds', generating further retaliatory crime, *Ag.* 153, 750–72, *Eum.* 534 etc., where the sins of the parents are replicated in those of their avenging children; conversely, if Zeus will secure Orestes' safety, there is hope that the Atreid house will flourish again from a small seed (*LB* 203–4 etc.). Injury to the fresh generations of the disordered family (and destruction for Troy) is mirrored in harm, deprivation, or death done to animals and particularly birds and their young: *Ag.* 50–9, 717–49 (Troy); 119–20, 134–45, etc. (Zeus' eagles devour the hare); *LB* 247–58 (Orestes and Electra are the injured young of their 'eagle' father—a blunt reminiscence of *Ag.* 119–20 etc.). Clytemnestra dreams that she gives birth to a snake which bites her breast (*LB* 523 ff., cf. 928), and Orestes infers that he is himself the avenger in that guise (549–50); then he likens Clytemnestra herself to a noxious serpent (994–5, cf. 1047) before her vengeful Furies derange him, snakes writhing in their hair (1049–50, cf. *Eum.* 128). These and further images from nature are common in all Greek poetry, but they get importance from their interactive deployment throughout the trilogy.[35]

One last field of imagery is again all-pervasive; although much discussed, not all critics agree upon its power. It is that of colour generally, but especially literal and metaphorical contrast between light and dark. The trilogy begins in the night; the beacon-signal shines suddenly, bringing joyful but anxious hope (*Ag.* 21–3)—joy to Clytemnestra (26–30, 264, 316, etc.) but anxiety to Agamemnon's loyal men (34–9, 99–103, 251–5, etc.): the new day's light bodes only a different darkness, it is a false

---

[35] On Aeschylean imagery and metaphor in general see Rosenmeyer, *AA* 117–42 and Sommerstein, *AT* 241–55. For 'hunting' see particularly Lebeck and Vidal-Naquet in Bibliography §7. For 'perverted sacrifice' see especially Zeitlin also in Bibliography §7. For animals see especially J. Heath, 'Disentangling the Beast: Humans and Other Animals in Aeschylus' *Oresteia*', *Journal of Hellenic Studies*, 119 (1999), 17–47, with copious bibliography. The Explanatory Notes draw attention to many thematic images, usually at the places cited in these paragraphs.

dawn. The family palace is threatened or overcome with metaphorical dark (*Ag.* 466–7, *LB* 51–3, 61–5, etc.); the underworld
dark belongs to the Furies and is one of their weapons (*LB* 285,
288, *Eum.* 72 etc.; it is the world of their own mother Night,
Eum. 321–3) and they attempt to submerge Orestes in it (378–
80). Theatrically dark with menace too, in other ways, are the
start of *Libation Bearers*, with the black-clad Electra and Chorus
bearing the tomb-offerings; and the start of *Eumenides*, where the
black Furies emerge incongruously from the bright Delphic
temple, their underworld message of death compounded by
Clytemnestra's ghostly presence; then brilliant Apollo emerges
in turn, and the visible contrast of meaning lasts throughout the
trial-scenes at Athens. Night too was the time of Troy's destruction (*Ag.* 355–6 etc.), like that of the returning Greek fleet (653–
68), so that the first daylight of the Herald's safe homecoming is
delightful to him (508 etc.); the compression of dramatic time
helps to suggest that Agamemnon's day of return will bring
daylight in the night (522), even if it is happy rather to
Clytemnestra (900). The night-beacon which releases her joy
as the first play begins (*Ag.* 21–30, 86–7, etc.) contrasts with the
nightmares which terrify her when the second starts (*LB* 32–6),
so that she has the whole palace blaze with reassuring light
(535–7); but in between those passages the light of hope and
relief is associated rather with Orestes' return (131), and
Aeschylus tempts us to hear him making the contrast explicit
in 320 ('light is a state opposite to dark'). Later, Orestes is
emphatically the light of salvation (810, 863–4, 961). Many of
these hopeful lights are born from, and borne by, fire; some
readers see them recalled and transformed in the torchlight
flames which accompany the Furies in the trilogy's happy
ending (*Eum.* 1005 ff.). Fire is red: there appears to be a thematic
continuity through this colour in the bloodshed so frequently
evoked (esp. *Ag.* 1018–21, 1092, 1505–12, etc., *LB* 66–74, 400–
2, etc., *Eum.* 261–3 etc.) and in the blood which the Furies seek
to draw from the living man (*LB* 578, *Eum.* 264–8 etc.). The
fabrics strewn for Agamemnon by Clytemnestra are irresistibly
interpreted as a path of blood into—or out from—the bloodstained palace (*Ag.* 909, 957, etc.).[36]

---

[36] Theatrical productions regularly exploit the opportunity; so does the cover of
O. Taplin's *Greek Tragedy in Action* (1978)—and note the central panel of Francis Bacon's

4. AESCHYLUS NOW: 'RECEPTION' AND PUBLIC RESPONSE

Aeschylus' plays were first translated into English in the later eighteenth century, and became widely accessible only in the mid-nineteenth. Until then they were read in the original Greek only by learned men and a few university and school pupils using Latin translations and commentaries which concerned themselves almost exclusively with the immediate meaning of the text. Commentaries with English notes which considered questions of form and poetic style began to appear from the 1840s. These and later nineteenth century studies, however, hardly touched the theatrical aspects of his plays and their deeper issues; these had to wait until the second half of the twentieth century.[37]

In England at least Aeschylus began to inspire graphic artists earlier than he attracted theatrical producers;[38] in the twentieth century this direction was almost completely reversed. Painters were drawn to the *Oresteia* and (perhaps in the distant shadow of Shelley) to the *Prometheus Bound* from the 1860s.[39] Two powerful paintings inspired by the *Oresteia*, one from those years and one from the later twentieth century, demonstrate the gulf in artistic

triptych, §4 below. At *Eum.* 1028 red clothing is worn in the Furies' procession, but the Greek text is insecure; various meanings can be asserted (see the Explanatory Notes).

[37] The first translation was into verse, by R. Potter (1771 etc.). Very literal prose translations ('cribs') started to appear in the 1820s; further verse translations came after 1840, including Robert Browning's of the *Agamemnon* (1877) made famous by Terence Rattigan's play of 1948. Translations into European languages began at about the same time, only France having a slight lead over England. Aeschylus was much slower in reaching modern translation than the other surviving Greek tragedians, Sophocles and Euripides. The first complete commentary in English was F. A. Paley's (1855).

Detailed critical appreciation of Aeschylus as a poet of the theatre began in Britain only with Gilbert Murray's *Aeschylus* of 1933 (he had earlier translated some plays for performance); the USA was a little quicker, with e.g. H. W. Smyth's *Aeschylean Tragedy* (1924). The greatest recent advance is due to Oliver Taplin, especially his *The Stagecraft of Aeschylus* (1977), a pointer in many fresh directions, not only theatrical. Note also his more general book *Greek Tragedy in Action* (1978), which discusses the *Oresteia* at length.

[38] See F. Macintosh, *CCGT* 284–8.

[39] The most significant earlier works were thirteen drawings to illustrate the *Oresteia* made by John Flaxman in 1793–5; Shelley's *Prometheus Unbound* was published in 1820. I draw these and other details here from *The Oxford Guide to Greek Mythology in Art* (1993) under the entries 'Agamemnon, Iphigenia, Orestes'. Incidents recounted in the *Oresteia* appear in European painting at earlier dates, but the source of inspiration was almost entirely Latin poetry, or the Electra and Iphigenia plays of Sophocles and Euripides.

response between the poet's new public of the mid-nineteenth century and our own time.

In 1869 the already famous painter Frederic (later, Lord) Leighton exhibited a striking impression of Electra at the start of *Libation Bearers*.[40] She has poured offerings at Agamemnon's tomb; now she stands there in exhausted grief and desperate hope that Orestes will return to avenge him. Her figure is statuesque, a 'Classical' pose influenced by statuary,[41] robed all in black, half-filling the narrow vertical scene; only her toes, neck and face, and one arm thrown up agonizingly round her head set off the blackness with white. The moment is well-imagined; viewers who knew the trilogy or just the myth could if they wished supply context, prelude, and sequel; but the bleak power of the painting seems to keep the viewer at a distance. It represents extreme emotion but discourages equal response, let alone a closer enquiry into the cause than the picture itself provides with its explicit title and content; and it hardly shows the artist's concern for, perhaps not even his awareness of, the tragic issues which dominate the trilogy. Leighton's scene allows Electra no other dimension than very great but stylized sorrow.[42]

Contrast a work of the later twentieth century, Francis Bacon's *Triptych inspired by the 'Oresteia' of Aeschylus* (1981), which he painted after nearly forty years' obsession with the trilogy.[43] The three panels allude to major issues of the trilogy

[40] *Electra at the Tomb of Agamemnon*, now in the Ferens Art Gallery, City of Hull; the best reproduction is S. Jones (ed.), *Frederic Leighton, 1830–1896* (Royal Academy of Arts, 1996), Pl. 57, with text and bibliography. A friend of Leighton recorded that he was inspired directly by the play; he imagines Electra's dress approximately as it is described in lines 16–18 and her actions as portrayed throughout 87–163. See cover picture.

[41] Leighton's technique was often to paint his Classical figures nude, practically as sculptural, and then to drape them: see R. Jenkyns, *The Victorians and Classical Greece* (1980), 311. Jenkyns's pp. 305-14 portray Leighton, amid a review of later Victorian 'Classical' art on pp. 308–30; pp. 87–111 examine the Victorian response to Greek Tragedy.

[42] Leighton's picture quickly had one pale successor, almost certainly an imitation as compliment. In 1877 (later, Sir) William Blake Richmond, an acquaintance of Leighton since his student years, exhibited his own *Electra at the Grave of Agamemnon* (now in the Art Gallery of Ontario, Canada). It forms the cover picture and Colour Plate XIV of S. Reynolds, *William Blake Richmond: An Artist's Life* (1995) and is discussed on pp. 111–12, 117–18 as 'more gracious in composition'; certainly it is pretty rather than impressive. Reynolds's Colour Plate XXII is of Richmond's *An Audience in Athens during the Representation of the 'Agamemnon'* (now in the Birmingham City Museum and Art Gallery), painted in 1884, which according to the exhibition catalogue showed the spectators reacting to Agamemnon's murder as described by Clytemnestra (*Ag.* 1384–7).

[43] Since his 1944 *Three Studies for Figures at the Base of a Crucifixion* (repainted in 1988); this is Pl. 1 in D. Ades and A. Forge (eds.), *Francis Bacon* (London, 1985). The *Triptych* is

and their theatrical representation, particularly bloodshed, but without confinement to individual scenes or their sequence. Unlike Leighton's self-contained picture, a knowledge of the trilogy is essential to the viewer's understanding, to his entry into the painter's imagination. Bacon presupposes the viewer's empathetic knowledge of Aeschylus, not simply of the myth in outline. The central panel is the most striking and the most immediately comprehensible. The background is a huge rectangle of monotone colour, that of the dark blood so vivid and constant in the plays' imagery, and Bacon's particular preoccupation. The rectangle carries the outlined steps and dais of a royal throne, and forms a seeming wall or even doorway behind it; it suggests that moment of the *Agamemnon* when purple fabrics are thrown down for the king to tread upon as he enters his palace-door. On the throne sits—or writhes—a contorted figure; its neck is grotesquely elongated and the vertebrae are exposed in Bacon's characteristic X-ray vision, and it is bent low so that apparent teeth in a featureless face seem about to devour the figure's own genitals. The figure may represent any or all of Atreus, Agamemnon, and Orestes; but it fits Orestes especially, who must torture himself in reclaiming his throne by avenging his father's death upon his mother. This royal family breeds crime and devours its own generations, on the first occasion quite literally: tricked into eating his own children's flesh, Thyestes cursed his brother Atreus' family-line with self-destruction.

Bacon's imagination seized upon this bloodstained plot to force his viewer inside its horrific tragedy, the simultaneous conflict and co-operation between a fated, dreadful duty of revenge and an individual will to act and survive. His art and its manner were no less historically determined—and made possible—than those of Leighton, whose *Electra* wrung powerful if limited impact from the classicizing conventions of his day.

The same developing imagination is revealed in the history of stage-performances of Aeschylus in Britain. The first certainly known were of the *Agamemnon* in Edinburgh in the 1870s and Oxford in 1880—but the latter was in the original Greek,

---

Pl. 110; Ades, ibid. 11, 17, and esp. 20–1, discusses it in association with the earlier work. Bacon said that he was haunted by *Eumenides* 253 in W. B. Stanford's translation, 'the reek of human blood smiles out at me': see Ades, ibid. 17.

simulated an 'ancient performance' as scholarship then imagined it, and was intended for a narrow, university-dominated public.[44] Occasional productions followed, mostly of the *Agamemnon* alone and particularly of *Prometheus Bound*, but only since the Second World War has the entire *Oresteia* enjoyed frequent performance, usually in translation and often in adaptation. Most famous, and a landmark in international theatrical history, was Sir Peter Hall's production for the National Theatre in 1981, in the forceful poetic version by Tony Harrison; it has been recorded on video-film. The physical frame and ambience of Aeschylus' own theatre were re-created (the production transferred readily to 'ancient' Greece itself, in the fourth-century-BC theatre at Epidaurus). All was power and tragic grandeur, with strikingly formalized masks for the actors and plangent music from Sir Harrison Birtwistle. The architecture and inevitable flow of the trilogy were measured out in scenes both static and mobile; the profound complexities of meaning were preserved in language as energetic as Aeschylus' own. A subsequent noteworthy production was of Ted Hughes's creative translation by L. Mitchell at the National Theatre in 2000.[45]

Aeschylus' Greek text is still being mined for deeper meanings, his artistry with language, verse, and staging is ever more subtly described. Scholars' work feeds continuously into new interpretations, and itself learns from new stage-productions. Translations intended not only for academic markets but for general readers and play-goers appear very frequently, but Aeschylus' secure return to the theatre is perhaps the most important of his modern revivals.

---

[44] The Edinburgh production is included in Hall and Macintosh, Bibliography §9 (forthcoming). The Oxford production, for which the set was designed by Edward Burne-Jones, was quickly repeated at Cambridge: see *CCGT* 290–1 and *Omnibus* 36 (1998). *Eumenides* was one of the first in the long series of Cambridge Greek Plays, in 1885.

[45] For the history of Aeschylus, and especially the *Oresteia*, on the stage world-wide see *CCGT* 281, 289–91, 314–18; Bierl and others in Bibliography §9. The *Agamemnon* was chosen both to inaugurate the production of Greek plays at Syracuse in Sicily from 1914 and to mark the foundation of the Greek National Theatre in Athens in 1932. An Archive of Performances of Greek and Roman Drama is now established in the University of Oxford, under the direction of Professors Oliver Taplin and Edith Hall; in 2001 the Archive hosted an international conference entitled '*Agamemnon* in performance, 458 BC–2001 AD', from which the papers will be published in 2002/3.

TEXT

THE basis of Aeschylus' Greek text is precarious. Only seven plays survive complete from his estimated total production of more than eighty; of these seven, only three are preserved in any considerable number of medieval manuscripts which have independent importance (*Persians, Seven*, and the disputably authentic *Prometheus Bound*), while the other four depend variously upon a very few quite closely related manuscripts or even upon one alone (the three plays of the *Oresteia* and *Suppliants*). In the *Oresteia*, in fact, *Agamemnon* survives complete in no single manuscript of authority, but in fragmentary manuscripts or in edited copies; *Libation Bearers* is found only in one manuscript of authority, and *Eumenides* in the same manuscript but also in a few others of a slightly different and inferior tradition.

The one manuscript of supreme authority for the *Oresteia* has suffered physical damage. It contains only 400 lines of *Agamemnon*'s 1,670, in two separated stretches; and it lacks the first 30 or so lines of *Libation Bearers*, from which we have only a few fragmentary quotations. Furthermore, this manuscript, like all others of Aeschylus, frequently offers a text so corrupt that editors cannot reconstruct Aeschylus' original words with any confidence; instead, they are often forced to make the best diagnosis they can of a corruption, and to emend it as best they can by conjecture. Scholarship has moved gradually to a consensus about the quality of the manuscript tradition, but there are very many doubts and disputes still about healing its damage.

The Greek text translated here is that edited by M. L. West (in the Bibliotheca Teubneriana, 1990[1], 1998[2]). It is acknowledged as the most thorough and authoritative modern edition in describing and evaluating the manuscripts; and its critical apparatus is generous in reporting manuscript readings and editors' corrections and conjectures. West's edited text is often adventurous in conjecture, but sometimes also surprisingly conservative where he retains what many other editors have condemned and emended. It is consistently honest in marking as desperately corrupt the numerous words or passages which he believes have yet to receive plausible conjecture, let alone convincing emendation. My translation replaces this corrupt wording with what seem to be the soundest conjectures from his apparatus (I have listed these in the Textual Appendix after the Explanatory Notes). Places where text has been lost are signalled in the translation with '*words missing*' or the like enclosed by square brackets; where there can be little doubt of the sense of the words lost, I supply it inside these brackets. I think it important that users of this translation, whether able to read the original Greek or not, should know the degree of authority for what they read and be careful accordingly when they interpret both drama and poetry. Many of these places, and some others where West's edited text is less secure but still problematic, are therefore discussed in the Explanatory Notes.[1]

TRANSLATION

The varying reliability of the Greek text adds to the difficulties of translating a poet as individual as Aeschylus. First, the primary meaning even where the text seems entirely secure and straightforward is often fiercely contested, and not only because the surrounding context may sometimes be ambiguous or damaged: Aeschylus is often abrupt in expression, and in changing ideas or topics, and the precise implication of a sudden new one can be hard to fix. Second, Aeschylus' verbal style is flexible and daring, sometimes clear and easy, especially in speech, sometimes complex, dense, and full of suggestive imagery: an attempt to describe it is made in the Introduction §3.4, above.

Can this singular richness be reproduced in translation? The translation which I offer here is not a poet's. I have tried above all to make it readable and accurate; but even with allowance made for the state of Aeschylus' text, there will be many places

---

[1] For a succinct description of Aeschylus' manuscript and editorial history see Sommerstein, *Eumenides* (1989), 35–6; longer in Rosenmeyer, *AA* 11–28.

where my translation can and will be disputed, and where other interpretations are not disprovable. I have tried to reflect the general tone and flow of the language, in particular the broad variations in diction and style which follow from the alternation between speech and lyric. I have been as consistent as possible in the translation of words and ideas which regularly recur and have thematic importance; and I have reproduced many close repetitions of words which may be not so much deliberate as unconsidered or even unconscious (the Greeks were apparently much less sensitive than we are to this kind of repetition). I have tried not to go too far from the imagery or idiom of the original if it can be kept without unnaturalness in English. I have occasionally adjusted the limited style of ancient Greek punctuation to the more flexible English kind, particularly by using exclamation marks; but I have very seldom changed its location, and then only to make clear the emphasis and sequence of ideas. Parenthesis is marked by dashes; I use square brackets to indicate or supplement brief textual defects (see 'Text', above); round brackets enclose italicized 'stage-directions'.

The translation of spoken dialogue, and of spoken verses set among lyric, is into prose (*Ag.* 1074–5, 1078–9, etc. are the first examples encountered in the *Oresteia*); but I have been more ambitious—or self-indulgent—in translating lyric. Those lyric verses which were apparently intoned or chanted, in an almost regular anapaestic rhythm, I have rendered line-by-line, but with no attempt at imitating the rhythmic regularity (*Ag.* 40–103, for example). Pure song, whether choral or antiphonal between chorus and actor (*Ag.* 1114 ff., for example), I have translated differently, in an attempt to show its distinctive nature and emotional intensity, and the importance of the choral songs to the action and meaning (see Introduction §3.3). This pure lyric is for the most part shaped by Aeschylus into stanzas in pairs which have identical form and rhythm, every line 'responding' between *strophe* and *antistrophe* (§3.3); in these stanza-pairs I have tried to achieve near-response in the number of syllables in the English line, and, where I can, also approximate rhythmic response in stressed and unstressed syllables. There has been some loss in the lyric, however: achieving readability in our language has often brought some sacrifice of exactly those effects of compression, juxtaposition, and sound described above as individual to

Aeschylus. I disclaim any pretension to have made these lyric parts more 'poetic' than the remainder of the translation; if they appear and read 'differently', that achieves my main object.[2]

Lastly, I must record a few special difficulties in translating Greek Tragedy over which all translators agonize. Words describing or evoking social or moral values and behaviour, injury, outrage, and suffering; their physical and emotional impact; and reaction to them in pain, anger, resentment, grief, and lamentation—these are the life-blood of Tragedy. Greek is rich with these words, and some individual ones appear in differing contexts which occasionally force on them differing translations in English; here any translator must choose as best he can from the idiom of his own day. In particular, English is losing from everyday use many words which seem appropriate for a vocabulary of extreme suffering; these are such archaic-sounding or almost self-conscious literary words as 'woe' or 'evils' and the exclamation 'alas!', and I have for the most part tried to avoid them. Commonplace and ritualized ancient reactions to hurt like constant tears and loud, demonstrative grief are also obsolescent in much of the modern English-speaking world and its culture; literal translation of the Greek terms inevitably sounds strange or exaggerated to the modern ear, and more than strange in its insistent repetition. Greek had also many exclamations, some of them apparently inarticulate; in Tragedy those of pain and grief naturally predominate. I have sometimes reduced these from their full and impressive sonority to a mere 'O-o-oh!' or the like; or I replace or accompany them with an articulate meaning such as 'Horrible!' or 'No!', or with an italicized 'stage-direction', much as a modern dramatist might use, like '(*shrieking*)'.[3]

---

[2] See Edith Hall's assessment of H. D. F. Kitto's very successful translation of Sophocles, made upon approximately similar lines: *Sophocles: Antigone, Oedipus the King, Electra* (1994, this series), pp. xxxiii–xxxiv. In his early life Gerard Manley Hopkins experimented with translations of *Prometheus*; and towards the end of it he contemplated a full study of *Libation Bearers*: if only in his poetic maturity he had translated the whole of the *Oresteia*, for in his own work he came perhaps nearer to Aeschylus' verbal brilliance than any other English poet.

[3] There is a huge international literature on the difficulties of translating Greek Tragedy. In addition to the remarks made by all translators themselves, see for Aeschylus in English especially P. Green, 'Some Versions of Aeschylus', in his *Essays in Antiquity* (1950), an essay reprinted more than once; K. J. Dover, 'The Speakable and the Unspeakable', *Greek and the Greeks* (1987), 176–81; and P. Burian, 'Translations Yesterday and Today', *CCGT*, 271–6.

Line-numbers are those of the Greek text, placed in the margin at the point of approximate correspondence.

The 'stage-directions' depend as far as possible on modern consensus how the plays were probably performed in the ancient theatre. Practically all are safe inferences from the text about the moments of entry and exit and their manner, and about costume, movement, posture, and gesture. Special problems are discussed in the Explanatory Notes.

In reproducing the names of persons and places I have followed the comfortable tradition of preferring familiar Latinized or Anglicized forms to the more accurately (and now modishly) transliterated Greek ones—for example, I use Clytemnestra rather than Klutaimestra, Athens rather than Athenai. In the usual pronunciation, all single vowels are voiced, especially final -*e*, which is long, as in (e.g.) Hecate (an exception is English monosyllabic Thrace). Adjacent vowels should be pronounced as a diphthong unless the second is marked with diaeresis, as in (e.g.) Deïphobus. The commonest diphthongs are -*ae*-, which in English convention varies between -*i*- as in *high* (e.g. Cithaeron) and -*ee*- (e.g. Aegisthus); -*au*- as in *noun* (e.g. Aulis—but many say 'Awlis'); -*eu*- as in *deuce* (e.g. Zeus); -*oe*- as in *subpoena* (e.g. Euboea). Both initial and internal *c* and *ch* (representing Greek *k* and *kh*) are hard, as in (e.g.) Calchas (Greek *Kalkhas*); but both initial and internal *c* are soft before -*e*- or -*i*-, especially in Latinized names, such as Cilicia. The Greeks frequently personified abstract concepts as gods or powers; I have rendered these as far as possible with a capitalized English translation, for example Justice for *Dikê*, Fate for *Moira*, Fury for *Erinus*. (In the Explanatory Notes Greek names and words are sometimes transliterated in underlined italics to serve etymological clarification.)

EXPLANATORY NOTES

The three plays of the *Oresteia* are very closely interwoven in themes, ideas, emotions, images both poetic and theatrical, and words. The Notes therefore have it as one of their chief aims to mark these connections, or to refer to discussion of them in the Introduction. For the rest, the Notes range very widely, in the hope that explanation or brief comment will help fuller appreciation of this astoundingly complex trilogy. Occasional note is made of comparable matter and language in the other plays of Aeschylus and in Homer's *Iliad* and *Odyssey*, but very seldom in other Greek drama. Purely textual notes are enclosed in bold square brackets and where possible given the final place in an extended discussion of a line or passage.

Bibliography and Further Reading

ITEMS listed are mostly recent books and a few articles, almost all in English or English translation. They are all important or useful; many contain their own bibliographies, so that readers may have a number of starting-points to follow up their own interests. Items in each section are arranged in chronological order; those which require a good knowledge of Greek are asterisked, but apart from text-critical works and linguistic commentaries (mostly in §§2 and 3), hardly anything is listed which will not yield most of its value to someone armed with this or any other translation which gives the line-numbers of the Greek text.

1.1. *Complete English translations of Aeschylus.* R. Lattimore in D. Grene and R. Lattimore (eds.), *Complete Greek Tragedies,* Vol. 1, 1953: still the 'standard' complete translation. H. W. Smyth, 2 vols. (Loeb Classical Library), 2nd edn. 1957: includes the great majority of the Fragments. M. Ewans, 2 vols. (Everyman), 1995–6 includes major fragments and is directed at a 'performance' text, with notes accordingly.

1.2. *Translations of the* Oresteia (a very small selection, in a range of styles). L. MacNeice *(Agamemnon* only), 1936: an admired verse-translation. R. Fagles (Penguin), 1977: with Introduction and Notes by W. B. Stanford: an extremely spirited and often free 'poetic' translation. H. Lloyd-Jones, 2nd edn. 1979: superbly accurate, with valuable notes (in part dependent upon important textual discussions reprinted in his *Academic Papers: Greek Epic, Lyric and Tragedy* (1990), 238–354). T. Harrison, 1981: a 'creative' and poetic translation, made for Sir Peter Hall's famous National Theatre production. F. Raphael and K. McLeish, *The Serpent Son,* 1981: a very free version, made for television. D. R. Slavitt, *Aeschylus I. The Oresteia,* 1998. Ted Hughes, *The Oresteia,* 1999: a vigorous verse-translation (published post-humously as a bare 'performance' text).

2. *Critical editions of the Greek text. Surviving plays*: *D. L. Page, 1972 (Oxford Classical Text); *M. L. West, 2nd edn. 1998 (Teubner Series), supplemented by his *Studies in Aeschylus,* 1990. Both these editions have introductory matter and critical apparatus in Latin; West's two volumes have full bibliography of text-critical work. See also Lloyd-Jones in §1.2 above. *Fragments*: *Tragicorum Graecorum Fragmenta, Vol. 3: Aeschylus,* ed. S. L. Radt, 1985: exhaustive critical edition, with some

interpretative matter, in Latin. English readers have Smyth (§1.1. above), Vol. 2, pp. 374–521, with Appendix by H. Lloyd-Jones, pp. 525–603 (Greek text, English translation and brief introductory notes) and Ewans (also §1.1 above), Vol. 2, English translation only.

3.1. *Complete commentaries on the surviving plays.* *F. A. Paley, The Tragedies of Aeschylus*, 4th edn., 1879: Paley's common-sense makes his work still useful. *H. J. Rose, *A Commentary on the Surviving Plays of Aeschylus*, 2 vols., 1957–8. J. Hogan, *A Commentary on the Complete Greek Tragedies of Aeschylus*, 1984: based on the Lattimore translation of 1953 (§1.1 above).

3.2. *Editions and commentaries of the individual plays of the* Oresteia. *Agamemnon*: *E. Fraenkel, 3 vols., 1950 includes a literal prose translation; a work of monumental scholarship, but largely philological. *D. L. Page (with J. D. Denniston), 1957, for university students, deliberately complements and often challenges Fraenkel, and is also heavily text-based. *Libation Bearers*: *A. Bowen, 1986: very useful brief general commentary. *A. F. Garvie, 1986: full-scale critical, linguistic, and interpretative commentary. *Eumenides*: *A. J. Podlecki, 1989: contains an English translation; a 'student' commentary, very well documented. *A. H. Sommerstein, 1989: excellent edition and commentary, more ambitious than Podlecki's. Also: *G. Thomson, *The Oresteia of Aeschylus*, 2nd edn., 1966. D. J. Conacher, *Aeschylus' Oresteia: A Literary Commentary*, 1987.

4. *Bibliographical surveys of Aeschylus.* The literature is vast; the most helpful starting point for all enquiries is now Sommerstein, *AT* 447–79, who categorizes and briefly evaluates a large range of publications. *CCGT* 355 has a list of Texts, Commentaries, and Translations of Aeschylus, and on pp. 359–79 a list of Works Cited in the entire volume. S. Ireland, *Aeschylus* ('Greece and Rome' New Surveys in the Classics 18), 1986 surveys the principal aspects of Aeschylean tragedy, with good bibliographic annotation.

5. *General studies of Greek Tragedy in English.* J. P. Vernant and P. Vidal-Naquet, *Tragedy and Myth in Ancient Greece*, trans. J. Lloyd, 1981 (original French edition of 1973). O. P. Taplin, *Greek Tragedy in Action*, 1978. A. Lesky, *Greek Tragic Poetry*, 1983 (the bibliography remains as in the original German edition of 1972). W. B. Stanford, *Greek Tragedy and the Emotions*, 1983. *CHGL* (1985), 258–345 (various authors). S. Goldhill, *Reading Greek Tragedy*, 1986. C. Segal, *Interpreting Greek Tragedy: Myth, Poetry, Texts*, 1986. P. D. Arnott, *Public and Performance in the Greek Theatre*, 1989. J. J. Winkler and F. I. Zeitlin (eds.), *Nothing to do with Dionysos? Athenian Drama in its Social Context*, 1990. B. Zimmermann, *Greek Tragedy: An Introduction*, 1991 (original German edition of 1985): a brief student's handbook. R. Rehm, *The*

Greek Tragic Theatre, 1992: concentrates on 'performance'. E. Csapo and W. J. Slater, *The Context of Ancient Drama*, 1993: the ancient evidence translated, analysed, and annotated. C. Meier, *The Political Art of Greek Tragedy* (translated from the German by A. Webber), 1993. R. B. Soodel (ed.), *Theater and Society in the Classical World*, 1993. J. R. Green, *Theatre in Ancient Greek Society*, 1994. R. A. Seaford, *Reciprocity and Ritual: Homer and Tragedy in the Developing City-State*, 1994. *CCGT* (1997): studies on the historical context of Tragedy, on the plays (the *Oresteia* is discussed throughout) and on Tragedy's reception since antiquity. D. Wiles, *Tragedy in Athens: Performance Space and Theatrical Meaning*, 1997. A. P. Burnett, *Revenge in Attic and Later Tragedy*, 1998. B. Goward, *Telling Tragedy: Narrative Technique in Aeschylus, Sophocles and Euripides*, 1998. S. Goldhill and R. Osborne (eds.), *Performance Culture and Athenian Democracy*, 1999. J. Griffin, 'The Social Function of Attic Tragedy', *Classical Quarterly*, 48 (1998), 39–61, with responses by R. Seaford, ibid. 50 (2000), 20–45, and S. Goldhill, *Journal of Hellenic Studies*, 120 (2000), 34–56. C. B. R. Pelling, *Literary Texts and the Greek Historian*, 2000 (cf. also his edited volume *Greek Tragedy and the Historian*, 1998). D. Wiles, *Greek Theatre Practice*, 2000. P. Wilson, 'Powers of Horror and Laughter: The Great Age of Drama', in O. P. Taplin (ed.), *Literature in the Greek and Roman Worlds: A New Perspective* (2000), 88–132.

6.1. *General studies of Aeschylus.* M. Gagarin, *Aeschylean Drama*, 1976 (a useful general study). J. Herington, *Aeschylus*, 1981. T. J. Rosenmeyer, *The Art of Aeschylus*, 1982: the fullest dramatic and literary appreciation. R. P. Winnington-Ingram, *Studies in Aeschylus*, 1983 (see also his chapter 'Aeschylus' in *CHGL* (1985), 281–95). Sommerstein, *AT*, 1996: comprehensive handbook. A. J. Podlecki, *The Political Background of Aeschylean Tragedy*, 2nd edn., 1999.

6.2. *Language and style in Aeschylus.* *W. B. Stanford, *Aeschylus in his Style*, 1942. *B. H. Fowler, 'Aeschylus' Imagery', *Classica et Mediaevalia*, 28 (1967), 1–74. *D. Sansone, *Aeschylean Metaphors for Intellectual Activity*, Berlin 1975. Cf. also Lebeck (1971) in §7 below and Conacher (1996) in §3.2 above.

6.3. *Characterization in Aeschylus.* R. D. Dawe, 'Inconsistency of Plot and Character in Aeschylus', *Proceedings of the Cambridge Philological Society*, 9 (1963), 3–19. P. E. Easterling, 'Presentation of Character in Aeschylus', *Greece & Rome*, 20 (1973), 3–19 = (*G & R Studies 2: Greek Tragedy* (1995), 12–28). Essays by P. E. Easterling, 'Constructing Character in Greek Tragedy' and S. Goldhill, 'Character and Action', in C. B. R. Pelling (ed.), *Characterization and Individuality in Greek Tragedy* (1990), 83–99, 100–27.

6.4. *Aeschylus on the ancient stage.* A. D. Trendall and T. B. L.

Bibliography and Further Reading

Webster, *Illustrations of Greek Theatre* (1970), 41–9. O. P. Taplin, *The Stagecraft of Aeschylus*, 1977: documents, subsumes, and qualifies all previous studies (cf. Taplin (1978) in §5 above). R. Green and E. W. Handley, *Images of the Greek Theatre*, 1995. Cf. also Arnott (1989), Rehm (1992), Csapo and Slater (1993), Green (1991), and Wiles (1997 and 2000) in §5 above, Sider (1978) in §7 below.

7. *Some studies and appreciations of the* Oresteia. J. Jones, *Aristotle and Greek Tragedy*, 1962. N. G. L. Hammond, 'Personal Freedom and its Limitations in the *Oresteia*', *Journal of Hellenic Studies*, 82 (1965), 42–55. F. I. Zeitlin, 'The Motif of the Corrupted Sacrifice in Aeschylus' *Oresteia*', *Transactions of the American Philological Association*, 96 (1965), 463–508, and 97 (1966), 645–53. J. Fontenrose, 'Gods and Men in the *Oresteia*', *TAPA* 102 (1971), 71–109. *A. Lebeck, *The* Oresteia*: A Study in Language and Structure*, 1971 (on the thematic imagery). D. Sider, 'Stagecraft in the *Oresteia*', *American Journal of Philology*, 99 (1978), 12–27. F. I. Zeitlin, 'The Dynamics of Misogyny: Myth and Mythmaking in the *Oresteia*', *Arethusa*, 11 (1978), 149–84. P. Vidal-Naquet, 'Hunting and Sacrifice in Aeschylus' *Oresteia*', in Vernant and Vidal-Naquet (1981), 150–74, in §5 above. C. W. Macleod, 'Politics in the *Oresteia*', *Journal of Hellenic Studies*, 102 (1982), 124–44 (*Collected Papers* (1983), 202–40). A. L. Brown, 'The Erinyes in the Oresteia', *Journal of Hellenic Studies*, 103 (1983), 13–34. H. Lloyd-Jones, *The Justice of Zeus*, 2nd edn., 1983 and the Introduction to his translation of the *Oresteia* (§1.2 above). D. H. Roberts, *Apollo and his Oracle in the* Oresteia, 1984. A. J. W. Prag, *The* Oresteia*: Iconography and the Narrative Tradition*, 1985. W. G. Thalmann, 'Speech and Silence in the *Oresteia*', *Phoenix*, 29 (1985), 98–118, 221–37. S. Goldhill, *Aeschylus: Oresteia*, 1992: a brief but comprehensive monograph (cf. the response by M. C. Clark and E. Csapo, 'Deconstruction, Ideology and Goldhill's *Oresteia*', *Phoenix*, 35 (1991), 95–125). R. Rehm, *Greek Tragic Theatre* (1992), especially pp. 77–108. A. M. Bowie, 'Religion and Politics in Aeschylus' *Oresteia*', *Classical Quarterly*, 43 (1993), 10–31. M. Griffith, 'Brilliant Dynasts: Power and Politics in the *Oresteia*', *California Studies in Classical Antiquity*, 14 (1995), 62–129. A. Maria van Erp Taalman Kip, 'The Unity of the *Oresteia*', in M. S. Silk (ed.), *Tragedy and the Tragic* (1996), 119–28, with 'response' by A. F. Garvie, pp. 139–48. See also Conacher (1987) in §3.2 above.

8. *Studies of the Individual Plays of the* Oresteia.

8.1. Agamemnon. B. M. W. Knox, 'The Lion in the House', *Classical Philology*, 47 (1952), 104–24 = (Knox, *Word and Action* (1979), 27–38). K. J. Dover, 'Some Neglected Aspects of Agamemnon's Dilemma', *Journal of Hellenic Studies*, 93 (1973), 58–69 = *Greek and the Greeks* (1987), 135–50. K. J. Dover, 'The Red Fabrics in the

Agamemnon', in *Greek and the Greeks* (1987), 151–60 (first published in Italian in 1977). M. W. Edwards, 'Agamemnon's Decision: Freedom and Folly in Aeschylus', *California Studies in Classical Antiquity*, 10 (1977), 17–38. T. Gantz, 'The Chorus of Aeschylus' *Agamemnon*', *Harvard Studies in Classical Philology*, 87 (1983), 65–86. H. Lloyd-Jones, 'Artemis and Iphigenia', *Journal of Hellenic Studies*, 103 (1983), 87–102. G. J. P. O'Daly, 'Clytemnestra and the Elders: Dramatic Technique in Aeschylus, *Agamemnon* 1372–1576', *Museum Helveticum*, 42 (1985), 1–19. G. Ferrari, 'Figures in the Text: Metaphors and Riddles in the *Agamemnon*', *Classical Philology*, 92 (1997), 1–45.

8.2. Libation Bearers. D. Wiles, 'The Staging of the Recognition Scene in the *Choephoroi*', *Classical Quarterly*, 38 (1988), 82–5. M. McCall, 'The Chorus of Aeschylus' *Choephori*', in M. Griffith and D. J. Mastronarde (eds.), *Cabinet of the Muses: Essays . . . in Honor of Thomas G. Rosenmeyer* (1990), 117–30. A. P. Burnett, 'Ritualized Revenge: Aeschylus' *Choephori*', in §5 above (1998), pp. 99–118.

8.3. Eumenides. K. J. Dover, 'The Political Aspects of Aeschylus' *Eumenides*', *Journal of Hellenic Studies*, 77 (1957), 230–7 = (*Greek and the Greeks* (1987), 161–75). A. Henrichs, 'Anonymity and Polarity: Unknown Gods and Nameless Altars at the Areopagus', *Illinois Classical Studies*, 19 (1994), 27–58. K. Sidwell, 'Purification and Pollution in Aeschylus' *Eumenides*', *Classical Quarterly*, 46 (1996), 44–57; 'The Politics of Aeschylus' *Eumenides*', *Classics Ireland*, 3 (1996), 182–203. Cf. also Meier (1993) in §5 above, pp. 102–36.

9. *'Reception' of the* Oresteia *in later times*. A. T. Sheppard, *Aeschylus and Sophocles: Their Work and Influence*, 1927. K. Mackinnon, *Greek Tragedy into Film*, 1986. J. D. Reid, *Oxford Guide to Classical Mythology in the Arts, 1300–1990s*, 1993, entries under 'Agamemnon, Iphigenia in Aulis, Orestes'. K. V. Hartigan, *Greek Tragedy on the American Stage* (1995), 68–81. A. Bierl, *Die Oresteia des Aischylos auf der modernen Bühne* ('Aeschylus' *Oresteia* on the Modern Stage'), 1996. P. Burian, 'Tragedy Adapted for Stages and Screens: The Renaissance to the Present', *CCGT* (1997), 228–83 (extremely well documented), especially 'Orestes and Electra in the Twentieth Century', 254–61 (on E. O'Neill, *Mourning Becomes Electra*, T. S. Eliot, *The Family Reunion*, J.-P. Sartre, *Les Mouches*). F. Macintosh, 'Tragedy in Performance: Nineteenth- and Twentieth-Century Production', *CCGT* (1997), 284–323 (with Bibliography on pp. 321–2), especially 290–1, 314–19 on the *Oresteia*). Wiles (§5 above, 2000), 179–208. A study by E. Hall and F. Macintosh, *Greek Tragedy and the British Stage, 1660–1914*, is expected in 2001/2002. See also §4 n. 45 above for a forthcoming collection of papers and essays on the 'reception' of the *Agamemnon*.

A Chronology of Aeschylus' Life and Times

c. 525 BC	Born into a prominent aristocratic family in Athens
510	Final expulsion from Athens of the sixth-century tyrants and the first movements towards full democracy
490s	Begins his career as a dramatist
490	Fights at Marathon against the first Persian invasion (King Darius)
484	First victory in the dramatic competitions
480–79	Fights, or is present, at the battle of Salamis and perhaps of Plataea, against the second Persian invasion (King Xerxes)
470s	Athens heads an anti-Persian alliance of Greek city-states which eventually becomes regarded as her 'empire'
	Aeschylus visits Sicily, by invitation—an indication of his already established fame
472	Victorious with *Persians*, narrating their disastrous defeat at Salamis, in an unconnected trilogy, the other plays having mythic plots
468	Sophocles enters the dramatic competition for the first time, and is victorious over Aeschylus
467	Victorious with *Seven*, in a connected trilogy on the Oedipus-story
460s	Further democratic advances and reforms at Athens, driven by Ephialtes and Pericles
463?	Victorious with *Suppliants*, in a connected trilogy on the Danaid-myth
458	Victorious with the *Oresteia* (see p. 114)
	Return visit to Sicily, again by invitation, probably in this year
456	Death in Sicily
455	Euripides' dramatic career begins

Only attested or confidently reconstructed dates, and events relevant to the plays, are given. For discussion of the poet's life and biography see M. Lefkowitz, *Lives of the Greek Poets* (1981), 67–74 and 157–60, Rosenmeyer, *AA* 369–76 (with a 'Table') and Sommerstein, *AT* 19–30

Family Trees of the Principal Characters of the Oresteia

The *Atreidae*, 'the sons of Atreus', are the royal house of Argos. Aeschylus has made their ancestry vague, with all three of Tantalus (*Ag.* 1469), Pelops (*Ag.* 1600, *LB* 503), and Pleisthenes (*Ag.* 1569, 1602) giving their name to the remoter family-line. Myth names Pelops consistently as the son of Tantalus but only sometimes as the father of Atreus; Pleisthenes is either ancestor of Atreus or his son. The family-tree in the *Oresteia* is:

(Tantalus/Pelops/Pleisthenes as ancestors of the brothers Atreus and Thyestes)

```
                  Atreus                              Thyestes
                                                         |
                                                      Aegisthus
Menelaus (marr. Helen)  Agamemnon (marr. Clytemnestra)  ("marr." Clytemnestra)
                              |
            Orestes        Iphigenia        Electra
```

Clytemnestra and Helen are half-sisters in myth: Clytemnestra is the daughter of Tyndareus (*Ag.* 83) and of Leda (*Ag.* 914), both of them mortals; Helen is the daughter of Leda and Zeus.

The *Priamidae*, 'the sons of Priam', are the royal house of Troy. Their name stands also for the Trojans generally. In the *Oresteia* the only family names which occur are:

```
                        Priam

Paris/Alexandros (marr. Helen)              Cassandra
```

For fuller details of the major mythical families see M. L. West, *The Hesiodic Catalogue of Women* (1985), esp. the Tables on p. 182 (Atreidae) and p. 180 (Priamidae).

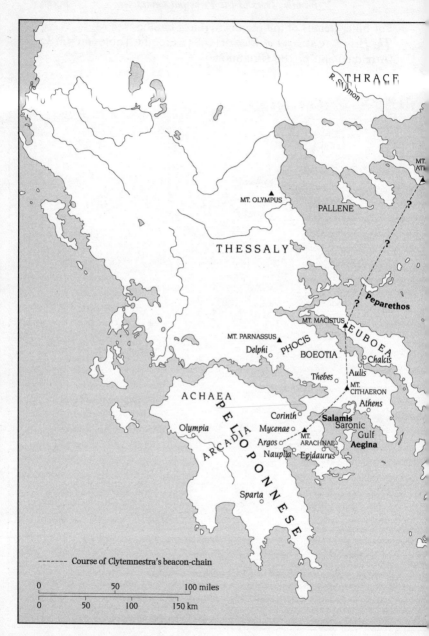

Greece and the Aegean Sea

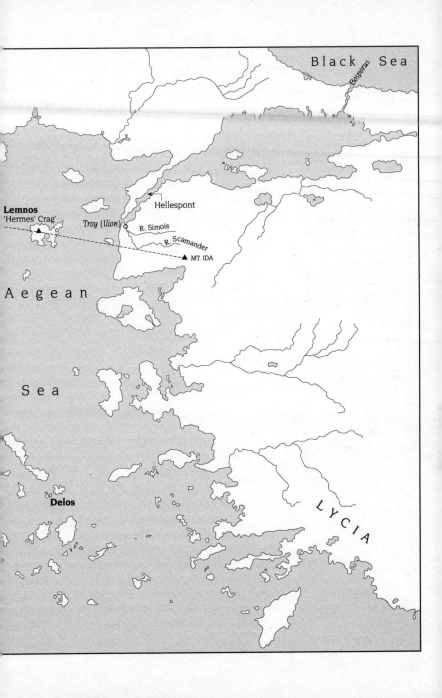

Agamemnon

Agamemnon

Characters

WATCHMAN at the palace of the Atreidae in Argos
CHORUS of old men of Argos
CLYTEMNESTRA, wife of Agamemnon King of Argos
HERALD from the Greek forces returning from Troy
AGAMEMNON
CASSANDRA, daughter of King Priam of Troy and war-prize
of Agamemnon
AEGISTHUS, son of Agamemnon's uncle Thyestes and now
Clytemnestra's lover

There are mute parts for Clytemnestra's serving-women, and for
attendants on Agamemnon and Aegisthus.

Scene: the palace-front at Argos. A WATCHMAN *appears on its roof,
on top of the stage-building. His words indicate that the action begins in
the night.*

WATCHMAN. I ask the gods for release from this misery, the
year-long watch I lie awake keeping on the roof of the
Atreidae, up above here like a dog; I am familiar now with
the night-stars' assembly, and those brilliant potentates which
bring men summer and winter, conspicuous in the heaven; I   5
mark them closely as they fade, and the risings of others. And
now I am on watch for a beacon's sign, a gleam of fire
bringing word from Troy and report of its capture: such is the
power here of a woman whose heart in its hope plans like a   10
man. Whenever I find myself shifting my bed about at night,
wet with dew, unvisited by dreams—because fear instead of
sleep stands at my side to stop my eyes closing fast in   15
slumber—and whenever I think to sing or to hum, dispensing
this remedy from music against sleep, then I weep in lament
for this house's misfortune; it is not managed for the best as it
was before. Now I wish for a happy release from misery when   20
the fire in the dark has appeared with its good news.

(*beginning to settle once more, but suddenly crying out*) The beacon! Greetings to you! You show daylight in the night, and mean the setting up of many dances in Argos to mark this good fortune!

(*shouting down into the palace behind him*) Ho there, ho! (*a slight pause*) I am making a clear signal to Agamemnon's wife, to rise up speedily from her bed and lift a joyful cry of celebration for the house at this beacon, if Ilion's city is indeed taken, as the flame prominently announces; and I shall dance a prelude of my own too, for I shall play on my master's good success now this beacon-flame has thrown me treble-six.

My real wish however, when the house's lord has come, is to clasp his well-loved hand in mine. The rest, I keep silent: a great ox is treading on my tongue—but the house itself, if it got a voice, would speak very plainly; I talk willingly to those who know, and for those who do not know, I choose to forget.

The WATCHMAN *disappears from the roof. The* CHORUS *of elderly men enter the orkhêstra from the side, chanting as they process; their words indicate that enough time has passed since the beacon-signal came for* CLYTEMNESTRA *to have reacted with orders for grateful sacrifice.*

CHORUS. Ten years it is since the great plaintiff against Priam,   40
    lord Menelaus with Agamemnon,
honoured by Zeus with their double throne and double
    sceptre,
the sturdy yoke-pair of the Atreidae,
sailed with a fleet of Argives from this land,   45
a thousand ships, an armada in support.
Their loud and ringing cry was of war, from anger,
like vultures which in extreme anguish for their young   50
wheel and spiral high above their nests,
oaring with their wings, oaring,
the labour of watching over nestling-chicks lost.
On high, someone—either Apollo or Pan or Zeus—   55
hears the birds' wailed lament, the sharp cry of these
    settlers in their home,
and for the transgressors' later punishment sends a Fury.
In just this way the mighty Zeus who guards hospitality   60
sends Atreus' sons against Alexandros,

because of a woman with many husbands—
to make many bouts of wrestling heavy on the limbs,
as the knee strains in the dust
and the spear shatters in the first-rites,   65
for Danaans and Trojans alike.
Things are now as they are;
they will be fulfilled in what is fated;
neither burnt sacrifice nor libation
of offerings without fire   70
will soothe intense anger away.

Ourselves disrated with our aged bodies,
left behind from the supporting force then,
we are waiting, our childlike strength moving upon staffs.   75
As the sap of youth when it rules inside the breast
is like old men's, and war is not in its place,
so extreme old age, its leaf now withering,   80
goes on its three-footed way and is no better than a child,
a dream appearing and wandering by day.

(turning towards the closed door of the palace)

You now, daughter of Tyndareus, Queen Clytemnestra,
what is the matter? What is new? What have you learned,   85
what report has persuaded you to send round
    and have sacrifices made?
All the gods who guide the city,
those on high, those below the earth,   90
those too at our house-doors and in our public places,
have their altars blazing with gifts;
flame from all sides rises tall to heaven,
bewitched by the pure and gentle soothing   95
of holy oils, in liquid offerings from the inmost palace.
Say about this what is both possible
and rightful; acknowledge and heal our concern here—
now, at one moment it brings grim thoughts;   100
at another, from the sacrifices you display,
hope defends the mind against insatiable anxiety
and pain devouring the spirit.

The CHORUS *stop circling the orkhêstra in their entry-march and take
position for their first sung dance.*

I have the power to tell of the command destined
    on its road, the command   Strophe 1
by men in their full prime—my age in life still breathes
    persuasion   105
from the gods above, the strength of song—
how the Achaeans' double-throned command,
one mind captaining the youth of Greece,   110
is sent with vengeful hand and spear
against the land of Teucer by an omen, a ferocious bird,
the king of birds for the kings of ships,
one bird black and one bird white behind,   115
appearing hard by their headquarters
on the spear-hand side, perching where they were seen
clearly all round as they fed
on a creature big with young heavy in its womb, a hare
stopped from its final run.   120
Cry 'Sorrow, sorrow!', but let the good prevail!

The careful seer of the army knew the warlike feasters on
    the hare   Antistrophe 1
at sight for the two sons of Atreus, two also in their mettle,
and the powers who led the force. He spoke,   125
interpreting the portent so: 'In time
our advance captures Priam's city,
and Fate before its walls will sack
its teeming herds of people, all of them there, in violence;   130
only let no jealousy from god
bring darkness on Troy's great bridle-bit
if that is stricken first, now it goes
on campaign! Pity makes holy Artemis
grudge her father's winged hounds   135
the wretched hare, unborn litter and all, their sacrifice;
she loathes the eagles' meal.'
Cry 'Sorrow, sorrow!', but let the good prevail!

'Such is Hecate's great goodwill   Epode
to the dewy, helpless young of ravening lions,   141
and her delight in the suckling whelps
of all beasts that haunt the wild;
she asks fulfilment for these omens.

The manifestation of the birds is favourable but means
    blame.   145
Apollo there! Healer indeed, I call on you,
lest she make contrary winds for the Danaans,
long delays that keep the ships from sailing,
in her urge for a second sacrifice,   150
one with no music, no feasting,
an architect of feuds born in the family,
with no fear of the man;
for there stays in wait a fearsome, resurgent,
treacherous keeper of the house, an unforgetting Wrath
    which avenges children.'   155
Those were the fated things which Calchas rang out for the
    royal house,
together with much good, from the road's omen-birds;
with them in unison
cry 'Sorrow, sorrow!', but let the good prevail!

Zeus, whosoever he is,   Str. 2
if to be called by this name is well pleasing to him,   161
with this I address him.
I have nothing to compare
though I measure all things against him—
only Zeus, if I am to cast out of my mind   165
its futile burden truthfully.

He who was formerly great,   Ant. 2
swelling and rash to fight all—his former existence
will not even be told;   170
while the one born next is gone
after meeting a champion wrestler;
but a man readily crying triumph for Zeus
will meet with wisdom totally—   175

Zeus who put men on wisdom's road,   Str. 3
who gave 'Suffer and learn'
authority.
Misery from pain remembered drips   180
instead of sleep before the heart; good sense
comes even to the unwilling.
Where is the gods' favour, seated
in violence at their majestic helm?

And then the senior in command   Ant. 3
of the Achaean ships,   185
blaming no seer,
going with fortune's wind as it struck
at him—the Achaean people now oppressed,
store-jars empty from not sailing,
facing Chalcis from their places   190
at Aulis with its noisy ebb and flow,

and the winds which came from Strymon   Str. 4
bringing bad idleness, starvation, difficult moorings,
with straying of men, ships and cables not spared,   195
redoubling the long delay—
they wore down and shredded the flower
of the Argives; when too the seer cried to the chiefs
a further, more heavy means   200
against the bitter storm,
he named Artemis as cause, enough
for the Atreidae
to thump their staffs upon the ground
and not be able to restrain their tears.

The senior lord spoke, declaring   Ant. 4
'Fate will be heavy if I do not obey, heavy as well   206
if I hew my child, my house's own darling,
polluting her father's hands
with slaughter streaming from a maiden   210
at the altar: what is there without evil here?
How can I desert the fleet
and fail the alliance?
Why, this sacrifice to stop the wind,
a maiden's blood,   215
is their most passionate desire;
but Right forbids it. So may all be well!'

When he put on the yoke-strap of compulsion,   Str. 5
his mind's wind veering round to the unholy,
the impious, the impure, from then   220
his purpose changed to hard audacity;
for men get overbold from the cruel derangement
and its ugly schemes that begin their affliction.
So he was hard enough to sacrifice

his daughter, in aid of a war   225
to punish a woman
and as first-rites for the fleet to sail.

Her entreaties and appeals to her father,   Ant. 5
and her maiden's years—in their love for battle
the officers set those at naught;   230
her father after praying gave an order
for the servers to take and lift her like a goat-kid
over the altar, when she had fallen forward
about his robes to plead with all her heart;   235
the lips in her beautiful face
were curbed to suppress
any word making the house accursed,

violently and with a bridle's muting power.   Str. 6
Her yellow-dyed dress streaming to the ground,
she struck each sacrificer with a bolt from her eyes   240
to move compassion; she stood out clearly
as in a picture, wanting to call them by name,
since she had often sung
in her father's men's-hall with its rich banquets,
and in the pure voice of an unwed girl   245
honoured with love her loving father's paean-hymn
at his third libation to good fortune.

What followed, I neither saw nor do I say;   Ant. 6
but Calchas' skills did not go unfulfilled.
Justice weighs down its scale for some to suffer and learn.   250
You may hear the future when it happens;
until it does, farewell to it!—or it's the same
as sorrowing too soon:
it will come sharp and clear, rising with dawn's rays.
Yet as for what follows, may good be done!—   255
as is the wish of this the closest guardian
of the land of Apis, its sole bulwark.

CLYTEMNESTRA *appears at the palace-door; the* CHORUS *now speak through their leader.*

I have come out of respect for your power, Clytemnestra; for it is right to honour the lady of a ruler, when the man leaves his throne empty. Whether or not you have learned something   260

trustworthy, and are making sacrifices in the hope of happy
news, I should gladly hear; but there's no grudge if you stay
silent.

CLYTEMNESTRA *(coming forward from the door)*. May happy
news come with the dawn from her mother night, as in the 105
proverb! You will learn of a joy greater than you hoped to
hear: the Argives have taken the city—Priam's!

CHORUS How do you mean? What you say escapes me, from
disbelief.

CLYTEMNESTRA. Troy belongs to the Achaeans, I say. Do I
speak clearly?

CHORUS. Joy is stealing over me and calling up my tears.   270

CLYTEMNESTRA. Yes, your face declares your loyalty.

CHORUS. What gives you your sureness then? Have you proof
of this?

CLYTEMNESTRA. I have, of course—unless a god has tricked
me.

CHORUS. Or are you too respectful of appearances in dreams,
with their easy persuasion?

CLYTEMNESTRA. I would not accept the fancies of a drowsing 275
mind.

CHORUS. Then has some unfledged rumour bolstered you?

CLYTEMNESTRA. You're quite faulting my intelligence, like a
young girl's!

CHORUS. And just how recent is the city's sack?

CLYTEMNESTRA. During the night which has now given birth
to this day, I tell you.

CHORUS. And what messenger could reach here with that 280
speed?

CLYTEMNESTRA. Hephaestus! He sent a bright gleam of fire
out from Ida; and beacon sent on to beacon here from the
messenger-fire in relays, Ida to Hermes' crag on Lemnos; and
Zeus' steep on Athos was third in taking up the great torch 285
from the island. Rising high in its strength to cross the ocean's
back, the journeying flare in pleasure [*at least two lines missing*]
the pine-torch, passing on the message of its brilliant golden
gleam like a sun to the watch-point on Macistus. The man
there made no delay at all nor failed his part as messenger by 290
carelessly letting sleep overcome him, and from far away the
beacon-light signals to the watchmen at Messapion that it has

reached Euripus' currents. They lit their flare in response
and passed the message forward, kindling fire in a heap of 295
ancient heather. Strong and not yet dimmed the flare leapt
above Asopus' plain like the shining moon to Cithaeron's
crag, and woke a further relay in sending on the fire. The
watch did not refuse the light sent from so far, the fire they 300
burned was more than had been ordered. Over the Gorgopian
lake the light dashed down; as it reached the Wander-Goat
Mountain it urged no delay in the orders for the fire; they
send it on, their ungrudging zeal making a great beard of 305
flame blaze upward, to cross also the foreland which looks
down on the Saronic narrows, onward as it flamed; then it
dashed down, then it came to the steep of Arachnae, the
watch-point neighbouring our city; and then it dashes down
to the roof-top here, of the Atreidae—this light which is a true 310
grandchild of the fire on Ida.

There you have my arrangements for the beacon-bearers!
One after another in succession they were performed in full;
the first and last to run were winners. Such is the token and
proof for my telling you that my husband has passed his 315
message on to me from Troy.

CHORUS. I shall pray again to the gods, my lady; but I should
willingly hear this account of yours right through once more,
and be full of wonder.

CLYTEMNESTRA. The Achaeans have hold of Troy this day! I 320
think, cries that do not blend must be very evident in the city:
just as if you were to pour oil and vinegar in the same vessel
and speak of them as unfriendly in their separation, so the
voices of captives and victors may be heard separately, in their 325
double fortune. The ones have fallen to embrace the bodies of
their husbands and brothers, and children the bodies of their
families' old men, lamenting the fate of their dearest from
throats no longer free; while the others' weariness had them
wandering through the night and sets them starving after the 330
battle to breakfast on what the city holds, with no discrimination in taking turns but as each has drawn fortune's lot. They
are living now in captured Trojan houses, released from the 335
frosts and dews of an open sky; as happy men they will sleep
the whole night without guards.

If they are showing due respect to the gods who hold the

if they are showing due respect to the g
who hold the

city, and to those gods' shrines, in a land now fallen, as
captors they may later not fall captive in their turn. Desire 340
however may first invade the army, I fear, to ransack what it
should not, overcome with greed; for it needs safety for its
return home, to round the race-track's other leg back in; and
if the army were to return without sin against the gods, the 345
injury to the dead which is awake [*words missing*] would be
[*words missing*], if no troubles occurred to break in.

There! You have heard that from a woman, from me. May
the good prevail, to be seen with no wavering! I choose the
enjoyment of many good things. (*turning to leave*) 350
CHORUS. Lady, you speak good sense like a prudent man. Now
I hear your convincing proof I am preparing due address to
the gods; a reward for effort has been achieved at its full value.

CLYTEMNESTRA *has now entered the palace. The* CHORUS *chant.*

O Zeus the King, and friendly Night 355
winner of great glories
in throwing your mesh to cover Troy's battlements
so that no one full-grown, nor any of the very young, might
    rise above
the great dredge-net of slavery which captures all. 360
I reverence great Zeus of Hospitality who has carried this
    through,
bending his bow long since against Alexandros
so he might not launch its shaft without effect 365
either short of the mark or beyond the stars.

The CHORUS *now dance and sing.*

Zeus' blow: they can speak of that; Str. 1
it is possible to track down this at any rate:
he fulfilled as he willed. Some person denied
that the gods deign to have concern about men 370
who trample grace
in untouchable things; but he was not pious.
Destruction is shown
exacting its price for their audacity, 375
aspirations greater than just,
houses teeming with excess
far beyond what is best.

Let things lead to no harm, and so suffice
men endowed with good sense.　　380
There is no protection
in wealth for a man who from its surfeit
has kicked Justice's great altar
into disappearing.

Cruel Persuasion uses force,　　Ant. 1
unendurable child of Ruin who plans in advance;　　386
all remedy is vain; there is no hiding
the havoc; it stands clear, its dreadful gleam bright.
But like bad bronze　　390
as it wears and is knocked, a man turns a fixed black
when judgement is made,
since he is a boy chasing a bird in flight,
scoring unendurable harm
on his city. And no god　　395
listens to pleas; instead
there is one to destroy the unjust man
who engages in these things.

Such in fact was Paris;
he came to the house of the Atreidae　　400
and disgraced his host's table
with the theft of his wife.

She left for the townsmen the tumult of warriors,　　Str. 2
companies forming, sailors arming;　　405
in place of a dowry she brought Troy its destruction.
She flitted lightly off through the gates
and was gone, her daring past all daring.
With much groaning the house-prophets spoke:
'The house! Oh, the house, alas, and its chiefs!　　410
The marriage-bed, the steps of a wife in love!
Here is silence, and dishonour seen
in those deserted; and they do not revile, they do not plead.
In his longing for her over the sea
her phantom will seem to rule in the house.　　415

The grace of shapely statues
is hateful to the husband;
in their lack of eyes
all love's being goes lost.

Apparitions in dreams and mournful imaginings   Ant. 2
come to him, which bring empty delight—   421
empty because when a man imagines his loved one,
the vision slips away through his hands
and is gone, never afterwards keeping   425
with its wings to the pathways of sleep.'
The house's sorrows are these, at its hearth,
and others far exceeding them; but in all,
for those starting out together
from Greece's land, an absence of grief was clear in each
    man's house,   430
as hard resolution entered his soul;
but yet there is much which touches the heart.

[The land] knows whom it sent out;
in place of human beings
their ashes in urns   435
come back to each man's house.

Ares who traffics in the gold of bodies   Str. 3
and holds his scale in the battle of the spears,
sends back to their kin   440
from Troy heavy dust burnt in the fire,
which brings hard tears; and in place
of a man, ash is the freight
of urns easily stowed.
Lamenting they praise the men,   445
one as knowing in battle,
another as fallen bravely amid slaughter.
'Through the wife of another'—
a man is snarling this quietly.
Resentment steals over their grief   450
against the Atreidae leading the case.

Others occupy tombs in the place itself,
in Ilion's earth around its wall,
handsome in death;
and a hostile soil hides its holders.   455

The townsmen's talking is heavy with rancour,   Ant. 3
paying its due to the people's solemn curse.
My anxiety waits
to hear of things veiled over by night;   460

those who have killed many men
are not unseen by the gods,
and black Furies in time
efface the man who succeeds
without justice, reversing   160
his success to wear out his life. There is no help
once a man has his being
among those lost to sight. Arrogance
from fame has heavy consequence:
the lightning of Zeus is hurled by his eyes.   470

I approve unresented prosperity;
I wish I may neither sack cities
nor as captive
myself see my life under others.

With the fire's good news   Epode
rumour has gone swiftly through the city;   476
whether it is true, who knows?—
or whether it is really a falsehood from god?
Who is so childish or struck so senseless
as to have his heart fired   480
by this new message passed on by flame,
and then to suffer from a change of story?
It is very like a woman in command
to concede gratitude before the facts appear:
too ready to persuade, a female ranges beyond her boundary, 485
quick to move; but doom is quick
for rumour when a woman spreads it, and it is destroyed.

(ending their dance and now speaking)

We shall soon know about the flares and the light they carried,
the passage of the fire along the beacons—whether in fact they 490
were true or whether this joyful light which came cheated our
minds like a dream: for I see a herald here *(pointing off-stage to one
side)*, from the shore, shadowed in twigs of olive; and the dust,
mud's thirsty sister and neighbour, is my witness that his news 495
for you will not be voiceless or given through the smoke of fire
kindled into flame from mountain-timber. What he says he will
either speak out more strongly for rejoicing—but I withhold any
love for the opposite words! I wish for happy addition to happy 500

appearances; and whoever makes a prayer otherwise for this city, I wish he may harvest his mind's error for himself!

A HERALD *now enters from the side.*

HERALD. Hail, my ancestral soil, land of Argos! Ten years' daylight now, and I have reached you, the one hope met after 505 so many broken! I was never confident I should die here in the land of Argos and have my share of the funeral most dear to me. Now, my greetings to the land, and greetings to the sunlight, and to Zeus supreme over the land, and to you the Pythian lord, no longer I hope shooting arrows at us with your 510 bow! You were implacable enough by the Scamander; but now be our saviour and our healer, lord Apollo! I address too all the gods in their assembly, and my own protector Hermes, herald whom heralds dearly revere, and the heroes who sent 515 us out—favour with your welcome back the army which has survived the war!

I hail the palace, dear house of kings, and their majestic seat, and you deities facing the sun! If ever you did in the past, welcome the king in due form with your faces bright, after this 520 long time; for when he comes he brings a light in darkness, for you and all these here to share, the lord Agamemnon! Greet him well, as is truly fitting: he has razed Troy with Zeus the justice-bringer's mattock, with which its ground has been 525 worked over and the seed utterly destroyed from the land. 526 Such is the yoke he threw over Troy, our lord the son of 528 Atreus, a man blest by god. Now he has come! He is the most 530 worthy to be honoured of mortals now alive: for not Paris nor his city as associate proclaim their deed greater than their suffering. Convicted of robbery as well as theft he both lost his 535 stolen prize and reaped total ruin for his father's house, soil and all; the sons of Priam have paid double for their misdeeds.

CHORUS. Happy greetings to you, herald of the Achaeans, for your news from the army!

HERALD. Yes, I am happy!—and I will no longer deny the gods my death.

CHORUS. Has love for your fatherland exercised you so hard? 540

HERALD. Yes, so that my eyes are filling with tears of joy.

CHORUS. A delightful disease, then, to have visit you all!

HERALD. How so then? If I have it explained, I shall master your meaning.

CHORUS. I mean, your being stricken with a desire for those who return your love.

HERALD. You say the land here is longing for the army which 545
is longing for it too?

CHORUS. Enough for me to groan aloud often, from a gloomy heart.

HERALD. What brought on this hateful despondency? Tell me.

CHORUS. I have long had silence as my medicine against harm.

HERALD. What? How is that? Were you in fear about any of the absent lords?

CHORUS. So much that now, to use your own words, even 550
death would be great happiness.

HERALD. Yes, because of our successes! Of those, over a long time, one might say that some have fallen out well, but some the reverse, in fact open to blame; but who except the gods is free from pain for his whole life-time? Why, if I told of the hardships we had, and the miserable sleeping-quarters [*a line* 555
missing] the narrow gangways with poor bedding—what did we not groan at, not get as our daily lot? The rest of it, moreover—on dry land there were even more hateful things too: our beds were near the enemies' walls; fields dewy-wet from the sky and from the ground kept us damp all through, 560
a constant plague, infesting the stuff of our clothes with creatures. And if one told of winter enough to kill the birds, what it was like to have it made beyond endurance by Ida's snow, or of heat when the sea fell calm and slept in 565
its midday rest, waveless—what need is there to grieve over those? The misery is past; it is past, so that the dead never 569
even care about rising again, while for us remnants of the 573
Argive army our gain prevails and the anguish does not 574
outweigh it. Why should those who perished be counted 570
up, and the living have pain from fortune's spite? Besides, I
think it right [to say] a long goodbye to our misfortunes [*a line* 572
missing] since it is natural for men passing swiftly over sea and
land to boast to this day's sunlight [*lines missing*] 'After taking 575
Troy long ago the Argive expedition nailed up these spoils for
the gods throughout Greece in their temples, to mark an
ancient glory'.

Such things once heard, men should praise the city and its   580
generals; and the favour of Zeus which accomplished this will
be given its due honour. You have the whole story.

CHORUS. I am not sorry to be convinced by what you say; the
old are always young enough to learn readily. This news
naturally concerns the house, however, and Clytemnestra   585
especially; but it enriches me as well.

CLYTEMNESTRA *appears at the palace-door.*

CLYTEMNESTRA. I cried out my joy long ago, when the first
night-messenger of fire came telling of Ilion's capture and
destruction. And someone said in reproof, 'Have beacon-
watchers persuaded you to think that Troy is now ransacked?   590
Truly like a woman to let her heart be lifted!' Words such as
those made me seem astray; nevertheless I went on sacrificing,
and people in all parts of the city shrilled cries of joy in   595
women's custom, in grateful triumph, lulling the fragrant
flame that devoured their sacrifice at the gods' seats. And
now, for the longer account, what need have you to give it me?
I shall learn the whole story from my lord himself; and I must
hasten to give my revered husband the best of welcomes now   600
he has come back. For what light of day is sweeter for a wife to
see than this, with the gates opened up when god has brought
back her husband safely from campaign? Take this message
away to my husband, to come as soon as possible; he is the
city's beloved darling. As to his wife, I wish he may find her   605
when he comes just as faithful in his home as the one he left
behind, the house's watch-dog true to him while hostile to ill-
wishers, and similar in everything else, with no seal broken in   610
the length of time; and I know no more of pleasure from
another man, nor talk of blame, than I do of dipping bronze.
There you have my boast; its fullness with the truth makes it
no shame for a woman of my nobility to proclaim.

CLYTEMNESTRA *withdraws into the palace.*

CHORUS. (*gesturing after her*). She spoke that way to you, words   615
which if you understand them with the help of clear interpreters, appear specious.

But you must tell me, Herald: I wish to know of Menelaus—

whether he has actually returned home with you, brought
safely back; he is a power dear to this land.

HERALD. Impossible I should report what is false as good, for 620
friends to harvest for the long future!

CHORUS. Then I wish you may give excellent news and be
telling the truth! Their separation is not easy to conceal.

HERALD. The man has disappeared from the Achaean fleet,
himself together with his ship. I tell no falsehoods. 625

CHORUS. Was it after he had set sail in clear view from Ilion, or
did a storm snatch him from the fleet, heavy on all alike?

HERALD. You hit the mark like a top archer, and describe long
suffering concisely.

CHORUS. Was there word of him rumoured by other sailors, as 630
alive or dead?

HERALD. No one knows enough to report clear news, except
the Sun which nurtures life on earth.

CHORUS. You mean that the storm came upon the fleet of
ships, and reached its end, through the gods' rancour? How? 635

HERALD. It is not fitting to pollute a joyful day by speaking of
bad news; the honour due to the gods is separate. When a
messenger with a grim face brings a city the pain it prayed to
avoid from its army's defeat, news that a single wound to all its
people has befallen the city, with many men given up from 640
many houses as victims to the double scourge which Ares
loves, the lethal pair of spears, a bloody partnership—a
messenger with such sufferings as his pack-load fittingly
tells this paean-hymn in honour of the Furies; but when a 645
messenger with good news that things are safe comes to a city
which rejoices in well-being—how am I to mix excellent and
bad together, by telling of the storm which did not come upon
the Achaeans except by the gods' wrath?

   For oaths were sworn together by those former worst enemies, 650
fire and sea, and the two demonstrated their pledges in jointly
destroying the ill-fated Argive fleet. In the night rose evil, stormy
seas; winds from Thrace smashed ships on one another amid
lightning, tempest and squalls of beating rain; others in this 656
violent buffeting were lost and vanished; an evil shepherd of the 655
storm whirled them all about. When the sun's clear light came 657
up, we saw the Aegean main blooming with the corpses of
Achaean men and the wrecks of ships. 660

Yet ourselves and our ship, its hull unscathed, some god
either stole away or begged us off, some god—it was no
human—with his touch on our helm; and saviour Fortune
was seated willingly on our ship, so we should have no squally
waves to prevent mooring nor be run on mighty rocks on land,   665
Then after we had escaped Death on the sea, in the white light
of day, with no trust in our fortune, we brooded anxiously on
the fresh disaster, with our fleet wrecked and badly pounded
by the waves.   670

And now if any of those men still breathe, they are talking
about us as if we are dead—what else?—and we ourselves
imagine, they are the same. May it turn out for the best! So, as
to Menelaus, first and above all you may look forward to his   675
return; in fact if a ray of sun finds him alive and flourishing
through the devices of a Zeus who is not yet willing to destroy
his family-line utterly, there is some hope he will come home
again. Now you have heard that much, know that you have
heard the truth.   680

The HERALD *exits by the side. The* CHORUS *dance and sing.*

CHORUS. Whoever was it gave this name so wholly true—   Str. 1
    unless it was someone not seen
by us, with forethought for what fate had predestined   685
and accuracy in guiding his tongue—
to her whom two sides disputed and whose bridegroom was
    war,
to Helen? For aptly to her name hellish
to ships, hellish to men, hellish to cities,   690
she came from her filmy chamber-curtains
to set sail on the wind of a giant Zephyr,
with many men bearing shields and hounding
on the vanished track of oars   695
once her ships beached on the leafy shores of Simois,
through the work of bloody Strife.

To Ilion purposeful Wrath drove on its way   Ant. 1
a wedding-bond—so right in name!—,   701
exacting later payment for the dishonour
to a host's table, to Zeus of the hearth,
from those whose song paid honour to the bride
    outspokenly,   705

the wedding-hymn which fell to the groomsmen then
to sing. Unlearning that hymn for another
of much lamentation, Priam's ancient   710
city I think is greatly bewailing Paris
and calling him 'Fatal in your marriage!'
It has brought its people's lives
utter ransack; with much lamentation, they endure   715
bloodshed's miseries in full.

Just so, a man once reared   Str. 2
a lion's offspring in his house
without mother's milk though still a suckling,
in these the first-rites of its life   720
tame, affectionate towards children,
delightful as well to the old;
it was often held in the crook of arms
like a new infant being nursed,
its face brightly turned to the hand   725
and fawning in hunger's need.

Brought on by time however   Ant. 2
it displayed the nature which came
from its parents; repaying its rearers'
favour with wild slaughter of sheep,   730
uninvited it made them a feast;
the house was a welter of blood,
an agony the housefolk could not fight,
a great havoc of many killed;
by god's will a priest of Ruin   735
was reared in the house as well.

At once there came to Ilion's city, I would say,   Str. 3
a notion of windless calm,   740
and—tranquil adornment to riches—
eyes throwing melting glances,
love blooming which eats at the heart.
The marriage was changed in its course, it ended
in a bitter fulfilment   745
by an evil settler,
an evil companion sped to Priam's sons,
escorted by Zeus god of hosts,
bringing tears upon brides, a Fury!

Long spoken among men, there exists an old saying   Ant. 3
that a man's prosperity grown   752
fully great has offspring, not dying
childless; his line's good fortune   755
bears shoots of insatiable woe.
I differ from others, alone in my thinking:
it is the impious deed
which later on begets
more deeds that resemble their own parentage;   760
for to houses upright and just
fine children are destined for ever.

Ancient insolence is wont to breed   Str. 4
youthful insolence in evil men   765
sooner or later, when the appointed day comes
for birth, rancour rising afresh,
and a demon unfightable,
invincible, unholy in boldness,   770
a demon of black Ruin
for a house, resembling its parents.

Justice gleams in houses foul with smoke,   Ant. 4
doing honour to the righteous life;   775
but gold-bespangled mansions where hands are unclean
she leaves with her eyes turned away,
and approaches those which are pure,
with no respect for riches and their power   780
when falsely stamped with praise;
she directs all things to their ending.

AGAMEMNON *drives into view from one side in a chariot;*
CASSANDRA *rides with him. There are attendants. The* CHORUS
change to chanting.

Come then, my king! Sacker of Troy's city,
child of Atreus—
how should I address you, how should I revere you,   785
neither overaiming nor undershooting the mark with what
  pleases?
Many among mankind hold appearances
in greater honour than reality once they transgress justice.
Everyone is ready to lament the unsuccessful,   790

but no distress bites deeply to his heart at all,
while men with the appearance of sharing others' joy
from forcing their unsmiling faces
[*at least one line missing*].
A good judge of his flock however   795
cannot fail to notice the eyes of a man
which seem out of loyal intention
to be fawning in watery friendship.
Yourself, at the time you were launching the campaign
to get Helen—I shall not conceal it from you—   800
you made a most unpleasing picture to me,
unwise too in guiding your mind's helm
[*words missing*] when you tried to recover
willing courage for dying men;
but now, from no mere surface feeling nor from insincere   805
loyalty [*words missing*]
'toil [*at least one word missing*] for those who have brought it
    to a good end'.
You will perceive and know with time
which of your citizens staying at home
acted rightfully and which improperly.

AGAMEMNON (*who remains in the chariot*). First I address Argos   810
and the land's gods: it is my duty to these accessories in my
return and in the justice I exacted from the city of Priam. The
gods heard a case without speeches, which brought men
death; they cast their votes for Ilion's destruction into the
bloody urn without division; the opposed vessel had Hope   815
approach it, but no hand began filling it. The city was taken;
its smoke even now makes it a clear mark; the storms of Ruin
live on; the ash of its dying sends out rich puffs of wealth. For   820
this the gods should be paid very mindful thanks, since we
punished an arrogant robbery, and it was for a woman that
Troy was ground into dust by the Argives' beast of destruction—the offspring of the horse, shield-bearers in a body,   825
launching their leap at the Pleiades' setting. Springing over
the battlements, the ravening lion licked its fill of royal blood.

This long prelude of mine has been for the gods; (*addressing
the* CHORUS) as to your sentiments, I heard and remember   830
them; I say the same, and you have me as fellow-advocate. It
is few men's nature to honour a successful friend without

jealousy; the poison of ill-will sits near the heart and doubles
the disease's burden for the man who contracts it: his own   835
injuries oppress him, and he groans at seeing prosperity by
another's door. I can speak from knowledge, for I well
understand companionship's mirror; its image is a shadow's,
persons appearing very well-disposed to me. Only Odysseus,   840
the one who sailed against his will, was my ready trace-horse
when joined to the team—he may in fact be dead or alive as I
speak of him. As for what else affects the city and its gods, we
will hold common assemblies and consult in a full gathering.   845
We must take counsel how what is good may remain so and
last well; but where healing remedies are needed, either by
sensible cautery or surgery we shall try to avert the disease's   850
harm.

　　Now I shall enter my palace and home, and at its hearth
raise my hand to greet first the very gods who sent me out and
brought me back again; and may victory, for its past attendance on me, remain steadfast!

CLYTEMNESTRA *appears at the door of the palace; her speech stops*
　　　　　AGAMEMNON *from dismounting.*

CLYTEMNESTRA. Men of the city, senior Argives here present, I   855
shall have no qualms in telling you how I love my husband; a
person's timidity dies away in time. I have not learned from
others, I shall tell my own life's hardship all the while this man
was under Ilion's wall. The first thing: for a wife to be separated   860
from her husband, and to sit at home alone, is a terrible misery,
when she hears many malicious rumours, with one man
coming and then another with his cries bringing worse pain
on top of pain for the house. (*pointing to* AGAMEMNON) Also, if   865
this man was receiving as many wounds as rumour kept
channelling homeward, he has more holes to count pierced
in him than a net; and if he had been killed as many times as the
stories came, he would have had three bodies for sure, a second
Geryon, and boast of getting three shares of earth as a great   870
cloak on him from above—I do not speak of that below him—
dying once in each of his forms. Because of malicious reports
like those there were many nooses hung high for my neck, from   875
which others forcibly took and released me.

　　(*speaking to* AGAMEMNON *now*) Those are the reasons why

our son Orestes is not standing with us here as he should, the
security of our pledges to each other; and do not wonder at this.
He is being brought up by the kindness of your war-ally 880
Strophius the Phocian; he warned me of disaster on two
counts, both the dangers under Ilion to yourself and the
popular clamour amid anarchy which might overthrow deliberation, and how it is natural to kick a man more who is down.
Such a plea in excuse, I assure you, carries no deception. 885

My gushing spring of tears is quenched, however, and there
is not a drop in it; but lying late awake has harmed my eyes as I
wept that the beacons set up for news of you were always idle. In 890
my dreams I kept waking at the thin whine of a gnat as it
buzzed, when I saw sufferings around you to exceed the time
which shared my sleep.

Now I have endured all this, with a heart free from grief I 895
would call this man his palace's watchdog, a ship's forestay
keeping it safe, a pillar to a lofty roof sure on its footings, an
only-begotten son to his father, and land appearing to sailors
against their hopes, daylight most beautiful to the eyes after 900
storm, a stream welling for a thirsty traveller; it is sweet to
escape from all stress.

I honour his worth with such addresses; and let jealous envy
have no place here, for the miseries we endured before were
many. (*turning fully to* AGAMEMNON) Now please, my dear 905
one, get out of this carriage, without putting to the ground that
foot of yours, my lord, which ransacked Ilion.

(*calling back through the door*) Women-slaves, why your delay
with the task laid on you, to spread the ground of his path with
fabrics? Let his way be strewn with purples immediately, so that 910
Justice may lead him into a home unexpected! As for the other
things, thoughtfulness unconquered by sleep will justly ensure
that they are done with the gods' help.

*The women strew the way between chariot and palace-door with richly
decorated purple fabrics.*

AGAMEMNON. Leda's child, guardian of my house, your
speech was appropriate to my absence: you drew it out at 915
length. Fair praise however is a reward which should come
from others. Besides, do not pamper me in a woman's fashion;
and do not give me gawping or obeisance crying from the

ground as if I were some barbarian, or strew my way with 920
vestments and open it to jealousy. It is the gods these things
should magnify; as a mortal it is impossible for me to walk on
beautiful embroideries without fear. I tell you, show me
respect as a man, not as a god. Foot-wipers and embroideries 925
cry out different meanings; a mind to avoid wrong is god's
greatest gift. The man to call blest with success is the man
who has ended his life in precious well-being. If I could fare in
everything as I fare now, I shall be quite confident. 930

CLYTEMNESTRA. Well, answer me this, without going against
your true opinion.

AGAMEMNON. Be sure, I will not falsify my true opinion.

CLYTEMNESTRA. Would you have vowed to the gods, if you
had been in fear, that you would do this thing?

AGAMEMNON. Yes, if anyone would, with sure knowledge I
would have proclaimed this duty.

CLYTEMNESTRA. And what do you think Priam would have
done, if he had achieved what you have? 935

AGAMEMNON. I think, he would certainly have walked on
embroideries.

CLYTEMNESTRA. Then have no regard for men's censure.

AGAMEMNON. But the people talk; their voice is very powerful.

CLYTEMNESTRA. Yes, but the man free of their jealousy never
draws envy.

AGAMEMNON. Surely it is not a woman's way to desire a battle?

CLYTEMNESTRA. No, but those blest with success fittingly 940
yield even victory.

AGAMEMNON. Do you really value victory in this contest?

CLYTEMNESTRA. Be persuaded; you are in fact the winner if
you give way to me willingly.

AGAMEMNON. (*beginning to get down*). Well, if you are determined on this, let someone quickly undo my shoes (*one of the
attendants comes to do it*), which serve walking feet as slaves; and 945
as I go upon these purples of the gods, may no jealous eye
strike me from afar! I have great qualms about destroying a
house's property underfoot, spoiling rich textiles bought with
silver.

Enough! Let it be so. (*turning to point to* CASSANDRA, *still
motionless in the chariot*) The woman stranger here: take her 950
inside kindly; god looks favourably from afar on the man

gentle in victory. No one puts on slavery's yoke from freewill;
she has followed with me as the army's gift, the flower chosen
out of many things.   955

Since I am subdued into obeying you in this, I shall go into
my palace-halls treading over purples

AGAMEMNON *begins walking over the fabrics towards the palace-door.*

CLYTEMNESTRA. The sea is there—and who shall quench
it?—nurturing the juices which yield much purple worth its
weight in silver, wholly renewable, the dye of vestments; there 960
is a remedy for these here with the gods' help, my lord, from
our reserve; the house does not know how to be poor. I would
have vowed treading over many vestments, if that had been
pronounced for the house at an oracle, when I was trying to
devise a safe return for this life here (*gesturing towards* 965
AGAMEMNON). When a root is there, leafy growth comes
to a house and stretches shade over it against the Dog-Star
Sirius; (*calling after* AGAMEMNON) so now that you have
come to your house's hearth, you signify warmth in winter
with your coming; and when Zeus makes wine from bitter 970
grapes, then already there is cool in the house when the man
its master moves about it.

AGAMEMNON *has now reached the doors, and disappears inside; the
women begin to gather up the fabrics in the direction of the door.*

Zeus, Zeus master-fulfiller, give my prayers fulfilment! And
may you indeed take care of whatever you mean to fulfil!

CLYTEMNESTRA *follows the women inside. The* CHORUS *dance
and sing.*

CHORUS. Why, why is this terror   Str. 1
hovering constantly   976
in front of my heart, to rule its divinations?
and why does my song act the seer, unbidden,
unpaid? and why is confidence   980
not enthroned at my mind's own seat,
easily persuading me to spurn my terror
like a doubtful dream?
Time has gone beyond its youth
since the stern-cables were jerked   985

aboard, the sand flying upward,
when the sea-going host started out for Troy.

I learn of its return   Ant. 1
by sight, I am myself
a witness within me however my spirit   990
is chanting self-taught that unlyrical dirge,
the Fury's; it does not possess
hope's welcome confidence at all.
My innermost senses in truth are not idle;   995
with my mind correct
in judgement, my heart whirls round
at the fulfilment to come.
I pray that my expectations
turn out false and do not come to be fulfilled.   1000

Great health as a condition   Str. 2
is truly insatiable,
[with no] limit; sickness shares its wall
as neighbour and leans on it.
Man's destiny too on a straight passage   1005
[*some words missing*]
can strike an invisible reef.
The caution which jettisons part
to save wealthy possessions,
by sizing it well for the sling—   1010
the house does not wholly go under
because plenty loads it too full,
nor its ship capsize;
truly the bounty of Zeus is great and all-embracing
and from the furrows year upon year   1015
does away with starvation's disease.

Once a man's blood has fallen   Ant. 2
on the ground in front of him,
black and fatal, who shall call it up   1020
again by incantation?
Not even to him with the right knowledge
to resurrect from the dead
did Zeus nod assent without harm as the price.
Were not one man's status in life   1025
set by heaven, preventing

another's from greater advance,
my heart would have anticipated
my tongue here in pouring this out;
but now it grumbles   1030
in the darkness, with my spirit grieving and not hopeful
ever of winding all to its end
effectively; my mind is ablaze.

CLYTEMNESTRA *reappears at the door.*

CLYTEMNESTRA. You, get yourself inside too—Cassandra, I   1035
mean—since Zeus without anger has given you a share in the
house's ritual sprinklings, to stand among many slaves near
his altar protecting its possessions. Get out of this carriage,
and do not be superior; why, they say that Alcmene's son was   1040
put on sale once and bore to touch the bread of slavery. So if
fate's balance does bring this fortune, there is much to be
grateful for from masters who have ancient wealth; but those
who never expected to reap a fine harvest are both cruel to
their slaves [*at least one line missing*] everything; and you have   1045
heard from me strictly what is our custom.

CHORUS (*to* CASSANDRA). It's you she's speaking to! She's
pausing, but what she says is clear. Since you've been caught
in the fatal net, please obey her if you're going to obey; but
perhaps you'll disobey.

CLYTEMNESTRA. Unless she's like a swallow and owns an   1050
unintelligible barbarian tongue, I am trying to persuade her
by speaking words within her comprehension.

CHORUS (*to* CASSANDRA). Go with her; she says what is best
in the circumstances. Leave your seat here in the carriage and
obey her.

CLYTEMNESTRA. I've no leisure to waste here out of doors!   1055
The sheep are already standing to be slaughtered before the
altar at the house's centre [*a line missing*] in that [we] never
hoped to have this pleasure. (*to* CASSANDRA) And you, if
you are going to do anything of this, make no delay; but if you
do not understand my words or take them in, then show your   1060
intention with an outlandish gesture instead of speaking.

CHORUS. The stranger seems to need a clear interpreter; her
manner is like a wild animal's just captured.

CLYTEMNESTRA. She's mad, and obeying wrong thoughts,

like one who comes here from a city just captured and does   1065
not know how to endure the bridle before foaming out her
temper in blood. I tell you, I am not going to throw more
words away and have them scorned.

CLYTEMNESTRA *re-enters the palace.*

CHORUS. I shall not get angry, though; I have pity for her.
Come, you poor wretch; abandon the carriage here and yield   1070
to this necessity; accept the new yoke.

CASSANDRA (*dismounting from the chariot; she moves towards the
door but quickly stops, bursting into cries of anguish and singing
wildly*)
    O-o-o-oh! Horror! No!   Str. 1
    O Apollo, O Apollo!

CHORUS. Why this loud wailing for Loxias? He is not of the
kind to meet a lamenter.   1075

CASSANDRA. O-o-o-oh! Horror! No!   Ant. 1
    O Apollo, O Apollo!

CHORUS. This woman blasphemes again in calling on the god;
it is not his part to assist at lamentations.

CASSANDRA. Apollo, Apollo!   Str. 2
    Lord of the streets, my destroyer!   1081
    You have destroyed me without effort for this second time!

CHORUS. She is going to prophesy about her own sufferings, it
seems; the god's power remains in her mind even as a slave.

CASSANDRA. Apollo, Apollo!   Ant. 2
    Lord of the streets, my destroyer!   1086
    Oh where, wherever have you led me? To what kind of
      house?

CHORUS. To that of the Atreidae. If you do not realize this, I
am telling you, and you will not call it false.

CASSANDRA. No—to a godless house, with much on its
      conscience—   Str. 3
    evil bloodshed by kin, carving like meat—   1091
    a place for slaughtering men, a floor sprinkled with blood!

CHORUS. The stranger has a keen nose it seems, like a hound;
she is searching for blood and will discover whose murder it
was.

CASSANDRA.—because I put my trust in this evidence
    here: Ant. 3
    these are infants weeping for their slaughter,   1096
    and over their roasted flesh which their father devoured.
CHORUS. Indeed we had heard of your fame as seer; but we are
    not searching for any prophets.

CASSANDRA. Oh, horror! Whatever is plotting now?   Str. 4
    What is this new affliction here?   1101
    Great evil, great, is plotting here in the house,
    unbearable for kin, difficult to heal;
    and help is standing far off.
CHORUS. I do not know of these divinations, but I recognize 1105
    those; all the city is shouting them.

CASSANDRA. Cruel woman, will you take this to its end?   Ant. 4
    After you bathe the husband clean
    who shares your bed—how shall I speak of the end?
    For this is soon to be; and hand follows hand   1110
    in stretching out and reaching.
CHORUS. I do not yet understand; I am now at a loss from
    riddles made in dark prophecies.

CASSANDRA. Oh horror! No! What is this which
    appears?   Str. 5
    Is it some catch-net of Death?   1115
    No, the trap-net sharing his bed, sharing guilt
    for his blood; now let insatiable discord
    for the family cry its triumph for the sacrifice which incurs
        stoning.
CHORUS (*also now singing*). What Fury's this you order to raise
    its cry over the house?
    What you say is bringing me no cheer.   1120
    Drops of blood yellow-dyed have run to my heart,
    the very drops which accompany men who fall by the spear
    in reaching their end, the sunset
    of life's rays; death follows swiftly.

CASSANDRA. No, no! Look, look! Keep the bull well
    away   Ant. 5
    from the cow! She has him caught   1126
    in the robing, in her black-horned contrivance,
    and she strikes; he falls in the vessel's water.

I am telling you here the outcome of the bath where
　　treachery does murder.

CHORUS. I would not boast of being expert in judging
　　prophecies,　　　　　　　　　　　　　　　　　　　　　　　1131
but I liken this to some evil
Do prophecies give rise to any good news
for men?—because evil is the means for oracle-singers
skilled and wordy in their verses
when they bring fear as their lesson.　　　　　　　　　　　1135

CASSANDRA. So cruel my fortunes, so evil my fate!　　Str. 6
The woes I cry out are my own, I add them
to the cup. So why did you lead me here, wretch that I
　　am—
for nothing at all, except to share dying! What else?

CHORUS. You are someone demented, possessed　　　　　1140
by a god, crying out unmusical music
about your own self, like a nightingale sounding
and calling insatiably, alas, heart full of sadness
in lamenting Itys, Itys, for a life
abundant all round with woe.　　　　　　　　　　　　　　1145

CASSANDRA. Oh the nightingale's end! So clear in her
　　song!　　　　　　　　　　　　　　　　　　　　　Ant. 6
The gods have put round her a wing-bearing form,
bestowing a life-time of sweetness, without any tears.
For myself cleaving awaits, by a blade with two sides!

CHORUS. Where do you have these agonies from,　　　　1150
violent onset of possession by a god
all to no purpose, terror borne on your chanting,
voice loud and ill-omened in your shrilly pitched music?
Where do you have your markers from, for your path
prophetic with evil words?　　　　　　　　　　　　　　1155

CASSANDRA. Oh, the wedding, the wedding of our
　　Paris　　　　　　　　　　　　　　　　　　　　　Str. 7
destroying his dearest!
Oh, Scamander, ancestral waters!
Then, I was reared and had my growing
along your verges, wretch that I am;
but now, it seems, I shall soon be singing my prophecies　1160
along the banks of Acheron and by Cocytus' stream.

CHORUS. What words are these you utter, and which are all
    too clear?
  An infant child would understand on hearing.
  I am stricken; your bloody fate bites deep
  as your song whimpers and cries at fortune's harsh pain;   1165
  and it shatters me to listen.

CASSANDRA. Oh, the anguish, the anguish of our city   Ant. 7
  destroyed so completely!
  Oh, my father's many offerings,
  grazing beasts slain in front of his walls!—
  but they secured no remedy   1170
  to stop the city suffering as was in fact its due;
  and I soon fall to Under-Earth, with my mind heated still.

CHORUS. You utter words which follow from those you said
    before;
  some god is putting misery in your mind,
  over-heavy in falling upon you   1175
  so disaster is your song, with death and sorrow;
  for the ending I am helpless.

CASSANDRA (*suddenly calm*). Now see! My oracle will no longer
be looking out from veils like a newly-wed bride, but clear and
keen its breath will seem to dart towards the sun's rising, so   1180
that there surges up like a wave against its rays a harm greater
than this by far. I shall no longer instruct you from riddles;
and you are to bear me witness that I track closely on the scent
of evil done long ago.   1185
    This house will never be abandoned by a choir of voices in
unison, unlovely in tone because it does not tell of good. No,
and now that it has drunk human blood for greater boldness,
the revel-band remains in the house, hard to expel, of family   1190
Furies. The hymn they sing as they besiege the house is to its
sinful folly from the very start; in turn they spit their disgust
with the brother's bed and their enmity to its trampler. Have I
missed, or do I score a hit like an archer? Or am I a false seer,
a hawker at the door, a babbler? Speak out in witness, under   1195
oath, that I know this house's crimes, ancient in story.

CHORUS. And how could an oath honestly struck bring
healing? But I marvel at you: you were born and bred
across the sea in a city which has a different language and   1200

you hit the mark with what you say, just as if you had been
standing by.

CASSANDRA. Apollo god of seers set me in this office.　　　1202

CHORUS. Smitten with desire for you, I fear you mean,　　　1204
although he is a god?

CASSANDRA. Before now, I was ashamed to speak of this.　　　1203

CHORUS. Everyone shows greater delicacy while in prosperity.　　　1205

CASSANDRA. But Apollo quite wrestled with me while
breathing his favours.

CHORUS. And did the two of you duly come to making a child?

CASSANDRA. Though I had consented to Loxias, I cheated
him.

CHORUS. Had you already been possessed by the skill the
god inspires?

CASSANDRA. I was already prophesying all their disasters to　　　1210
the citizens.

CHORUS. So how were you unscathed by Loxias' anger?

CASSANDRA. I could convince nobody of anything, after I
committed that sin against him.

CHORUS. Yet we at least think that you prophesy convincingly.

CASSANDRA (*suddenly crying out*). Oh! Oh, this misery! Deep
down again the fearsome work of truthful prophecy agitates　　　1215
and whirls me round with its stormy prelude. You see these
young ones seated by the house, resembling dream-shapes?
They are children killed, as if by people outside their family!
Their hands are full of their own flesh for meat, clearly　　　1220
visible, holding their entrails and the vitals with them, most
pitiable burden, which their father tasted. For that, I say that
someone is planning retribution, a cowardly lion who roams
free in the marriage-bed and has stayed at home—alas, it is　　　1225
against the master on his return. The ships' commander and　　　1227
overturner of Troy will meet with underhand destruction,　　　1230
through evil fortune; he does not know the kind of bite　　　1228
behind the hateful bitch's tongue when it brightly laid back　　　1229
its ears and licked. Such is the male's female murderer in　　　1231
her audacity. What loathsome monster should I be accurate
in calling her—an amphisbaena, or a Scylla living in the
rocks, destruction for sailors, a hellish mother raging and
breathing war without truce on her dearest? How she cried　　　1235
in triumph, in her total audacity, just as at a battle's turn!

Yet she appears to rejoice at the safe homecoming.

And it's all the same if nothing of mine persuades you, of course: the future will come; and you will soon be at my side to pity and call me too true a prophet. 1240

CHORUS. I understood Thyestes' feast upon his children's flesh, and shuddered, and fear possesses me now I have heard things that truly are no images; but when I listen to the rest, I stumble and run off the track. 1245

CASSANDRA. I say that you will look upon the death of Agamemnon.

CHORUS. Still your tongue, you wretched woman! Say nothing inauspicious!

CASSANDRA. But the Healer cannot aid my words at all.

CHORUS. No, not if this is to be; but may it never happen!

CASSANDRA. You pray, but others have killing as their concern. 1250

CHORUS. Which man is to bring this evil thing about?

CASSANDRA. You have indeed been thrown a long way off the course my oracles are running!

CHORUS. I did not understand the contrivance the accomplisher will use.

CASSANDRA. And yet I know the Greek language only too well.

CHORUS. So do the Pythian decrees, but they are still hard to understand. 1255

CASSANDRA (*crying out and singing suddenly again in prophetic seizure*). O-oh!
How the fire invades me!
O-o-oh! Lycean Apollo! Oh me, my [pain]!

(*speaking once more*). This two-footed lioness, bedding with the wolf in the absence of the noble lion, will kill me, wretch that I am; and as if preparing a drug she will put in the drink a wage paid for myself as well. As she whets her sword for the man, she boasts he will pay in blood for bringing me here. 1260

Why then am I keeping these (*gesturing at her dress and emblems*) to mock myself, and the staff and seer's bands around my neck? (*pulling at them*) You! I will destroy you, before my own fate! (*hurling them all to the ground*) Fall there and be damned! And I shall keep company with you; make some other woman rich with ruin in my place! See, it is 1265

Apollo himself who strips me of my prophetic dress! He 1270
watched over me while I was greatly mocked even in this attire
by friends who became undividedly my enemies, while I
vainly [*a line missing*]. I was abused, like a fortune-teller
wandering about for alms: I endured wretched beggary half-
dead from hunger. And now the prophet-god has exacted his
due from myself as prophet and led me into captivity for a 1275
deadly fate like this; and in place of my ancestral altar there
waits a butcher's block warm from the blood-rite of one cut
down before.

Not, I swear, that he and I shall die without retribution
from the gods: there will come another in turn to avenge us, a 1280
child born to kill his mother, one to exact penalty for his
father. A fugitive, a wanderer, an exile from this land he will
come home to put a coping-stone on these ruinous acts for his
family; his father thrown on his back on the ground will bring
him back.

Why then do I lament so piteously? Now that I have seen 1285
Ilion's city faring as it fared, and those who took the city
getting their outcome like this in the gods' judgement, I shall
go and do it: I will submit to death. (*moving towards the door*) I 1289
address these as the gates of Hades. I pray I may get a fatal 1291
blow, and close my eyes without convulsions as my blood
streams out in easy death.

CHORUS. So much misery as yours, but so much skill, lady, 1295
and you spoke at length! If you truly know your own fate, how
can you tread bravely towards the altar like an ox driven on by
god?

CASSANDRA. There is no further escape, no, none, strangers,
through time.

CHORUS. Yet the final part of one's time is the most valued. 1300

CASSANDRA. That day is here; I shall gain little by flight.

CHORUS. Your resolution is from a brave heart, I tell you.

CASSANDRA. None of the truly fortunate hears that said.

CHORUS. But a famous death is welcome to a mortal.

CASSANDRA (*with sudden intensity*). Oh, I grieve for you, my father, 1305
and for your noble children! (*moving again towards the door*) Now I 1313
shall go to keen in the house as well, over my fate and over 1314
Agamemnon's. Enough of life! (*halting at once in horror*) Oh! 1315
Strangers!

CHORUS. What is it? What fear turns you back? 1306

CASSANDRA (*retreating in sudden revulsion*). Ugh, horrible!

CHORUS. Why your cry of 'horrible'?—unless there is some revulsion in your mind?

CASSANDRA. The house is breathing murder, with the drip of blood.

CHORUS. How? Not so! That is the smell of sacrifices at the 1310 hearth.

CASSANDRA. The vapour is just like that from a tomb; it's so evident!

CHORUS. No Syrian splendours for the house in your descrip- 1312 tion!

CASSANDRA. My cry of distress is not like a bird's at a thicket, 1316 from alarm to no purpose: bear me witness to that, once I am dead, when woman dies in place of woman, in place of me, and man with evil wife falls in place of man. I claim this from you as a stranger here, now I am to die. 1320

CHORUS. Poor wretch, I pity you the fate you predict.

CASSANDRA. There is one speech more I wish to make—or my own dirge: I pray to my last daylight from the sun, that my master's avengers requite my murder too on our enemies; 1325 mine is a slave's death, an easy victory.

Oh! Mortal men and their dealings! When they succeed, a shadow may turn them round; if they fail, the wipe of a wet sponge destroys the picture. I pity the second much more than 1330 the first.

CASSANDRA *enters the door. The* CHORUS *are now alone, and chant.*

CHORUS. Success by its nature brings mortal men no satiety;
no one forbids and bars its way to palaces which fingers
point out,
declaring 'Enter no more!'
And so to this man here the blessed gods granted the taking 1335
of Priam's city,
and he has come home with the gods' honour;
but now if he is to pay for the blood of those before,
and by his death to ordain vengeance
for the dead in other deaths,
who of mortal men, when he hears this, 1340
would boast of birth to a destiny without harm?

A sudden cry is heard from within the house.

AGAMEMNON (*offstage*). O-oh! I have been struck deep, a fatal
blow!

CHORUS. Quiet! Who shouted of a blow as if dealt a fatal wound?

AGAMEMNON. O-oh! Again! Struck a second blow!   1345

CHORUS. The deed has been done, it seems to me from the
king's cries of pain. Let us share our thoughts, in case there
may somehow be safe plans.

—— I tell you my proposal, to have criers call the townsfolk here
to the house, to help.

—— No, my idea is to rush in at once and prove the deed   1350
together with the freshly streaming sword.

—— I share a proposal like that, and I vote for action; it's a
moment for no delay!

—— It's here to see: this is their prelude to actions which mean
tyranny for the city.   1355

—— Yes, we are taking our time while they trample down delay's
reputation, and their hands are not asleep.

—— I do not know what plan to hit on and say; for the man of
action has also to plan for it.

—— I'm like that too, at a loss for words to resurrect the dead. 1360

—— Are we really to drag out our lives in submitting like that to
these violators of the house as our rulers?

—— That is not tolerable, it is better to die; it is a fate milder
than tyranny.   1365

—— Why, are we to divine from the evidence of his groans that
the man is dead?

—— We should be discussing this from clear knowledge; guessing is different from knowing clearly.

—— I am getting a majority from all sides for approving this   1370
course, to know exactly how things are with the son of Atreus.

The CHORUS *have not moved. The door opens and* CLYTEMNESTRA
reappears, standing by the bodies of AGAMEMNON *and* CASSANDRA
which are brought into view through it.

CLYTEMNESTRA. After saying much before that suited the
moment, I shall not feel shame to say the opposite. How else
would someone preparing hostilities against enemies who had
seemed to be friends, make a net-fence of harm too high for   1375

them to leap? This challenge had all my thought from long
ago; victory has come in fulfilment—late, but come it has.

I stand where I struck, over a deed completed; I did it this
way, and I shall not deny it, so there should be no escape,   1380
no fending off death. A net with no way through, just as for
fish, I stake out round him, an evil wealth of clothing; I
strike him twice, and with two groaning cries his legs gave
way on the spot; and I deal him a third blow on top now he   1385
has fallen, a thank-offering vowed to the Zeus below the
earth, the saviour of the dead. And so he speeds his life away
after his fall; he gasps out quick blood from his throat-
wound and hits me with a dark shower of gory dew, and I   1390
rejoice no less than a sown crop does in Zeus' sparkling gift
when the sheathed ears swell for birth. If it were possible to 1392
pour a libation to the corpse from what is fitting, it would   1395
justly be from this blood—no, more than justly: so great a
mixing-bowl in his house did this man fill with curse-laden
evil, and now on his return he drinks it up himself.   1398

Things being so, you senior Argives here present,   1393
rejoice if you should be for rejoicing; I myself am for
boasting!   1394

CHORUS. We marvel at your tongue, at your bold mouth in   1399
vaunting such words over your husband.   1400

CLYTEMNESTRA. You test me like a witless woman, but I
speak with a fearless heart to those who know; and whether
you yourself wish to approve or to blame me, it's all the same!
This is Agamemnon, my husband, but a corpse, the work of   1405
my right hand here, a just architect. This is how things are.

The CHORUS' *distress increases and they turn to lyric;*
CLYTEMNESTRA *at first continues in speech, then her emotion
increases too.*

CHORUS. What evil thing, woman,   Str. 1
  grown in the earth to eat,
  or to drink from a source in the flow of the sea,
  did you taste to perform this rite of death, incurring the
    people's spoken curse?
  You have thrown them off, you have cut them off, and you
    shall be put out of the city,   1410
  a mighty hate to the townsmen.

CLYTEMNESTRA. Now your sentence is my exile from the city,
and to have the townsmen's hatred and the people's spoken
curse, although earlier you made no opposition to Agamemnon here. He took no special account, just as if it were the   1415
death of an animal from his teeming woolly flocks of sheep,
when he sacrificed his own daughter, the darling of my womb,
as a spell against Thracian winds.

Is not he the one you should have driven from the land in
penalty for pollution? But now you have witnessed my action   1420
you are a harsh judge. I tell you: make threats like those, and I
am prepared on similar terms, for one who wins by force to
rule me; but if god ordains the opposite, you shall be taught,
late it may well be, to learn discretion.   1425

CHORUS. You are great in your plans,   Ant. 1
arrogant in your talk—
exactly as your mind is mad from this event
and the gore which drips from it; the thick smear of blood
    in your eyes is obvious.
Payment in return you have still to make, and you shall be
    deprived of your friends;
a blow is to pay for a blow.   1430

CLYTEMNESTRA. And now you are to hear my oaths, in their
full right: I swear by Justice fulfilled for my child, by Ruin
and by the Fury, for all of whom I slew this man, that for me
no expectation treads in fear's palace so long as fire is burned   1435
at my hearth by Aegisthus, loyal towards me as in the past; he
is no small shield of confidence for us.

(*pointing to Agamemnon*) Here he lies, his own wife's defiler,
me here, the charmer of any Chryseis under Troy, and here is
the woman captive, both portent-seer and sharer of his couch,   1440
the prophecy-telling faithful bedmate, plying the ships'
benches like a loom. The two of them have not done without
their proper honour: that is why he lies here like this, and she
does too, his lover, after singing her last death-laden lament   1445
like a swan; and for me their bed has brought an added relish
for my luxuriance.

CHORUS. Oh for a fate without excessive pain   Str. 2
and not long-watchful by the bed,
to come and bring to us quickly   1450

the sleep which never ends, now that our most kind guardian
has been brought down in death
after enduring
much through a woman; by woman too his life was lost.

O you demented Helen,   Ephymnion 1
singly destroying those many,   1456
all too many lives under Troy!
Now you have decked for yourself, with the flowers of
    fulfilment,
the Strife which was then in the house, long to be
    remembered
because of blood not to be washed away,   1460
strong to subdue a man, a great agony of woe.

CLYTEMNESTRA (*joining the lyric mode, but chanting*).
Make no prayer for death as your fate under the weight of
    these things,
nor turn your anger away upon Helen
as destroyer of men, for singly destroying   1465
the lives of many Danaans
and causing anguish impossible to fight.

CHORUS. You demon who are falling on the house   Ant. 2
and its two brother Tantalids,
the power you wield is from women,
equal in their temper—a thing which bites to my heart!   1470
Over the body it stands
like a hostile crow
tunelessly boasting and singing [evil in its] song.

CLYTEMNESTRA. You have corrected now the thought in   1475
    your words,
in calling on the thrice-fattened demon of this family:
from the demon a craving to lick blood afflicts it,
with fresh pus fostered before the old hurt has ceased.   1480

CHORUS. Great indeed and heavy in its anger   Str. 3
for this house is the demon you praise—
no! no! it is wrong, this praising is wicked—insatiable for
    ruin's success—
oh, grief indeed!—through Zeus   1485
the all-causing, the all-doing.

For what is fulfilled for mortals without Zeus?
What is there in things here which god has not ordained?

Oh! O my king, my king, how am I to weep for
    you?   Ephymn. 2
What am I to say from a heart of friendship?   1491
You lie in this spider's web
breathing out your life in a death which is impious;
oh, oh me!, your lying here is ignoble,
laid low in a treacherous death   1495
by a hand with double-bladed weapon.

CLYTEMNESTRA. You say confidently, this deed is mine;
    but you are not to reckon in that I am Agamemnon's mate:
    taking the semblance of this dead man's wife,   1500
    the ancient bitter demon of revenge
    upon Atreus the cruel banqueter
    has made this man the price, a full-grown sacrifice made
        over the young ones.

CHORUS. That you have no responsibility   Ant. 3
    for this murder, who will bear witness?   1506
    How, how have you none? The demon coming from his
        father would be your accomplice!
    Forcing a way in streams
    of fresh bloodshed among kinsmen,   1510
    black Ares goes forward to where he will bring
    justice for clotted blood, for those children devoured.

Oh! O my king, my king, how am I to weep for
    you?   Ephymn. 2
What am I to say from a heart of friendship?   1515
You lie in this spider's web
breathing out your life in a death which is impious;
oh, oh me!, your lying here is ignoble,
laid low in a treacherous death
by a hand with double-bladed weapon.   1520

CLYTEMNESTRA. I think, neither was this man's death
    ignoble,
[*a line missing*]
for did he not also bring ruin on the house through treachery?

Yes, my child by him which I raised, 1525
the much lamented Iphigenia,
[her father sacrificed].
What his actions deserved he deservedly suffers;
so let him make no great boast in Hades,
now that he has paid for just that deed, felled in death by
the sword.

CHORUS. I am helpless, bereft of thought   Str. 4
and resourceful meditation, 1530
where to turn now the house is falling.
I fear the beat of rain which wrecks a house,
the rain of blood; the shower gives way,
but in aid of Justice, for further retribution, Fate 1535
is whetting harm on other whetstones.

O earth, earth! I wish you had received me   Ephymn. 3
before I saw him here, occupying
a base couch in the silver-sided bath! 1540
Who will inter him? Who will lament him?
Will you be hard enough yourself to do this—after you killed
your own husband, to keen for him,
and to perform a graceless grace unjustly to his ghost 1545
in return for his great deeds?
And whose task will it be to utter the tombside praise
over the godlike man amid tears,
with a true heart? 1550

CLYTEMNESTRA. It is not your business to take care of this
duty: from us
he had his fall, he had his death, and we shall have his
interment,
not to the accompaniment of weeping by outsiders,
but Iphigenia shall welcome him, 1555
daughter meeting father as she should,
at the swift ferry-crossing of sorrow,
to throw her two arms around him and kiss him.

CHORUS. This is insult matching insult;   Ant. 4
these are issues hard to decide. 1561
The robber robbed, the killer paying;
while Zeus remains enthroned, this too remains:
'the doer suffers'; that is fixed law.

Who is there to expel the curse and its stock from the   1565
   house?
The family is glued fast to ruin.

CLYTEMNESTRA. The oracle you entered on has truth;
but I myself wish to swear a pact with the demon of the   1570
   Pleisthenidae
to acquiesce in all this, hard though it is to bear;
while for the future it is to go from this house
to wear away another family with kindred murders.
To have a little share in the house's possessions quite   1575
   contents me,
if I remove from it the madness of mutual killings.

     AEGISTHUS *enters suddenly from the side.*

AEGISTHUS. O kindly day, bringing justice with its light!
   Now at last I would say that the gods keep watch from
above upon earth's evil deeds, as avengers of mankind, when I
see this man lying here in the woven robes of the Furies; as I   1580
dearly wanted, he pays in full for what his father's hand
contrived.

   Atreus his father, the ruler of this land, when his power was
disputed, banished my father Thyestes, his own brother—this
is a true account—from city and home. By returning as   1585
suppliant to the hearth the wretched Thyestes found for
himself security against being killed and bringing blood
upon his ancestral soil himself; but for his hospitality this
man's godless father Atreus, eager rather than amiable   1590
towards my father, while cheerfully seeming to celebrate a
day for butchered meat, provided him with a feast from his
children's flesh. He broke up small the feet and the combs of
fingers; and Thyestes, seated separately at a distance, at once   1595
takes the unrecognizable parts and eats them in ignorance, an
ugly meal which ended the safety, as you see, for Atreus' line.
Then, as he realized the monstrousness of the deed he cried
his revulsion; he falls backward vomiting the slaughter out,
and invokes an intolerable fate upon the Pelopidae: his kick   1600
overturning the meal makes joint sentence with his curse, that
thus should perish totally the line of Pleisthenes.

   That, I tell you, is the cause of the man's fall you see here;

and I had the right in justice to scheme this killing. I was the third child after ten others; while I was tiny, in my swaddling, 1605 Atreus expelled me together with my hapless father; and when I was grown up, Justice brought me back again. I laid my hands on this man from outside, fitting together every device of ill intent. So even death is well for me too, now I have seen 1610 this man in Justice's toils.

CHORUS. Aegisthus, I have no respect for arrogance amid others' disaster. Are you saying that you killed this man deliberately, and that you alone planned this pitiable murder? I tell you that in the court of justice you will not escape the people's curse, for 1615 stones to be hurled at your head; be sure of it!

AEGISTHUS. Is this your language when you sit at the oars below, while those at the helm control the ship? Old as you are, you shall know how heavy it is for one of your years to be taught, when the word has been given to show good sense. 1620 Chains and the pangs of starvation are the most excellent diviner-doctors for the mind in teaching even old age. You can see—but can you not see this? Do not kick against the pricks, in case you hit yourself and get hurt.

CHORUS. You—you woman! Against those who were newly 1625 from the fighting, while you had kept the house at home and violated the husband's bed as well—did you plan this death for their commander?

AEGISTHUS. Those words too are the begetters of tears to come. Your tongue is the opposite of Orpheus': he would lead everything after him through its delight in his voice, but your 1630 provocation with your silly yelping will have you led away. Once under control you will appear more tame!

CHORUS. As if I shall see you ruling the Argives—you who planned death for this man but had no courage to carry out the deed by killing him yourself! 1635

AEGISTHUS. That was because the deception was clearly a woman's role, while I was a suspect enemy from long ago. From this man's wealth I shall try to rule the citizens; any man who does not obey me I shall put under a heavy yoke— he will be no trace-horse fed with barley! That hard friend 1640 hunger which houses with darkness will see him softened.

CHORUS So why did you not slay and strip this man out of your evil heart yourself, but a woman did the killing with you, in an

act polluting land and native gods? Is Orestes alive some-   1645
where, to come back home with fortune's favour and to be the
all-victorious killer of these two here?

The altercation is suddenly more excited,

AEGISTHUS. Well, since you think to act and speak like this,
you shall soon learn!

CHORUS. Come on then, our band of friends! The action here   1650
is not far off!

AEGISTHUS. Come on then: every man have his sword ready,
hilt to hand!

CHORUS. Look, my hilt is to hand as well, and I do not refuse to
die!

AEGISTHUS. You die? We accept the omen of your words, we
choose this outcome!

CLYTEMNESTRA (*breaking the silence she has held since*
AEGISTHUS' *entry*). No! No, dearest of men, let us inflict no
more trouble! Even this is much to have reaped, an unhappy   1655
harvest. There is enough harm already; let us bring no further
ruin on us!

Go to the house, you esteemed elders; yield to fate before you
suffer [*words missing*]. These things had to be as we have done
them. If there were a remedy for our afflictions here, we would
welcome it, now a demon's heavy hoof has miserably struck us.   1660
That is what I say, a woman, if anyone thinks it worth hearing.

AEGISTHUS. But that these men should glory over me with
empty talk like this, and throw out such words to test their
fate, and in default of sensible moderation [insult] their
master!

CHORUS. It would not be like Argives to fawn upon an evil   1665
man!

AEGISTHUS. But I shall still pursue you in later days!

CHORUS. No, not if fortune directs Orestes to come here.

AEGISTHUS. I'm well aware that men in exile feed on hopes.

CHORUS. Go on then, do it, get yourself fat, polluting justice
since you can!

AEGISTHUS. You shall pay me the penalty, be sure of it, in   1670
return for this foolishness!

CHORUS. Vaunt away while you have the confidence, like a
cockerel near the hen!

CLYTEMNESTRA (to AEGISTHUS). Take no account of this empty yelping! In our twin mastery of this house [I] and you will make things [well].

She and AEGISTHUS *go in together, and the bodies of* AGAMEMNON *and* CASSANDRA *are hidden by the closing door. The* CHORUS *leave by the side.*

Libation Bearers

Libation Bearers

Characters

ORESTES, son of the murdered King Agamemnon of Argos
PYLADES, Orestes' close friend
CHORUS of women slaves from the palace of the Atreidae at
  Argos
ELECTRA, daughter of Agamemnon
DOORMAN at the palace
CLYTEMNESTRA, Agamemnon's wife who murdered him
  and now rules at Argos
NURSE of Orestes when he was a baby
AEGISTHUS, son of Agamemnon's uncle Thyestes and now
  ruling at Argos with Clytemnestra
HOUSE-SLAVE of Aegisthus

There are mute parts for servants and attendants.

Scene: in front of the palace, as in Agamemnon. *The characters at the
beginning speak as if they are at Agamemnon's tomb; later the action moves
more precisely to the palace-front.*
  ORESTES *and* PYLADES *in travelling clothes and carrying pack-
    baggage enter from one side.*

[*The beginning of the play is lost. Fragments 1 to 7 come from quotations
in various ancient Greek authors.*]

ORESTES.
  (Fragment 1) Hermes of the Underworld, watching over
  paternal powers! I ask you, be my saviour and my ally; for
  my coming to this land is my return from exile.   1-3
  (Fragment 2) . . . in my wish to avenge my father . . .   3a
  (Fragment 3) . . . he died . . . violently at his wife's hand 3b, c
  through unseen trickery . . .
  (Fragment 4) . . . Here on my father's grave-mound I cry to him
  to listen, to hear . . .   4-5

(Fragment 5) . . . a lock of my hair to Inachus, for my up-
bringing, and this second one here in mourning . . . 6–7
(Fragment 6) . . . on the rock-hard ground . . . 7a
(Fragment 7) . . . for I was not there to lament over your death,
father, and I did not stretch out my hand when your body was
carried out for funeral . . . 8–9

The CHORUS *and* ELECTRA *begin to enter from the side in
procession.*

What's this I see? Whatever is this company of women approach- 10
ing, so conspicuous in their black dress? What misfortune am I
to picture from it? Has some new disaster befallen this house, or
would I be right in guessing that these women bring libations for
my father, appeasements of the dead? It could never be any- 15
thing else! Why, I think my sister Electra is there too, conspicuous in bitter grief. O Zeus! Grant me vengeance for my father's
death! Be my ally if you will!

Pylades, let us stand aside, so I may learn for certain what this 20
act of supplication by the women is.

ORESTES *and* PYLADES *withdraw to one side; in stage-convention
they remain unseen by the entering women.* ELECTRA *moves clear of
the* CHORUS *and approaches the tomb. The* CHORUS *dance and sing.*

CHORUS. I have been sent here from the house; I come Str. 1
in procession with libations, hands in the quick beat of
grief,
cheeks torn into bright crimson-red,
my nails cutting furrows afresh— 25
life-long my heart is fed upon wailing!—
fine linens and their weave destroyed,
noisily rent, ripping in grief,
the folds of the robe over my breast 30
battered by laughterless disaster.

Piercing and shrill, standing the hair on end, Ant. 1
the dream-prophet of the palace, breathing rancour out of
sleep,
yelled screaming at full dead of night
in terror from the inmost house, 35
falling heavy on the women's chambers.

The interpreters of this dream
pledged the gods' meaning and cried
the passion of those under the earth,   40
their blame for the killers, and rancour.

In seeking to do this grace that is graceless,   Str. 2
to turn away harm—O Earth our good mother!—   45
the godless woman has sent me—I fear to utter her words!
What amends can there be, once blood falls to the ground?
Oh, this hearth and home are all woe!
This house is now razed to the ground!   50
Sunless and loathsome to men,
blackness covers the house
through the death of its master.

Invincible once, unconquered, unsubdued,   Ant. 2
the awe of respect, which entered people's   56
ears and minds, abandons them, and they fear. To have
    good success—
this is god among men, and more, even, than god.   60
Justice weighs down with its dark,
quickly upon some in the light;
for some mid-way to the dark,
delay grows full with time;
some have night with no fixed end.   65

The bloodshed drunk up by Earth its nurse—   Str. 3
the vengeful blood is set hard, and it will not dissolve.
Ruin lasting for ever
torments the guilty man,
[and] all-powerful disease.   70

For one who assaults a bridal bower   Ant. 3
no cure whatever exists; and all ways which converge
in one road, to purify
blood on polluted hands,
go straight onward in vain.

And for myself—because the gods brought   Epode
my city its fate by siege, and from my father's house   76
led me into the lot of a slave—,
right or wrong, it is proper I accept
a rule over my life in violence to my heart,

and conquer my bitter loathing; 80
yet these garments hide my weeping
for my masters' helpless fortunes,
in secret, curdling grief.

ELECTRA. You servant-women, who set our house in order,
since you are here with me in procession with this 85
supplication, help me with advice in the matter: what am I
to say as I offer these mourning-libations? How am I to speak
sensibly to my father, how am I to pray to him? Am I to say
that I bring them to a dear husband from a dear wife, from my 90
mother? I have no courage for that, no words I should say as I
pour this offering on my father's tomb. Or am I to follow
men's custom and make my speech this, that he should well
repay those who send these offerings, and with a gift which
their goodness deserves? Or in silence, in dishonour to him— 95
and so exactly as my father died—once I have poured this
libation for the earth to drink, am I to go off again like
someone who discards the dregs at a purification, throwing
the vessel away with averted eyes? Share the responsibility for
this decision, my friends; why, inside the house we share 100
hatred as a habit! Don't keep things hidden in your heart
through fear of anyone: what is destined waits for the free as
well as for those subjected to another's hand. Please tell me, if
you have anything better than this. 105
CHORUS. I respect your father's tomb like an altar; so I will tell
you, since you order me, what speaks from my heart.
ELECTRA. Please tell me, just as you have respected my father's
grave.
CHORUS. When you make the libation, say good words for
those of kind intention.
ELECTRA. Which of those dear to me am I to name as that? 110
CHORUS. Yourself first, and anyone who hates Aegisthus.
ELECTRA. Then I will make this prayer for me and you
together.
CHORUS. Since you already understand this for yourself, put
your mind to it.
ELECTRA. Who else then is there for me to add to our side?
CHORUS. Remember Orestes, even if he's abroad. 115
ELECTRA. That's well said, and not the least of your advice.

CHORUS. And while you remember him, upon those guilty of
the murder . . .

ELECTRA. What am I to say? Explain, and instruct me; I have
no experience.

CHORUS. . . . pray there comes upon them some god or man

ELECTRA. A judge, you mean, or a just avenger?   120

CHORUS. . . . state it simply: someone to kill them in return.

ELECTRA. And I may ask this from the gods in proper piety?

CHORUS. And why not, to requite an enemy with harm for harm?   123

ELECTRA. [*one line perhaps missing*] supreme messenger of those
above and those below, [*words missing*] Hermes of the Under-   165
world, carry my cry to the gods below the earth, to hear my   124
prayers in their watch over my father's house; and to Earth   125
herself, who gives birth to all things, nurtures them, and
takes their increase back again. As I pour these libations to
the dead, my own words too call upon my father: have pity   130
on me, and kindle our dear Orestes as a light in the house!
For we are outcasts now, as it were, sold off by our mother;
and she has taken a man in exchange, Aegisthus, her very
accomplice in your murder. I am like a slave myself, while   135
Orestes is in exile from his property; and their great and
extravagant luxury is the fruit of your labour. That Orestes
may come here through some fortune is my prayer to you;
and you must hear me, father! Grant me also to be much
more chaste than my mother, and my hands to have greater   140
piety. Those are the prayers I say for ourselves; for our
enemies I pray for your avenger to appear, father, and for
your killers to die justly in return. In speaking this curse for
evil upon them, I am putting it in the open before those   145
whose concern it may be. For ourselves, send up here above
the good which we ask, with the help of the gods, and of
Earth, and of Justice who brings victory!

Such are the prayers with which I pour these libations; and
it is the custom that you crown them with laments, voicing   150
the dead man's paean-hymn.

ELECTRA *pours the libations. As the* CHORUS *dance and sing, their
increasingly irregular rhythm matches their increasing passion.*

CHORUS. Let your tears fall splashing
for your master who died,

on to this bulwark here for good men (*gesturing to the tomb*),
this defence against abominable pollution by bad,   155
now the libations are poured.
Listen, please, majesty!
Listen, master, with your mind in the darkness!
(*uttering a prolonged rhythmic wail of grief*)
Oh, what man [will come] to deliver the house,   160
strong with his spear, brandishing Scythian arrows
in hand in the War-god's work,
and wielding a hilted blade in close fight?

ELECTRA. My father now has his libations for the earth to   164
drink—(*starting in surprise*) but here's a new thing for talk!   166
Share it with me.

CHORUS. Please tell it me; my heart is dancing in fear.

ELECTRA. I can see a lock of cut-off hair, here on the tomb.

CHORUS. Whosoever is it—a man's, or some slim-waisted girl's?

ELECTRA. That's easy to conjecture; anyone can guess.   170

CHORUS. So how may I learn whose it is, an older from a
younger woman?

ELECTRA. There is no one except myself who would cut it off.

CHORUS. No, because those with a duty to offer hair in
mourning are enemies.

ELECTRA. See here, too! To look at it, this strand seems very
like . . .

CHORUS. Whose hair? This is what I want to know.   175

ELECTRA. . . . my own; it's very close, to look at it.

CHORUS. You surely don't think this is a secret gift from
Orestes?

ELECTRA. It's *his* hair which it resembles!

CHORUS. And how did Orestes dare to come here?

ELECTRA. He cut and sent the lock to honour his father.   180

CHORUS. What you say makes me no less ready with my tears,
if he is never to set foot in this land.

ELECTRA. A surge of bitterness reached my heart too; it was
like a piercing shaft that struck me. Tears drip and fall from
my eyes uncontainably in their thirst, in a flood like a winter   185
storm, now I have seen this lock of hair. How can I hope that
anyone else among our townspeople is the owner of this hair?
And I swear it wasn't she, the killer, who cut it off either—yes,
my own mother, quite untrue to that name because of the   190

godless thoughts she possesses towards her children. But for
me to agree outright that this tribute is from the dearest of
beings to me, from Orestes—well, hopes of this do fawn on
me! Oh! If only it had a voice and intelligence in it, like a   195
messenger, so that I wasn't shaking with uncertainty, and it
was quite clear whether to reject this lock of hair, with
loathing, if it really has been cut from an enemy's head—or
as a kinsman's it could share my sorrow, a glory for this tomb   200
and an honour for my father! So I call upon the gods: they
know the kind of storms which swirl us round like sailors; and
if we are destined to reach safety, a little seed might grow into
a great root-stock.

(*starting in surprise again*) Look, footprints! Further evidence,   205
the feet equally like mine! In fact there are two pairs of feet
outlined here, Orestes' own and some fellow-traveller's. [*a line
missing*] the heels and impressed contours of the soles when I
measure them match my own prints. This is agony for me, my   210
wits are quite destroyed!

ORESTES *and* PYLADES *have come nearer, unnoticed.*

ORESTES. Pray for the future and success! Tell the gods, your
prayers are now fulfilled!

ELECTRA. Why, what help am I getting thanks to the gods at
this moment?

ORESTES. You have come in sight of the very persons you were   215
praying for just now.

ELECTRA. And which among men was I calling for? How can
you be aware of him?

ORESTES. I am aware that you are wonderfully intent upon
Orestes.

ELECTRA. And just how have I obtained my prayers?

ORESTES. Here: here I am! Seek for no one more dear to you
than me.

ELECTRA. What? Are you weaving some trickery round me,   220
stranger?

ORESTES. If I am, in that case I am forming schemes against
my own self.

ELECTRA. What, are you wanting to laugh at me in my misery?

ORESTES. In my own misery too, in that case, if I really am
laughing at yours.

ELECTRA. Why, is it actually Orestes I'm speaking to? Is it you?

ORESTES. Yes, and though you see my real self, you are slow 225
to know me; but when you saw this hair cut off in mourning
your excitement took wings and you thought you saw me;
and while you were looking at traces in my footprints [*a line
missing*] of your brother's, exactly similar to your own head.
Look: put one of your braids beside the lock of hair! And see 230
this piece of weaving, your own handiwork, with its batten-
marks and the picture of a beast (ELECTRA *starts in
delight*)—control yourself! Don't let your mind be overcome
with joy; I know that our nearest and dearest are bitterly
against us.

ELECTRA. O you dearest darling of our father's house! You are 235
its hope we have been weeping over, for the germ of its safety! 236
Oh, to see your face delights me! It has four parts to play for me: 238
I am compelled to address you as father; and it falls to me to
show you the love I would towards our mother—for she is most 240
justly detestable—and towards our sister who was ruthlessly
sacrificed; and you were my faithful brother, quite alone in 243
bearing me respect. [*a line missing*] with trust in your strength, 237
you will recover your father's house.

ORESTES. If [only] Might and Justice, with Zeus the third 244
and greatest of all, may be with me! 245
Zeus, Zeus! Observe our circumstances here! See the
brood bereft of their eagle father, killed in the twisted coils
of a dreadful viper! Starving hunger presses hard on the
orphans, for they are not grown enough to bring a father's 250
prey to the nest. This is the state in which you can see myself
and her, I mean Electra, children deprived of their father, both
of us in the same exile from our house. If you destroy these
nestlings of the father who made the famous sacrifice and did 255
you great honour, where will you get the tribute of rich feasting
from a hand such as his? You could never again send mankind
trustworthy signs if you destroyed the eagle's nestlings, just as
this royal root-stock, once it is all withered, will not help at 260
your altars on days of ox-sacrifice. Take the house into your
care, and from little you would raise it up to greatness although
it now seems quite fallen.

CHORUS. Children, you saviours of your father's hearth, be

quiet, so that no one hears and for the sake of gossiping 265
reports this to those in power. If only I may see them dead one
day, on fire in oozing pitch!

ORESTES. Loxias' great and powerful oracle will not betray me, I
tell you, which orders me to go through this danger. Loud and 270
often it cried out, proclaiming ruin wintry-cold to strike up into
my heart's warmth if I do not pursue those guilty for my father's
death in the same way; it says I am to kill them in return. It 274
asserted I should pay for this with my own dear life, and have 276
much unpleasant evil, maddened like a bull in a punishment 277
which will keep me from my property. The oracle's words to 275
men in part revealed angry acts from the earth's hostile powers,
in part decreed diseases that invade the flesh, ulcers eating 280
away its original nature with cruel jaws and then white hairs
springing up on these lesions; and it spoke of further
visitations from Furies, exacted for a father's blood. [*a line
missing*] seeing clearly, eyes roving in darkness. Those below 285
have a weapon from the dark, from men killed within their
family and supplicating vengeance: it is madness and empty
terror in the night; it attacks, it harasses and it drives a man
from his city, with his body maimed under a yoke of beaten 290
bronze. Such men, the oracle said, may share neither wine-
bowl nor friendly libations, and they are kept away from altars
by a father's unseen anger. No one either welcomes or shares
his roof with such a man; lacking all honour and friends he 295
dies in time, withered dry as a mummy in an evil death of
total extinction.

Are not such oracles to be trusted? Even if I do not trust
them, the deed has to be done. Many desires are falling
together into one; there are the gods' commands, and my
great grief for my father; besides, it oppresses me to be 300
deprived of my property, so that our citizens, who have the
finest glory among men, and honour for their heart in sacking
Troy, should not be subjects like this of a pair of women.
Why, the man is effeminate at heart; and if he is not, he shall
soon find out! 305

ORESTES, ELECTRA, *and the* CHORUS *arrange themselves at
Agamemnon's tomb to chant and sing;* PYLADES *remains to one side.*

CHORUS (*chanting*). You great powers of Fate, may Zeus
    grant an ending here   (A)
  in which justice changes to the other side!
  'In return for hostile words, let hostile words be paid!'—   310
  in exacting what is due, Justice shouts that aloud,
  and 'In return for bloody blow, let bloody blow repay!'
  'For the doer, suffering' is a saying three times old.

ORESTES. O father, my father in doom,   Str. 1
  what word or action of mine
  might I waft from afar and reach to you,   316
  where you are held in sleep's bed?
  Light is a state opposite to dark; all the same, a lament   320
  which gives renown is said to be pleasing
  to the Atreidae who lie here in front of their house.

CHORUS. My son, this dead man's proud spirit   Str. 2
  is not subdued in fire's ravening maw,
  but shows its anger later on.   325
  The one meeting death is bewailed,
  the one doing harm is revealed;
  the lament for fathers and parents,
  which claims justice, goes on its search;   330
  it is roused in its full abundance.

ELECTRA. O father, do hear our sorrow,   Ant. 1
  and our many tears in turn!
  See, your two children are here at your tomb,
  voices raised loud in their dirge!   335
  Both of them exiles and suppliants, your grave is their
    welcome.
  What here is good, and what without evil?
  Is not the ruin beyond reversal with three throws?

CHORUS (*chanting*). Yes, but out of this still the god if he
    wishes
  may make your loud singing more cheerful;   (B)
  instead of dirges at the tomb   341
  let us wish that the paean-hymn in the king's palace
  brings in the welcome newly-mixed bowl!

ORESTES. If only there under Troy   Str. 3
  some Lycian with his spear, father,   346

had cut you down and stripped you!
You would have bequeathed fame in your house,
founded a life for your children making eyes turn in the
    streets,   350
and in a land overseas
had your tomb heaped high,
an easy thing for your house to bear.

CHORUS. Comrade conspicuous below earth   Ant. 2
    among comrades who died bravely at Troy,   356
    an honoured and majestic lord,
    and minister serving the kings
    who are great there under the earth—
    for he was a sovereign while he lived,   360
    his hands holding fate's appointment
    and a sceptre which all men obeyed.

ELECTRA. Not even under Troy's walls   Ant. 3
    do I wish you had died, father,
    buried near Scamander's ford
    with our other folk slain by the spear!   365
    Sooner his killers had died so, laid low in fate bringing
        death
    [to enemies], for someone
    far off to find out,   370
    unaffected by these troubles here!

CHORUS (*chanting*). You are voicing things beyond the power
    of gold,   (C)
    greater, my child, than any great fortune
    outside this world; voice them, indeed you can.
    Yet here is the thud of a double lash coming: 375
    Orestes has helpers below earth already,
    and our rulers' hands are impure.
    [*words missing*] of these hateful sorrows;
    but they have come more to his children.

ORESTES. That went sharply right through my ears,   Str. 4
    like a bolt striking.   381
    Zeus, Zeus! You send up from below
    the ruin from later punishment
    for mortals' reckless and criminal hands;
    likewise for the parents shall it be paid.   385

CHORUS. Oh to chant the piercing victory-cry   Str. 5
  over the man when he is struck
  and the woman when she is killed—
  how I wish it! Why hide
  what hovers despite all
  at the front of my mind, where my heart's anger   390
  is blowing fiercely from the prow,
  in rancorous loathing?

ELECTRA. And when may Zeus almighty launch   Ant. 4
  his hand to strike them—
  ah, ah!—cleaving their heads apart?   395
  If only our land might trust in it!
  From the unjust, justice: that I demand.
  Earth, hear me, and you in honour below!

CHORUS (*chanting*). Certainly there is a law that bloodshed   (D)
  dripping to the ground demands another's blood.
  The havoc from those slain before   401
  shouts the Fury on
  who brings fresh ruin upon ruin.

ORESTES. Oh, horror! No! You underworld rulers!   Str. 6
  Look, you mighty Curses of the slain!
  See here the remnants of the Atreidae,   406
  helpless exiles from their house
  in dishonour. O Zeus, which way to turn?

CHORUS. My own heart too has been trembling in turn   Ant. 5
  when I hear this piteous cry.
  Then at times I scarcely have hope   411
  and my mood becomes gloom,
  black at hearing your words;
  but in turn [when you say something] to strengthen,   415
  new courage moves distress away,
  for good expectations.

ELECTRA. What should we tell, for success? All the hurt   Ant. 6
  we had from a parent, yes, from her?
  Fawn she may, but there's no mitigation:
  wolf-like and savage, my heart   420
  has a rage no mother's fawning will soothe.

CHORUS. The beat of my grief was Arian, and its measures
    were those   Str. 7
  of a Cisslum wailing-woman,
  hands to be seen hitting relentlessly,   425
  wandering, ceaselessly bruising,
  reaching right down from above, down from a head
  ringing and sounding from blows in my wretchedness.

ELECTRA. Oh! Brutal, you were brutal,   Str. 8
  mother, so cruel with the funeral then,   430
  cruel enough to bury the king
  with his people not there, your husband
  without mourning, with no lament!

ORESTES. Wholly dishonoured, you say: oh, the hurt!   Str. 9
  For my father's dishonour she shall pay, then,   435
  with the aid of the gods
  and with the aid of my own hands.
  Oh to take her life from her, and then to die!

CHORUS. Mutilated too, he was, you must know,   Ant. 9
  and the deed was hers who buried him like that,   440
  seeking to make his death
  unbearable for your own life.
  You hear your father's torment and dishonour!

ELECTRA. You tell of my father's dying; but they kept me
    away   Ant. 7
  in dishonour, worth no regard,   446
  fenced off inside like a dangerous dog,
  tears rising readier than laughter,
  so many poured out in my hidden lament.
  Such things, now you hear [them, you must write] in your
    mind.   450

CHORUS. Yes, write them! Help the story   Ant. 8
  pierce through his ears, to his mind's quiet depth.
  All that is as it is; the rest
  he is eager to learn for himself.
  The fight needs unbending resolve!   455

ORESTES, ELECTRA, *and the* CHORUS *share the climax of the
appeal to Agamemnon.*

ORESTES. You, I mean you, father! Be with your
      friends!   Str. 10
ELECTRA. And my voice calls on you too, in my tears!
CHORUS. Our side is loud in its cry, all in concord!
      Hear us by coming into the light;
      be with us now against our enemies!   460

ORESTES. War will meet war, and justice meet justice! Ant. 10
ELECTRA. O you gods, in justice sanction [my prayers]!
CHORUS. I hear your prayers, and trembling fear invades me.
      What is destined has been waiting long;
      it may well come to those who pray for it.   465

      Oh the troubles of this house   Str. 11
      born in it, and the discordant music
      of Ruin's bloody stroke!
      Oh harsh, unbearable sorrows!
      Oh harsh, unstoppable anguish!   470

      It is the house that must stanch   Ant. 11
      and heal this, and with no help from others
      outside, but by itself,
      because of Strife, bloody and raw.
      The gods below: this is their hymn!   475

      You hear this invocation, you blessed underworld dead:
      now be eager to send the children aid for their victory!

ORESTES. Father, your death was not kingly; grant me now I
      ask it the power over your house.   480
ELECTRA. Father, I too have such a request from you, to
      escape from great [misery] by inflicting it on Aegisthus.
ORESTES. Yes, because if this were so, men would establish
      regular banquets for you; otherwise you will be without
      honour beside those who feast well when the earth gets its
      savoury burnt sacrifices.   485
ELECTRA. And I shall bring you libations at my wedding, out
      of my complete inheritance from my father's house; the first
      thing of all for my special honour shall be this tomb.
ORESTES. O Earth, send me up my father to watch over the
      fight!
ELECTRA. O Persephassa, grant us as well his power in all his 490
      handsomeness!

ORESTES. Remember the bath in which your life was taken from you, father!

ELECTRA. Remember too how they invented a net to throw over you!

ORESTES. Fetters from no forge had you trapped, father!

ELECTRA. Yes, in coverings shamefully devised!

ORESTES. Are you roused to waking by these insults, father?   495

ELECTRA. Are you lifting your head which we hold so dear?

ORESTES. Either send Justice as ally to your friends, or grant our seizing an equal hold in return, if you really wish to return victory for defeat.

ELECTRA. Hear this final cry too, father, as you see your   500 nestlings seated here on your tomb. Take pity on a daughter's and a son's laments together!

ORESTES. And do not wipe out this seed-stock of the Pelopidae; for in this way you are not dead, not even though you died. A man's children preserve his fame when he is dead; they hold it   505 up as corks do a net, preserving its deep flax-line. Listen to us; these lamentations are for you, we tell you, and your preservation lies in honouring our words here.

CHORUS. Now, there can be no blame for you two in   510 prolonging your words here; it is compensation to the tomb for its unlamented fortunes. (*to* ORESTES) But the rest is action; since your mind is rightly set on that, you should try your fortune and act now.

ORESTES. It shall be done; but it is not at all off the course we run to learn why she sent the libations, for what reason, too   515 late with amends for a harm beyond healing. They were a cowardly grace to send to a dead man without senses. I could not imagine why this was; the gifts are less than the offence. 'Someone pouring away his all in return for a single   520 bloodshed, it's work wasted', as the saying has it.
   Tell me if in fact you know; it's what I want.

CHORUS. I do know, my son, for I was there. It was dreams and terrors wandering in the night that made the godless woman shudder and send these libations.   525

ORESTES. Have you actually learned details of the dream, enough to give a true account?

CHORUS. She thought she gave birth to a snake, as she tells it herself.

ORESTES. And the end of her story? Its culmination?

CHORUS. She laid it up in swaddling, like a child.

ORESTES. What food was it wanting, this new-born monstrosity? 530

CHORUS. She gave it her own breast in the dream.

ORESTES. What? How was her nipple not wounded by the abominable thing?

CHORUS. It was; it drew a clot of blood out with her milk.

ORESTES. This vision should not prove idle, I am certain!

CHORUS. She shrieked in terror in her sleep; because it was 535 the mistress many lights blazed up in the house, which the dark had put out like blinded eyes. Then she sends these mourning-libations, hoping for some surgeon's cure for her troubles.

ORESTES. I pray to Earth here, then, and to my father's tomb 540 that this dream may be fulfilled for me. I tell you, my judgement makes it fit closely: for if the snake left the same place as I and was wrapped in my swaddling, and mouthed the breast which nurtured me, and mingled its loving milk 545 with a clot of blood; and if then she wailed in fright at this evil experience—clearly she must die violently for nurturing the ghastly portent, and I have been made into the snake and am to kill her, as this dream tells. 550

CHORUS. I choose your interpretation of this portent; I wish it turns out that way! Now take your friends through the rest, ordering action for some, and for others to do nothing.

ORESTES. It's simply said: Electra here is to go inside [*a line missing*]. I urge keeping these arrangements secret, so that for 555 killing a man of high honour by trickery they may be caught by trickery too, dying in the same noose, exactly as Loxias declared, the Lord Apollo, in the past a prophet without falsity. I shall come in the guise of a stranger, complete with 560 baggage, to the outer doors, together with this man here—he is Pylades, guest-friend and fighting-ally to the house; and we shall both of us speak Parnassian, imitating the sound of the Phocian language. Now, suppose none of the doorkeepers 565 should receive us cheerfully, since the house is indeed possessed by evil: we shall wait as we are, so that anyone who passes by the house will make an inference and say, 'Just why is Aegisthus keeping his door closed against the suppliant, if he's in the house and is aware of him?' But if I get 570

across the threshold of the outer doors and find him on my
father's throne, or if he actually comes back and speaks to me
face to face—you can be sure, as soon as I get sight of him,
before he can say, 'What country's the stranger from?', I'll   575
make a corpse of him; I'll cover him with blows from my swift
blade. The Fury will not be stinted of bloodshed, she will
drink pure blood to the third draught.

(*to* ELECTRA) You must therefore now keep a good guard
upon things inside, so that all this succeeds in fitting closely   580
together. (*to the* CHORUS) You, I urge you to keep your tongues
to what is auspicious, silent where necessary and speaking when
opportune. For the rest, I call on him here (*gesturing to Apollo's
image at the door*) to keep watch in this direction and bring me
success in the battle where I take my sword.

ELECTRA *goes inside the palace;* ORESTES *and* PYLADES *withdraw
to one side. The focus moves from Agamemnon's tomb to the palace-door.
The* CHORUS *dance and sing.*

CHORUS. The earth nurtures many terrors   Str. 1
    which frighten and cause grief;   586
    the ocean's rounded arms
    teem with hostile brute creatures;
    lightnings too between sky and earth,   590
    high in the air between,
    do harm to both winged and earth-walking things;
    and these may speak of tempests with their angry winds.

But a man too bold in spirit—   Ant. 1
    who is to tell of him?—   595
    or women's reckless mind,
    bold all round in those passions
    which are partner in men's ruin?
    Passion rules the female,
    selfishly subverting the bond which unites   600
    in shared dwellings brute creatures and mankind alike.

It should be knowledge for whoever's mind   Str. 2
    does not lightly take wing,
    to learn of the resolve
    formed by the cruel child of Thestius,   605
    the woman who destroyed her son, kindled a fire

and burnt up the dark-red brand
which dated from the time
her son came crying from his mother's womb,   610
its life keeping measure with his
till the day ordained by futu.

There is another in myth to detest,   Ant. 2
that murderous daughter,
for bringing her own kin   615
death at the hands of his enemies,
persuaded by the Cretan necklace, worked in gold,
which was given her by Minos;
she despoiled Nisus
of his immortal hair while slumber's breath   620
unguarded him, the heartless bitch;
and then Hermes came for him.

Since I made mention of pitiless wrongdoing,   Str. 3
not inapposite too
are a union hateful and deprecated by the house,   625
and the planned designs of a woman's mind
against a husband who bore arms,
a man who enjoyed his enemies' respect.
I honour a hearth unheated by passion,
its women not emboldened to assume command.   630

In evils from myth the Lemnian ranks supreme;   Ant. 3
but ours is lamented
as unique in abomination; yet people compare
its horror anew to the Lemnian crime.
In an outrage hateful to god,   635
a race of men perishes in dishonour;
no one has respect for heaven's displeasure.
I collect those examples; is any unjust?

They are a sword to go near my lungs,   Str. 4
its point piercing   640
as it wounds all the way through,
because Justice is being trampled—
against all right—and heeled into the ground—
men offending the majesty of Zeus
absolutely in ways not lawful.   645

But Justice has her foundation laid;   Ant. 4
Fate is early
to the forge as her swordsmith.
The child of older bloody murders
is being brought as well into the house,   650
to pay for their pollution at the last,
by the famous deep-scheming Fury.

ORESTES and PYLADES now move back to centre-stage, with their
baggage; ORESTES bangs on the door.

ORESTES. Slave! Slave there! Hear the knocking at the outer
door! Who's at home, slave? One more time: slave! Who's in
the house? This is my third call for someone to come outside   655
the house, if it does welcome strangers because of Aegisthus.

DOORMAN (*speaking from inside the door*). All right, I hear you!
What country's the stranger from? Where from?

ORESTES. Take a message to the masters of the house; they're
the ones I've come to, and with news! Be quick! Besides,
night's dark chariot is hurrying on, and it's the hour for   660
travellers to let their anchor down in a house open to guests.
Have someone with authority in the house come out, the lady
in charge—but a man is more seemly: the constraints of
conversation blur one's words; a man speaks to another   665
man with confidence and reveals his meaning with clarity.

The door opens, and CLYTEMNESTRA appears; she has attendants.

CLYTEMNESTRA. Strangers, please say if there is anything you
need; all the kinds of thing proper to this house are near to
hand, hot baths as well as bedding to soothe weariness, and   670
the presence of honest faces. If there's need to do anything
requiring more deliberation, it's work for men, and we'll
communicate it to them.

ORESTES. A stranger I am indeed, a Daulian from Phocis; I
was on my way, portering my pack myself, to Argos—exactly   675
where I've ended my journey here—when a man fell in with
me—we were unknown to each other—and he said, after he'd
questioned me about my route and made his own clear—
Strophius the Phocian, as I found out in our talk: 'Since
you're going in any case to Argos, stranger, you can remem-   680
ber with absolute right to tell his parents that Orestes is dead;

don't in any way forget it! Then if his family decide in favour
of bringing him back home, or rather of burying him as a
settler there, a stranger for all eternity, convey these in- 685
structions back again. The walls of a bronze urn now contain
the man's ashes; he has been well mourned.'

I have told you as much as I heard. Whether I am actually
speaking to those in authority and his relations, I do not
know; but it is reasonable for his parent to know. 690

CLYTEMNESTRA. Ah me, alas, you speak of our utter ruin! O
you Curse upon this house, so hard to wrestle down! You
watch over so much, even what was well put out of the way!
With arrows well-sighted from afar you overcome and strip me
of my dear ones, for my utter misery. And now Orestes—he 695
was well-advised, in moving his feet clear of destruction's
mire—but now this very hope, which was healer of the evil
revelry in our house, you must write down as traitorous.

ORESTES. I should myself prefer becoming known to hosts as 700
prosperous as this, and being given hospitality, thanks to
happy news; for what is more agreeable to hosts than their
guest? I thought it would be near impiety in me however not
to bring such a matter to a head for friends when I had agreed 705
to, and now that I have been welcomed as their guest.

CLYTEMNESTRA. Be sure, you will not receive less than you
deserve, nor would you be less of a friend in the house.
Another could equally have come to bring this message. But
it's well time for guests who have been a whole day on a long 710
journey to get what is appropriate to them: (*to a servant*) lead
him into the house, to our hospitable men's quarters, with his
followers and fellow-travellers here, and there let them have
what is appropriate to the house; I urge you to do this as one 715
who must answer for it! (*turning back to* ORESTES) We shall
communicate this to the house's rulers, and with no shortage
of friends deliberate on this disaster.

> ORESTES *and* PYLADES *are led inside by a servant;*
> CLYTEMNESTRA *follows. The* CHORUS *chant.*

CHORUS. Well then, loyal servants of the house!
When shall we show the power of our tongues in Orestes'
    cause?
                                    720
O holy and sovereign Earth, and this high-mounded tomb

our sovereign too, you who now lie
over the admiral's royal body,
now listen to us, now come to aid us: 725
now the time is ripe for guileful Persuasion
to come down and join in our fight,
and the moment is here for Hermes of the Underworld to
    stand as reserve
in these dark struggles where the sword deals death.

A woman-servant, Orestes' childhood NURSE, *comes out from the
house, in visible distress.*

That man the stranger seems to be causing trouble: I can see   730
Orestes' nurse here, all in tears. Where are your steps taking
you, Cilissa, in front of the house? Grief is your fellow
traveller, and takes no wages.

NURSE. The mistress bade me summon Aegisthus to the
strangers as soon as possible, to come and inquire into this   735
newly reported account more definitely, and man from man.
She made a melancholy face to the servants, but she was
hiding her inner laughter at things which had worked out well
for herself; but it's total ruin for this house according to the 740
tale the strangers reported clearly. Certainly, when Aegisthus
hears, it will cheer his heart, once he learns the story. Oh, it's
misery for me: the mixture of ancient griefs beyond bearing
that have happened in this house of Atreus agonized the heart   745
in my breast, but I never yet endured any hurt like this. My
other troubles wrung me dry though I was steadfast; but my
dear Orestes, who wore away my being, whom I nurtured
once I received him from his mother, and [*a line missing*] his   750
shrill commands which had me wandering in the night,
frequent and wearisome, without benefit to myself—I put
up with them. A thing which cannot reason must be nurtured
just like an animal, of course with due attention; a child still in 755
its swaddling cannot say at all whether hunger or thirst or its
bladder affects it; and children's young stomachs are a law to
themselves. Although I tried to divine these things in advance,
as laundress of the child's swaddling, I was I think frequently
mistaken; so launderer and nurse had both the one duty.   760
Those were my hands' two occupations in bringing up
Orestes for his father; now he is dead, and I have the

misery of learning it! I am going to fetch a man who has
ruined this house foully; and he will want to hear this story. 765

CHORUS. So how do her orders tell him to come? How is he to
be attended?

NURSE. What do you mean with 'How'? Tell me again, so I
may understand more clearly.

CHORUS. Whether he is to come with bodyguards, or make his
way alone?

NURSE. Her orders are to bring armed attendants.

CHORUS. Then don't make that your message to our hated
master, but bid him with a cheerful heart, so that he hears 770
without being frightened, to come by himself as soon as he
can. It depends on the messenger to make bent words
succeed.

NURSE. What, are you in your right mind, with the news just
brought?

CHORUS. But what if Zeus will one day bring a wind-change in 775
our troubles?

NURSE. And how? The hope of the house has perished with
Orestes.

CHORUS. Not yet; it would be a poor prophet who gave that
opinion.

NURSE. What do you mean? Do you know something different
from what's been told?

CHORUS. Go and give your message, do what you were sent to
do; the gods take care of whatever it is they care for.   780

NURSE. Then I will go and obey what you tell me. May it turn
out for the best, with the gods' giving!

The NURSE *leaves by the side. The* CHORUS *dance and sing.*

CHORUS. Father of Olympian gods,   Str. 1
I beseech you now, Zeus,
grant good fortune and success   785
lasting and sure for this house,
for those who are yearning to see them.
Justice speaks out through my every word;
and, Zeus, may you keep it safe!

Listen, [Zeus]! The one inside the palace—   Str. 2
oh, set him over his enemies! If you raise him high,   790

then he will be willing to make
a double or triple repayment.

Know that the orphan young colt   Ant. 1
of the man you held dear   795
is now yoked to the chariot,
setting a pace for his steps
as he runs, and keeping its rhythm.
Grant us this sight, for his feet to win home,
stretching straight over the ground!

You gods too who inside the house   Str. 3
provide for its joy from wealth deep within,   801
listen now and give us your favour!
Bring [*words missing*],
expiate the blood of those deeds
long ago with fresh justice; I wish   805
the old murder breeds no more in the house!

And you who dwell in that great and well-built vault,   Mesode
grant that the man's house may look up again in well-
        being,
and he may see freedom's
brilliant [light] with welcoming eyes   810
after the veil of darkness!

A part in things would justly go   Ant. 3
to Maia's son, since his willing support
wafts any action best on its course.
Much appears different if he desires,   815
working his deception unseen;
in the night he brings dark on the eyes,
but cannot be seen more clearly by day.

We shall be voicing quite soon now   Str. 4
a glorious song of freedom   820
for the house, of winds set fair,
a women's song, [high]-struck, of magical power.
The voyage goes well;
it is my gain, mine, which is growing here;
and ruin keeps away from my friends.   825

Orestes! When the moment for action   Ant. 2
comes, cry out over her appeal of 'My son!' and say, 'No,
my father's!' Then go to complete
a ruin which brings you no censure.   830

[You must be brave], and in your heart   Ant. 4
keep up the courage of Perseus;
for your friends below the earth
and those above, perform this duty and grace.
Make bloody ruin   835
of the noxious Gorgon inside the house,
a death which Apollo frees of guilt.

    AEGISTHUS *enters from the side; he is alone.*

AEGISTHUS. I am not here unsummoned but in answer to a
    message; there is a recent report, I am told, that some
    strangers have come with news—in no way desired—of the   840
    death of Orestes. For the house to bear this as well would be a
    burden dripping blood, when it has open sores and lacera-
    tions from killing in the past. What of this news—am I to think
    of it as true and living fact? Or are these frightened tales from   845
    women, which spring up in the air but die away with no
    effect? What can you tell me of this, to get it clear in my
    mind?
CHORUS. We did hear; but go inside and enquire from the
    strangers. There's nothing as strong in messengers as the
    enquiries one man makes for himself from another.   850
AEGISTHUS. I want to see the messenger and interrogate him
    well whether he was himself close by the dying Orestes, or if
    his account was learned from faint rumour. He won't deceive
    a mind that has good eyes.

    AEGISTHUS *quickly goes inside. The* CHORUS *chant.*

CHORUS. Zeus, Zeus! What am I to say?   855
    Where should I begin these prayers and invocations to the
      gods,
    and after words of goodwill equal to the need, how make an
      end?
    Now the polluted cutting-edge
    of cleavers which butcher men   860

is destined either to make destruction
of Agamemnon's house absolute for all time,
or by kindling fire and light to signal his freedom
Orestes shall have the rule to manage his city [*words missing*],
his ancestors' great wealth, 865
Such is the bout of wrestling which godlike Orestes is
   destined
to join against two as sole adversary in waiting;
may it be for victory!

A loud and wailing cry of grief is heard off-stage.

What? What's that? 870
How do things stand? How has it been determined in the
   house?
   (*speaking*) Let us stand aside from the business as it reaches
fulfilment, so as to seem innocent of these troubles; the issue
of the fight has surely been decided!

As the CHORUS *move to one side, a house-slave runs out in panic.*

HOUSE-SLAVE. Oh, woe, utter woe for our master struck 875
   down! Oh woe, again; three times I call the words! Aegisthus
   is no more! (*calling back inside*) Open up there at once, and
   undo the bars to the women's doors! And there's need for
   someone young and strong—but not to help the one done 880
   away—of course not! (*shouting*) Ho there, ho! I'm shouting to
   the deaf! I'm calling in vain to people uselessly asleep!
   Where's Clytemnestra gone? What's she doing?
CHORUS. It seems her head is now about to fall at the butcher's
   block, with Justice the striker!

CLYTEMNESTRA *appears at the door.*

CLYTEMNESTRA. What's the matter? What's this shouting for 885
   help you've set up? Help for the house?
HOUSE-SLAVE. The dead are killing the living, I tell you.

The HOUSE-SLAVE *goes back inside.*

CLYTEMNESTRA. Ah me, alas, I understand the meaning from
   the riddle. Trickery will be our death, just as we killed by it.
   Someone give me an axe to slay a man, at once! Let us see if

we are to win or lose the victory! That is where I have come to 890
now in this evil business.

ORESTES *and* PYLADES *now come out and move forward.*

ORESTES. It's you I'm seeking! This one here (*pointing back inside to where Aegisthus lies dead*) has all he needed.

CLYTEMNESTRA. Ah me, alas, you are dead, my dearest, mighty Aegisthus.

ORESTES. You love the man? Then you shall lie in the same tomb; and you shall never desert him now he is dead. 895

CLYTEMNESTRA. Stop, my son! Hold back, from respect for this breast! You often drowsed at it while your gums drew out its rich milk.

ORESTES. Pylades, what am I to do? Is such respect to stop me from killing my mother?

PYLADES. Then where's the future for Loxias' oracles, deliv- 900
ered by the Pythia, and the pledges sworn on oath? Think of all men as your enemies rather than the gods!

ORESTES. I judge, you have the victory; your advice to me is good. (*to* CLYTEMNESTRA) Follow me! Right by this man's side is where I wish your slaughter. While he was alive you thought him superior to my father; so go and sleep with him 905
when you are dead, since you love this man but hate the one who should have had your love.

CLYTEMNESTRA. I nurtured you, and I want you with me as I grow old.

ORESTES. What, will you share my house when you are my father's killer?

CLYTEMNESTRA. Fate has some responsibility for that, my 910
child.

ORESTES. Well, Fate has dealt you this death too.

CLYTEMNESTRA. Have you no reverence for a parent's curse, my child?

ORESTES. No, for though you gave me birth you threw me out into harsh fortunes.

CLYTEMNESTRA. Indeed I did not throw you out—it was into the house of a fighting-ally.

ORESTES. It was an outrage: to be sold away, when I was a free man's son. 915

CLYTEMNESTRA. Then where was the price I got in exchange?

ORESTES. I feel shame at putting that reproach to you plainly.

CLYTEMNESTRA. Don't, unless you speak equally of your father's follies too.

ORESTES. Don't find fault with the worker while you sit about indoors.

CLYTEMNESTRA. It is painful for wives to be kept from a 920 husband, my child.

ORESTES. But it is a husband's toil which maintains them while they sit indoors.

CLYTEMNESTRA. You are about to kill your own mother, my child, it seems.

ORESTES. It is you who will be killing yourself, not I.

CLYTEMNESTRA. Mind out, be on your guard against a mother's fury-hounds and their rancour!

ORESTES. And how am I to escape my father's if I fail now? 925

CLYTEMNESTRA. I seem to be singing a dirge to my tomb, alive but with no effect.

ORESTES. Yes, it is my father's destiny which determines this death of yours.

CLYTEMNESTRA. Ah me, alas, this is the snake I gave birth to and nurtured; my fear from my dream was truly prophetic!

ORESTES. You killed the man you ought not; so you must suffer the thing you should not. 930

ORESTES *with* PYLADES *takes* CLYTEMNESTRA *inside; the door closes. The* CHORUS *resume a central position.*

CHORUS. I lament even these two in their double disaster; but now that Orestes has come steadfastly to the most extreme among these many bloodsheds, our choice is nevertheless for this eye of the house not to fall utterly in destruction.

The CHORUS *dance and sing.*

There came justice at last to Priam's children,   Str. 1
heavy and just in punishment;   936
there came to Agamemnon's house
a double lion, double warfare;
there drove absolutely forward
the exile, as Pythia   940
enjoined, well sped by warnings of the gods.

Come! Cry celebration for our master's house   Mesode 1
in escaping evil and its wealth's erosion
by two polluters,
its lamentable fortune.   945

There came stealthy fighting, the favourite means   Ant. 1
plotted by guile in punishment;
there lent her hand's touch in the fight
a true daughter of Zeus—as Justice
we mortals name and address her   950
with happy accuracy—
breathing rancour's destruction on her foes.

This very Justice Loxias, who keeps   Str. 2
the great inner vale of Parnassus, cried loud and clear—
without guile, though guile brought harm to Justice;   955
mature now with time, she attacks.
The gods' will somehow prevails
in everything, refusing to serve wicked men;
respect is due to the power which rules in the sky.   960

The light is here to see! The great chain-bridle   Mesode 2
has been taken from the house!
Arise now indeed, O you house! For too long a time
you lay on the ground where you fell.

Soon now, as absolute head of his house,   Ant. 2
Orestes will come through the doorway, when he expels 966
all defilement from his hearth, with cleansing
to expel ruin's destruction.
Its fortunes, their glad face seen
in everything, will turn out in glory again;   970
their favour comes as they move to live in the house.

The door opens and the bodies of CLYTEMNESTRA *and* AEGISTHUS
are revealed, covered by the robing in which they had snared and killed
Agamemnon. ORESTES *is standing by them, and carries the emblems of*
a suppliant and his bloody sword. There are attendants.

ORESTES. See the double tyranny which ruled the land, the
ransackers of the house who killed my father! They had state,
sitting on their thrones then, and they are dear to each other 975
even now, as one may picture by their fall; and their oath stays
by its pledges: they swore together upon death for my poor

father, and to die together; and here (*pointing*) their oath holds
true.

And see, moreover, as you hear these troubles told, the ₉₈₀
device which made bonds for my poor father, manacling his
hands and coupling his feet! (*to the attendants*) Stretch it out
and stand round it in a circle: show the thing which covered a
man, so that a father may see—not my own father, but the one ₉₈₅
who watches over all this—so that I may have a witness in ₉₈₇
justice one day that I pursued this death justly—my own
mother's! Aegisthus' death I do not count, for he has had the
justice customary for an adulterer. What would I be correct in ₉₉₀
calling it with temperate words—a thing to catch a wild beast, ₉₉₇
or a dead man's bath-wrap tented over him down to his feet?
You might rather call it a net and snare, and foot-length
robing to trap his legs. It's the kind of thing a cheating rogue ₁₀₀₀
would get for himself, with a habit of swindling strangers and
a life spent stealing money; his trickery with it would make
away with many men, and bring his heart much warmth. ₁₀₀₄
And a woman who contrived this hateful thing against a ₉₉₁
husband whose children she had carried heavy in her womb—
they were dear to her for a while, but now a bad enemy, as she
shows—what do you think of her? If she had been born a sea-
snake or a viper, would she have caused more putrefaction by
her mere touch, in one she had not bitten, thanks to her audacity ₉₉₅
and lawless spirit? I wish for no such mate to share my house! ₉₉₆
May the gods kill me first, and childless! ₁₀₀₅

CHORUS. Sorrow, [sorrow] for these unhappy deeds!   Str.
You were done away in a hateful death!
Oh sorrow! but suffering comes into flower also for one
    who waits.

ORESTES. Did she do it, or not do it? This robe is my witness ₁₀₁₀
that Aegisthus' sword dyed it; the ooze of blood contributes
over time to spoiling the many dyes in the embroidery. I
praise my father now, I lament him now, while I am here and
addressing this woven thing which killed him. I grieve for the ₁₀₁₅
deeds and the suffering and the whole family; and there can
be no envy for the pollution my victory here brings to me.

CHORUS. There is no mortal man who'll pass his life   Ant.
unharmed throughout, with no price to pay.
Oh sorrow! One misery is now, another is soon on its way. ₁₀₂₀

ORESTES. You are to know, I have no knowledge how it will
end. I am like a charioteer with his horses well off the track; I
am carried away, overcome by senses hard to control. Fear is
ready with its song close to my heart, and my heart ready with
its dance to Rancour—but while I still have my reason, I
proclaim and tell my friends that it was not without justice
that I killed my mother, the pollution who killed my father
and an abomination to the gods; and the inducement to this
resolute act I attribute mostly to Loxias the Pythian prophet,   1030
whose oracle told me I was to be without the evil of blame if I
did these things, but if I failed—I will not say the punishment,
for no one will come within a bowshot of describing its
torments.

And now you see me about to go in supplication, ready
prepared with this wreathed and leafy branch, to the shrine at   1035
mid-earth's navel, Loxias' holy ground, and its bright fire called
undying, as I flee pollution for this family blood; and it was
Loxias' order to turn to no other hearth. I tell all Argives [to   1040
remember] for me in later time the evil dealt me here, and to be   1041a
my witness [if] Menelaus [comes]. Myself a wanderer banished   1041b
from this land [*a line missing*] living and dead with this fame left   1042
behind me.

CHORUS. But what you did was good; and do not let your lips
be linked to damaging speech, nor put your tongue to things   1045
of bad omen, now you have set all Argos' city free by your
clean severance of the two snakes' heads.

ORESTES (*in sudden terror*). A-a-ah! These grim women here—
like Gorgons with their dark clothing and snakes twined
thickly in their hair! I can't stay here longer!   1050

CHORUS. What fancies are swirling you round, you dearest of
men to your father? Hold on, do not be afraid; your victory is
great.

ORESTES. They are not fancies to me, the torments I have here:
these are clearly my mother's rancorous fury-hounds.

CHORUS. That is because the blood is still fresh on your hands;   1055
this is the source of the agitation now invading your mind.

ORESTES. Lord Apollo, here they are, multiplying now! They
drip and trickle from their eyes—loathsome!

CHORUS. You have a single means to purification: Loxias'
touch will set and keep you free from these torments.   1060

ORESTES. You don't see them yourselves, but I can see them!
I'm being driven, I tell you; I can't stay here longer!

ORESTES *rushes out by the side.*

CHORUS. Good fortune be with you then, and may the god
watch over you kindly and keep you safe in critical times!
(*chanting*) In the royal palace this is the third family-storm in   1065
turn
to have blown itself out and come to fulfilment.
Children devoured began the first,
misery hard and cruel;
second were a husband's sufferings, a king's,   1070
and slaughter in a bath was his death for the Achaeans'
leader in war;
now in turn a third has come from somewhere to bring
safety—or should I say, death?
Where indeed will fulfilment be, where will lulling asleep   1075
stop the energy of Ruin?

The CHORUS *leave the orkhêstra by the side.*

Eumenides

Eumenides

Characters

PROPHETESS of Apollo's temple at Delphi
ORESTES, avenger upon his mother Clytemnestra of his father
  Agamemnon King of Argos whom she murdered
PHOEBUS APOLLO, the oracular god of Delphi
CHORUS OF FURIES persecuting Orestes for the matricide
GHOST OF CLYTEMNESTRA
PALLAS ATHENA, patron goddess of Athens
SECONDARY CHORUS of Athena's female temple-servants on
  the acropolis of Athens

There are mute parts for citizens of Athens who act as officers
and jurors in Orestes' trial there.

*Scene: the play begins in front of Apollo's temple at Delphi; later the
action moves to Athens. The* PROPHETESS *enters from one side.*

PROPHETESS. With first place among the gods in this prayer I
  give special honour to Earth, the first prophet; and after her,
  to Themis, for she was the second to sit at her mother's oracle
  here, as one story has it. The third to have this office
  assigned—it was at Themis' wish and with no violence to 5
  anyone—was another of Earth's daughters by Titan, Phoebe.
  She it was who gave the office as a birthday gift to Phoebus,
  who has his name from hers. He left Delos with its lake and
  spine of rock; he beached on Pallas' shore where the ships put
  in and came to this land and his seat at Parnassus. The sons of 10
  Hephaestus escorted him here with great reverence and made
  a road for him, taming an untamed land. After his arrival the
  people magnify him in honour, as does Delphos, this land's 15
  lord and helmsman. Zeus inspired his mind with skill, setting
  him as the fourth prophet on the throne here; so Loxias is his
  father Zeus' spokesman.
    These gods are the prelude to my prayers, and I give special 20
  honour in my words to Pallas Before the Temple; and I do

reverence to the nymphs of Corycus' rocky cave, welcoming to birds, the haunt of gods. Bromios has possessed this place—and I do not omit his mention—since the time he led his Bacchants in an army as their god, scheming a death for 25 Pentheus like a hare's. Next, with invocations to Pleistus' waters, to mighty Poseidon and to Zeus most high, the fulfiller, I go to take my seat on the throne as prophetess. And now I wish they may grant me better success by far than 30 at my entrances before. If there are any here from among the Greeks, let them come as the lot assigns them, in the normal way; for I give my prophecies as the god may lead me.

The PROPHETESS *enters the temple-door—only to burst back out again almost at once, stumbling and reeling around on all fours.*

Terrifying! Terrifying to describe, and to see with one's eyes—things to send me back out of Loxias' house, so that I 35 have no strength and cannot stand upright. I am running on my hands, without the quickness of feet and legs. An old woman in terror is nothing—no more than a child!

(*pulling herself together*) I go to the inner temple, with its many garlands, and I see at the navel-stone a man polluted 40 before god, sitting there in supplication, his hands dripping with blood and holding a new-drawn sword, with a tall-grown branch of olive duly wreathed with much wool, from a white fleece—with these details my account will be clear. In front of 45 this man an amazing band is asleep, of women, sitting on the chairs—no, I do not mean women, but Gorgons; but on the other hand I can't compare them to Gorgon-figures. I did see those in a painting once before, carrying off Phineus' ban- 50 quet; these however have no wings to be seen; and they are black, utterly revolting in their manner, snoring out a breath which is unapproachable, while their eyes run with a loath-some fluid. Clothing of this form is not right to be brought near gods' images or into men's houses. I have not seen the 55 race this company is from, nor the land which can boast of nurturing this progeny without harm or sorrow afterwards for its labour.

Let what happens from now on be mighty Loxias' own concern, who is the master of this temple! He is doctor and 60 diviner together, and interpreter of portents and cleanser of others' houses. 63

The PROPHETESS *leaves by the side she entered. The door opens for* ORESTES *and* APOLLO *to come out, and closes behind them.*

ORESTES. Lord Apollo, you know how not to do injustice; and 85 since you have that knowledge, learn also how not to be neglectful. Your strength is the guarantee of doing good. 87

APOLLO. I will not betray you, no; and through to the end I will 64 be your guard in standing near you, but also when I stand far 65 off; I will not be gentle with your enemies. And now you see these rabid creatures overtaken (*gesturing towards the closed door*): they have fallen into sleep, abominations that they are, maidens in old age, ancient children, whom no god mixes with, nor 70 man, nor beast, ever. It was for evil's sake that they even came into being, since their sphere is the evil dark of Tartarus under the earth; and they are objects of hate to men and the Olympian gods—but make your escape from them never-theless, and do not soften! For they will drive you throughout all the long mainland as your steps take you constantly 75 wandering the earth beyond the ocean and the cities round which it flows. Do not weary before then by brooding on this ordeal, but go to Pallas' city and seat yourself there, clasping her ancient statue; and there we shall have judges for this 80 matter, and words to win them over, and find means to release you once and for all from these miseries. The fact is, I did 84 persuade you to kill your own mother! Remember that; do not let fear overcome your mind. 88

ORESTES *leaves by one side, to go to Athens.*

And you, Hermes, my own blood-brother by the father we share, keep guard over him; be quite true to your name and 90 bring him on his way, shepherding this suppliant of mine. Zeus respects this sanctity in outcasts when they are sped among men with good fortune as escort.

APOLLO *goes into his temple; the door remains open. The* GHOST OF CLYTEMNESTRA *enters from the side and calls to the* FURIES *within.*

GHOST OF CLYTEMNESTRA. Hey! Stay asleep, then, do! And what's the use of your sleeping? Here am I dishonoured like

this among the other dead because of you, and with the slain   95
ceaselessly reproaching me for those I killed; and I wander in
shame. I tell you solemnly that they accuse me very much; and
that although I have suffered so terribly from my closest kin,   100
not one divine power is angry on my account, although I was
slaughtered by the hands of a matricide. See these blows, see
them with your heart!—the mind asleep is given clear light by   104
the eyes. You licked up many enough things from me,   106
libations without wine, plain offerings of appeasement.
Meals too, solemnized by night in burning altar-hearths,
were my sacrifices, at an hour shared by no god; and yet I
see all these heeled and trodden down, while the man has   110
made his escape and is gone like a young deer, and lightly at
that: he bounded from your nets' midst, with a great mocking
leer at you. Hear me! I have been talking about my existence;
give it thought, you goddesses under the earth! I am Clytem-   115
nestra, and I call on you, in your dream!

The CHORUS OF FURIES *moan from within.*

CLYTEMNESTRA. Moan, then, do!—while the man is already
far away in his escape! Suppliants are no friends of mine!

The FURIES *moan again.*

CLYTEMNESTRA. You are too sleepy, you have no pity for my   120
suffering! This is the mother Orestes murdered, and now he
is gone!

The FURIES *groan.*

CLYTEMNESTRA. You groan, you are sleepy—be quick and
get up! What work is set for you except to wreak evil?   125

The FURIES *groan again.*

CLYTEMNESTRA. Those conspirators with authority, Sleep
and Weariness, have enfeebled the dreadful serpent's energy!

The FURIES *moan with redoubled intensity and now cry out.*

Seize! Seize!
Seize! Seize! Put your mind to it!   130
CLYTEMNESTRA. In a dream you are! You're chasing a wild
beast, and baying like a hound which never gives up its intent

on the work. What are you doing? Get up, don't let weariness
overcome you! Don't forget to do harm because sleep has
softened you! Feel the pain from my just reproaches deep in   135
your heart! They are like goads to rightful minds! Waft your
bloody breath at the man, wither him with its blast, the fire
from your belly; keep with him, waste him away, pursue him
again!

CLYTEMNESTRA'S GHOST *disappears by the side. The* CHORUS
*begin to come out through the door irregularly, jostling and calling to one
another.*

CHORUS. Wake her up! Wake this one here as well, and I'll do   140
the same for you! You're asleep? Get up, kick slumber away
and let's see if any of that prelude is in vain!

The CHORUS *assemble in the orkhêstra for their first and excited dance.*

Oh, the outrage!   Str. 1
We have suffered, my friends—
I laboured so much, and all of it in vain—
we have suffered a blow hard to heal—oh, it hurts us!—   145
an unbearable wrong.
The beast has slipped from our nets, and is gone:
sleep overcame me, and I lost my prey.

Son of Zeus there!   Ant. 1
You are turning to theft!
Young god against old, you have ridden me down;   150
and the suppliant has your respect, a man godless
and harsh to his parents;
you stole the matricide away—you, a god!
Which of these things will be said to be just?

I myself get abuse, which came in dreams   Str. 2
and struck like a chariot-driver   156
with his goad held at the middle,
deep to my heart, deep to my core.
I can feel the scourging,
brutal as a public hangman's,   160
cruel, so very cruel, a frozen agony to have.

Such things as these are done by younger gods   Ant. 2
with power wholly beyond justice

at the throne dripping with murder
all round its foot, all round its head.   165
I can see before me
the earth's navel, which has taken
bloodshed on itself, a ghastly defilement to have.

A prophet with pollution sitting at his hearth,   Str. 3
he tainted its inmost place at his own urge, at his own call;   170
his honour of men against the gods' law
has also destroyed the Fates so ancient in birth.

To me he is offensive; nor shall he release   Ant. 3
this man, who after he flees below is never to be free;   175
a suppliant still, he is to go where
he shall get another vengeful power on his head.

APOLLO *comes out angrily through the door; he now carries bow and*
arrows.

APOLLO. Out of this temple, I command you! On your way
quickly, take yourselves off from this inner place of prophecy,
so you receive no winged and flashing shaft sped from my   180
golden bowstring, and under the pain bring up a dark froth
from your lungs, vomiting the clots of blood you drew off! It is
quite improper that you approach this temple—go rather   185
where justice is decapitation and gouged-out eyes, and
slaughtered throats; where boys' downy virility is foully
destroyed by castration; where extremities are amputated
and stonings done; and where men impaled up into their
spine moan long and piteously. Do you hear? This is the kind   190
of festivity for which your fondness makes you abominable to
the gods. Every aspect of your form points that way; those
such as you should likely inhabit the cave of a lion which
slurps down blood, not rub off defilement on nearby people in   195
this place of oracles. On your way, grazing without a herdsman! A flock like yours has no god's friendly favour.

CHORUS. Lord Apollo, hear me in my turn. You are yourself no
mere accomplice in these things, but you have been the single
agent completely, as taking the whole responsibility.   200

APOLLO. How so then? Extend your speech that far in length.

CHORUS. Was it your oracle's injunction for the stranger to kill
his mother?

APOLLO. It was my oracle's injunction to bring vengeance for his father. Of course!

CHORUS. And then did you promise to give refuge to the murderer with the blood still fresh on him?

APOLLO. It was also my order to him to this temple in 205 supplication.

CHORUS. And do you then abuse us for escorting him on his mission here?

APOLLO. Yes, for you are not fit to come to this temple.

CHORUS. But this is our prescribed duty!

APOLLO. What prerogative is this? Make a boast of your fine privilege!

CHORUS. We drive matricides from their houses. 210

APOLLO. What then of a woman who does away with her husband?

CHORUS. Such killing would not be murder of one's own blood.

APOLLO. You quite dishonour the pledges given Hera and Zeus for a marriage's fulfilment! You make them of no account! Cypris too is rejected with dishonour in your argument, Cypris 215 the source of what is dearest to mankind. A man and wife's marriage-bed once under destiny is greater than any oath, with justice as its guardian. If therefore you are lax in exacting payment from them when they kill each other, and in watching over them with your rancour, I say you are driving Orestes 220 into exile unjustly. I know that you lay the one thing very much to heart, but evidently you pursue the other more gently. Pallas however will watch over the pleas in this case.

CHORUS. I will never leave this man alone! 225

APOLLO. In that case go on pursuing him and make yourself more work.

CHORUS. Don't you try to curtail my prerogatives by what you say!

APOLLO. I wouldn't even consent to have your prerogatives.

CHORUS. No, because you're accounted great in any case, with a place by Zeus' throne. I will pursue this man for justice, however, because a mother's blood is drawing me on, and I 230 will hunt him down.

The CHORUS *leave by the same side as* ORESTES *used, to follow him to Athens.*

APOLLO. And I will aid and protect the suppliant; the anger over one seeking refuge is terrible among both men and gods if he is willingly betrayed.

APOLLO *too leaves in the same direction; after his disappearance there is a short interval during which both scene-front and orkhêstra remain empty. Then* ORESTES *enters from the other side, and his opening words reveal a change of scene from Delphi to the acropolis at Athens.*

ORESTES. Queen Athena, I have come at the command of   235
Loxias. Be kind in your reception of one accursed—no polluted suppliant, nor one with hands not cleansed, but with his guilt already blunted and also worn away in other men's houses and journeyings with them. Land and sea alike   240
I have crossed in observing Loxias' oracular injunctions; now I approach your house and statue, goddess; and I shall keep watch here where I am, and await the outcome of judgement.

As ORESTES *takes up his position in sanctuary, the* CHORUS *enter from the same side, intent on his traces and probably in separate small groups or even individually, spreading out into the orkhêstra.*

CHORUS. Well, here is a clear mark of the man! Follow the signs of this voiceless informant! Like a hound after a   245
wounded deer we are searching him out by the dripping of blood. Our many wearying efforts make our lungs gasp! Our flock has been ranging the earth's whole extent. Over the ocean too I have come in pursuit in wingless flight, no slower   250
at all than a ship. And now he is cowering somewhere here; the scent of human blood smiles its greeting to me.

The FURIES *break into excited and irregular song.*

Keep looking, and again! Look in the [place] on every side,   255
so the matricide doesn't escape unseen and without paying!
Look, here he is himself, with no defence,
clasping the statue of the immortal goddess:
he wants to undergo trial for his accountability!   260
That is not possible; a mother's blood on the ground
is not to be recovered—horror, no!
What soaks into the earth when shed, is gone!
(*to* ORESTES) You must repay us with a gruel of red
to slurp from your limbs while you live;   265

I shall want my food from you by drinking this grim
   draught.
And when I have withered you I will lead you off below,
   alive,
to pay penalty for the matricide and its horror.
You shall see too every other mortal man who has sinned
in not reverencing a god or a stranger   270
or his own parents,
each one with his just deserts.
Hades is mortal men's great auditor
beneath the earth;
with the written tablets of his mind he watches over   275
   everything.

ORESTES. I have been taught amid my ordeal to know the
moments for many things, and when speech and silence alike
are justifiable; and in this matter I was instructed to speak by
a wise teacher. The bloodshed is now drowsily asleep and
wasting away from my hand, with the pollution of my   280
mother's killing washed off; for while still fresh it was driven
out at the hearth of the god Phoebus in a purification where
young pigs were killed.

It would be a long story for me from its beginning, all the
people I approached harmlessly with my company; time   285
cleanses everything with it as it ages. Now my lips are pure
as I call reverently upon Athena, this land's queen, to come to
me with her help; and without warfare she will gain myself,
and my land, and the Argive people as her true and ever-   290
faithful allies. So, whether she is marching straight forward or
standing defensively to aid her friends in Libyan places along
Triton's flow, her natal stream, or surveying the plain of   295
Phlegra like a manly captain bold in command, I wish she
may come—a god can hear even when far away—to set me
free from what I have here.

CHORUS. Not Apollo, I tell you, nor mighty Athena could save
you from wandering exile and neglect, with happiness   300
unknown anywhere in your heart, a shadow drained of
blood to feed divine powers. (*There is a pause while* ORESTES
makes a violent gesture of rejection)—Do you not even speak in
reply, but spit my words back at me, when you have been

nurtured and consecrated for me? Even while living you shall
be my feast, not even slaughtered at an altar; and you shall ₃₀₅
hear this song to bind you.

The CHORUS *now chant*

Come, let us link in dancing too, since we have a mind
to display our hateful music,
and to say how our party manages ₃₁₀
its allotted roles among men.
We think we are straight in our justice:
no anger from us comes against those
who hold out pure hands,
and each walks through his life without harm; ₃₁₅
but to any who sins like this man here
and conceals bloody hands,
we appear as true witnesses in support of the dead,
exacting payment for bloodshed with authority. ₃₂₀

The CHORUS *now dance and sing.*

O mother who bore me—O Night　　　　　　　Str. 1
my mother—as retribution for the blind and the seeing,
listen! Leto's child does dishonour to my rights,
taking from me this cowering wretch, a victim sanctified by
　　right ₃₂₅
to expiate his own mother's blood.

Over the one who is made our sacrifice　　　Ephymnion
this is our song: derangement,
distraction, ruination of the mind ₃₃₀
in a hymn from the Furies
which binds the mind, no lyre's music,
withering mortal men dry.

This role was allotted, spun off　　　　　　Ant. 1
by Fate in a piercing blow, for us to possess securely: ₃₃₅
mortal men whose own wanton acts cleave fast to them,
these are ours to accompany until each comes down below
　　the earth;
and after death he is not too free.

Over the one who is made our sacrifice　　　Ephymnion
this is our song: derangement,

distraction, ruination of the mind
in a hymn from the Furies
which binds the mind, no lyre's music,   345
withering mortal men dry.

When we were born we had these rules decreed,   Str. 2
with our hands to be kept from immortals; there is   350
no god who shares a common table with us;
all-white clothing I was given no part in, no share   353
[*a line missing*].

I have taken for myself the overturning   Mesode 1
of houses; whenever Warfare reared tamely at home   355
kills family or friend,
we go in pursuit of the man—On! On!—
however strong he is,
and enfeeble him, draining youth's blood.

Eager to free every god from that care,   Ant. 2
and establish immunity from my prayers   361
and from conducting first interrogations,
Zeus deemed our tribe, rightly hateful for its dripping
    blood,   365
unworthy of his converse.

The self-opinion of men, so proud beneath a living
    sky,   Str. 3
melts away on earth and dwindles into dishonour
through our assaults clad in black   370
and the vindictive dance of our feet.

So, leaping from a great height above   Mesode 2
I launch my swift feet
downward in heavy fall—
with pace in my legs to trip [even] runners at full stretch—   375
a ruin not to be borne.

A man does not know he falls, the maiming takes his wits
    away;   Ant. 3
such a darkness of pollution hovers over him.
Rumour and much groaning speak
of a murk misting over his house.   380

For this is our care; resourceful   Str. 4
we are, and we bring to fulfilment,

remembering sin,
awesome, implacable to mortal men,
pursuit our allotted role, yet dishonoured   385
and kept separate from gods, in slime without sunlight,
on a path hard and rocky
for seeing and sightless eyes alike.

Who then can there be of mortals   Ant. 4
not in holy awe and fear of this,   390
in hearing from me
fate's decreed ordinance, a power bestowed
by god to the full? An ancient privilege
is resting with me, and I meet with no dishonour
although I have my station   395
below earth, in dark without sunlight.

The goddess ATHENA *enters in majesty from the side.*

ATHENA. From far away I heard a cry summoning me from
Scamander, where I was taking first possession of a land
which the Achaean leaders and chieftains had assigned to me
for ever, root and branch, a great portion from their captured   400
spoils, a gift picked out for Theseus' sons. From there I have
come in swift pursuit with unwearied feet, wingless and with   404
the fold of my aegis flapping. (*starting in surprise*) I see strange   406
company here for this land! I have no fear but the sight
amazes me. Whoever are you? I speak to all in common, both
this stranger seated at my statue [*a line missing*], and you who
are like no kind of begotten things, neither belonging to   410
goddesses seen by gods nor yet resembling human forms.
But to speak ill of people at hand who give no cause for blame,
is to assume a right far distant from justice.

CHORUS. You shall learn the whole of it concisely, daughter of   415
Zeus. We are Night's eternal children, and in our home
beneath the earth we are called the Curses.

ATHENA. I know your descent and your names in their
meaning.

CHORUS. Yes, and you shall soon learn our prerogatives.

ATHENA. I should learn, if one of you gave a clear account.   420

CHORUS. We drive murderers from their homes.

ATHENA. And where has the killer an end to his flight?

CHORUS. Where happiness has no currency at all.

ATHENA. Is it flight like that with which you howl and harry this man?

CHORUS. Yes; he saw fit to shed his mother's blood.   425

ATHENA. When no necessity overcame him, or did he fear someone's rancour?

CHORUS. What can be great enough to goad a man into killing his mother?

ATHENA. With two parties here, that is only half the story.

CHORUS. He would not accept an oath; he will not give one.

ATHENA. You want a name for justice rather than to do it!   430

CHORUS. How so? Explain; you are not poor in cleverness.

ATHENA. I say that an unjust case is not to prevail by oath.

CHORUS. Put the truth to the test; give a straight judgement in a trial.

ATHENA. Would you actually entrust me with the issue of your accusation?

CHORUS. Why not, if you return our deserved respect with   435 deserved respect?

ATHENA. What do you wish to say to this, stranger, in your turn? Name your country and descent and fortunes; then defend yourself against their censure, if you really trust to justice in sitting watchfully by this statue near my hearth, a   440 solemn suppliant like Ixion. Give me an answer on all these points which I can understand easily.

ORESTES. Queen Athena, first I shall remove the great anxiety in your last words. I am no suppliant for refuge, and I had no pollution on my hands when I sat by your statue; and I   445 will tell you a great proof of this. There is a custom that a man with murder on his hands does not speak until the slaughter of a suckling beast makes him all bloody, by a   450 man who can cleanse from bloodshed. Long ago I was given this purification at other men's houses, with beasts as well as river-water. This concern of yours is thus to be dismissed, I tell you; and you shall quickly hear the facts of my descent. I am an Argive, and you do well to enquire   455 about my father—Agamemnon, the men's commander in their fleet, with whom you yourself made Troy's city of Ilion a city no more. He did not die well, when he came home, but my black-hearted mother killed him, trapping him in

embroidered stuffs to cloak his sight, which witnessed his 460
murder in his bath. And when I came back home myself, an
exile for the time before, I killed the mother who bore me, I
shall not deny it, in retribution for the killing of my dearest
father. For this, Loxias shares a common responsibility, for 465
he warned me of pains to pierce my heart like goads if I
should take none of this action against the guilty ones. But
whether I acted justly or not, it is you who must decide the
case; for however I come out of it, I shall accept your
decision.

ATHENA. To judge this matter is greater than any mortal 470
thinks—and I certainly have no right to decide between
pleas about shed blood where angers are sharp, especially
since you, Orestes, have been submissive to custom and come
in supplication to my temple purified and harmless; and I
respect you as giving the city likewise no cause for blame— 475
but these persons have an allotted role not easy to dismiss, and
if they do not get an outcome which brings them victory,
poison from their proud spirit will later fall to the ground and
be the land's intolerable, everlasting sickness. This is how the
matter stands: both courses, for you to stay, Orestes, and for 480
me to send you away, bring harsh pain if there is to be no
wrath against me. But since this matter has descended
suddenly upon us here, [I shall appoint] judges for murder-
cases, with respect for oaths under an ordinance which I shall 484
lay down for all time, [*a line missing*] with no transgression of 489
their oath through unjust minds.

(*addressing both* ORESTES *and the* FURIES) You are to 485
summon your witnesses and evidence, the sworn support
for your cases; after choosing the best of my citizens I shall
come back to resolve this matter in the truth.

ATHENA *leaves by one side. The* CHORUS *dance and sing.*

Catastrophe now is coming   Str. 1
from new ordinances, if a justice   491
which is harm to justice shall prevail
for this man here, the matricide.
This day's work will at once accustom
all men to licence;   495
and much veritable suffering, which their own children

will inflict, lies waiting for parents
in time hereafter.

For neither will any rancour   Ant. 1
against such actions come upon them   500
from our madness-driven watch on men:
I shall launch every death at them;
and all men from all sides, proclaiming
their neighbours' troubles,
will be eager to stem or escape from the long torment,   505
and prescribe uncertain remedies
in useless comfort.

And let no one call out and implore   Str. 2
when disaster strikes at him,
crying the words,   510
'O Justice!'
and 'O Furies enthroned!'
Thus perhaps a father or mother
with her pain still fresh
may wail in lament and sob   515
when Justice's house falls.

There is a place where terror is good,   Ant. 2
and a watch on minds by fear
seated above.
It is well   520
to learn wisdom through grief.
Would any that nurses no terror
in his heart's clear light—
both man and city the same—
revere Justice still?   525

Do not praise a way of life   Str. 3
which is anarchic,
nor one which despots rule.
To the mean in everything god has given power,   530
but he oversees all in differing ways.
The words I say are consistent:
insolence is child to irreverence, truly,
but out of minds which are healthy   535
is born that prosperity
which is dear to all and greatly prayed for.

In all things I say to you: Ant. 3
respect the altar
of Justice; and do not,   540
with an eye to profit, insult and kick it down
with godless feet, for retribution results;
an end is appointed and waits.
Let a man therefore rightly put first in honour   545
the reverence due to parents,
and respect attentiveness
to a house's guests which does them honour.

A man righteous by his own will,   Str. 4
under no compulsion, will not fail to prosper;   551
total destruction would never be his.
But I say that the man who defies out of boldness,
    transgressing
[while he carries] his great cargo, one randomly got without
    right,
in violence, will lower sail with time,   555
once trouble catches him up
and his yard-arm shatters.

He calls on those who do not hear,   Ant. 4
from the whirlpool's centre so hard to struggle with;
and god laughs over a hot-headed man,   560
when he sees one who was confident that he would never
    be caught
impotent in helpless torment, and not surmounting the
    wave-top.
His prosperity, life-long till then,
is dashed upon Justice's reef;
he dies unwept, unseen.   565

ATHENA *re-enters from the side, accompanied by a herald and
trumpeter and followed by the citizens chosen to act as jurors; seats for
the jurors, and two voting urns, are brought on. The scene is now the
Areopagus.*

ATHENA. Make your proclamation, herald, and keep the
people back! And let the Etruscan trumpet which pierces
[to the heaven] be filled with human breath and sound its
shrill note clearly to the people! While this council is filling 570

up, it helps for the whole city as well as these parties to be
silent and to hear my ordinances for all time, so that the case
may be well judged.

APOLLO *enters suddenly from the side.*

Lord Apollo, keep your authority to what is your own! Say
what part you have in this matter. 575
APOLLO. I have come both to give evidence—for this man is
legally a suppliant and refugee at my hearth, and I am his
purifier from bloodshed—and to support his case myself. I am
responsible for the killing of his mother. (*to* ATHENA) You 580
must bring this case to trial and determine it with the best
knowledge you have.
ATHENA (*to the* FURIES). It is for you to speak—I now bring
this case to trial—because the plaintiff should properly be first
to tell the matter from the beginning, and to explain it.
CHORUS. We are many, but we shall speak concisely. (*to* 585
ORESTES) Make answer, putting word against word in turn.
Say first whether you are your mother's killer.
ORESTES. I killed her; there's no denying it.
CHORUS. Here's one already of our three throws!
ORESTES. Your boast is spoken over one who is not yet down. 590
CHORUS. But you must say how you killed her.
ORESTES. I say it: drawn sword in hand I cut into her throat.
CHORUS. And at whose persuasion and by whose design?
ORESTES. By the oracles of Apollo here; he is my witness for
this.
CHORUS. The prophet authorized your matricide? 595
ORESTES. Yes, and up till now I do not blame my fortune.
CHORUS. But if the vote gets you caught, you will soon say
differently.
ORESTES. I have my trust; and my father sends me support
from the grave.
CHORUS. Yes, put your trust in corpses now you have killed
your mother!
ORESTES. I did so because she incurred a double pollution. 600
CHORUS. How so? Explain this to the jurors.
ORESTES. In killing her husband she killed my father.
CHORUS. So you have your life, and she is now free through her
murder?

ORESTES. But why didn't you drive her in flight while she was alive?

CHORUS. She was no blood-kin of the man she killed. 605

ORESTES. And am I blood-kin of my mother?

CHORUS. How else did she nurture you in her womb, you foul murderer? Do you disavow a mother's blood, your nearest and dearest?

ORESTES (*turning to* APOLLO). Now is the time for your evidence, Apollo, to set out on my behalf whether I killed 610 her justly. I shall not deny I did it, as it is the fact; but you are now to give your judgement whether in your opinion this blood seems justly shed or not, so I may tell them here.

APOLLO (*to the jurors*). I shall say to you, who are here by Athena's great ordinance, that it was shed justly; and as 615 prophet I shall not lie. I never yet said at my prophetic throne, not about man, not about woman, not about city, except what Zeus the Olympian Father might command. I tell you plainly: understand how strong this just plea is, and heed 620 the Father's will; an oath is in no way stronger than Zeus.

CHORUS. Zeus, do you say, granted your telling Orestes this oracle, that in vengeance for his father's killing he was to hold his mother's prerogatives of no account?

APOLLO. Yes, for it is not the same that a man of noble birth, 625 magnified in honour by the sceptre which is Zeus' gift, should die, and that by a woman's hand, not from any furious strike of an arrow like an Amazon's, but in the way you are about to hear, Pallas, together with those sitting to decide by vote upon 630 this matter. Because—when he came from the campaign, his trafficking done mostly for the better, she welcomed him with loyal [*a line missing*] when he was completing his bath, and at the vessel's edge she threw a cloak over him like a tent; she fettered her husband in cunning, endless robing and cut him 635 down. This is the man's death now told to you, a man absolute in his majesty, the commander of the fleet; it is the ending of my speech, to sting to anger the people appointed to determine this case.

CHORUS. Zeus values a father's death more highly, from what 640 you say, yet he himself put his old father Cronus in bonds. Is what you are saying not contradictory? (*to the jurors*) I call you to witness that you hear this!

APOLLO. You brutish, hateful creatures, altogether detested by the gods—fetters can be undone! There is a remedy for that, 645 and many a way to contrive freedom; but when the dust sucks up the blood of a man once he is dead, there is no raising him up at all. For this, my father has made no spells; but everything else he turns up and down and disposes in his 650 might, with no panting for breath.

CHORUS. See how you are pleading for this man's acquittal! When he has shed his mother's blood—his own kin's!—on the ground, is he then to live in his father's house in Argos? And what altars is he to use—the public ones? What brother- 655 hood will admit him to its rituals of sprinkled water?

APOLLO. I have this to say as well, and you are to understand that what I shall say is right. The so-called mother is no parent of a child, but nurturer of a newly seeded embryo; the parent is the one who mounts her, while she conserves the child like a stranger for a stranger, for those fathers not thwarted by god. I 660 will show you proof of this argument: there can be a father without a mother; a witness is close at hand, the daughter of Olympian Zeus [*a line missing*] nor nurtured in the darkness of 665 a womb, but the kind of child no goddess could give birth to.

(*turning to* ATHENA) Pallas, I shall make your city and your people great in other ways, as I know how, but above all I have sent Orestes here as suppliant at your temple's hearth to pledge loyalty for all time, and for you to gain him as your 670 ally, goddess, and those after him; and in order that these things should remain to eternity, for the Athenians' later generations to honour the pledges sworn.

ATHENA (*speaking generally*). Shall I now order these men to bring in a considered and just verdict, on the ground that enough has been said?   675

CHORUS. For our part, every bolt we have is already shot, and I wait to hear how the issue will be decided.

ATHENA (*to the* FURIES). And so? How am I to escape your blame in what I arrange?

APOLLO (*to the jurors*). You have heard what you have heard; bring in your vote, strangers, with respect for your oath in your hearts.   680

ATHENA. Now hear my ordinance, people of Athens, who are judging the pleas in the first trial for shed blood. For the future too this council of jurors shall always exist for Aegeus' people; it shall have its seat on this hill, the Amazons' position 685 and camp when they came in an army out of jealous anger against Theseus, and at that time fortified here a new and high-walled city over against the acropolis, and made sacri-fices to Ares, from which it is named Ares' rocky hill. In this 690 place the city-people's reverence and the fear which is its kin will keep them from wrong-doing, by day and night alike, if the citizens themselves make no innovation in the laws through evil infusions: if you pollute a clear spring with mud you will never find a drink. I counsel the citizens to 695 maintain with their respect what is neither anarchic nor despotic, and not to throw all fear outside the city—for who among mortal men is righteous if he fears nothing? If you go righteously in dread of such a revered body, you may have a 700 bulwark to keep land and city safe such as none of mankind have, either among the Scythians or in Pelops' regions. Untouched by desires for gain, revered, quick to anger, the 705 land's wakeful guardian of those asleep, this council I now establish.

This has been my lengthy exhortation to my citizens for the future; (*turning to the jurors*) and you must rise and take your votes for casting and decide the case with respect for your oath. My speech is said. 710

While the FURIES *and* APOLLO *continue their altercation the jurors file from their seats and pass between the two voting-urns to cast their votes.*

CHORUS (*to the jurors*). Our company here is very heavy for the land! I advise that you do it no dishonour in any way.

APOLLO (*also to the jurors*). I too command you, to go in dread of my own and Zeus' oracles, and not to render them fruitless.

CHORUS (*to Apollo*). But you concern yourself with matters of blood when they are not your province! The prophetic shrine 715 you occupy will no longer be pure of taint.

APOLLO. Was father Zeus mistaken in his decision when Ixion supplicated him after the first blood-killing?

CHORUS. You say not; but if I do not win the case, I shall be heavy company for this land in future. 720

APOLLO. But you are without honour among gods both new and old; the victory will be mine.

CHORUS. You acted like this in Pheres' house too; you persuaded the Fates to make men immortal.

APOLLO. Was it not right to benefit a pious man, above all 725 when he was actually in need?

CHORUS. You destroyed the age-old dispositions! You distracted the ancient goddesses with wine!

APOLLO. And you, when you do not win the verdict, will soon be vomiting that poison which does no heavy harm to your 730 enemies!

CHORUS. Since you are riding me down, young god over elderly goddess, I am waiting till I learn the verdict, in two minds whether to be angry against the city.

ATHENA (*coming forward now the jurors have finished voting*). It is my business in this case to give my judgement last; and I shall cast this vote of mine for Orestes. (*She drops it into one of the* 735 *urns.*) I do so because there is no mother who gave me birth, and I approve the masculine in everything—except for union with it—with all my heart; and I am very much my father's: so I will set a higher value on the death of a woman who killed her husband, a house's guardian. And Orestes wins even if in 740 the judgement he has equal votes.

 Empty the votes from the urns at once, you jurors who have this duty put on you!

Some jurors, perhaps two for each urn, empty the votes and begin counting them.

ORESTES. O Phoebus Apollo! How will the issue be decided?

CHORUS. O Night, black mother! Are you seeing this? 745

ORESTES. A noose is the end for me now, or to see the daylight!

CHORUS. Yes, and for us it is extinction, or maintaining our prerogatives hereafter!

APOLLO. Count the emptied votes correctly, strangers, with reverent care against a wrong determination! (*The jurors approach Athena to give her the count.*) When good judgement's gone away, great harm happens; but if a single vote comes in, 750 it can set a house upright.

ATHENA (*pointing to* ORESTES). The man here goes free on the charge of bloodshed. The numbers of the votes are equal.

ORESTES (*coming forward to centre-stage*). O Pallas! O saviour of my house! You have restored me to my home when I was 755 deprived of my father's land. Among the Greeks they will be saying, 'The man is again an Argive, and living on his father's property'—thanks to Pallas, and to Loxias, and to him the third, the Saviour, who accomplishes everything, who from proper regard for my father's death has brought me safety, on 760 seeing these advocates for my mother.

Now I will go to my home, after I have sworn on oath to your land and people here, for the whole greatness of future time, that no helmsman of my country will come to bring war 765 against it, well-armed and equipped. Though we shall ourselves be in our tomb by then, we shall bar the road with impossible disasters for those who transgress my oaths sworn now; we shall bring despair and ill omens to their 770 passage, so that they repent of their effort; but if oaths are fully kept and if they always honour this city of Pallas with their army in alliance, we are to be more kind towards them.

And so rejoice, and fare well, both you, goddess, and your people in their city; may your grip in wrestling with your 775 enemies give them no escape, bringing safety and victory for your spear!

ORESTES *and* APOLLO *leave by the side. The* CHORUS *burst into angry dancing and singing.*

CHORUS. You younger gods! The ancient laws—   Str. 1
  you have ridden them down! You have taken them out of
    my hands for yourselves!
I am dishonoured, wretch that I am; my heavy rancour   780
releases on this land—woe to it!—
a poison, a poison from my heart to requite my grief,
dripping from below the earth, intolerable. From this
a canker destroying leaves, destroying offspring—O Justice
    [Justice]!—   785
will sweep over and strike the land
with a blight killing men.
I am groaning—what am I to do?
I am laughed at; what I suffer
from the citizens is hard to bear.   790
Oh, your ruin is great,
you ill-fated daughters of Night
grieving for your dishonour!

ATHENA (*using speech still*). Let me persuade you to bear it
without heavy groaning! You have not been defeated, but the
verdict came out with the votes truly equal, with no dishonour 795
for you. On the contrary, there was bright and clear testimony
to hand from Zeus, and the giver of the oracle himself was
himself the giver of the evidence, that Orestes was to take no
harm for doing these things. And you should neither launch
your rancour heavily upon this land—do not stay angry—nor 800
make its crops sterile with droplets released from your lungs,
ungentle spears which devour the seed. I here give you my
promise, in all right, that you shall have an abode, a hidden
place, in a land that is righteous, seated on gleaming thrones 805
by your altar-hearths, richly in honour from these citizens.

CHORUS. You younger gods! The ancient laws—   Ant. 1
   you have ridden them down! You have taken them out of
     my hands for yourselves!
I am dishonoured, wretch that I am; my heavy rancour   810
releases on this land—woe to it!—
a poison, a poison from my heart to requite my grief,
dripping from below the earth, intolerable! From this
a canker destroying leaves, destroying offspring—O Justice,
   [Justice]!—   815
will sweep over and strike the land
with a blight killing men.
I am groaning—what am I to do?
I am laughed at; what I suffer
from the citizens is hard to bear.   820
Oh, your ruin is great,
you ill-fated daughters of Night
grieving for your dishonour!

ATHENA. You are not dishonoured—and do not from excessive
anger blight the land of mortal men, goddesses that you are! I 825
too have my trust—in Zeus; and what need I say? Besides, I
alone of the gods know the keys of the house in which his
lightning is sealed—but there is no need for it: be ready to let
me persuade you, and do not throw out a wild tongue's
threats against the land, for all things which bear crops to do 830
badly. Lull the waves of your black anger in its bitter force to
sleep, for you are to be honoured with awe, and be the sharer

of my home. When you have the first-fruits of this great land
for evermore, sacrifices made for children and for marriage's 835
fulfilment, you will be grateful for my speech.

CHORUS. That I should suffer this, alas—   Str. 2
I the ancient in wisdom—[and] live on earth
[where] pollution goes, alas, without punishment!
All my force is in my breath,   840
and all my rancour.
(*violently*) Oh no! The shame! The hurt!
What is the pain going deep in my side?
Listen, mother Night!
I am taken from my age-old prerogatives   845
by the gods' irresistible trickery, I am made into nothing!

ATHENA. I shall bear with your anger: you are the older. Yet
while there are things in which you are very much wiser than
I, Zeus gave good sense to me also in no mean way. If you go 850
to the country of a different people, you will long passionately
for this land here, I foretell; because time as it flows onward
will bring ever more honour to these citizens; and you yourself
with an honoured abode by the temple of Erectheus will 855
receive from processions of men and women more than you
would ever get from other mortals. And in those regions which
are mine, you are neither to throw down whetstones for
bloodshed, harmful to young spirits, crazing them with a
rage unhelped by wine, nor to excite my citizens' hearts like 860
those of fighting-cocks and set up reckless warfare between
their families and against one another. Let war stay abroad; it
makes no difficulty in coming, for the man who will have in
him a strong desire for glory. I disapprove a bird's battling in 865
its own home.

Such are the things you may choose from me—doing good,
receiving good, with honour that is good when you share in
this land which the gods love most.

CHORUS. That I should suffer this, alas—   Ant. 2
I the ancient in wisdom—[and] live on earth   871
[where] pollution goes, alas, without punishment!
All my force is in my breath,
and all my rancour.
(*violently*) Oh no! The shame! The hurt!   875

What is the pain going deep in my side?
Listen, mother Night!
I am taken from my age-old prerogatives
by the gods' irresistible trickery, I am made into nothing!   880

ATHENA. I will not tire in telling you the good things, so you
may never say you are dismissed from this land without
honour or hospitality, an ancient goddess rejected by a
younger one, myself, and by the mortal men who hold the
city. No, if you hold Persuasion sacred in her majesty, who   885
gives my tongue its soothing and winning way—well then,
please remain; but if to remain is not your wish, you would
not be right to let any wrath or rancour weigh down upon this
city, or harm for her people. You may have a settled holding   890
in this land and be rightly held in honour for ever.

CHORUS. Queen Athena, what abode do you say I have?

ATHENA. One untroubled by all distress. Accept it, I beg you!

CHORUS. And suppose I have accepted—what prerogative
remains for me?

ATHENA. That no house is to thrive without you.   895

CHORUS. Will you yourself ensure this, for so much power to be
mine?

ATHENA. Yes, the man who reveres you will have me keep his
fortunes safe and sure.

CHORUS. And will you make me a guarantee for all time?

ATHENA. Yes, for I may not say anything which I shall not
fulfil.

CHORUS. You will win me over, it seems; I am giving up my   900
rancour.

ATHENA. So now that you are in the land, you will acquire new
friends.

CHORUS. What then do you bid me invoke for this land?

ATHENA. Such things as attend victory not badly won, and for
these to come from the earth, and from the waters of the sea,
and from the heaven; for the winds to come to the land   905
blowing their breath amid happy sunshine; for an abundant,
thriving yield for citizens from soil and beasts not to fail with
time; and for safety for its human seed. May you bring more
to birth who are reverent—because like a man husbanding his   910
crops I cherish this nation of righteous men in freedom from

sorrow. Such things lie with yourselves; and in war's glorious
conflicts I shall myself not tolerate a lack of honour among
men for this city and its people's victories.   915

CHORUS. I shall accept a home with Pallas,   Str. 1
and I shall not dishonour
this city which Zeus the almighty and Ares
hold as a gods' outpost;
they delight in its guarding the altars of Greek deities.   920
For this city I make my prayer,
and prophesy with kind intent
good fortune in profusion to benefit its life,
burgeoning up from the earth   925
in sunshine's bright gleam.

ATHENA (*now chanting to take up the* CHORUS' *singing*).
I do this from goodwill to the citizens here,
in settling in this very place
great deities who are hard to placate;
for these have all that men do allotted them to manage.   930
The man who may not [have sinned overmuch] but meets
      with their heaviness,
does not know where the blows to his life are from;
for it is the sins beginning with his ancestors
which lead him towards these goddesses.   935
Silent destruction through their hostile anger
makes even the loud-voiced into dust.

CHORUS. I wish no breath of harm blighting trees—   Ant. 1
I speak now of my favour—
to blow the flaming heat that robs plants of their buds   940
over the land's borders;
and may no persistent disease invade, destroying the crops.
I wish Pan to foster the sheep,
to thrive in carrying twin young;   945
and may the produce growing from richness in the soil
drink at the appointed time
the gods' gift of rain.

ATHENA (*to the jurors*). Do you hear this, you guardians of the
      city—the nature of these undertakings?
The sovereign Furies have great power   951
among both immortals and those under the earth;

and in the case of men it is clear that they work their will to
    fulfilment,
giving some cause for singing, but others
a life with eyes dimmed by tears.   955

CHORUS. I forbid misfortunes killing men untimely   Str. 2
Give to the lovely young women
lives which get husbands, you powers, I pray,   960
and you goddesses the Fates,
my mother's sisters,
divinities just in apportioning,
sharing a place in all homes,
bringing your weight at all times   965
to your lawful visitations,
the most honoured of gods in all ways!

ATHENA. I am delighted by this, these undertakings to my land
from goodwill. I gladly accept that Persuasion and her eye   970
watched over my tongue and words
in response to their savage refusals.
The power however was with Zeus the god of assemblies;
and our struggle for good wins out for all time.   975

CHORUS. I pray too that faction, insatiable for harm,   Ant. 2
never clamours in this city,
nor the dust drinks its people's black blood   980
from counter-killings in rage,
in retribution,
the city's ruin its eager pursuit;
may they reciprocate joys,
resolved on sharing friendship,   985
and show hate with a single mind:
for this remedies much among men.

ATHENA. Are they minded to find a path for their tongues to
    be kind?
From their fearsome countenance   990
I see great benefit to these citizens.
(*to the jurors*) If with goodwill towards goodwill you always
    do them great honour,
you will be wholly pre-eminent for keeping
both land and city on the straight way of justice.   995

CHORUS (*to the jurors*). [Greetings! and] rejoicing in your
destiny of riches! Str. 3
   Greetings, people of Athens,
   so dear to the dear maiden,
   daughter seated hard by Zeus—
   and wise amid surfeit! 1000
   Beneath Pallas' wing
   you have due respect from her father.

ATHENA (*to the* FURIES). Rejoicing to you as well! But I
   must go in front
to show you your chambers,
by the holy flame-light of these escorts. 1005

While ATHENA *continues, a* SECONDARY CHORUS *begins to
enter from the side in procession, bearing torches.*

   Come! Hasten below the earth while these solemn sacrifices
     are made!
   Keep ruin in check and away,
   but send what gives the city advantage, for victory!
   (*to the jurors*) And you are to lead these settlers in our home, 1010
   you children of Cranaos who hold the city.
   May the citizens be disposed to goodness to answer their
     goodness!

CHORUS. Greetings, and rejoicing again—I repeat my
   wishes— Ant. 3
   all of you here in the city, 1015
   both deities and mortals!
   While you manage Pallas' city,
   and hold in reverence
   my settling among you,
   you will have no blame for life's fortune. 1020

ATHENA (*now speaking*). I thank you for the words of these vows,
and I shall have the women who serve me and guard my
statue escort you by gleaming torch-light to the places within
and below the earth, and rightly. The very eye of all Theseus'
land will therefore please come forward, a glorious band of 1025
children, wives and older women in procession with red-dyed
clothing put on [*lines missing*] give [them] honour! And let the 1028
light of fire set out on its way, so that this company for the

land may in future be pre-eminent for its goodw.
fortune of noble manhood!

CHORUS OF WOMEN TEMPLE-SERVANTS.
Go to your home, you great and honour-loving
children—not children!—of Night, in cordial procession.
—Countrymen, keep holy silence!   1035

Deep in the earth's primeval hidden places   Ant. 1
may you receive high respect from sacrificial honours!
—All people, keep holy silence!

Gracious and with straight intentions towards the
   land,   Str. 2
over here! Come, [goddesses,] The Awesome Ones,   1041
delighting in the gleaming torches on your way!
—Cry out your joy now, in song!

Enter with eagerness your house all of torches!   Ant. 2
Thus have Zeus the all-seeing and Fate come down   1045
together to support the people of Pallas!
—Cry out your joy now, in song!

*There is a ceremonious exit, as the procession circles the orkhêstra and
then leaves by the side.* ATHENA *leads the way, followed by the*
FURIES *in retinue with her servants carrying torches; the jurors are at
the rear.*

Explanatory Notes

AGAMEMNON

THE medieval manuscripts preface the play with a *hypothesis* or 'introduction', a narrative summary written probably in the Roman era. It ends with some details of the trilogy's original production at Athens; they are taken from an older *hypothesis* compiled by Aristophanes of Byzantium in the third century BC (for whom see also the start of the Notes on *Eumenides*): 'The play was produced in the archonship of Philocles, in the second year of the eightieth Olympiad (i.e. 459/8 BC). Aeschylus won first prize with *Agamemnon, Libation Bearers, Eumenides* and the satyr-play *Proteus.* The expenses of production were paid by Xenocles of the deme of Aphidnae.' A now damaged inscription of the 340s was probably the source of these details; it implies that Aeschylus was his own producer.

stage directions: *the action begins in the night*: about half a dozen surviving Greek tragedies begin then. The device in itself marks the coming day as important; often the night contains a not less important precipitating incident, here the beacon-message; cf. Ajax's derangement by Athena in the night at the start of Sophocles' play.

1 *I ask the gods for release from this misery*: a headline which will echo through the trilogy; it is repeated in 20 (see n.) and culminates in the god Apollo's promise to release Orestes from his misery, *Eum.* 83, cf. *LB* 1060, so that he is 'saved', *Eum.* 754, 761.

3 *up above here like a dog*: watch-dogs slept on the roof.

5 *potentates which bring men summer and winter*: the major constellations associated with the changes of season; for these see the Herald at 563–7.

7 [For *I mark them closely*: the MSS have 'the stars', superfluous and metrically unsound. The line's uneven syntax is of questionable style, so that many editors delete it.]

10 *such is the power . . . plans like a man*: Aeschylus at once presumes that his audience's familiarity with the myth will identify the 'woman' as Clytemnestra, with her design against Agamemnon. He gives early and forceful warning of her exceptional and unfeminine dominance; the hint recurs at 258, immediately before her

entry, and subsequently: n. to 348. The successful beacon-chain from Troy will be her woman's triumph over the sceptical male Chorus, 348 ff., 590 ff.

17 *dispensing*: literally 'cutting into', a metaphor from medicine which may refer to cutting roots or stems to make drugs, or to surgery. This is the first of many explicit medical images, as cure is sought for the family's wounds: *LB* 472. At 13 'unvisited' and 15 'stands at my side' may also allude to medical practice.

19 *not managed for the best*: understatement, consistent with the Watchman's veiled anxiety in 36–9.

20 *release from misery*: completing this first section of the prologue-speech with repetition of its opening idea ('ring-composition'), in 1, and thus emphasizing it for the audience; similarly in the prologue-scenes at *LB* 2/19, *Eum.* 1/20 and 2/33/(62).

23–4 *show . . . and mean*: one verb in the Greek; it is used both of ordinary disclosure and of divine revelation or decree, e.g. *LB* 279, *Eum.* 620. *daylight* is both literal and metaphorical for 'salvation', like 'light in darkness' at 522; cf. Introduction, p. lvii and e.g. *LB* 131 (n.). *setting up of many dances*: that is, formal and communal celebration. *Argos*: Aeschylus uses this name for both territory and city as the ancestral home of the Atreidae. Myth locates them both in Argos and at their chief citadel there, Mycenae (see n. to *LB* 232).

26 *I am making a clear signal*: the Watchman's cry carries in the night as Clytemnestra's shriek carries in her nightmare with piercing clarity at the start of *LB* (32). Her bed there is very much visited by dreams, unlike the Watchman's here, 13.

28 *joyful*: the Greek word implies also 'of good omen, respectful to the gods'. *cry of celebration*: one made by the women of a house, often when a sacrificial victim is killed. Clytemnestra uses the same phrasing with 'joy' at 595–6 (cf. also her 587): perhaps in both places Aeschylus alludes already with black irony to the 'sacrificial' killing of Agamemnon. The converse 'cry of celebration', for the deaths of Aegisthus and Clytemnestra, is anticipated by the female Chorus of *LB* 386, 821, 942.

29 *Ilion*: Troy; both names derive from its mythical kings, Ilos and Tros.

32–9 For the rest of his speech, the Watchman's language veers to a sequence of colloquial expressions and images, phrased with special terseness in 36–9. This is how Aeschylus suggests the pressure of the man's anxieties; cf. n. to 251–5.

32–3 *dance a prelude of my own too*: looking back to 23 'many dances'. *play on my master's good success*: Agamemnon's capture of Troy means an end to the Watchman's misery, 1, 20. *treble-six* with the dice enabled the player to capture all eighteen end-positions on the board and to win the game outright (it was not unlike draughts); the metaphor compares with our own 'double six'. Line 30 can mean, less well, 'I shall reckon my master successful (now that the beacon signals also the end of my watch)'.

36 *a great ox ... tongue*: a folk-saying; cf. English 'cat got your tongue'.

40–257 The longest choral sequence in surviving Tragedy. The Chorus's chanted entry-song (40–103) not only gives the background to the immediate scene but also the moral and theological implications of Trojan Paris' offence to man and god in abducting Helen. Six pairs of sung and danced stanzas (104–257), the first extended by an epode (140–59), focus the scenes at Aulis where the Greek fleet gathered to punish Troy. Zeus' favourable omen for its success is simultaneously disastrous for the commander Agamemnon: he must sacrifice his daughter Iphigenia to placate the goddess Artemis offended by the same omen. The long narrative is dramatized, with speeches from Calchas the omen's interpreter (126–55) and Agamemnon its agonized recipient (206–17), and with vivid close-ups (114–20 the omen, 188–98 the suffering of the fleet, 228–47 Iphigenia's brutal death)—but interpretation and sacrifice surround a 'Hymn to Zeus' which expounds his stern but wise justice (160–83: see n.). The first lyric stanzas (104–59) are given an epic cast through the use of Homeric metre and sometimes of vocabulary.

The whole sequence 40–257 constantly examines wrongdoing and its punishment, however delayed, for Troy and for Agamemnon as member of a family cursed with inherited criminality. The same general purpose and style, mixed narrative and commentary, shape also the next two Choral odes: 355–487 narrates Troy's arrogant misuse of its riches and the consequent misery for both Troy and Greece; 681–782 is a second examination of Helen's and Troy's wrongdoing, ending with the *Oresteia*'s most profound and extended sermon upon sin, its cause and just punishment (750–82).

40 *plaintiff*: the first occurrence of the legal imagery pervading the trilogy (Introduction, §3.4).

45 *a thousand ships*: the impressive round number became canonical in poets after the *Iliad*, which in the 'Catalogue' of Book 2 counts 1,186.

46 *in support*: a military but also a legal term, continuing the image of 40 'plaintiff'.

48 *ringing cry*: preparing for the far-carrying bird-cries in the following simile, 56.

50–9 The vulture-image derives (with a different reference) from Homer, *Odyssey* 16.216 ff. See also 57 and n.

50 1 *young*: translates literal 'children'; see n. to 718. [*extrema*; the context forces this easy emendation upon a word in the MSS which means literally 'off their (usual) path' and is retained by West; but the birds' *anguish* has no point unless demonstrated close by their haunt, their nests (the simile does not extend to the Atreidae in this regard, who have already left their homes). West marks corruption in *high above their nests*, because the grammar is questionable; '(young) in high nests' is conjectured.]

53 *oaring*: the metaphor corresponds with the literal ships of 45.

55 *Apollo*: named to anticipate his later role, helping Orestes' vengeance for his father, esp. *LB* 269 ff., *Eum.* 64 ff., etc. *Pan*: named as god of mountain and wilderness, and of their creatures, here the robbed vultures; Artemis' concern for the hare (134 ff.) is thus anticipated. *Zeus*' name connects the simile directly with what precedes (43) and follows (60).

57 *settlers in their home*: and so protected by them—but the comparison with the 'crying' (48) Menelaus is breaking down: he has lost a wife, not children; he and Agamemnon are natives of Argos (45); both were like the vultures in being robbed, but in 60 they themselves are sent by Zeus to punish the robbers—as eagles, 114 and n. 'Sharers' however perhaps implies that the two Atreidae are closer to Zeus, as kings by his right (43, *Eum.* 626). For the Greek word here, and its special meaning at Athens, see n. to *Eum.* 1010.

59 *for . . . later punishment sends:* similarly 703, *LB* 383. *a Fury*: postponement to sentence-end emphasizes this important identity, as 749, *LB* 652, etc. For the name 'Fury' as a translation of Greek *Erinus* see Introduction, §2.3 n. 17.

60–1 *Zeus who guards hospitality*: overseeing both hosts and guests, the bad guest Paris above all, 362–3, 401–2, 703, 748 (Introduction, p. xli). *Alexandros*: (also 363) the other name of Paris, used apparently without discrimination.

62 *woman with many husbands*: Helen, who married Paris (687–716) after abandoning Menelaus (404–26), and after the former's death Deïphobus (Homer, *Odyssey* 4.276).

63 *bouts of wrestling*: a metaphor which becomes frequent in the *Oresteia* for the struggles of the Atreid house, *LB* 339 etc. (Introduction, §3.4).

65 *first-rites*: a grim image from prenuptial sacrifice evoking the fatal marriage of Helen and Paris and here pre-echoing the more sinister first-rites of Iphigenia's sacrifice which were necessary to let the ships sail against Troy, 227; for the image of the 'perverted sacrifice' throughout the trilogy see Introduction, §3.4.

66 *Danaans*. 148, 1400, etc.: the Greeks collectively, but properly a name for the people of Argos itself, from its mythical king Danaus.

67 *Things are now as they are:* terse, cryptic, and euphemistic, but an everyday idiom; see n. to 251–5 and cf. *LB* 453.

68 *fulfilled in what is fated*: the first occurrence of this motif dominating the trilogy; see Introduction, §2.3, at start.

70 *libation of offerings without fire*: for their nature see n. to 94–6.

71 *intense anger*: of the gods, implacable even if delayed, 59.

72 *disrated*: translation disputed; 'dishonoured' and 'not paying our debt (to our aged bodies, i.e. to death)' are also ventured. *our aged bodies*: the 'superannuated' Chorus are therefore plausibly ineffectual while Agamemnon is killed, 1347 ff., but offer resistance afterward, 1617 ff.—with their staffs (75): see n. to 1652.

76 *rules*: this does not make a clear anatomical image [nor does the conjectural alternative 'leaps up']. Youth's *sap* (literally 'marrow') is still too weak or soft, age has lost its firm strength.

77 *war is not in its place*: within the person, cf. *Suppliants* 749 'war is not in her' [both text and interpretation are insecure here].

81 *three-footed way*: using staffs, 75. There is possibly an allusion to the famous riddle of the Sphinx solved by Oedipus, approximately 'What is it which goes first on four feet, then on two, and finally on three?' 'Man.'

84–7, 97–101 The Chorus address Clytemnestra in her absence; she enters only at 258 (see Taplin, *Stagecraft*, 280 ff.). In the 'dramatic time' which has elapsed since the Watchman disappeared, Clytemnestra has begun her thanksgiving.

90 *gods . . . below the earth*: paired automatically with those *on high*, but important to a city's well-being, *Suppliants* 25.

94–6 *bewitched by . . . soothing . . . oils*: a verbal echo only, not a reversal, of 71 'soothe away'. There is an imprecise allusiveness here; the oils burn both as lights and as offerings, but the Greek word means literally 'unguents'. *liquid offerings*: a viscous mash of cereals or fruit with oil, milk, honey, wine, etc.; expressly without wine at *LB* 92, *Eum.* 107 (nn.). *from the inmost palace*: made with the richest

ingredients, therefore (cf. 1312, *LB* 800–2), symbolic of the offerings' importance.

102–3 *anxiety and pain*: distrust, that the beacon-message may be false
(268 ff.), likely pain at news of the war-dead (445 ff.), and fear for
Agamemnon (255 ff., 1149 ff.).

104–5 *I have the power to tell*: a typical poetic beginning, claiming
privileged knowledge and insight, 105–7; so *Iliad* and *Odyssey* begin
with appeals to divine inspiration (*breathes*, 105). The beginnings of
Str. 1 and Antistr. 1 (104–6, 123–5) are couched in suitably solemn
dactylic rhythm—like Homer's own beginnings. *command destined on
its road*: that of Agamemnon and Menelaus against Troy (109–10),
destined by Zeus (42, 60–2) and his confirmatory omen as they set
out (111 ff.).

105–7 *my age in life*: literally 'congenital life-time', conformably with
the Greek idea that time accompanies men through life, e.g. at 894.
Persuasive old age: Nestor with his lessons from experience, in
Homer, *Iliad* 1.260 ff. etc., is probably the model. For 'persuasion'
in the trilogy see Introduction, p. xxxvii. [*men in their full prime*: so
the MSS, but long disputed; many editors change to 'men in full
authority'.]

108 *Achaeans*: 185, 189, etc.: one of Homer's collective names for the
Greeks at Troy, but by Aeschylus' day Achaea defined more limited
territories.

109–10 *double-throned command*: repeating 43 and preparing for the
images in 114–15, 122–5.

113 *Teucer*: a founding king of Troy. *omen, a . . . bird*: a single word in
the Greek, carrying both meanings, 158; cf. *Eum.* 770 and n.
ferocious: the adjective is Homer's for the furious onslaught of Ares
the War-god; cf. 124.

114 *the king of birds*: the eagle, Zeus' bird (135), symbolic of his will
and power—but at once pictured as two eagles appearing to the two
Atreidae, 115 ff. In the omen described at 114–30 Zeus' two fierce
eagles, and the nature of their prey, transparently imply Troy's
capture by the two Atreidae.

115–16 *one bird black*: and implicitly more menacing and strong,
Agamemnon; *one bird white behind*: and weaker, Menelaus (he
mopes after Helen's elopement, 414–22). This difference in mettle
between the heroes (123) is conventional in poets after Homer, *Iliad*
6.55 ff. *hard by*: the archaic Greek preposition has solemnity; also
Eum. 997.

119–20 *stopped from its . . . run*: as the whole expedition may be stopped from its road (104, 158) or its advance (126) if the danger in the omen is fulfilled. *final*: that is, this run proved to be its last. [*a hare stopped* is grammatically precarious, so that many editors write '(the eagles) having stopped (it)'.]

121, 139, 159 *cry sorrow . . . prevail!*: a refrain in hymnic style, closing the first set of three stanzas 104–59 and preceding the true 'Hymn to Zeus' 160–83. For the wish *let the good prevail* cf. 217 (Agamemnon), 255 (the Chorus again), 349 (Clytemnestra), 574 and 674 (the Herald), and the echo at *LB* 867.

125 *powers who led the force*: the translation personifies an ambiguous abstraction in the Greek and may mean 'the favourable beginning of the expedition', for this is where the seer's interpretation concludes, 145 ff.

126–55 The seer (Calchas: 156 and n.) appropriately mixes direct reference to the ominous phenomena with allusive and metaphorical interpretation, esp. in 132–4 (not all the details correspond: cf. n. to 717–49).

126 *captures*: as prey, the first of many hunting images in the trilogy; cf. e.g. 135–7 (n.) and Introduction. p. lv.

129 *herds of people*: 'animal' for 'person' is typical of the prophetic style; cf. 140–5 and the seer Cassandra at 1125–6 'keep the bull from the cow' (Agamemnon and Clytemnestra), 1258–9.

132–4 *bring darkness on*: obscure, obliterate it, imagery as at *Eum.* 378, cf. *LB* 60–3. *bridle-bit*: Troy's curb and destruction. It is difficult not to hear a later echo of this image in the 'bridling' and gagging of Iphigenia, 238. *if that is stricken first*: the seer fears the effect of Iphigenia's sacrifice. *now it goes on campaign*: translation insecure, in this forceful personification of the 'bit'.

135–7 *winged hounds*: Zeus' eagles as (hunting) dogs, as at *Prometheus* 803, 1022. *their sacrifice*: anticipating the compensatory 'sacrifice' of Iphigenia, 150, 215, 224, 240.

140–5 The vocabulary in these lines is often unusual in form, register, and usage, probably to simulate prophetic style; the whole Epode 140–59 is bleak in tone.
    Hecate: originally an underworld goddess, her concern for births and the newly born overlaps with that of Artemis (134–43, 202; cf. *Suppliants* 676), and they are sometimes identified. Artemis' hostility to the Greeks at Aulis perhaps reflects her traditional support of Troy, e.g. Homer, *Iliad* 20.39; but she must be placated by a compensatory sacrifice of 'young' by those who as hunters (the

eagles as Agamemnon and Menelaus, 114 and n.) have killed the mother and young of animals in her protection—this although she is herself the patron-goddess of hunters. See Introduction, p. xxxii. *lions*: startlingly incongruous after the pregnant hare of 136. *means blame*: i.e. it is simultaneously inauspicious, portending fault, blame, and consequence in the act. It symbolizes (144), the sacrifice of Iphigenia; 552–3 has a similar verbal antithesis.

[Both text and interpretation are strongly disputed here. In West's text (translated), the emphasis is upon Artemis' ominous insistence that the killing of the hare's litter is repaid (144) within Agamemnon's family—by his own murder for the child he killed—so that the Epode is uniformly bleak. Some editors create a preliminary optimism with a concessionary clause in 140, roughly 'Although . . . has such great goodwill . . . she asks fulfilment etc.']

146 *Apollo . . . Healer*: invoked not least as brother to Artemis-Hecate; cf. n. to 55. For the cult-title 'Healer' see also n. to 246–7.

151 *with no music*: suitably for a rite honouring Fury or Death, 990, 1142, *Eum.* 332, etc. *no feasting* has a double meaning: the rite is joyless, and reverses the normal aftermath of a victim's sacrifice, the sharing out of the meat (cf. n. to *LB* 483); Iphigenia's sacrificers will not enjoy a meal like the eagles (138).

152–5 *born in the family . . . resurgent*: Aeschylus introduces the family curse, disguised in *Wrath*; its 'breeding' of wrongdoing and retribution becomes a dominant image, e.g. 751–5 and Introduction, §3.4. Agamemnon, as himself born to be both agent and victim of wrongdoing, will kill his daughter. The sacrifice (150) is progressively personified and becomes first an *architect* (a metaphor repeated at 1406); then it has *no fear of the man* (Clytemnestra's revenge on her husband is meant); finally it *stays in wait* as the *Wrath* (155) and *keeper of the house* (154—as Clytemnestra has been in Agamemnon's absence, 607 and n., 809), and is *treacherous* (again like her, 1636 etc.). *Wrath* is also Zeus' agent against Troy (701).

156–9 *fated . . . the road's omen-birds*: recapitulating the first words of the whole sequence 104–59, and rounding it off, an effect aided by the incorporation now of the refrain 159 into the syntax of the Epode. *Calchas*: the seer, anonymous (122) until now; important in the *Iliad*, especially at 1.69 ff., where Agamemnon upbraids him for never giving sound advice, no doubt in allusion to this incident.

160–83 This so-called 'Hymn to Zeus' divides Zeus' omen for the Atreidae (104–159) from its awful corollary, Iphigenia's sacrifice (184–251), which is nevertheless part of Calchas' interpretation of

Zeus' will, 249. *whosoever he is*: an archaic precautionary and all-embracing formula beginning prayer-hymns. Lines 160–83 are conventional in sequence: 160–6 formal and full address of the god, 167–75 his powerful history, 176–83 the benefit of his power.

165 *its futile burden*: of trying to find a comparison, 163–4. *truthfully*: pointedly placed at stanza end, like 'totally' in the antistrophe, 175. The particular Greek adverb hints at the habit of seeking the 'true' explanation of a name in its meaning: see n. to 681 'Helen'. The etymology of Zeus is certain, 'the (sky-)god of bright light'; cf. 1014–17, *LB* 951, and nn.

168–9 *He who was formerly great*: Uranus ('Sky', 'Heaven'), deposed by his son Cronus (meaning unknown) who was in turn deposed by his son Zeus, 171–2. This succession-myth appears first in Greek poetry at Hesiod, *Theogony* 154 ff., 453 ff. *rash to fight all*: the Greek perhaps evokes an arrogant contestant in the pancration, a brutal no-blows-barred combination of boxing and wrestling. It is the first of three images from athletics here: 172 and n., 174 literally 'the victory-cry' at the games.

172 *champion wrestler*: literally 'victor-with-three', a wrestler winning with three throws; cf. *LB* 339 and n., *Eum.* 589. There is allusion also to Zeus Saviour and Third: see n. to 246–7.

177 *'Suffer and learn'*: a major theme of the *Oresteia*, quickly repeated at 250; see Introduction, §2.3, at start. Aeschylus fits the elliptical maxim (two nouns in the Greek) ingeniously into the clause's syntax, as in 1564.

180–1 *Misery . . . drips . . . before the heart*: like fear, 1121–2, cf. 976–7. *pain remembered*: like a nagging wound: evil done must eventually be punished.

182–3 *Where is the gods' favour . . . helm?*: a pessimistic question follows the confidence of 176–81, whose optimism is borne out only at the trilogy's very end. The pessimism is at once illustrated in the Chorus's gloomy review of Aulis and its consequences, which fit Zeus' and the gods' hard justice here. *seated in violence*: the paradox is expressive [but the text has been doubted]. *helm*: literally 'steersman's bench', a nautical image often applied to men in power, e.g. 1618.

184–204 One long irregular and incomplete sentence in the Greek, as the hurry of pictures outstrips syntax. 184 *the senior in command* is however resumed at 205 'The senior lord'.

187 *going with fortune's wind*: a common metaphor (cf. 219, 376), here perhaps ironic in both contrast and consistency with the real 'contrary winds' then blowing, 193 and n.

190–1 *Chalcis*: on the island of Euboea. *noisy ebb and flow*: the Aulic strait, the Euripus (292), has conflicting, irregular, and audible currents; at Sophocles, *Antigone* 1145 they 'groan'.

193 *Strymon*: a Thracian river; the winds are northerly therefore, preventing the northerly voyage to Troy, 148–9; cf. n. to 654–7.

200–2 *a further, more heavy means*: heavier than others by implication already tried, e.g. ordinary sacrifices to get a wind, all short of the real need to placate Artemis, who is *named* (201, cf. 964) both *as cause* (134 ff.) and solution ('another sacrifice', 150 ff.).

207 *hew*: a purposely violent and brutal verb; of cloven heads *LB* 396.

211 *what is there without evil here?*: so too Electra at *LB* 338, of the correspondingly hideous and inescapable matricide.

215–17 *So may all be well!*: that is, despite Right's forbidding it, there is no escape from the sacrifice; it is heavy either way, 206–7, and the Chorus's anxiety now is for its long-term consequence, 255. Cf. the refrain at 121 etc. [West's text here (translated) is partly conjectural; most editors follow the MSS, roughly 'It is right (not personified) to desire (instead of *right forbids it*) eagerly and most passionately a sacrifice . . . blood.']

218 *yoke-strap*: yoking is a ready metaphor for unpleasant compulsion, 1640.

221, 222, 224 *hard audacity . . . cruel . . . hard*: an attempt to reflect three variations of a single Greek word-root which ranges from 'daring' through 'hardihood' and 'endurance' to 'cruelty'; cf. 385 'cruel Persuasion'.

223 *derangement*: Aeschylus commonly attributes ruin to this, when realization follows the event: Introduction, p. xxxiii.

227 *first-rites*: see n. to 65.

231 *servers*: a Greek dialect word; it may suggest distancing in the narrator. *like a goat-kid*: the pathos is the narrator's, not part of Agamemnon's orders; Iphigenia is like a helpless young animal held face forward over an altar, for the throat to be cut.

233–5 *fallen forward . . . with all her heart*: a famously disputed passage. Four of the five Greek words alliterate upon 'p'; that effect, and their embracing order, favour the translation given rather than 'lift her . . . with all their (the servers') heart, when she had fallen forward enveloped in her robes'.

237 *any word making the house accursed*: any cry from Iphigenia, let alone an imprecation.

238 *violently and with a bridle's muting power*: possibly 'with a bridle's violent muting power'; the line defines the momentary puzzle of 236 'curbed', the bridle being more harshly literal than 'bridle-bit' in 132 (n.). The unusual enjambment of this one line from the end of one stanzaic pair to the next gives lively continuity, as well as emphasis to its ~~mounings~~ ~~any~~ ~~noise~~ ~~as~~ ~~struggling~~ from a sacrificial victim was ominous: cf. Cassandra at 1293, 1298.

239 *yellow-dyed dress*: the colour either of the wealthy (royal, *Persians* 660) or, here, alluding perhaps to a woman participating in ritual, which Iphigenia has forcibly become. There may be an allusion also to the yellow clothes of a bride ('a bride of death', cf. 749, of Helen)—for Iphigenia is poignantly never to wed (245).

241–2 *clearly as in a picture*: the focus both of silent action and of eyes watching inside and outside the picture. The girl's brilliant yellows draw the gaze as much as her shocking inability to use her voice; contrast Euripides' defiant victim Polyxena who stands free and bares her breast for the sacrificial knife (and is compared with a statue), *Hecuba* 560. *call them by name*: the Greek verb of 162. The next clause reveals how Iphigenia knew their names.

245 *unwed*: literally 'not-bulled, unserved by a bull'. The image is perhaps less vigorous in Greek than it is for us; Aeschylus may allude with the Greek adjective *(a)tauro(tos)* to Tauro as cult-name of Artemis, as if the maiden Iphigenia at home is as yet 'not given to Tauro'. The Tauropolia was an Athenian festival for the goddess; in myth she rescued Iphigenia from the sacrifice at Aulis and made her her priestess among the remote Taurians, as in Euripides' play.

246–7 *paean-hymn*: a paean was any communal hymn, of celebration (here and e.g. *LB* 343; with bitter irony at *Ag.* 645) but also of sorrow (*LB* 151); it was so often dedicated to Apollo, inviting or celebrating his gift of success, that he became known as Apollo Paeon, 'Healer' (146 and n., 512, etc.). *third libation*: to Zeus Saviour, or Third, final and greatest in any ritual trinity: 172, 284–5, *LB* 244–5, 578 and n., *Eum.* 759–60. The unmarried daughter pictured among her father's male guests replicates but reverses the sacrificial feast (n. to 151); the girl's freedom there is for pathetic contrast and Homeric in ambience (e.g. *Odyssey* 3.464 ff., 8.457 ff.); it was against contemporary Athenian manners.

248 *What followed*: deliberately vague, like 255.

250 *Justice . . . scale*: image as in *LB* 61, *Eum.* 888; Fortune's scale *Ag.* 1042. *to suffer and learn*: emphatic recall of 177 (n.), but here probably a general statement, or a reference to the Trojans.

251–5 *You may hear . . . good be done!*: these few lines are colloquial in tone throughout and employ proverbial expressions, suggesting an uncomfortable retreat into commonplaces, like the Watchman at 32–9; and indeed Clytemnestra may already be visible to the Chorus (see n. to 256–7). Aeschylus uses or simulates proverbs very frequently, e.g. 265, 943, *LB* 521 (n.). The fatalism of 251 approximately recurs at 1240. *with dawn's rays*: today's dawn has in fact come: 264–5, 279.

255 *may good be done*: see 121 and n. [The text of this line is insecure, and *with dawn's rays* conjectural.]

256–7 *closest guardian*: ambiguous. The Chorus probably mean themselves, but Clytemnestra is closest by relationship, as wife to Agamemnon guarding his house in his absence (259–60)—but she is also physically close, for her entry is imminent and she may be already visible. At 808–9 the Chorus and Clytemnestra are implicitly contrasted in their loyalty. *Apis*: mythical king of Argos, son of Apollo, *Suppliants* 262–70. *bulwark*: a Homeric metaphor for a mighty warrior; if the reference is to Clytemnestra, it is another hint of her unusual male-like dominance (11); cf. 348 and n.

265 *dawn from her mother night*: the notion again in 279.

268–80 This is the first of two short spans of stichomythic dialogue (see Introduction, §3.2) in which Clytemnestra overcomes challenges to her authority; the other is 931–43 (n.), and both show this form of concentrated exchange at its best. The tone here of the Chorus's questions increasingly riles Clytemnestra.

274 *too respectful of appearances in dreams*: Clytemnestra will later have good reason to heed her dreams: *LB* 31 ff. etc.

276 *unfledged*: or 'wingless', translation insecure; an ancient commentator paraphrases with 'flying, swift'—but that is commonly expressed by the converse, 'winged'. So *unfledged* perhaps suggests 'immature, half-grown', as in English 'fledgling rumour'. *bolstered*: literally 'fattened', metaphorically 'cheered'; the Chorus use the word as a taunt to Aegisthus, 1669.

281–316 Clytemnestra's 'proof' (272, cf. 315) of the beacon's veracity is a long narrative, which has something of the style of a messenger-speech (cf. the Chorus's doubt of any 'messenger' at 280). Her second long speech at 320–47 is corroborative, as she imagines the aftermath of Troy's fall; and her imaginative picture is implicitly confirmed when the Herald reports the actual suffering of the Greeks both before the fall (555–83) and on their stormy voyage home (648–79). For the approximate course of the beacon-chain see the Map. It is suggested that Aeschylus' audience would have been reminded of the chain of couriers set up by Xerxes to send news back to Persia that he had captured Athens in 480 as described by Herodotus 8.98; but the imagery evokes also the ritual torch-races at Athens, implicit in line 314 (see n.).

281 *Hephaestus*: god of fire, often depersonalized.

284 *Zeus . . . third*: counting inclusively, but the allusion is to 'Zeus the Third', i.e. 'Victor' (172 and n.) and 'Saviour'. Most mountain-peaks were sacred to Zeus, like Olympus itself; cult-sites there were the closest man could come physically to the sky-god controlling the weather (165 and n.).

287–8 The missing text named an island as an intermediate stage (Peparethos: West; see the Map.). [Probably two main verbs and predicated ideas are missing, to complete the subject-nouns *flare* and *pine-torch*.]

292–3 *Messapion*: another peak, location unknown; at Aeschylus, *Fragment* 25e.8 it is 'leafless, tree-bare'. *Euripus*: the strait at Aulis: see n. to 190–1.

297 *Asopus*: the river of the Theban plain, as *Cithaeron* is the moun-tain-range to its south.

300–1 *had been ordered*: this translation makes a neater point, devel-oping *did not refuse*, than 'those (fires) already mentioned'; cf. 304 'orders for the fire', 312; Clytemnestra's orders, 10–11.

302 *Gorgopian lake*: not certainly identified, but presumably near Corinth.

303 *Wander-Goat Mountain*: unidentified; if not invented, a purely local name. Some think it an allusion to the island of Aegina in the Saronic gulf, whose name suggests 'Goaty'.

304 [*no delay*: the best conjecture from among many for MSS 'no indulgence'.]

306–9 *narrows*: where the gulf narrows towards Corinth. *Ara-chnae*: the ridge dividing the Saronic gulf from the inlet to modern Nauplia. The name means 'Spider('s Mountain)', but is unex-plained. [The text is most insecure, the grammar being astray. Some editors write 'and (the flame) . . . as it blazes' or suppose loss after 307.]

311 a *true grandchild of the fire on Ida*: literally 'not ungrandfathered', a unique metaphor; the litotes helps to close the narrative with a final emphasis on the unbroken chain of beacons which began at Ida, 281.

312 *arrangements*: cf. n. to 300–1.

314 *first and last to run were winners*: the line of beacons 'won', i.e. successfully reached Argos, like a team all sharing their victory in the Athenian festival Torch-Races, the analogy unspoken but familiar to the audience.

320–8 A similar image of instantly recognizable natural enmity, between fire and water, at 650–1.

326–9 War's reversal of normal grief into that of old for young is a pathetic commonplace. The mourners are the wives and sisters of the fighting men already slain, and the very young who grieve for their elderly grandfathers—for all the male survivors were killed in the aftermath of a siege, 358–60 and n., 528, 715, 814. [The text of these lines is insecure.]

338–45 *the gods who hold the city*: (90 and n.) protective even amid or after capture; for these gods see especially *Seven* 211–36. Clytemnestra disguises as fear her hope that the Greeks may commit sacrilege (and Agamemnon thereby imperil himself: cf. 459–60 and n.). There was a story that when the Greek Ajax (the 'Lesser Ajax', son of Oileus) desecrated Athena's Trojan shrine, the goddess in her anger (649) had storms destroy the fleet on its way home (650–70); see the opening of Euripides, *Trojan Women*, 69–86.

344 *race-track's other leg*: the victorious return from Troy. Greek races regularly had a 'leg out' and a 'leg in'.

346–7 *the injury to the dead*: alludes to the Greeks dead at Troy and resentment for them at home (445 ff.); but the words missing from the text might also have shown an allusion to Clytemnestra's and Aegisthus' intentions to avenge both Iphigenia (1413 ff., 1525 ff.) and Thyestes' children (1580 ff.). *to break in*: imagery of sudden sea-storm: as actually happens, 650 ff. [Editors generally agree that the missing words contained at least the idea '(would be) assuaged'.]

348 *from a woman, from me*: further emphasis on her abnormal dominance: 10 (n.); cf. 1661.

349 *May the good prevail*: see 121 and n.

350 *I choose the enjoyment of many good things*: alternatively, 'I prefer its enjoyment (the truth's) to many good things.' Both are enigmatic; she seems to mean her enjoyments in Agamemnon's absence, but privately also their guaranteed continuation if she kills him (1673; cf. however 1574–5).

352–7 *convincing proof*: Clytemnestra has given no 'proof' in 320–50, only pictured the aftermath at Troy compellingly, so that the words may just repeat 317–19; but the Chorus now give due thanks to Zeus, and draw the moral from his justice upon Troy.

354 *a reward for effort has been achieved at its full value*: a truism typically
closing a scene; there is no allusion to specific effort, Clytemnestra's
with the beacons or the Greeks' at Troy.

355–487 For the general purpose and style of this ode see n. to 40–
257.

355–6 *O Night . . . glories*: early Epic had Troy fall in the night, as the
Greeks broke from the Wooden Horse before dawn (824–6, cf. 330);
much less apt is the purely decorative translation 'Night . . .
possessor of great ornaments', i.e. the stars (cf. 6).

358–60 *no one full grown . . . captures all*: the Greek masculine gender
may suggest the total extinction of the male population regular when
a city was sacked, worse even than the slaughter imagined at 320–9;
the women were taken into slavery, *LB* 75–7. *mesh to cover . . . dredge-
net*: the first occurrence of this thematic image; Agamemnon nets
Troy, then is himself netted and covered, 1115 ff. etc., Introduction,
§3.4.

363 *Alexandros*: Paris; see n. to 60–1.

369 *he fulfilled as he willed*: a typical and part-rhyming equation,
euphemistic and near-sacral: cf. e.g. 1287, Introduction, §3.3 n. 33.

374–5 [I translate wholly uncertain conjectures by West. The MSS
give no sense, but appear to relate the crime of Troy and its
destruction to 'family' history, an idea appropriate rather to the
Atreidae; but the reference here is exclusively to Trojan arrogance.]

376–7 *aspirations . . . excess*: my translation cannot reproduce the
exactly assonantal words beginning these two lines in the Greek.
In 'aspirations' I conceal the metaphor for mental impulse expressed
by 'wind' at 187 (n.), 219.

382–3 *no protection . . . surfeit*: a better continuation of the thought in
374–80 than the translation 'no protection for a man who in wealth's
surfeit'. *kicked*: recalling 372 'trample'. *Justice's . . . altar*: again at
Eum. 539.

385 *Persuasion*: here personified for the first time in the trilogy: see
Introduction, p. xxxviii and n. to 105–7.

386 *Ruin who plans in advance*: she warps men's own plans, 223 (n.).
The Greek wording may reflect the Athenian constitutional practice
of 'preliminary deliberation and proposal'.

390–5 The translation tries to preserve the pervasive imagery: a base
man is like a base coin, shown up by knocks and scoring and by
justice's test as himself knocking and rending his city. *chasing a bird in
flight*: the criminal's aims are vain, like his attempts at avoiding

justice (387). *unendurable*: completing 386; so Paris cannot escape, 532 ff.

400 *the house of the Atreidae*: Agamemnon and Menelaus inhabit the same house at Argos, it seems: 43, 109 and n.; both are involved, 41, 400, 410; but sometimes just one is emphasized, Agamemnon 184 and 524 ff., Menelaus here, 412 ff., and particularly 617 ff.

405 *companies forming, sailors arming*: corresponding and near-rhyming terms in the Greek.

408 *daring past all daring*: perhaps an echo of 375 'audacity', but the Greek words seem to recall Agamemnon's 'hard audacity' at Aulis, 221, 224 (n.). Helen (again at 1455 ff., cf. 745 ff.) shares her half-sister Clytemnestra's audacity, for which see 1231, *LB* 433, 630, 996.

409 *the house-prophets*: private functionaries, both interpreters (cf. *LB* 37) and predictors (here, as far as line 426); for the word 'prophet' see n. to *Eum.* 19, cf. n. to *LB* 32–3.

410 *chiefs*: both Menelaus and Agamemnon; 109.

412–13 The plural in *those deserted* alludes only to Menelaus in his bedroom deserted by Helen (414); *dishonour* recalls 401 'disgraced'. Menelaus is incapable of recrimination or pleading (perhaps cf. 396). The silence is then plausibly filled by his imagination of Helen's ghost, 415. The translation does not reproduce three consecutive negative adjectives in the Greek, literally 'without honour, without reviling, without pleading'; for this heavily emotive figure cf. 769. [The text is partly conjectural.]

415 *phantom*: possibly an allusion to the myth-version which had only a phantom of Helen going to Troy, her real self being taken by the gods to Egypt.

416–19 *shapely statues*: of Helen herself, or any recalling her; their blank gaze frustrates passionate feeling. 'Love in the eyes' is an erotic commonplace, 742 again of Helen. Some translators dissociate the 'eyes' from the statues: either Helen's own eyes are not there to fire Menelaus, or his own eyes are starved of seeing her—but these ideas underlie rather 420–6.

420–1 *mournful imaginings*: fanciful visions of Helen, perhaps of her remorse, perhaps of his own regret. Any *delight* they bring disappears as they fade.

422 [*when a man . . . his loved one*: the Greek clause lacks a verb and is usually emended to give this sense.]

429–31 [*absence of grief*: text conjectural, and some other words insecure.]

433–6 The pathetic image of ashes returned in place of living men (also 441–4) was much imitated, e.g. at Sophocles, *Electra* 1129–42, but the practice was not itself Homeric. The dead were given a funeral where they fell, 452–5.

438 *traffics in the gold of bodies*: I leave this as imprecise as in the Greek, which may mean either 'exchanges heavy (i.e. with grief) ashes for the (heavier) gold of living bodies' or 'weighs bodies in his scales like a gold-assayer'. *gold* may allude to the idealized beauty of the slain hero (n. to 454–5).

448 *'Through the wife of another'*: Helen, 1453; cf. 62 (n.) 'a woman with many husbands'.

451 *leading the case*: an explicit back-reference to the legal imagery introduced with 'plaintiff' at 40.

454–5 The repeated 'h's' aspire to match remarkable assonances in the Greek, apparently emphasizing the paradox of slain and buried conquerors 'occupying' the soil they have occupied by conquest. *handsome in death*: I have added 'in death', for the full sense; for the idea see also *LB* 439 and n.

458 *paying its due . . . curse*: translation disputed. The rancour voiced now (456) in some sense fulfils a curse pronounced before the many deaths (461) occurred; cf. 799–804.

459–60 *My anxiety waits*: cf. the Chorus at 99 ff. *veiled over by night*: that is, either still obscure and uncertain, despite the beacon in the night, or, as suggested by the Chorus's words in 461 ff., dark as the black-clad, night-like Furies (463); annihilation by them follows any unjust killing, not only the Greeks' immoderate slaughter of Trojans.

465–7 *to wear out his life*: perhaps an unconscious echo of 390 ff.—but *There is no help* clearly echoes 381.

469–70 *the lightning of Zeus is hurled by his eyes*: text suspect; if sound, it is remarkably compressed for 'Zeus' eyes when they see arrogance hurl jealous resentment (947, cf. 462) and with it his immediate lightning'.

478 *falsehood from god*: 273, cf. 492. [*really*: a conjecture for unmetrical MSS 'not', and itself of doubtful metre.]

479 *childish*: as Clytemnestra supposed the Chorus thought her at 277.

480–1 *fired . . . by flame*: the punning metaphor is probably deliberate.

483 *woman in command*: literally 'a woman's spear', as if she were a male at war; cf. Agamemnon to Clytemnestra, 940, 942; Cassandra at 1237; *LB* 630.

485 *too ready to persuade . . . boundary*: the abnormal woman moves beyond the 'boundary' conventionally set for her, that of her home. There seems to be a parallel for this metaphor at 1154. [The translation is disputed. Some render 'too credulous (against the useage of the Greek adjective), a woman's boundary is soon invaded', for Clytemnestra is accused of credulity at 66, 274 ff., 591.]

486 *quick to move; but doom is quick*: the first 'quick' contains an allusion to the barely credible speed of the beacon-flame (480–1, cf. 280) and the second anticipates the speed with which Clytemnestra's own claims (613, 1394) will collapse (1498 ff., 1569 ff.). The word-play and sound-pattern approximate to ones in the Greek.

489–502 The MSS give this speech to Clytemnestra, with the consequence that she is present throughout 355–488 but exits at 537 only to return at 587. Taplin, *Stagecraft*, 294–7, argues cogently against this.

492 *cheated our minds like a dream*: cf. 274.

493 *shadowed in twigs of olive*: that is, wreathed with them, normally a very visible intimation of victory and its report; there is a certain tension with the Chorus' scepticism of 491–2 and 498–9.

495–7 *dust, mud's thirsty sister and neighbour*: where the mud's edge dries into dust. With this curious kenning (allusive name), whether poetic or folksy, compare *Seven* 494 'black smoke is sister to flickering fire'; at 1641 below, hunger 'houses' with darkness. The kenning perhaps registers the moment's importance, just as the overfull description of the beacons emphasizes that a verbal report may confirm what they signalled as *voiceless* and establish Clytemnestra's triumph (587–98). Logically the Herald's dust-clouded and therefore hasty approach is seen before his wreath.

496 *you*: addressed to a fellow-member of the Chorus. [Such self-reference also *Eum.* 140; but editors who assume Clytemnestra's presence here (see n. to 489–502) replace 'you' with 'assuredly'.]

500 *happy appearances*: ambiguous; the Chorus wish for the beacon's plausibility to be confirmed; the wording recalls and partly inverts 484 'before the reality appears'.

503 *s.d.*: *A* HERALD *now enters from the side*: the preceding Choral ode has covered a long interval of dramatic time, between the arrival of the beacon-flame and now the arrival of a messenger; a similar interval was noted on 84.

504 *Ten years' daylight now*: compare the Chorus's words at their first entry, 40. [Literally 'in this tenth light of a year', in which the

dislocation of the adjective perhaps expresses excitement: see n. to 555–83. Almost all editors emend to give the sense translated.]

508 *greetings to the sunlight*: 'code' for thankfulness to be still alive, like 575, 668; contrast 1324. The welcome of the daylight recalls the Watchman's joy at 'light in darkness', 22–3: cf. 519, and for the image in general, 23–4 and n.; cf. 522.

509 *Pythian lord*: Apollo; for the name's origin see n. to *Eum.* 2–19, first paragraph.

511–12 *Scamander*: one of Troy's rivers, apostrophized also by Cassandra at 1157. The allusion is to Apollo's enmity towards the Greeks throughout the *Iliad*, but especially to the pestilence his arrows send them in Book 1.45 ff. *healer*: cf. Calchas at 146.

513 *gods in their assembly*: imagined collectively; a precautionary, all-embracing formula of address.

515 *Hermes, herald whom heralds dearly revere*: see n. to *Eum.* 90.

516 *heroes who sent us out*: those of local tradition and cult (cf. *LB* 483–5), invoked and offered sacrifice no less than gods upon departure from home.

519 *deities facing the sun*: cult-statues facing its rising, in anticipation of brilliant and successful days (such as this day of home-coming); facing east therefore, roughly towards defeated Troy; cf. 575–9.

522 *light in darkness*: a common image of salvation; especially at *LB* 131, 810, etc.; cf. n. to 508.

525 *Zeus the justice-bringer*: explicitly recalling 40–1, 355–84.

[527 'and the gods' altars and shrines made invisible' is deleted because it disrupts the imagery of 526–8 and shows an arrogance inappropriate to the Herald. It was perhaps interpolated to confirm Clytemnestra's hope of Greek sacrilege at 341 ff. It may have been modelled on *Persians* 811.]

533 *deed greater than their suffering*: an allusion to the law 'the doer suffers', *LB* 313; cf. 177 above, 'Suffer and learn'.

534–5 *robbery*: not 'rape', since Helen left with Paris voluntarily, 407–8, cf. 822; in Homer, Paris also stole property with Helen, *Iliad* 3.282, 285, etc.

536–7 *total ruin . . . soil and all*: formulaic terms from extinction-curses. *paid double*: losing both Helen and their everything.

538–50 This stichomythic dialogue has a certain awkwardness, perhaps helping to express the awkwardness it uncovers in the Chorus; contrast the more natural 620–35 and particularly 268–80.

539 [MSS 'death' is obelized by West because the Greek word is faulty in form; any conjecture must keep roughly the same sense.]

540 *exercised . . . hard*: the metaphor from athletic training implies 'exhausted you, worn you out'.

547 [*Tell me*: a conjectural replacement for '(brought) to the army'.]

548 *silence . . . medicine against harm*: cf. the Watchman at 36.

549 *fear about . . . lords*: the Greek can mean both 'fear of' and 'fear for'; the Chorus feel the latter, the Herald reassures them about the former, at 551 misunderstanding their reply in 550.

551–4 Aeschylus apparently makes the Herald qualify (again? cf. the deleted line 527) the actions of victorious Agamemnon at Troy, for the mixed joys and pains of the ordinary soldiers are yet to be described, 573 ff. With 552–3 *some . . . well, but some . . . open to blame* Aeschylus no doubt intends us to recall Calchas at 145, interpreting the ambivalent omen. The continuation *but who except the gods is free from pain* perhaps anticipates the disastrous storm they send the returning Greeks, 648–70.

555–83 The Herald's account is disjointed, and his syntax often violently strained, perhaps expressing his violent relief, and his jaggedly emotional reminiscences of discomfort; so too in 638–49, as he prepares uncomfortably to add unwelcome news to the joy of victory. The realistic detail of the speech helps to increase Clytemnestra's credibility and confidence: see n. to 281–316. The hardships of 555–7 were those of the outward voyage; the missing line may have had something like 'which exhausted us as we crossed the Aegean'.

556–7 [*what . . . not get as our daily lot?*: text and interpretation are insecure.]

558–62 *damp all through*: as already imagined by Clytemnestra, 335–6. Such complaints from foot-soldiers have never been rare; and the *Independent*'s obituary of the last known British survivor of the Gallipoli (i.e. 'Troy') campaign of 1915, Percy Goring, who died at the age of 106 in July 2001, included his recollection: 'What with poor food and shortage of water, illness, particularly dysentery, soon began to make itself felt. We were permanently filthy. Food was covered in flies, billions of them, and our blankets and uniforms were full of lice.'

568 *the dead never even care about rising again*: their experience of life was too grim to make them want to leave the underworld.

570–9 [The text and sequence of ideas at the end of the Herald's speech are full of uncertainties. Editors either emend or transfer lines quite freely, and the transfer of 570–2 seems inescapable if they are to be retained in this play (the language is certainly Aeschylean). West suggests after 572 something like 'the army will now be caught up in thanksgiving', and as preparation for 577–9 'spoils will be dedicated in temples with this inscription: . . .'.]

574 *our gain prevails*: an echo (ironic—or unconscious?) of 'let the good prevail', 121 and n.

575 *sunlight*: see nn. to 508, 519.

577–9 The three lines are in the style of a dedicatory inscription, to be read by future generations.

580–1 *praise the city and its generals*: collective human victory, aided by the gods (*Zeus*, 582): see Agamemnon's words on entry, 810–12.

586 *enriches me as well*: the meaning appears to be, Agamemnon's return is not less a concern to the Chorus, but the news strengthens their confidence.

590 *someone said in reproof*: she means the Chorus, 268–80 (n.).

596 *lulling*: the idea may be that of quieting, not extinguishing, the flames by regular pouring on of wine or incense. [*lulling* is marked corrupt by West; 'regulating' or even 'stirring up' has been conjectured.]

600 *revered husband*: Clytemnestra's sardonic tone continues in 605 *beloved darling*, an endearment here almost contemptuous; cf. her exaggeration in his hearing at 896 ff.

606–7 *wife . . . just as faithful . . .*: dissembling, not ironic. Clytemnestra betrayed her faith only after Agamemnon left, when her daughter was sacrificed and she turned to Aegisthus. *watch-dog*: she calls Agamemnon this, 896. The idea of 'house-minder' pervades the play: 155, 809 and n., 1225, etc.

610 *no seal broken*: for this practice of securing the house's most precious goods during the master's absence see also *Eum.* 828. There is no allusion to the 'seal' of her own chastity; that comes in 611–12.

612 *dipping bronze*: to make it more workable; but Clytemnestra means simply 'metal-working'.

617 *Menelaus*: see n. to *LB* 1040–3.

619 *dear to this land*: as Agamemnon's brother, Menelaus commands the land's duty; see n. to 400.

626 *set sail in clear view*: watched by the rest, including the Herald. One version of the myth had Menelaus quarrel with Agamemnon after Troy's fall: Homer, *Odyssey* 3.136 ff. The storm which shatters

the main fleet (648–70) was the gods' angry punishment (635, 649) for Greek sacrilege in victory: n. to 338–45.

637 *the honour . . . separate*: the aphoristic form of this sentence makes it opaque in context. The idea appears to be that bad news pollutes normal thanksgiving to the gods, because it honours rather the Furies (645) who cause disaster.

638 [*grim*: an extremely rare Greek adjective, conjectural both here (the MSS have 'loathsome') and at *LB* 1045.]

643 *lethal pair of spears*: Homeric warriors carried two spears each.

654–7 *winds from Thrace*: probably an unconscious echo of 193–4, the winds which prevented the Greeks from sailing on their outward journey. *buffeting*: the forces of the storm are like a bull's charge. *an evil shepherd*: the storm personified, continuing the animal imagery; cf. n. to 669. [West adopts 656, 655 as the order of the lines, and makes the change to *lightning* from MSS 'storm', so restoring the idea of fire (651).]

659 *blooming*: for this metaphor of unpleasant abundance cf. *LB* 1009, *Persians* 821.

665 [*prevent mooring*: the MSS have 'at our mooring', but the two perils make better sense if the god aids their avoidance while the ship is still at sea, 667.]

669 *brooded*: an almost dead metaphor, also at *Eum.* 78; literally 'grazed (cattle)', it often carries the idea of feeding with false hopes, deceiving either self or others.

673 *May it turn out for the best!*: cf. 121 and n.

678 *Zeus . . . not yet . . . destroy his family-line*: Aeschylus has the Herald anticipate the intention of Thyestes' curse upon his brother Atreus (1601–2)—which is fulfilled, as much part of Zeus' justice as that upon Troy, e.g. 1481–8, *LB* 308–9, etc.

681–783 For the general purpose and style of this ode see n. to 40–257.

681, 689–90 *name so wholly true . . . Helen . . . aptly to her name hellish*: the obvious and nearest way for English to attempt this play on the name; *hel-* in Greek is 'capture, overcome, destroy'. Such etymological inference or omen was taken seriously, not only by poets; cf. 700 and n., 1081, *LB* 951, *Eum.* 69, 90, etc.

683–5 *someone not seen by us*: discreetly allusive. The child was named by its parent, but Helen's father was simultaneously the god Zeus himself, who had *forethought for what fate had predestined*, and the mortal Tyndareus, *not seen* because he is now among 'those lost to sight', the dead, 466. See the Family Tree.

691 *filmy chamber-curtains*: a literary echo perhaps of Helen's luxurious bedroom (at Troy, however), Homer, *Iliad* 3.382. Tragedy makes Helen fastidious of her beauty, in poignant contrast with the mayhem she causes, 745 ff., 1455 ff.

692 *giant Zephyr*: almost jarring hyperbole for a 'powerful west wind'. Herodotus 2.177 cites a (now lost) Epic account of the speed of Helen's voyage; cf. 747 below, 'sped'.

693 *hounding*: the imagery begun at 135.

696 *Simois*: one of Troy's two rivers, its mouth a landing-place.

697 *bloody Strife*: associated again with Helen at 1461, in the consequences for Agamemnon when he returns home—and this further connection appears at *LB* 474. For the personified force see Introduction, p. xxxiv.

700–1 The antistrophe begins by heavily repeating the 'correct and ominous naming' which opens the ode, 681 and n.; in the Greek *so right in name* and *purposeful* are pointedly juxtaposed. *wedding-bond*: the Greek noun means 'care, concern', both as 'betrothal, marriage' and as 'anxiety, grief'. This double meaning is attempted with English *bond*. For *drove on its way*, a verb of oracular pedigree, see *LB* 939. *Wrath*: active also at Aulis, bringing on Iphigenia's sacrifice, 155.

713 *'Fatal in your marriage!'*: this particular kenning for Paris originates in Homer, *Iliad* 3.39 and was much copied by lyric poets; it is paraphrased at *Ag.* 1156. Cf. also 749 and n.

717–49 This fable of the lion-cub (note the indicatory headline *Just so . . . once . . .*; cf. 60) provides a telling but not wholly exact allegory for Helen's (and Paris') effect at Troy. Like the lion-cub, at first harmless because dependent, endearing, and pampered (717–26), so is Helen at first quiescent, seductive, and spoiled (739–44); Aeschylus gives full colour to the Trojans' initial fascinated indulgence. The cub's maturity inevitably brings out its instinct for bloodshed, destroying its rearers' prosperity (727–34)—but Helen's change is different, for while her marriage to Paris brings inevitable retribution (744–6), it comes from outside, sent to Troy by Zeus when outraged by Paris' insult to his host Menelaus, Helen's husband (747–9, cf. 61, 361–4, 701–3). Moreover, the cub's behaviour is only nature's course, but Paris (like Helen) has abused wealth and inevitably afflicts his house (771, 'justly' 774–82; contrast 761–2, 779). Yet the effect of both cub and Helen is presented as the same, the will of gods (735, 748, phrases deliberately put by Aeschylus near the end of the consecutive Antistrophe 2 and Strophe 3), and as the action of personified powers (Ruin, 735, Fury 749, also placed at those ends; cf. Wrath, 701).

718 *a lion's offspring*: the Greek word denotes human offspring (reversing the commoner source of metaphor: 129 and n.), and is part of the allegory: the cub's effect is like that of the human counterpart. Similarly at 50, in the simile of the vultures distraught for their young lost from the nest, the Greek word for the chicks is 'children', prefiguring both the hare's young (119) and Agamemnon's child (150–1) who is to be killed in compensation.

720–2 *first-rites*: as at 65, 227. The word maintains the ideas both of marriage and of sacrificial killing: see 737 and n. *delightful as well to the old*: but at Homer, *Iliad* 3.150 ff. it is the old men who advise Priam to send Helen back to Menelaus.

737 *priest of Ruin was reared . . . as well*: as the man unwisely took in the cub, so the Trojans unwisely took in Helen; both brought bloodshed, an idea implicit in Greek *priest*, an officer of sacrifice.

742 *melting glances*: Helen's seductive (and fatal, 744–9) eyes; for the idea see n. to 416–19.

744 *The marriage was changed in its course*: an artifice in translation. The Greek sentence begins with a feminine active participle, 'changing the course', as if referring to Helen herself; but the identity of the subject is reserved to the very end, 749 *a Fury* (for this device, see 59 and n.). The meaning of the participle is much disputed; some translate '(Helen) changing her ways' (an explicit link with the fable of 717–49), others as '(a Fury) bedding them side by side', i.e. Helen and Paris. See also on 749 below. *ended . . . fulfilment*: a sardonic play upon the near-formula 'fulfil the rite of marriage'.

748 *Zeus god of hosts*: resuming 703, the motif occurring first at 61 (n.).

749 *bringing tears upon brides*: if this is the meaning (it is the strictly correct translation), the brides are those of the war-dead, 438–44; but the plural may be allusive and mean no more than 'bringing tears to the bride', that is, Helen alone. If the Greek participle cunningly placed in 744 (n.) half-conceals Helen, she is simultaneously the *Fury* in 749 here and the strictly incorrect translation 'a bride bringing tears' becomes attractive.

757 *I differ . . . alone in my thinking*: to emphasize the higher truth, that wrong mentality and actions in a prosperous family bring on disaster (758 ff.), not prosperity in itself (751–5), Aeschylus pretends originality in setting out what is in fact traditional belief, e.g. in Solon

(early sixth century) *Fragments* 1.7 ff., 3.7 ff., 5.9 f. Same moral theme, same didacticism *Eum.* 550 ff., cf. above 369–72. 'Breeding' by personified abstractions (754–5, 756, 759–60, 762, 764, 772) is common in these sermons, and the metaphor is not rare in the *Oresteia* generally, e.g. *LB* 806: n. to 152–5

769–72 III 769–70 *a demon* is the further 'child' of insolence, 763. It is feminine in the Greek, implicitly therefore the Fury of 749. For the three negative adjectives in 769–70 compare *LB* 55. In 772 *resembling its parents* pointedly recalls 760. [Text and translation are insecure in these lines.]

776–80 [Text again insecure, containing several conjectures.]

778 *eyes turned away*: to avoid pollution; cf. *LB* 99.

781 *falsely stamped with praise*: a paradox: false praise of 'unclean' wealth (776) makes it seem sound, like a counterfeit coin made from base metal (the imagery of 389–93).

782 *she directs all things to their ending*: cf. *Eum.* 544, Introduction, §2.3, at start.

785 *how should I address you . . . revere you*: the questions resemble the cautious formulae of address to gods, e.g. 160–2, but no irony can be meant, despite Agamemnon's apparent condescension to the gods in his first words, 810–12. Compare Orestes' doubt, how to address the robing which trapped his murdered father without blasphemy, *LB* 997.

788–9 *Many among mankind . . . justice*: the first note of warning that some of those who welcome Agamemnon will be disloyal.

794 [Both text and metre are suspect here, and loss appears certain.]

798 *fawning*: perhaps an unconscious echo of the fawning lion-cub of 725, but the image recurs at *LB* 194, 420.

801 *picture*: the metaphor is suggestive only, not directive like the simile at 242.

802 *your mind's helm*: this metaphor at *Persians* 767.

803–4 *for dying men* may mean 'for those dying at Aulis', whom the Chorus described at 188–98 as starving, angry, and dispirited; the phrase may hint too at the Chorus's condemnation of Iphigenia's sacrifice (151, cf. 215, 248). [Something is badly wrong with the text hereabouts, and the translation gives only a possible outline of the sense.]

806–7 [West cites editors' supplements, '. . . *loyalty*. (I commend this saying of men gone by:) *Toil* (is sweet) *for those etc.*', but himself prefers in 807 '(There is sleep from) *toil for those etc.*']

808–9 *staying at home . . . rightfully . . . improperly*: there is a double allusion. The Chorus were too old for the campaign (72–5) and faithful in their king's absence (259–60, 996 ff.); Clytemnestra and especially Aegisthus have been treacherous and cowardly stay-at-homes (607 and n., 1223–5, 1626; cf. 'unjust' 1546)—but he too claims to be 'just' (1604), as does she (1396, 1406, etc.).

810–54 Agamemnon's entry-speech in part resembles a second prologue (cf. Orestes' arrival at Athens, *Eum.* 235–43 and n.); his greeting to his home on his return from abroad will be echoed in Orestes' true prologue-speech in *Libation Bearers*. The speech is at the same time carefully styled as the opening of the confrontational scene with Clytemnestra. He begins, and she follows (855–913), both of them with defences of their conduct, but they speak as if to a third party, for external approval, not to each other; he addresses only the Chorus, 830, as does she at her start; he becomes 'second person' only at 877, and in turn he acknowledges her in the second person only at 914. Cf. n. to 931–43.

811–17 The language of judicial process resumes (40 and n.), as later at 822–3, 831. *accessories*: as if Agamemnon had at least an equal role, if not one greater than the gods. The word recurs at *LB* 134, of Aegisthus sharing Agamemnon's murder, and particularly at *Eum.* 199, where the Furies accuse Apollo of having a role greater than accessory in Clytemnestra's death. 813–14 *case without speeches*: summary justice, *Eum.* 360–4 and n. West compares *Suppliants* 934 'Ares judges this without the evidence of witnesses'.

824–8 *beast of destruction*: literally 'biting thing'; this almost dead metaphor is used of the murderous Clytemnestra at 1232, and of the menacing dream-snake at *LB* 530 (n.). The Trojan Horse (825) leapt the battlements (827); it dropped its concealed warriors like a mare its foal, and before dawn (the poetic implication rather than strict sense of *near the Pleiades' setting*; cf. 355–8, Night's part in Troy's capture). The lion is also the emblem of Agamemnon's own kingdom, *LB* 232, 938 (nn.).

830 *your sentiments*: the Chorus's avowals at 782–809.

834–7 *the poison . . . door* seems to contradict 832–3, and may be a parallel passage interpolated by some early reader; cf. also n. to *LB* 997–1004. *sits near the heart*: for the imagery see 978 and n., *Eum.* 519.

839 *companionship's mirror*: exposing the false friend, described by the Chorus at 786–96. *image is a shadow's*: a common conceit, applied usually to the insubstantiality of fortune or existence; cf. 1328 and n.

841–3 *Only Odysseus*: for his closeness to Agamemnon see Homer, *Iliad* 4.360 f.; his initial reluctance to go to Troy is also in Sophocles, *Philoctetes* 1025. *trace-horse*: harnessed alongside the yoke-pair, and chosen for its strength to wheel the whole team; also 1640. *dead or alive*: perhaps a reference to Telemachus' search for his father Odysseus, Homer, *Odyssey* 2.132, but the idea is that of 871–9.

845 *common assemblies*: cf. 884, perhaps an echo of the *Iliad*'s 'democratic' consultation, e.g. Book 2.50 ff.; cf. the king consulting the people, *Suppliants* 369.

849 *cautery or surgery*: Agamemnon contemplates execution of the disloyal, but is himself cut down by Clytemnestra for his treachery, 1521–9.

853–4 *gods who . . . steadfast*: Agamemnon ends where he began, 812. *may victory etc.*: for the audience an ironic echo of the Chorus's prayer at 121 (n.) etc.

857–8 *timidity dies away in time*: Clytemnestra sets the tone for her combative defiance, which astonishes Agamemnon, 940 ff.; cf. her 879.

861 *wife . . . separated . . . husband*: cf. Clytemnestra at *LB* 920, again defensively.

864–5 *with one man coming . . . pain for the house*: the translation slightly mitigates awkward Greek syntax, which expresses Clytemnestra's emotional intensity like the rather contorted sentences which follow.

867 *channelling*: imagery from irrigation.

870 *Geryon*: a three-bodied herdsman, symbolic perhaps of nature's multiple danger to man, rather than a mere monster like the three-headed Cerberus of the underworld; Heracles killed him in one of his Labours.

871–2 *cloak*: a common metaphor for burial, first at Homer, *Iliad* 3.56–7. *I do not speak of that below him*: extraordinarily flat in sense and tone to our ear (for this occasional impression see n. to 1120); perhaps Clytemnestra means the earth literally below the living Agamemnon now but soon to receive him in death's finality: 1386–7, 1552. [Some editors delete these two verses as clumsy (and 871 and the genuine 875 begin very similarly in the Greek), but *Seven* 949–50 also have the idea of 'earth beneath the buried man'.]

875 *nooses*: conventional means of suicide for despairing or guilty women, e.g. *Suppliants* 160; but Orestes too contemplates such suicide at *Eum.* 746.

881 *Strophius the Phocian*: father to Pylades, Orestes' close friend, *LB* 562, cf. 679. For Phocis, whose territory abutted Delphi, see the Map.

884 *deliberation*: some translate as 'the council', recalling 845–6.

886 *Such a plea in excuse . . . deception*: by explaining Orestes' absence as Strophius' well-intentioned interest, she hopes to mask her own treachery. In other versions the child Orestes is smuggled into his keeping for eventual vengeance.

887–94 Clytemnestra seems to say that her eyes have dried, in part because she cried so much in watching late for the beacons; her interrupted dreams also harmed her appearance.

894 *time which shared my sleep*: for this concept of time 'living' with a person cf. 105–7 and n. Clytemnestra is not repeating to Agamemnon her claim of chastity made to the Chorus, 611.

896–902 A flurry of images; Clytemnestra and Cassandra share the most colourful language of the play: cf. Introduction, p. lv. [The text in 899–902 raises problems of co-ordination and style; some editors delete 902 *it is sweet etc.*, others move 901 *a stream welling etc.* to follow 898 *his father.*]

904 *jealous envy*: by the gods, of the victory at Troy, 907; the danger is seen by Agamemnon, 921, 947.

905 *my dear one*: until now he has been third person, 860, 867, or an unspecified second, 877–9, 890, 893. The sudden and surprising endearment is at once followed by the ingratiatingly respectful *my lord*, and by the invitation to tread like sublime royalty, 907.

908–9 *s.d.*: *calling back through the door*: the effect of Clytemnestra's appearance at 855 and long speech would be weakened if the women slaves carrying the purples entered with her. *fabrics*: woven stuffs ('textiles', 949). Although subsequently described as 'vestments' (921), 'tapestries' or 'embroideries' (923, 936, etc.) are meant, used as wall-hangings. Trampling them is arrogance suggestive enough; their purple-red is brilliantly ominous of the bloodshed inside to which they lead: see Introduction, §3.4, at end, with n. 36.

911 *Justice*: ironically recalling the tone of Agamemnon's thanksgiving for his return, 811 ff. *unexpected*: ambiguous and ironic in its recall and reverse of 899 'against their hopes'.

912–13 *unconquered by sleep*: inverting Agamemnon's prayer at 854 (n.), but 'sleep' perhaps also recalls Clytemnestra's own sleeplessness at 889–94: she will be watchful still. [*are done*: a conjecture replacing MSS 'fated'.]

917 *Fair praise . . . from others*: he means, from outside his family.

919–20 *obeisance . . . barbarian*: like the Persians greeting their royalty at *Persians* 151, 694–701.

922 *magnify*: the Greek verb has cultic provenance; it recurs at *Eum.* 15, 626. Rich robes were often dedicated to gods, to clothe their statues, most famously in the great festivals honouring Athena at Athens.

924 *without fear*: picked up at 930 (n.). He fears that he may not dissuade Clytemnestra from her intended welcome; cf. 946–7.

926 *Foot-wipers . . . different meanings*: about the mentality of those who walk on them. Some translate as 'fame cries out (loud enough) without foot-wipers and tapestries'. The word *foot-wipers* is invented (and unique), perhaps in order to convey Agamemnon's contempt—and alarmed surprise (924, 927, 947–9).

930 *If I could fare . . . confident*: Agamemnon is trying to quiet his fears of divine retribution (924; cf. Clytemnestra at 933). [The syntax is suspect. Some editors change to 'I have said how I should myself act in this with full confidence', i.e. 'how I would confidently avoid divine jealousy.']

931–43 An extraordinarily compressed exchange, cast in stichomythia (cf. especially 268–80 and see n.). Clytemnestra swiftly concentrates unbearable pressure upon Agamemnon, with a few exactly targeted questions and crushing ripostes to his qualms. The very speed of it all increases our impression of a man uneasy and defensive from the moment of his entry.

931–8 The sequence of thought from 931, and indeed some of the precise meaning, are famously uncertain. Clytemnestra twice manipulates Agamemnon, inviting him to revalue his scruples: first, as if he had been in fear and with no alternative to vowing this act of triumphant celebration if he should escape from that fear (933; he yields to this negative hypothesis, 934); second, as if his disliked model Priam had vowed such ostentatious triumph should he achieve a victory of Agamemnon's magnitude (935). He concedes this second and flatteringly positive point (936), but tries to preserve the difference between himself and the defeated Priam. Clytemnestra exploits both concessions as if they were real (937), and his answer is weakly evasive (938).

943 *you are in fact the winner . . . willingly*: the idea is proverbial. [The text is nevertheless conjectural: the MSS have approximately 'but yield the superiority willingly to me.']

945 *which serve walking feet as slaves*: the pedestrian comparison seems obtrusive, almost incongruous, as if to suggest awkwardness; per-

haps Aeschylus is hinting that Agamemnon is himself behaving slavishly (cf. his words about Cassandra at 953).

948–9 *I have great qualms*: Agamemnon tries to reduce his blasphemy by removing his shoes at least. *bought with silver*: see n. to 958–74.

950–5 Agamemnon's first offence is to god, by walking as a mortal man over his wealth; now he violates men's morality too by inviting his wife to welcome a concubine captive into his house (as Deianeira is deceived into doing in Sophocles, *Women of Trachis* 375 ff.)—only for her to turn this insult into further triumph in his death, 1058, 1444–7. Cassandra is booty, but her arrival is also like that of a bride drawn to her new husband's home in the wedding-chariot.

956–7 *Since I am subdued . . . treading over purples*: transparently emphatic recapitulation for the audience of the scene's significance—but also avoiding Agamemnon's mention of Cassandra as his exit-lines.

958–74 *The sea is there, etc.*: Clytemnestra disingenuously consoles Agamemnon against the material loss of the trodden purples, easily replaced from the house's wealth (961–3, *a remedy for these here*). Purple dye was extracted from a shellfish. The demonstrative brilliance she intends for his return, to relieve the house of its cheerless emptiness (861 ff.), makes black irony: she was contriving *a safe return for this life here* (965) only to kill him once he is inside (n. to 973–4).

961 [*remedy* is West's conjecture for MSS 'house'; he compares 1169. The MSS may mean 'the house has sufficient of these'; most editors read 'there is a reserve of these for the house to have etc.']

964–5 *pronounced . . . at an oracle*: the word with which the seer Calchas 'named (Artemis as cause)', 201.

966–72 The general illustration from nature in 966–7 is made particular to Agamemnon's house in 968–72 through similar imagery, giving the appearance of duplicated ideas. [Some editors suspect textual interpolation or try to unify the thought by translating 966–7 as 'Since the root is there, leafy growth has come . . . and stretched'.] *cool*: i.e. in early summer; grapes are not then ripe enough to make sound wine.

973–4 *master-fulfiller*: the Greek adjective applied in 971 to the man who moves about his house, and translated as *its master*, is the same as that applied here to Zeus (cf. 1487 and *Eum.* 974 etc.); both are echoed in the cognate verbs translated *give . . . fulfilment* and *fulfil* in 973–4. I have done my best to reflect this deliberate and blackly ironic effect. *take care of whatever*: for this vague phrasing of a definite wish see *LB* 145 and n.

975–1034 Agamemnon's entry to his house brings the Chorus to express suddenly sharpened fear, at the start and end of their song (975–1000, 1025–34). Their forebodings surround further reflections on the frailty of human prosperity (1001–24, cf. 750 ff.). This song is quite different in character from the preceding ones, which draw their moral truths from extended narratives (see n. to 40–257); and subsequent lyric in the play is shared between two voices (1072–1117: see n.; 1406–1576), except for a further brief outburst by the Chorus immediately before Agamemnon's murder (1331–42, on the same theme as 1001–24 here).

978 *in front of my heart, to rule*: more pointed than the simple location 'before my heart' in 179, for the Greek here echoes the popular Athenian name for one who 'stands before, presides over, champions' the democratic interest; the Chorus fear for the community. Cf. *Eum.* 518 f. 'the watch on minds by fear'. *heart* means here both emotions and intelligence: 983, 993, 995–6.

979 *my song act the seer*: like *LB* 1024. *unbidden, unpaid*: unlike a hired and predictable singer and therefore frighteningly irregular; it is 'self-taught' and 'unlyrical' in 990–1 (n.). At *LB* 733 'grief . . . takes no wages'.

985–6 *cables . . . jerked aboard, the sand flying upward*: ships were beached by the stern and then roped. [All these words are conjectural; the MSS are very corrupt here.]

991 *unlyrical dirge*: something of a cliché for the Furies' song: see n. to 151. Dirges were sung not to a stringed instrument, but to a droning pipe.

1001–13 The danger of insatiety threatening supreme well-being is thematic to *Agamemnon*, e.g. 382, 756 'insatiable' (750–62 and nn.), 1331, cf. *Eum.* 1000; Introduction, p. xxxviii. [*Great health . . . limit*: a very free translation of a hopelessly corrupt passage, to create an acceptable preparation for *sickness etc.*]

1005–6 [Even the location of the missing words is uncertain; I have attempted no supplement.]

1008–13 *The caution . . . capsize*: the Chorus return to the ideas of 757 ff., that moderation can forestall disaster for rich and poor alike. The metaphor of safe sailing for a laden ship runs from 1005 to 1013, suitably to Agamemnon pictured as a ship's safeguard (897), to the Greeks' voyage against Troy (984–7), and to the fatal voyage of Paris and Helen (691 ff.). The metaphor recurs at *Eum.* 554–65.

1010 *sizing it well for the sling*: jettisoning enough to prevent foundering, 1011; the *sling* is tackle for (un)loading. The image in 1008–13 occurs at *Seven* 769–71 in the same moral context. The sentence resumes in 1011 with its subject transformed from *caution* into *house*, its location.

1014–17 *the bounty of Zeus . . . disease*: the Sky-god (11. to 165) controls the climate, but especially the vital rainfall (1391–2, *Eum.* 947–8).

1018–21 *Once . . . blood has fallen . . . incantation?*: an idea thematic in the trilogy, e.g. *LB* 48 and *Eum.* 980 (nn.: for the imagery cf. Introduction, §3.4, at end). *incantation* was part of religious medicine; ineffectual to restore life, *Eum.* 649.

1022–4 *Not even to him . . . the price*: the doctor-hero Asclepius, although a son of the doctor-god Apollo, was destroyed by Zeus when he restored men to life. [*nod assent* is West's conjecture for MSS 'stop'.]

1025–7 *one man's status . . . advance*: translation insecure; the Chorus seem to regard Agamemnon's rule over them as divinely fixed, and to think that their inferiority prevents their speaking out to him in warning (cf. e.g. 805–9—but at 799–804 they did voice misgiving at his conduct). Others translate 'were not fate set by heaven preventing (an individual's) fate . . .'.

1028 *heart . . . anticipated . . . tongue*: reversing the commoner, proverbial conception.

1030–3 *grumbles in the darkness*: the language recalls the animosity snarled quietly against Agamemnon, 449–50. *winding all to its end*: i.e. 'achieving an end', a weakened metaphor from winding yarn. The Chorus are inhibited from intervention; Aeschylus is preparing once more for their helplessness during Agamemnon's murder itself, 1348 ff. (n.).

1035 *get yourself inside*: peremptory and colloquial, pointedly shifting the tone of Agamemnon's polite request at 951 to take Cassandra inside. The Chorus match Clytemnestra's tone at 1047.

1036–8 *without anger*: implication unclear, but perhaps preparing for Clytemnestra's advice to Cassandra that as a captive she could be much worse off, 1040–5. The words are much less likely to register just Cassandra's sharing in the house's rites as a stranger without incurring its anger. *ritual sprinklings*: washing of hands and the sprinkling of purifying water, *Eum.* 656. Aeschylus may be alluding to her murder together with Agamemnon as a ritual 'sacrifice' (Introduction, §3.4). *altar protecting its possessions*: such an altar was regularly set in storerooms, and it was sacred to Zeus of Possessions himself (cf. *LB* 800–1 and n.). The Greek however hints at the meaning 'altar of the house's possessor', that is, near Agamemnon when Clytemnestra 'sacrifices' him (alluded to in 1057).

1039 *Get out of this carriage*: Clytemnestra's command to Agamemnon, 906.

1040 *Alcmene's son . . . slavery*: Heracles, for a time punished for bloodshed by humiliating slavery to Omphale, Queen of Lydia.

1045–6 *what is our custom*: what is said and provided to new slaves by their masters. [The extent of the textual loss in indeterminable.]

1048 *fatal net*: over Troy, 358; but Aeschylus alludes also to Clytemnestra's net of robing thrown over Agamemnon, 1116, 1382, etc.

1050–2 *like a swallow . . . comprehension*: a common comparison for speech heard as a kind of meaningless twittering, e.g. in Aristophanes' description of some feeble tragic poetry itself, *Frogs* 93, 681. [*I am trying etc.*: syntax and sense are both in doubt.]

1057–8 [The text of these two lines is wholly insecure; a connection with 1059 is missing.]

1061 *show your intention*: whether she will get down, not whether she understands. In performance Clytemnestra would accompany her words with explicit gestures of her own. *outlandish*: the tone of this rare dialect and possibly abusive word expresses her impatience. Cf. n. to 1120.

1063 *wild animal*: Cassandra is already in prophetic seizure (1067) before she bursts out at 1072. *captured* however continues the imagery of the net, 1048.

1066–7 *bridle . . . in blood*: many Greek horse-bits were sharp-edged or even serrated. *foaming out her temper* contains also the idea of 'foaming out her life'—in an agonized death such as Cassandra later prays to avoid, 1293–4.

1072 Cassandra's immobility and intriguing silence since her entry with Agamemnon at 783—despite Agamemnon's explanation of her presence at 950–5, and despite Clytemnestra's baffled attempt to get her to respond at 1034–71—make the violence of her sudden outburst all the more effective. Her cries are allusive and riddling, and initially beyond the Chorus's comprehension, except that they perceive her prophetic seizure.

1072–1177 In this long exchange, the Chorus at first answer Cassandra's lyric outbursts with speech (in the first four pairs of stanzas, 1072–1113). At 1114, as Cassandra's visions become more fantastic, the Chorus's own greater incredulity and horror are given a lyric voice as well (in the final three pairs of stanzas, 1114–78). The

beginnings of all Cassandra's stanzas show remarkable 'responsions', especially in ejaculations of horror and in phrasing of ideas,
e.g. 1072 and 1076 (n.),1080–2 and 1085–7, 1156–8 and 1167–8.
On these features see Introduction, p. li.

1072 = 1076 *O o o oh!*: attempts to reproduce Greek *ototototoi*, a wild
cry of pain, anguish, despair, etc. associated with non Greeks —
which Cassandra is and as the Chorus of *Libation Bearers* appear to
be at *LB* 159 (see n. to 423–8 there), like the off-stage servant
wailing at *LB* 869. *Horror! No!*: similarly extreme; Orestes cries it at
LB 409.

1074–5 *Loxias*: etymologically, the name Loxias is generally understood as 'The Slanter, The Oblique One', registering the indirect-
ness of the oracular Apollo who is nevertheless always right, as
Orestes trusts at *LB* 559 and as Apollo himself states, *Eum.* 615 (cf.
Emily Dickinson's 'Tell all the truth, but tell it slant'). The name is
in fact used indifferently, often occurring where there is no allusion
to Apollo's obliquity, e.g. 1208, 1211 below. *He is not of the kind . . .
lamenter*: as god of healing, youth, and music Apollo has no part in
death or dirge; also 1079, cf. *Seven* 859.

1081 = 1086. *Apollo . . . of the Streets*: large houses had a column
symbolic of the god at the door, for greeting upon entry and prayer
upon leaving; cf. n. on 'Lycean Apollo' at 1256–7. As Apollo's
victim and servant (1202 ff.), Cassandra responds to his symbol in
front of the palace-door at once. (*Apollo*) *my destroyer*: a play on the
god's name, whose spelling is close to that of a verb 'destroy'; cf. the
biblical Apollyon, 'The Destroying Angel'. See also n. to 681 'hellish
Helen'.

1082 *for this second time*: see 1202–12 for the first, Apollo's attempted
rape of her at Troy.

1091–2 Aeschylus suddenly gives Cassandra specially coined compound adjectives and nouns, to intensify the horror of her vision; she
sees both Tantalus' dismembered son Pelops (1592; see the Family
Tree), and Thyestes' children butchered and fed to him by Atreus
(1590–7 and n.); the latter are almost tangible to her at 1095–7.
[The phrase *carving like meat* replaces MSS 'and nooses' and the
phrase *a floor sprinkled with blood* approximates to the likely sense of a
very doubtful word marked corrupt by West.]

1093 *hound*: the Furies track the house's bloodshed by its scent,
Eum. 246–7, 253.

1098–9 *Indeed . . . prophets*: the Chorus recognize Cassandra's accurate 'divination' of the past in 1093–4; they do not (want to)
understand her prophecies, 1105, 1112–13.

1100—2 *Whatever is plotting . . . is plotting*: the Greek verb in both places has no grammatical subject expressed, suitably to Cassandra's cryptic vision and enigmatic speech; she names Clytemnestra only at 1107.

1105 *I do not know . . . divinations*: even out of Clytemnestra's hearing the Chorus will not yet admit her menacing intentions (1100—4) but they do allude more openly to anger stored up against Agamemnon as son of the infanticidal Atreus (1106).

1108 *bathe the husband clean*: 1128 ff.; Clytemnestra takes over the function of Homeric maids, *Odyssey* 4.49 ff. etc.

1110 *hand follows hand*: Clytemnestra's hands, imagined as busy at the bathside pouring water, washing, handing things, entangling Agamemnon in robing like a net (1115—16) to make him helpless when she strikes (1126—8).

1116 *trap-net sharing his bed*: vivid condensation: the instrument of death becomes its human agent; cf. n. to 1125—9.

1117—18 *discord*: that which caused the original quarrel of Atreus and Thyestes; it is 'Strife' at 1461 (the word is Greek *stasis*, used of political faction or discord, as at *Eum.* 977. Here, it translates less well as 'company', as if anticipating the 'company of the Furies', 1120: see the wording of *Eum.* 311). *cry its triumph*: a women's ululation of joy (28 and n.), here for the *sacrifice* (of Agamemnon, like his own of Iphigenia, 130, 240). Kin-killing, as destructive to the community, was regularly punished with *stoning* by the population, 1409, (any homicide) 1616; Orestes is condemned to it in Euripides, *Orestes* 50 etc.

1119 *What Fury's this*: half-colloquial, expressing alarmed astonishment, cf. 1087.

1120 *What you say is bringing me no cheer*: expression and tone create bathos in English, like the corresponding lines 1130—1; cf. also e.g. 1060—1, 1088—9. Many of these 'flat' expressions, and the bizarre exchange between Clytemnestra and the mute Cassandra above (1035—68), were cruelly imitated in A. E. Housman's brilliantly parodic *Fragment of a Greek Tragedy*, which draws heavily on the *Oresteia*.

1121—3 *blood yellow-dyed*: fear turns the complexion yellow (*Suppliants* 566) and runs *to the heart*, as at 976—7 it flies there. *drops which accompany . . . their end*: the Chorus seem to equate their fear with the terror of a dying warrior.

1125—9 *the bull . . . the cow*: for persons as 'animals' in prophecy see n. to 129; also 1258—9. Clytemnestra's attack on her husband reverses the role of the weaker female (cf. 1231), as she uses a woman's cunning to prevent his defence against her blow. There is much dispute about the meaning of *black-horned contrivance*. I follow the view that 'contrivance' can refer only to the robing which ensnares Agamemnon and makes him vulnerable in the bath to *treachery* (1129, cf. 1253, *LB* 981, 1003), and not to the weapon; then 'black(-horned)' connotes 'sinister, lethal', the colour of death; '-horned' both suggests the shape of the cloth lifted on her outstretched arms (1111) and continues the image of the cow. Many editors take the allusion in '-horned' to be to a double-bladed axe used by Clytemnestra or to her two 'horns' as the *cow* goring the *bull* —but there is dispute whether she used an axe or a sword: see n. to 1149.

1129 [*the outcome*: translation insecure; and some editors read 'the clever trick'.]

1134 *wordy in their verses*: oracles were phrased in hexameter verses employing Epic diction; many are quoted by the historian Herodotus, for example.

1135 *fear as their lesson*: another echo of the motif 'learning through suffering', 177 and n..

1138 *why did you lead*: addressed to Apollo: cf. the wording of 1087.

1142–8 *nightingale sounding . . . any tears*: Procne punished her husband Tereus' adultery (with her sister Philomela) by killing their son Itys (1144) and serving him the flesh (a common mythic motif; there is no necessary allusion here to Thyestes' children, 1096–7). To save her from his vengeance the gods transformed her into a nightingale; the Greeks heard the son's name in the bird's call ('ee-tis', two sharp syllables) and so the myth became aetiological. [The text and interpretation of 1143–6 are endlessly disputed; West preserves the MSS almost entirely.]

1148 *without any tears*: the meaning apparently is that after her transformation nothing further could befall Procne for which to weep, even if she continues to mourn her son.

1149 *a blade with two sides*: the description here fits either a sword with two cutting edges or an axe with a double head; cf. 1496 and 1520 'double-bladed weapon'. At 1262 Cassandra describes Clytemnestra's weapon against Agamemnon as a sword; at 1343 Agamemnon is struck 'deep' (if the text is sound); at 1351 the Chorus picture a sword; at 1389–90 the gasp of blood from Agamemnon suggests a sword-thrust rather than a blow to the head; at 1529 the Chorus again describe a sword; at *LB* 1011 Aegisthus had used a sword against Agamemnon (although in *Agamemnon* he takes no part in the killing, 1635). At 1277 Cassandra expects her death on a 'chopping-block',

which suggests an axe for both her and Agamemnon; but Clytemnestra's own death from Orestes' sword (*LB* 584, *Eum.* 42, 592) is also
upon a chopping-block, *LB* 884; at *LB* 889 Clytemnestra calls for an
axe to defend herself against Orestes (and it is therefore inferred that
she must have used an axe against Agamemnon; cf. also 860 there,
'cleaving'). These are the most significant passages adduced in the
debate; in my view they point much more to a sword than to an axe,
LB 889 being the only unequivocal reference to the latter—but that is
not in this play. Two further arguments seem to me conclusive in
favour of a sword: first, the one advanced in the note on 1127 above,
on 'black-horned contrivance' as the robing rather than the weapon;
second, the effective parallel between the deaths of the husband and
his murderous wife if both die by the sword. The question is
constantly reviewed.

1154–5 *markers*: bounding and defining her ominous prophecies; for
this image drawn from property-boundaries see 485 and n..

1156 = 1167 Each translated as two lines: the correspondences of
syllables and sound are approximately as in the Greek. For Cassandra's heavy stress here on Troy's just destruction, see Introduction,
pp. xxviii and xxxix.

1157 *Scamander*: one of Troy's rivers, 511.

1160 *Acheron* (the name means 'Sorrow, Mourning') and *Cocytus*
('Wailing') were rivers of the Underworld (cf. 1172 in the Antistrophe).

1164 *your bloody fate bites deep*: the same image of distress as in 791.

1166 *shatters me*: a more vigorous image in Greek than in the dying
English metaphor.

1171 [*as was in fact its due*: a conjectural replacement of the insecure
MSS 'as in fact it was'.]

1172 *Under-Earth* translates 'Empedos', a name for Hades meaning
approximately '(Fixed) In The Ground'. *my mind heated still* probably
refers to Cassandra's continuing prophetic seizure; and she is still
possessed by its 'fire' at 1256. The phrase may however mean no
more than 'in extreme passion': cf. the Chorus at 1033 'my mind is
ablaze'. ['Empedos' is West's venturesome reading of the Greek; the
name has very little ancient evidence. All emendations are unsatis-
factory, however.]

1174 [*putting misery in your mind*: so the MSS and West; most editors
write 'some evil-minded god . . . is making disaster your song'.]

1178 From this point until her exit at 1330 Cassandra uses speech,
except when she is again briefly overtaken by prophetic seizure at

1214 and 1256–7, and except for broken cries of horror immediately before entering the house of her death, 1305, 1307. *out from veils like a newly-wed bride*: perhaps an unconscious echo of Helen's elopement (690–1), but Aeschylus is emphasizing Cassandra's change from ironuled lyric to clear speech; and she perhaps alludes to the moment when Apollo repaid his frustrated seduction of her with the gift of riddling prophecy (1206–12).

1180–3 *clear and keen:* one adjective in the Greek, which can describe both brilliant light and a wind's fresh force. The images are fused: harm rises to be seen clear like a wave driven with the wind against the rising sun.

1185 *on the scent*: Cassandra at 1093 had 'a keen nose like a hound'.

1186–90 *choir*: Greek 'chorus', a band of singing dancers. The metaphor is only slowly developed: harsh voices, ill-omened words, wassailers not to be expelled and revealed only at sentence-end as the Furies, a word-manoeuvre like those of 59 (n.) and 749. The Furies invoke their own dancing, *Eum.* 307, 371; the voice of the family demon is raven-harsh, 1471 below. *family Furies*: native to the house, its kindred: it is the idea of 153, but this is the first explicit naming of the Furies as bloody persecutors in the house. They drink *human blood*, *Eum.* 264–5 etc.

1192–3 *sinful folly from the very start*: 386; Agamemnon's own, 223: see Introduction p. xxxiii on Atê, 'Ruin'. *brother's bed*: Thyestes' seduction of Atreus' wife is naturally omitted by Aegisthus when he defends his vengeance for his father Thyestes, 1583 ff.; but Aegisthus in turn seduced Agamemnon's wife, 1224–5—as the Chorus later accuse him, 1626 (cf. Orestes at *LB* 990).

1194 *like an archer*: the same image as at 628.

1196–7 *Speak out in witness*: heavily repeating 1184; cf. Cassandra again at 1317. The implication of the command here is that if Cassandra is proved right, the inevitable retaliation by the Fury will again demonstrate her prophetic accuracy, 1240, 1317: cf. the Chorus at 1249, 1337–42. Seers claimed accuracy if they could also narrate the past accurately, 1173. *in story*: West points out that Cassandra knows through divine prompting, not human report. [West nevertheless marks the words as corrupt.]

1198–1200 *bring healing*: probably unconscious irony: the healer Apollo (246 and n.) will not heal Cassandra herself (1275–8). [*born and bred . . . a different language*: the expression is insecure; and at 1254 Cassandra claims to know Greek well.]

1202–4 *Apollo . . . god*: the Chorus at once infer that the relationship between the god and his human servant was sexual (priestesses were regularly dedicated in this sense); Apollo was fairly promiscuous (cf. the plot of Euripides' *Ion*).

1206 *wrestled:* an uncompromisingly physical image, like the animal metaphor at *Eum.* 666; cf. n. to 1443. Apollo's rape of Creusa at Euripides, *Ion* 939, is described as a 'struggle'.

1207 *duly*: perhaps the idea is that (in myth) divine seductions normally lead to children. *making a child*: wording from the Athenian marriage-oath; cf. *Eum.* 835.

[1216 *stormy*: purely conjectural, an adjective displaced in the MSS by 'seated close by' duplicated from the end of the next line.]

1219 *people outside their family*: the sight in dreams of children killed so savagely immediately suggests their death by enemies; but the full horror of their death is that they were indeed killed by their own kin [which is indeed the reading of the MSS, but which West rightly alters]. *as if* makes a rather strained connection; Aeschylus has Cassandra rely upon the Chorus's knowledge.

1224 *cowardly lion*: Aegisthus, not expressly named until 1436. The perversion of the lion-image (n. to 824–8) makes a strong point; Clytemnestra too is a 'lioness' at 1258, but the real 'lion' of the house is Agamemnon, 1259 (the animal is his house's emblem: Note on *LB* 232). The Chorus later abuse Aegisthus' cowardice, 1625 etc., even if Clytemnestra naturally praises him as bold, 1437. *stayed at home*: recalling the Chorus's allusions at 809 (n.); cf. Clytemnestra's own pretences at 606–12, 861–94.

1227–31 (1226 is omitted from the translation): *The ships' commander and overturner of Troy*: the insistence on Agamemnon's status doubles the outrage of his murder: 1335–6, 1547, 1627, and frequently in *LB* (55–6, 723–5 and nn.). *tongue when it . . . licked:* Clytemnestra's hypocritical but triumphant rhetoric, especially 931 ff. The fawning bitch with subsequently dangerous bite recalls the fawning lion-cub of 725–6 (*brightly* there too). [West's rearrangement of the lines is bold. All editors differ in handling this widely corrupt passage, but most delete the intrusive 1226 'my (master on his return: 1225); the yoke of slavery must be endured'.]

1231 *the male's female murderer*: such portentous gender-reversal is common in oracles; cf. 1125–6 and n.

1232–6 *What . . . should I be accurate in calling her?*: this style of question is a device of emphasis; again at *LB* 997–1000. *accurate*: for the idea cf. 681 and n. *amphisbaena*: (literally 'a female who goes both ways') imagined as a snake, perhaps with dangerous jaws at both ends (*monster*, literally 'biting-creature': n. to 824–8). *Scylla*: a monster described first at Homer, *Odyssey* 12.85 ff., with six heads, each with three rows of teeth, and twelve 'tentacles'. [*hellish mother*: 'mother' is doubtful, because it can only allude to Clytemnestra as mother potentially lethal to her son Orestes—but that idea appears first at 1281.]

1236–7 *cried in triumph*: at 973–4. *total audacity*: compare the wording for Agamemnon's audacity at Aulis, 221. *rejoice at the safe home-coming*: 895–905; cf. the Chorus's warning to Agamemnon at 793–8.

1239–41 *it's all the same*: colloquially direct; again at 1404. *the future will come*: similarly 251–4, the Chorus themselves. *too true a prophet*: so Cassandra began this speech, 1215 ('ring-composition': nn. to 20 and 810–54).

1242–5 *Thyestes' feast*: Cassandra at 1091–7, *understood* by the Chorus, 1093–4—unlike her allusive prophecy of Agamemnon's death, 1107–29, which she now therefore repeats in unequivocal clarity, 1246. *off the track*: cf. the Chorus's imagery for Cassandra's own accuracy, the hound on the scent, 1093, 1185.

1247 *Say nothing inauspicious*: even naming Agamemnon, not merely speaking of death.

1248 *the Healer*: (for this title see 246 and n.) more than ambiguous: Apollo very much has his part in her words, he inspires her (1202, 1256–7); yet by the same token he will not prevent the death she prophesies (1275). Then, the Greek word 'healer' doubles also as the word for 'the song to invite victory' (247 and n.): so Cassandra is taking up the Chorus's 'Say nothing inauspicious!' with this word in its further sense of 'victory-hymn' (e.g. 645).

1252 *the course my oracles are running*: the reference is once again to a hound losing the scent, 1245. [*a long way*: a conjecture, the MSS being unintelligible.]

1253 *contrivance*: a reference to 1127 (see n.).

1255 *the Pythian decrees*: Apollo's at Delphi: cf. 509 and n. to *Eum.* 2–19, first paragraph.

1256–7 Cassandra's fresh and more violent seizure is conveyed by her sudden brief reversion to lyric. *Lycean*: in popular etymology the name meant '(slayer) of wolves', Greek *luko-*. Similar titles for Apollo suggest a belief that he offered safety for those leaving home to go into the wild; cf. n. on Apollo of the Streets at 1081. At *Seven* 146 Lycean Apollo is invoked to destroy enemies: here too? [The text of these lines is much damaged and disputed.]

1258–9 *two-footed lioness . . . noble lion*: allusive abuse followed by warm evocation. 'Noble' lion in contrast with Aegisthus as 'cowardly' lion, 1224 (see n.)—who is now also unfavourably called *wolf* for his cunning. For people as animals in the prophetic style see 1126, n. to 129.

1261 *a wage paid for myself*: ambiguous, like the Greek. The wage paid to Cassandra herself is her death, and Agamemnon with his death pays Clytemnestra a wage for bringing her; both wages are paid by putting them in the *drug* and *drink* (metaphorical only, it seems) which she prepares as she *whets her sword*: a remarkable fusion of images. [*drink* is conjectural for MSS 'anger'; 'vessel' is also suggested.]

1264–70 Euripides' *Trojan Women* 451 ff., cf. 256 ff., repeats Cassandra's theatrical rejection of her seer's emblems, but while she is still at Troy. Here, she wears them still (despite her long captivity) not only for this stage-effect, but so that the audience would identify her by sight immediately upon her entry at 782. [In 1266 the text is suspect because *You!* is in the singular, awkwardly interrupting the plurals of 1264–5 which are resumed in *fall* in 1267. Some editors therefore delete 1266.]

1267 *be damned*: harshly colloquial, cf. 1239 and n.

1270 *Apollo himself who strips me*: to be explained perhaps from 1275–6 'And now the prophet-god, etc.'.

1272 *friends who became . . . enemies*: fellow Trojans, before the city's fall. *fortune-teller wandering*: recalling the picture of 1195. Such mendicants have been an age-old target of suspicion and dislike; they recur at e.g. Plato, *Republic* 364b. [The text of 1270–4 is very badly damaged. The reference of *vainly* is quite uncertain; West suggests the missing line contained approximately '(vainly) made reliable prophecies, he gave me no protection'.]

1275 *exacted his due from myself as prophet*: in further return for her deception, 1208; now he rescinds the gift of prophecy, and so her life must end.

1277–8 *ancestral altar* may allude to the story, attested only in later works, that her father Priam was hacked down at its side. *butcher's block*: brutally echoing Atreus' block for Thyestes' children, 1092. *blood-rite . . . before*: Agamemnon's death (*one cut down*) which precedes and 'sanctifies' her own: the imagery once more of the 'perverted sacrifice', cf. e.g. n. to 1036–8. Clytemnestra would kill Agamemnon before Cassandra, to prevent his alarm; the play naturally emphasizes his death, in the enactment 1343 ff., in Clytemnestra's boasting 1372 ff., and in the Chorus's recrimination

1399 f., 1490–6, 1541–6. [For *one cut down* the MSS have 'a woman cut down', i.e. Cassandra dying before Agamemnon.]

1282–3 *exile . . . come home*: cf. 1607, and Orestes of himself at *LB* 3 (= Fragment 1), 1142. *Eum.* 462 *coping-stone*: a frequent metaphor for completion, from building. Cassandra is again ambiguous: Orestes will bring further disaster, but his matricide will also end the ruinous acts, *Eum.* 799.

1284 *thrown on his back*: as he was left by Clytemnestra after his murder, and will be displayed by her at 1372, cf. 1404. In *Libation Bearers* compare especially 980 ff.

1287 *faring as it fared*: a euphemistic redundancy (like 67), for the hard truth; at 1171 Cassandra was less explicit.

1288–91 *s.d.*: for Cassandra moving towards the door see the Chorus at 1298. *getting this outcome*: a bad one (cf. Clytemnestra at 340). Aeschylus makes Cassandra view the outcome for Agamemnon and the Greeks, even though it brings her own death, as no less just than that which the gods ordained for Troy itself, 1156 (1167) and n., 1171, cf. Agamemnon at 813–16. But now she seems quickly to abandon her sympathy for Agamemnon (cf. 1225 ff.), only to return to it at 1314. [*do it* is insecure; some editors write 'make a start' (i.e. upon the ritual of sacrificial death). 1290 'For a great oath has been sworn by heaven' is omitted from the translation; it is clearly foreign to the context.]

1293 *without convulsions*: a sacrificial victim's placid death (see 1298) was well-omened: so Iphigenia was firmly held and gagged, 238–9.

1296 *you spoke at length*: this is strange in tone, unless there is poignant contrast with 1300. Any echo of Agamemnon's response to Clytemnestra at 916 is unconscious.

1298 *towards the altar*: artfully placed in the Greek, so that it seems part both of Cassandra's own ritual path (1292–3) and of the simile.

1299 [*no further*: text conjectural, but suiting the following line. The translation too is approximate rather than certain.]

1304 Cassandra's death is in itself inglorious, so that *famous* probably alludes to subsequent mythical fame; for this Epic and poetic idea cf. perhaps *LB* 302, 349 of Troy's victors. [Because of this doubt over *famous*, some editors give 1303 to the Chorus, preceded by 1304 from Cassandra.]

1313–15 [The transfer of these lines gives a better sequence overall from 1305, because placing Cassandra's sudden halt before 1306 removes a second halt which is otherwise implied by 1315 'O strangers!' and might weaken the effect of the first.] This appeal to strangers (cf. 1320) conforms with contemporary Athenian practice; Aeschylus makes Cassandra as the victim of an outrage cry out for witness, 1317, cf. 1196.

1307–8 [*Ugh, horrible!*: raw exclamations, a correction of the weaker MSS 'Alas! . . . Alas,']

1312 *Syrian splendours*: costly, sweet-smelling incense. Cf. n. to 94–6.

1316 *My cry of distress*: a verb in the Greek, of uncertain meaning; but the comparison is clear enough: Cassandra has stopped and cried out at 1315 not from useless fear like a bird crying out at danger from limed twigs to trap it near its nest, but from the horror of it all.

1318–19 *woman dies . . . in place of woman . . . and man . . . of man*: the killings of Clytemnestra and Aegisthus in *Libation Bearers*.

1319 *I claim . . . as a stranger here*: another verb of disputed meaning, but cf. Cassandra's cries of 'strangers!' at 1299, 1315. The Greek word 'stranger' is also both 'guest' and 'host': see Introduction, p. xli n. 22.

1321 *the fate you predict*: you are not only doomed, but doomed to its foreknowledge.

1324–5 *last daylight from the sun*: regularly invoked to witness life's end; cf. 1300. *an easy victory*: somewhat strained in expression, but Cassandra prays that her own murder, though a trivial feat, should get the same revenge as Agamemnon's. [The text is heavily corrected from MSS 'to pay my (*noun missing*) to my avengers, hostile murderers, too.']

1328–30 *shadow*: a metaphor usually of insubstantiality, rather than insubstantial force effecting it: 839. *a wet sponge*: an image of total obliteration, from wall-painting; less vivid at *LB* 503. *the second*: the finality of death, like her own and Agamemnon's, is more pitiful than *the first*, survival of disaster.

1331–42 For the dramatic function of this brief chant by the Chorus see *LB* 719–29; Introduction §3.3, at start.

1331 *no satiety*: see 1002 and n.

1333–4 *which fingers point out*: cf. *LB* 35. '*Enter no more!*': as if addressed to personified 'Success' itself.

1337–40 *those before*: all the family's dead, including Iphigenia; *the dead* may have the same reference but probably is Thyestes, since *other deaths* can be only his children's; but some translate less well 'vengeance causing other deaths', i.e. of Clytemnestra and Aegisthus. [*to ordain* is strained in sense, and faulty in metre; no conjecture satisfies.]

1343 [*deep, a fatal blow*: this is the MSS text, although marked as corrupt by West; no conjecture gives sense as apt. Some translate 'deep' as 'inside the house', which is superfluous information for spectators, since Agamemnon is not visible; it makes a very heavy 'in-built' stage-direction.]

1348–71 The Chorus dither when Agamemnon is killed; we can accept this hesitation, which their physical frailty (72–5) excuses. The debate is not Aeschylus' helplessness in the face of any convention which prevented the Chorus from leaving the scene (the Chorus leaves it at *Eum.* 231), still less from entering the central stage-door, but a further indication of Clytemnestra's dominance in the palace and over its males—soon to be confirmed in her triumphant display of her victims, 1372 ff. The dithering also adds a little to the sense of inevitability.

   The twelve members of the Chorus each have here a couplet; such dramatic fragmentation is found nowhere else in surviving Tragedy. The Chorus-leader alone spoke 1344 and 1346–7, which are in trochaic tetrameters, the excited dialogue-metre which recurs in the fraught final scene 1649–73 (see Introduction, §3.2, at end). The Leader probably spoke the final couplet, 1370–1.

1351 *freshly streaming sword*: i.e. catch the killer red-handed.

1356 *delay's reputation*: that is, in a well-known proverb; the language itself suggests a maxim (like 1359, 1369; for this habit of Aeschylus see 251 and n.). This speaker reverses the attitude of 1353.

1359 [There is a problem of idiom in the Greek words *for it*, with both text and translation disputed.]

1367 *divine*: sounding artificial in English, but inoffensive in the Greek, with an echo of Cassandra's divinations, 1098–9 etc.

1370 *I am getting a majority*: a rather free translation of 'I am being filled', the verb apparently being used figuratively in an image from a voting-urn filling up; the literal picture occurred at 817.

1371 *how things are with the son of Atreus*: another seemingly 'flat' sentiment; but the Greek is in fact extraordinary in expression, ending the verse-line (and the whole sequence since 1346) with the word 'how'.

1372 *s.d.*: a blood-spattered Clytemnestra (1390–2) is revealed standing over the bodies of Agamemnon, still in the bath (1539–40) and enveloped in robing (1382–3, 1492 and 1516), and of Cassandra (1444–6). The theatrical moment will be matched by the exposure of Clytemnestra and Aegisthus, with their killer Orestes standing over them, at *LB* 973—enveloped in the very robing they had used to trap Agamemnon (981–2 etc.): see Introduction, §2.4, at n. 28.

1373–5 *not feel shame*: echoing her words at 856; cf. 614. *hostilities . . . enemies . . . friends*: see the Chorus's hints at 788–92, 797–8, Agamemnon at 840 (and for the idea Cassandra at 1272). *net-fence of harm*: ensnaring Agamemnon, as forecast by Cassandra at 1115–16; cf. 1382 and n.

1377–8 [The text is very uncertain; *in fulfilment* (cf. Clytemnestra at 973–4) is conjectural.]

1380 *I shall not deny it*: so also Orestes after his matricide, *Eum.* 463, 588, 611; it is a law-court defendant's anticipatory manoeuvre.

1382–3 *with no way through*: literally 'without limit', the first implicit in the second; the fatal garment is an 'endless robe' at *Eum.* 634, cf. n. to *LB* 980. Aeschylus' own order of words puts the phrase immediately after *death* in 1382. *stake out round*: the net is properly one thrown to catch fish but seems to have only a broad meaning also at *LB* 492, of the same picture. Clytemnestra's present tenses (1383–90) are typical of vivid narrative (e.g. 325–36), but seem here to convey her continued relish in the moment of vengeance. *evil wealth of clothing*: fatal in its heavy richness and extent.

1385–6 *deal him a third . . . Zeus below the earth . . . saviour*: grim reversal, like *LB* 577–8, of the usual third libation to Olympian Zeus the Saviour (246 above and n.), 'Zeus of the dead' here refers to Hades, as at *Suppliants* 156 f. 'Zeus of the earth, the most hospitable to the many dead', 231.

1388–9 [*after his fall*: marked as corrupt by West; 'as he breathes' is conjectured. The whole expression of these two lines is imperfectly understood. *quick blood from his throat-wound*: somewhat freely rendering an awkward phrase exactly paralleled in the possibly derivative fourth-century BC anonymous melodrama *Rhesus* 790–1.]

1391–2 *Zeus' sparkling gift*: rainfall, n. to 1014–17. The simile becomes metaphor at 1533, a 'rain of blood'; both pervert the idea of fertility, alluding to extinction of Agamemnon's line: cf. *LB* 502–9.

1395–8 *mixing-bowl*: normally celebrating a victorious return, *LB* 344. *curse-laden evil*: apparently anticipating the imminent realization of the family-curse's power (1468–84, 1501–76), but also an echo of Aulis, 237. [West moves these lines, with a small change in 1395–6, to create a challenging conclusion in 1393–4, immediately answered by the Chorus, 1399–1400.]

1393–4 Scornful politeness in 1393 (cf. the more placatory 855 and 1657), near-contempt in 1394 (cf. 1049).

1401–2 *like a witless woman*: a reversion to Clytemnestra's earlier scorn for these males, 275–7, cf. 348, 613. *those who know*: for this idiom inviting complicity from those who matter (Aegisthus) cf. the Watchman at 39.

1405–6 *architect*: the Wrath in the house was this, 153. *This is how things are*: repeating 1393, in triumphant finality.

1407–1575 For the style of this alternating sequence first of lyric and speech and then of lyric and chanting, compare 1072–1177 and n. Clytemnestra begins with spoken arguments against the Chorus's lyric protests, but from 1462 her own growing passion and anxiety move convincingly into lyric as well.

1407 *did you taste*: the Chorus can imagine Clytemnestra's evil acts only as the result of evil potions; cf. Cassandra's confused picture of Clytemnestra poisoning her, 1261–3 and n.

1408–11 In 1409 *rite of death* looks back to 1118, Cassandra's prophecy of Agamemnon's murder as a 'sacrifice' which leads to stoning. For the rhythm and sound of 1410 cf. e.g. 1541 (n.). *put out of the city*: the penalty in historical Athens for involuntary homicide, but such outlawry is the Furies' punishment for kin-murder, *Eum.* 210, 421. *mighty hate*: the adjective is Homeric, usually describing huge warriors, as at *Seven* 794. [In the words *incurring* as far as *cut them off* both punctuation and interpretation are insecure; some editors make *curse* the object of *thrown off* and *cut off*, which seems very forced.]

1412–13 *sentence*: the legal imagery again; cf. 1420–1, 1431, etc. *people's spoken curse*: the exact repetition from 1409 is striking; similar wording at 1616.

1415 *He took no special account*: Clytemnestra's imagination of Aulis is naturally very different from that of the Chorus at 206–27.

1420 *witnessed*: 1196; as at *LB* 980, *Eum.* 732 a quasi-legal term.

1422 [*for one . . . to rule me*: the Greek syntax is very strained, and some editors suspect loss of text.]

1424 *you shall be taught*: an idiom of threats, 1619, 1649 (both from Aegisthus).

1427–8 *smear* translates 'fat', which suggests half-congealed blood. *in your eyes*: blood-shot, symptomatic of crazed killing. [*exactly as etc.*: some editors join this clause rather with *the thick smear etc.*; also *obvious* is insecure.]

1429–30 The law of exact retribution again, 1318 etc.; 'blow for blow' also at *LB* 310–12. *deprived of your friends*: Clytemnestra will lose her 'friend' Aegisthus (1435 ff., cf. *LB* 893, 976).

1431 *you are to hear*: admonitory, like 1421 'I tell you', and the language echoes the assertion of oaths in a law-court.

1432 *Justice fulfilled*: 996–7 from the Chorus, but we recall just again Clytemnestra's own 973–4.

1434–6 *no expectation treads in fear's palace*: she does not expect to be fearful. Abstractions operating in a house, 774 ff.; cf. Introduction, pp. xxxiii ff. *Aegisthus*: the first time he is named, emphasized by the Greek word-order. Clytemnestra is answering 1429 (n.).

1438–43 *Here he lies*: the switch from Aegisthus to Agamemnon is very sudden and awkwardly phrased, so that some editors suspect a loss of text. A crescendo of abuse: Agamemnon is a philanderer; *any Chryseis* (a contemptuous plural in the Greek) is a reference to Homer, *Iliad* 1.112–15, where Agamemnon is said to prefer this captive girl to his wife, because of her looks, intelligence, and handicrafts. Cassandra is twice abused in derogatory terms; *faithful* too is scornful—this is what Clytemnestra claimed for herself, 606. The final insult *plying . . . loom* is much debated. West insists that the Greek compound adjective 'plying, wearing away a loom' is to be understood from the *Iliad*, as if the praise there of Chryseis' work is contemptuously transferred to a Cassandra reduced to captive drudgery; but no loom-work could be done on shipboard, so that the image connotes Cassandra's nightly work as a concubine, and not only of Agamemnon. The explicit translation 'wearing away the ship's benches' is also suggested, and some scholars find in it a second meaning, 'wearing away . . . like a mast', in obscene allusion to Agamemnon's personal 'mast' (the Greek noun can mean both). Tragedy can be astonishingly direct in sexual imagery: cf. 1206, *Eum.* 660.

1443 *their proper honour*: sardonic; they are lying together still, in death as in life; cf. on 'his lover': in the next note.

1446–7 *like a swan*: the first literary appearance of the swan's death-song, but the point is rather that the bird was sacred to Apollo, Cassandra's prophetic inspiration. It does not matter that Clytemnestra was not on stage to hear it. *his lover*: the particular Greek word insinuates that Cassandra took the initiative. At *LB* 906–7 Orestes cruelly mocks Clytemnestra's love for Aegisthus before he kills her, and again when they lie together in death, 976–7, cf. 894–5. *their bed*: the union with Agamemnon adds spice to her triumphant vengeance. *added relish*: colloquially elsewhere connotes adultery. [*their bed* is West's conjecture; the MSS have 'he brought in an added relish for my bed for my luxuriance', but such a hint of her own sexual frisson seems improbable.]

1449 *long-watchful by the bed*: in protracted final illness.

1452–3 *guardian*: Agamemnon himself applied this term to Clytemnestra, 914. *through a woman*: the wording of 448: Helen.

1455–61 *demented Helen this conforms* with the idea that Agamemnon's own madness began his troubles, 223: see on 'Atê' in n. to 1192–3. *destroying . . . many . . . lives under Troy*: phrasing drawn from Homer, *Iliad* 1.3 (Achilles' lethal anger); for destructive Helen cf. 62–5, 405–6, 689–90 above and *Odyssey* 11.436 ff., 14.68 f. *decked . . . with . . . flowers*: the image recurs at *LB* 150, but of keening which 'adorns' grief. The shift from the cause, *Strife*, through the act, *blood* (that of Thyestes' children; Iphigenia's), to the effect, *woe*, is allusive: Helen is the agent of the *house*'s personified destruction. *Strife . . . strong*: the assonance reflects the Greek, which juxtaposes the two words for etymological play. 'Bloody Strife', also *LB* 474. [The translation 'strong to subdue' is insecure; possibly 'strongly-founded'.]

1462–6 *death as your fate*: recalls 1451, just as *singly destroying . . . lives . . . many* deliberately repeats 1456–7.

1468–70 *demon*: of bloody persecution, 1476–9 etc.: Introduction, p. xxxiii. *house and its two brother Tantalids*: an indication that the family curse began its power three generations ago (cf. 1476), even before Atreus and Thyestes; see Introduction, p. xxii and Family Tree. For Tantalus' crime see n. to 1091–2; he was given special punishment in Hades. Only Agamemnon and Menelaus are meant here, however; they inhabit one house in the *Oresteia*, 400 and n. *equal in their temper*: i.e. Helen and Clytemnestra (half-sisters) are identically 'driven' women: they are both adulterous, and both bring death.

1472–4 *it stands . . . boasting*: that is, the demon (1467), a remarkable change to third person from second [but some editors make the participle feminine, that is, Clytemnestra, to echo her words at 1394]. *tunelessly*: cf. the Chorus on Cassandra at 1142. An ancient commentator suggests that the Greek word has a double meaning: (the crow caws) tunelessly, (the demon boasts) lawlessly (both are indeed possible); but in 1481 ff. the Chorus accept that everything is Zeus' doing. [The words [*evil in its*] plausibly fill up damage at the end of the Greek line.]

1476 *thrice-fattened*: upon three generations, those of Thyestes' children, Agamemnon, and Iphigenia (and her brother Orestes), cf. 1468–70 and n.

1478–81 The imagery in 1480 is from an obstinately suppurating wound (cf. *LB* 471 and n.). [The text here is most insecure: *afflicts it* is a conjecture for MSS '(is) in the bowels'.]

1481 [*for this house* gives good sense but contains a metrical problem so far unsolved.]

1484–7 *oh, grief indeed!—through Zeus*: despairing recognition that it is not the house's demon, still less human agency, which is the ultimate cause of ruin, in this as in everything, but the working of Zeus' justice (Introduction, §2.3, at start). Contrast the optimism of the 'Hymn to Zeus' at 160 ff., which nevertheless contains a premonition, 176–8. With 1487 compare *Suppliants* 823–4 'What is fulfilled for mortals without you?', part of a prayer to Zeus Almighty (*Eum.* 918, cf. 781, 973 above).

1490–6 = 1514–20 Responding stanzas of this type mark great passion: see n. to 1072–1177.

1492–3 = 1516–17 *spider's web*: it is also literally a woven garment, 1580. [*breathing*: the present tense is hard to understand, and the Greek form is metrically suspect.]

1494–6 = 1518–20 *ignoble*: literally 'unfree', lacking dignity in the manner of death and now its display; again at 1521, cf. 1539–40.

1499 *reckon in*: the apparent meaning. Since Clytemnestra is indeed Agamemnon's wife (1404), she asks for the physical fact to be discounted from the moral reckoning. The equivocation anticipates those about the relationship in blood between husband, wife, mother, and son in Orestes' trial, *Eum.* 212, 605–66.

1501 *demon of revenge*: 1508 again, a more explicit name for the 'demon' of 1468 etc.

1503 *full-grown sacrifice . . . young ones*: adult paying for infants, Thyestes' children, themselves seen as ritual victims (once more in 'perverted' sacrifice, 1592–8).

1507 *How, how . . . ?*: a colloquialism expressing extreme incredulity. *The demon coming from his father*: Atreus' crime is punished in his son.

1511–12 *black Ares*: the War-god is to join in Orestes' revenge, *LB* 938, cf. 461, *Eum.* 355: Introduction, p. xxxiv.

1522–4 The reference of *treachery* in 1524 is possibly to Agamemnon's deceitful bringing of Iphigenia to Aulis, purportedly to marry Achilles, a detail of the myth not explicit in the *Oresteia*: see Introduction, §2.1, at n. 10. [The incompletely logical sequence, and a metrical problem, prove the loss of a verse, exemplified by

West as 'and death through treachery was his lot, not unjustly'; some editors delete 1521.]

1526–7 *What his actions deserved . . . suffers*: the idea of 533, 1529, 1564; cf. n. to 177. Here it is expressed in two phrases similar in grammar, rhythm, and sound, a device common in axioms; cf. 1562–4 and n. to 1541. [West marks *Iphigenia* corrupt (and there is a metrical problem); perhaps the name was introduced to help supply the loss of wording; a verb such as *sacrificed* is certainly missing.]

1534 *the shower gives way*: to (continuous) *rain*, apparently meaning that Agamemnon's death will soon be followed by a greater storm, 1535–6.

1535–6 Fate arms Justice also at *LB* 646–8. [The text of these lines is much emended by conjecture.]

1540 *base couch*: cf. 1518.

1541 *Who will inter . . . lament him*: solemnity, 'liturgical' or 'sacral' in character, by means of two rhythmically equal clauses; similar effects at e.g. 1410, 1552; Introduction, §3.3, at n. 33.

1543 *Will you be hard enough*: she is similarly accused after the interment, *LB* 433.

1545 *graceless grace*: a description repeated at *LB* 44.

1549–50 *godlike man*: a Homerism, used of the living Orestes at *LB* 867—and of the dead Darius at *Persians* 634, 642. *with a true heart*: cf. the Chorus at 787–98, 1491.

1552 *he had his fall . . . his interment*: calculated assonance in a distinctively rhythmic line.

1554 *by outsiders*: cf. *LB* 430–3. [This is West's adventurous conjecture for MSS 'from the house'; it produces an unattested word but is consistent with *LB* 430–3. Even in the underworld the mourning Iphigenia (1555) would be 'from the house'.]

1555–9 *Iphigenia . . . welcome . . . swift . . . crossing . . . kiss*: grim reversal of almost all the details of the scene at Aulis, 228–47 (the 'crossing' at 190–1 is here the swift crossing of Death's river). *sorrow*: the Greek noun <u>ach-</u> ('sorrow') plays on the name Acheron, river of Sorrow (1160 and n.); for the 'sorrows' at Aulis see 194–8, for Agamemnon's 204.

1560–6 The Chorus again confess their ambivalence (cf. 1530–2); the law of retaliation (1429–30 etc.) is also a moral dilemma: 1576, 1600–2 and n. Their *issues hard to decide* in 1561 and Clytemnestra's pronouncement in 1567 appropriately surround lines of consistently gnomic and allusive expression (cf. n. to 1356)—and the implicit prediction ('oracle', 1567) of future ruin, 1562, 1566. For 1562–4 *'the doer suffers'* cf. 177 and n. *glued*: not a rare metaphor, from carpentry.

1567 *the oracle*: the Chorus's words in 1563–6 are perceived as a poetic truth: while Zeus' law remains, the family will not escape destruction.

1571 *Pleisthenidae*: the whole family line, named from Pleisthenes (1602), a remote ancestor, like the 'Tantalids' from Tantalus at 1469: see the Family Tree.

1575–6 On these lines, Clytemnestra's recognition that she too is caught in the Curse's working, see Introduction, p. xxxiv. The present tenses imply she has already realized her hopes, and the colloquial *quite contents me* perhaps registers some unease.

1577 *kindly day*: cf. the Herald's grateful greeting, 508 (n.), 636.

1580 *woven robes of the Furies*: fatal instruments of the Curse (1114–20), as Aegisthus seems to recognize in 1600. *woven*: the spider's web, 1492.

1585 *his power was disputed*: Aegisthus' narrative of his father's curse (Cassandra gave some allusive details at 1095–7, 1217–22) was well known to the audience. The allusion here is to Thyestes' seduction of Atreus' wife, partly to gain the golden ram which was the god-given emblem of the kingship (cf. Introduction, §2.1, at end).

1586–9 *banished . . . suppliant . . . security*: as cuckold Atreus could have killed the adulterer; by returning as suppliant to his own hearth Thyestes averted his own death but provoked his children's.

1591–2 *eager rather than amiable*: this understatement of Atreus' vile intention both emphasizes the sentence's shocking end and adds colour to Aegisthus' clumsy exultation; Aeschylus perhaps designs to provoke attention in the audience. Aegisthus means, 'Atreus was only too eager to serve his brother a far from amiable meal'; hence 1592 *cheerfully seeming*. [The text is nevertheless questioned because of the flat expression.] *a day for butchered meat*: marking festivity and only in rich houses; meat otherwise eaten was generally from sacrificial animals (cf. *LB* 483–5 and n.). The word for 'butchered meat' perhaps recalls the initial butchery by Tantalus of his own son Pelops, 1091–2.

1595–6 *combs of fingers*: a vivid and characteristically Aeschylean metaphor. *seated separately*: reflecting his status as a polluted suppliant—just as Euripides describes the matricidal Orestes at Athens, *Iphigenia in Tauris* 949, but as Orestes denies at *Eum.* 237. [*seated . . . indistinguishable parts*: only an approximation to what Aeschylus may have meant; corruption of the text is certain, and loss possible.]

1597 *ended the safety . . . for Atreus' line*: Orestes' anxiety at *LB* 505.

1598 *monstrousness of the deed*: literally 'deed contrary to immutable fate'; so dire, it signalled dire consequence.

1600–2 *intolerable form* with this apparently insipid phrase Thyestes intends death for death, to extinguish the line, and for each death to be 'intolerable'—kindred murder, requiring the same retaliation. The *Pelopidae* (also *LB* 503) and the Pleisthenidae (1570 above) are both family names. *thus should perish totally*: a formula of curses. [Either 1600 or 1602 is deleted by some editors, to remove adjacent references to one family through different ancestors.]

1604 *scheme*: literally 'sew, stitch'; the weak metaphor again at *LB* 221, *Eum.* 26. Aegisthus repeats his claim at 1609, but at 1636 he backs away from the Chorus's attack on his cunning by disclaiming it as Clytemnestra's.

1605 *third child after ten others*: if sound, an archaic formulation perhaps intended to evoke Aegisthus' terrible duty to avenge his father. The number thirteen was variously significant, not always unluckily.

1607–9 *Justice brought me back again*: Clytemnestra claimed this for Agamemnon (911); then Cassandra forecast it for Orestes (1280–4), and the Chorus hope for it, 1647–8, 1667—and the event proves it, *LB* 3, 946–52, *Eum.* 402. *from outside*: like Orestes later, *LB* 115. Aegisthus means, he began scheming before he entered the house as Clytemnestra's lover, although Cassandra located him firmly inside it (1225), as Clytemnestra appeared to do at 1435–7 and as the Chorus do at 1626. *ill intent*: Aegisthus seems to recognize the questionable morality of what he and Clytemnestra have done; as does she, 1571, 1654–6.

1610 *death is well for me too*: either almost crudely ironic or alluding to a common prayer, e.g. 539, *LB* 438.

1612 *arrogance amid others' disaster*: the Chorus rebuke Clytemnestra similarly, 1399–1400, 1426–8.

1615–16 *in the court of justice*: *LB* 987. *people's curse, for stones*: see n. to 1117–18, cf. 1413. Such executions took place amid communal execration. *at your head*: English idiom slightly misrepresents a poetic circumlocution ('your head will not escape . . .') which is also part of a curse-formula.

1617–18 *those at the helm control the ship*: for this metaphor of government see *Eum.* 16.

1619–20 *you shall know . . . to be taught*: repeating Clytemnestra's words at 1425; cf. Aegisthus again at 1649.

1621–3 *diviner-doctors*: one word in the Greek, registering the fusion of the two arts (particularly in the patron-god of both, Apollo, *Eum.* 62). The 'diviners' will reveal the Chorus's folly and its consequences, the 'doctors' cure it by starvation. For the metaphor here cf. *LB* 699, hope as a 'doctor'. [*even old age* is placed anomalously between *chains* and *floggings* in the Greek word-order, probably to emphasize it; but some editors change it to a third torment, e.g. 'flogging-straps'.]

1623–4 *see . . . kick . . . hit . . . get hurt*: three successive commonplaces, effecting harsh but empty bluster; cf. n. to 1628–32. Line 1623 may also be translated 'Do you not see, when you see this?'

1625–7 The Greek syntax is severely disjointed, suggesting the Chorus's outrage. *kept the house at home*: Cassandra's jibe at his cowardice, 1224 (n.).

1628–32 *begetters of tears to come*: Aegisthus' language varies between the high-flown (here, 1621–3, 1639–42) and the everyday (1623–4); he is all uneasy threats. *lead . . . led away* (to prison, 1621): a crude word-play, again suggestive of weakness. *silly yelping*: unlike the tuneful and effective singing of Orpheus (1629). Clytemnestra repeats this insult, 1672.

1638 *this man's wealth*: implicitly as much a motive for the killing as revenge: 1669, Clytemnestra at 1673 (and perhaps 350: n.), cf. Electra's accusation at *LB* 137 (n.); cf. Introduction, p. xxxix.

1640 *trace-horse*: fed for strength, and loosely harnessed: 842 and n.

1641 *hard friend hunger . . . softened*: expanding the threat of 1621; *houses with*: metaphor as in 1004, but phrased here in a 'kenning' like 'mud's sister', 495–7 (n.).

1643 *slay and strip*: the (single) Greek verb pointedly evokes the Homeric battlefield (cf. *LB* 347), where such stripping inevitably follows death (e.g. of Patroclus at *Iliad* 17.187). The Chorus mean, Aegisthus had not been there and is no hero.

1645 *in an act polluting land*: cf. 1669. Alternative translation: 'a woman with you, a pollution to land . . .'.

1648 *all-victorious*: the adjective connotes the brutal athletic pancration, 169 and n.

1649–end [The text is badly damaged throughout, in part because the metre changes to a 'quicker' spoken rhythm, as at 1348–71; see n. In 1649–53 the distribution of the voice-parts is that now generally accepted by editors; the MSS give 1651 to the Chorus: see next n.]

1652 *hilt is to hand*: because the Chorus use not swords but staffs (75), these words mock Aegisthus.

1653 *You die?*: a mild subterfuge in translation; literally '(your words) that you are dead'. Aeschylus has Aegisthus exploit also the Greek ambiguity of 1652 *I do not refuse to die*, which can be understood as 'I do not deny I am dead': so *we choose this outcome* follows.

1656 [*ruin*: West's conjecture, the idea of 1524, 1566; 'let us shed no (more) blood' is generally read.]

1657–8 *esteemed elders*: after her scorn at 1393–4, Clytemnestra is placatory again (cf. her 855)—but at 1672 she is back to abuse, once the Chorus have continued their hostility. [The text of these two lines is extremely insecure and in part conjectural, including the word *esteemed*; some text may have been lost.]

1659–60 *heavy hoof*: for a 'demon' *heavy* in jumping on the afflicted see the Furies at *Eum.* 372–4; cf. the dream at *LB* 37 and fortune falling heavily 1175 above, 1463. [*a remedy for* is conjectural for 'enough of'.]

1661 *what I say, a woman . . . worth hearing*: Clytemnestra is now less combative than at 277, 348, 592, 1401, 1421–5.

1662–4 *glory*: sense uncertain: the Greek verb seems to mean 'pick the flower from', and to be a metaphor like that at 1458 'wreathed yourself with flowers'. [*glory* has found no convincing conjecture—and much of these three lines in the MSS is uncertainly interpreted or subject to conjecture.]

1665 *Argives*: i.e. none who are loyal to the royal line; cf. the Chorus at 805–9 and Orestes at *LB* 302–4, 503.

1668 *I'm well aware . . . hopes*: derisively alluding to a proverb; but Aegisthus was himself an exile, 1606.

1669 *get yourself fat*: counter-derision, and colloquial; cf. 276 and n., and 1638.

1671 *like a cockerel*: loud, proud and quarrelsome—and only indoors (cf. *Eum.* 861–3). *near the hen*: i.e. by implication Aegisthus is uxorious.

1672–3 *yelping*: Clytemnestra repeats Aegisthus' contemptuous 1630. [The words *I* and *well* are missing from the end of the two Greek lines in the MSS.]

LIBATION BEARERS

THE text of this play depends upon a single medieval manuscript which is often damaged or corrupt over long passages. Any introductory matter which may have survived from antiquity is also lost: see the beginning of the Explanatory Notes for the other two plays.

Scene: the small permanent altar to Dionysus which stood in the centre of the *orkhêstra* seems to have represented Agamemnon's tomb. The tomb would not be so close to the palace-door in real life, but it focuses the ritual nature of the play's first part (1–584), in the formal approach of the Libation Bearers to it (10–21), the Chorus's first song at it (22–83), the intense scene round it which reunites Electra and Orestes and draws out their hopes and fears (84–305), the invocatory lyrics over it (306–475: see separate n.) and Orestes' plan to avenge its occupant (479–584). In the second part (585–end), where the palace-door resumes the importance it had in *Agamemnon*, the tomb remains significant, for the intentions it has focused are put into effect in the same theatrical space.

1–3 *Fragment 1. paternal powers*: two meanings appear possible. Orestes' appeal to *Hermes of the Underworld* indicates that the god is to secure the dead Agamemnon's influence for his son (40, 405–19, 727, etc.) and to uphold Orestes' eventual succession to his father's kingly power (480, cf. 126); but Hermes is also to exercise his own father Zeus' powers in Hades, for just revenge (18, 124 ff., 382 ff.). A symbolic image of Hermes stood at house-doors, marking his power over the crossing of important boundaries like thresholds; Orestes must soon enter the palace (cf. n. to 583). The god's name means 'sender, escorter' (cf. *Eum*. 90 and n.), and he is invoked here also as the intermediary between the living and the dead (165, 124–5, 622). *watching over*: a constant belief and appeal of the avenging parties in this play and the next: 126, 489, 693, 985, 1063, *Eum*. 220, 224, 275, 296, 518, 531, 740 (cf. also *Ag*. 1579). *I ask*: cf. 480; 'asking' begins also *Ag*. 1. *my return from exile*: Orestes uses the term regular for such returns (cf. 'exile' at 136, 254 etc.); his greeting to his home echoes that of Agamemnon at *Ag*. 810 ff..

3a *Fragment 2*. This is a prose paraphrase of Aeschylus' original words and drawn from an ancient commentator on Aristophanes' *Frogs* (we owe all of *Fragments 1–4* to quotation in *Frogs*, where Aeschylus' style is often ridiculed).

5 *Fragment 4. on my father's grave-mound*: that is, standing directly above the dead man (501), where offerings were put or poured (87, 129, etc.). *to listen, to hear:* the apparent tautology expresses an intense appeal; 'hear' implies 'act upon', cf. 459, 500, 508.

6–7 *Fragment 5. a lock of my hair*: later found by Electra, 168 ff. *Inachus:* river-god of Argos, native rivers like native soil being prime recipients of thank-offerings. Hair is a (safe) sacrifice from the living body, and the cutting signifies the reversal of normal growth; cf. n. to 22–31.

7a *Fragment 6* is possibly not authentic; *rock-hard ground* seems to contradict the leaving of footprints (205 ff.).

8–9 *Fragment 7. stretch out my hand*: in a gesture of ritual farewell (cf. n. to 1015). Orestes expressly repairs the lack at 1014; Electra too was not at her father's funeral, 444 ff.

15 *appeasements of the dead:* to avert their ill-will, cf. 44 etc.; to placate the dead Darius, *Persians* 610 ff. Orestes is made to anticipate that Electra's offerings are not her own; cf. 21.

19 *Be my ally*: closing the prologue with a heavy echo from its first lines, 2, *Fragment 1*; for the device cf. *Ag.* 1 and 20. The appeal is thematic in Orestes' 'fight' for vengeance, 245, 456–60, 478, 497, etc.

21 *s.d.*: *Orestes and Pylades withdraw to one side*: or, it has been suggested, either behind the symbolic image of Apollo of the Streets which stood outside street-doors (*Ag.* 1081 and n.), or into the doorway itself.

22–83 The entry of the Chorus is not a marching song, as in *Ag.* 40–103, but fully danced lyric; the Chorus have had time during Orestes' last words (10–21) to take their position in the *orkhêstra*. They are Electra's slave-women (75–9, cf. 84), supporting her endless and frustrated grief for her father (22–31, 81–3). Here they report Clytemnestra's terror in response to her nightmare (32–41), which has led to her sending the libations (42–54); she may have cowed the people (55–9), but justice for the polluting murder of Agamemnon will come inevitably (60–74). In this way the Chorus enlarge on the meaning of Orestes' return (which for them is still only a hope, 115, 182), and prepare the audience for the circumstances which will both encourage and challenge him.

22–31 One of the fullest poetic descriptions of the *kommos* ('beating'), the rhythmic striking and tearing of head, face, arms, and body in ritual grief, and of clothes, all signifying the damage done by a death to normal life; cf. 423–8.

31 *laughterless disaster:* the same pathetic expression at 448, voiced by Electra.

32–41 *dream-prophet*: the dream prophesies the terrible future (523 ff.—its content becomes reality, 928–9) and takes on the screaming voice of the dreamer, Clytemnestra (35–6, 535). The dream's mere fact implies its fulfilment; the house's *interpreters* (37, cf. *Ag.* 409) guarantee the gods' meaning. *rancour*: this word for the nursed anger of the house's 'demon' (*Ag.* 1468, 1501, etc. and nn.) and of the Furies becomes frequent: *LB* 41, 393, 593, 924, 952,

1025, 1054, *Eum.* 220, 426, 501, 800, 841, 900; cf. Introduction, p. xxxiv. [Line 32 in the MS contains also the name 'Phoebus', described by *piercing and shrill*, for which ancient commentators give the variant 'terror'; some editors rewrite the line in order to preserve it, with 'terror prophetic in dreams', and compare 070 and (g. 9)0 9 for the idea]

44–7 *this grace that is graceless*: the Greek words deliberately echo the 'graceless grace' of Clytemnestra's funeral for Agamemnon, *Ag.* 1545; cf. 517 below. Now, the 'grace' is to avert his ill-will. *Earth, our good mother*: invoked not only as the mother and nurse of all life and its receiver again upon death (127–8, cf. 67), but also as the origin of dreams (*Suppliants* 890 ff.), as potential averter of menace from the dead (41–2, 45, 66–7), and as 'drinker' and avenger of blood wrongly shed (47, 66, 399, cf. 149). *her words*: her hypocritical instruction; even to name them risks more harm (cf. *Ag.* 1247). Electra has the same reluctance, 87 ff. The word *fear* has the same place in the responding line 59.

48 *once blood falls*: Agamemnon's, as in the same image at *Ag.* 1018 ff. The images of blood falling and requiring retaliation pervade the trilogy from *Ag.* 134 ff., 209, 1018 (n.),1092, etc. onward, e.g. below, 400–2, 468. The play moves towards hope that Aegisthus' and Clytemnestra's blood will make the amends, cleansing the pollution (963–8: cf. 50), but the hope is quickly falsified (1038 etc.).

52 *blackness covers the house*: 811, *Eum.* 380.

55–6 The *respect* never lost by a majestic king like Agamemnon (157, 357, 723–5 and n.) is replaced by fear of his materialistic usurper Aegisthus (*Ag.* 1669, *LB* 137 etc.).

61–5 *Justice weighs down . . . no fixed end*: lines both insecure in text (a good deal is conjectural) and obscure; they seem to describe punishment successively as evident and immediate; dimly perceived but inevitable even if delayed; invisible but absolute and endless. The lines perhaps evoke the terrifying and inevitable punishment of bloodshed by the Furies, 66–70.

66–7 *bloodshed drunk up by Earth its nurse*: 127–8, cf. n. to 48 above. *the vengeful blood is set hard*: the equation of blood soaked away with the same blood congealing is deliberately striking: one part remains immovably to avenge the other, cf. *Ag.* 1511–12.

68–70 The images of disease and cure again, for the threatened or criminal house of Atreus, e.g. 472, 516, 539; n. to *Ag.* 17. [After *disease* the MS impossibly repeats the final words of Antistrophe 2, 64–5 'grow full; some have right with no fixed end'.]

71 *who assaults a bridal bower*: virginity once taken is irreparable, but the allusion is to Paris' crime (*Ag.* 402, 1156, etc.), which was as irredeemable as the family blood-letting to which it has led.

77–9 [*led me . . . to my heart*: text, metre, and sense are all insecure.]

81–2 *these garments hide my weeping*: the women veil their heads in inexpressible sorrow.

92 *offering*: for its nature see nn. to *Ag.* 94–6, *Eum.* 106–9.

95 *their goodness deserves*: sardonic inversion of a formulaic prayer; Electra means 'wickedness'.

97 *libation for the earth to drink*: in 164 it reaches Agamemnon through the earth.

99 *with averted eyes*: cf. *Ag.* 778–9, Justice abandoning impure men.

101 *hatred as a habit*:: towards Aegisthus (111) as well as Clytemnestra.

108–23 In this first exchange of the play, stichomythia suits the measured and precisely directed answers with which the Chorus guide a diffident Electra towards appropriating Clytemnestra's offerings, and turning intended appeasements into incitements of her father's pity and aid.

113 *understand this*: the identities of 112. *put your mind to it*: the Chorus encourage Electra to take the chief role in invoking her father, 117.

114 *our side*: the idea recurs at 458, by which time Orestes has joined 'the side'.

120 *judge . . . or a just avenger*: some see here the first hint in the trilogy that the vengeance for Agamemnon may also be subject to judgement, and not go uncontested; the idea is however already clear enough at *Ag.* 1505–12, 1535–6, 1615–16, etc.

123 *to requite an enemy with harm for harm*: *Ag.* 1374, cf. Electra at 144 below, Orestes at 273–4; the wording varies the 'law of retaliation', 310–14 and n.

165, 124 Aeschylus makes Electra repeat the style of Orestes' initial prayer, 1–3, *Fragment 1. those above and those below*: both gods and men. [While loss of text between 123 and 124 is not certain, 165 (if genuine to this play) cannot keep its place and may reasonably be repositioned here. West suggests '(be my aid)', comparing Orestes' appeal at 2, *Fragment 1*.]

131 *kindle . . . as a light*: 961; for this metaphor of salvation see n. to *Ag.* 22–3.

132 *sold off*: like slaves (135); so too Orestes reproving Clytemnestra, 915. *a man in exchange* implies that Aegisthus too is worth no more than someone bought in; cf. Orestes' sneer at 916–17.

140 *more chaste*: as a faithful wife. *my hands to have greater piety*: Clytemnestra's are polluted (378) and her conduct is godless: Electra at
191, Chorus 46, 525.

145–6 *before those whose concern it may be*: for this precautionary
vagueness in an intended curse or prayer of 780 and n., *Ag.* 974.
[These words are conjectural, replacing a line-end in the MS which
duplicates that of 146.]

150 *crown . . . with laments*: as if the laments are wreathed flowers, of
praise (imagery as at *Ag.* 1459). Such laudatory lament is exactly the
content and sequence of the ensuing elaborate *kommos* 306–475 (see
n. and esp. 320–2).

151 *dead man's paean-hymn*: full and proper lament will lead to his
victory (476–8; the hymn again at 343). There is a similar paradox at
Ag. 645, where men's lamentation is a paean-hymn for the powers
which destroyed them. For such hymns, see n. to *Ag.* 246.

152–6 The *bulwark* is Agamemnon's tomb, which will protect his
children from his polluting murderers. The metaphor is used of
Clytemnestra at *Ag.* 257 and of the Areopagus Council at *Eum.* 701.
[The text of these lines is insecure throughout.]

159 *s.d.*: *wail of grief*: their noise is the wild cry associated with
Orientals (Cassandra makes it at *Ag.* 1072, on which see the note):
the Chorus reveal their origin as such at 423 ff. A similar wild cry
comes from inside the palace at 869.

160–3 The Chorus seem to envisage any or all of spear, bow, or sword
as the deliverer's weapons. *Scythia*: approximately the modern
Ukraine and eastward, famous for its archers, *Prometheus* 711. *the
War-god's work*: a Homerism originally, e.g. *Iliad* 11.734, cf. *Seven*
414. [The text of these lines is in part conjectural, but the general
sense is clear.]

164–82 Stichomythia aptly conveys the rapid sequence of surprise,
doubt, and hope which follow Electra's discovery of the hair left by
Orestes on Agamemnon's tomb (5, *Fragment 4*).

167 *my heart is dancing*: metaphor as at 1025, cf. 'leaping' 410, 524.

169 *some slim-waisted girl's*: that is, a lock of elegantly coiffeured hair
could come only from a girl of noble birth and free, not a plainly
combed and clothed slave. *slim-waisted* translates 'deep-waisted', a
Homeric adjective for a woman richly dressed in clothes falling fully
over the waist-band; it describes court-ladies at *Persians* 155.

171 *older from a younger woman*: Greek habitually completes an antithesis when the first idea makes the point adequately ('you're younger,
but tell me'), cf. e.g. 448, 553. The same idea is at *Ag.* 584.

[Lines 170–1 are sometimes moved to follow either 175 or 179, but the Chorus's polite request in 171 suits an early point in the dialogue.]

172–3 Electra prompts the Chorus: 'since there's only myself here to cut off a mourning lock, and you know that I didn't cut this one, you can surely realize that it must belong to Orestes.' *enemies*: only Clytemnestra is meant.

185 *in their thirst*: two implications here: the flood of tears by its simple plenty expresses in reverse Electra's need for relief; the flood is inadequate to her longing for Orestes' return and revenge.

197–9 *whether to . . . or . . . it could*: the uneven syntax expresses Electra's excited hopes.

200 *a glory . . . my father*: perhaps the ideas overlap: 'a glorious honour for my father's tomb'.

201–4 [Moved by some editors to follow 210 'exactly' or (better) 211.]

204 *little seed . . . great root-stock*: (cf. 236, 503; 260) the line of the Atreidae might flourish again; the proverbial imagery perhaps reflects 128 and its implications. The image reappears at Sophocles, *Electra* 420 ff. in Clytemnestra's dream of Orestes resurgent like a tree growing from his father's sceptre.

205–10 Aeschylus' wording is loose here: *contours of the soles* translates Greek 'tendons', but these do not show in a footprint; male and female feet do not match, only perhaps resemble each other in general proportions (the idea comes from Homer, *Odyssey* 4.149, where a father's and a son's feet match). In 206 *equally like* means, equally with the hair. [But the translation *the feet equally like mine* is only an approximation to what Aeschylus may have written. The lines are very corrupt and deleted by some editors, who see in them a duplication of 228–9, similarly suspect; both places seem to have lost verses. West suggests supplementing after 208 '(His [i.e. the fellow-traveller's] *heels* (are in no way akin, but this man's on the other hand,) *and his impressed contours etc.*']

212–24 As in 164–82, the regular but quick pace of stichomythia conveys well Orestes' urgency to reveal himself convincingly to his sister.

215 *the very persons*: allusive plural; Orestes means, only himself.

221 *forming schemes*: for the metaphor in the Greek see n. to *Ag.* 1604.

228 The mechanisms of recognition and reunion between Orestes and Electra became an apparent issue of rivalry between tragedians as each tried to make them more plausible than his predecessors. The scene at Sophocles, *Electra* 1209 ff. is most convincing in its

emotions, while that at Euripides, *Electra* 518 ff. is often thought to be a dismissive parody of Aeschylus' episode here, if not actually inauthentic. [The missing line contained perhaps (West) '(you thought you saw mine; well, here are the feet, here is the hair!)'. But 229 weakly repeats 227, and deletion or rearrangement of 228 and 229 is sometimes suggested.]

232 *picture of a beast*: part of the weaving: see n. to *Ag.* 908–9. It was probably a lion, the family emblem: *Ag.* 1259 and perhaps 825, cf. 938 below (but at Euripides, *Iphigenia in Tauris* 813–14, in the recognition-scene, Iphigenia has woven the golden ram which was at issue between Thyestes and Atreus: see n. to *Ag.* 1584). The famous 'Lion Gate' still stands at the entrance to the royal citadel of Mycenae near Argos.

234 *our nearest and dearest*: Clytemnestra, cf. 173.

238 *it has four parts*: as if the face were a theatrical mask; the four parts (239–43) are: as our father; as our mother, who should be receiving the love I now give you; as our sister, to receive it too were she alive (Iphigenia: 242); and as the faithful brother you have proved to be. This pathetic motif became a commonplace after its first appearance when Andromache addresses her doomed husband Hector at Homer, *Iliad* 6.429–30.

242 *ruthlessly sacrificed*: together with 255–6 the only clear reference to Iphigenia in the play (but see n. to 695). With 'ruthlessly' Electra may seem to make an unfavourable comment on her father's conduct, but the word is intended to evoke her loneliness after his death; it also anticipates Orestes at 255.

237 [The line makes a better climax to Electra's emotion here than after 236, and provides a better immediate cause for the prayer of 244–5, which is appropriate only to Orestes. This necessary transfer can however be made at smaller cost than the supposition of a missing line.]

244–5 *Zeus the third*: see nn. to 578 and Ag. 246–7. *be with me*: the appeal to Agamemnon himself at 456, 460; cf. 2, *Fragment 1*.

246–51 A complex of allusions. Orestes and Electra (offspring of the dead king, Zeus' eagle-agent against Troy, *Ag.* 111 ff.) are caught in the coils of the snake Clytemnestra—but the coils both allude to the 'nets' in which Clytemnestra snared and killed Agamemnon (491–4, *Ag.* 1115 ff. and n., etc.) and which Orestes will use against her (981 ff. below), and are metaphorical. The viper bites rather than strangles its victims, coiling, it was believed, only in copulation with its mate which it then killed (Agamemnon again); in fable the offspring thus engendered break from the womb to avenge the father—as snake-Orestes will emerge and wound Clytemnestra in her dream, 526 ff. and kill her in the event, 928 ff. Both Clytemnestra and Orestes kill with the 'bite' of an edged weapon (see n. to 995, *Eum.* 803). For the animal imagery in this passage see also Introduction, p, lvii.

Zeus is invited to *observe* (246) like a spectator at a sacred rite or in a theatre (metaphor as at *Prometheus* 118, 302; and cf. 238 ff. above)—where Orestes will in fact prove *grown enough* (250) to bring *a father's prey* (251), his treacherous wife's corpse, to display it theatrically: see 973 and especially 980 ff. They do therefore bring 'their father's prey', in the sense of his wife killed to avenge him, *to the nest*, for the Greek word translated 'nest' can also bear the meaning 'stage back-cloth, stage-building, scene'. Alternative interpretations of *prey* are either 'their father's inheritance', his palace and its wealth (135–7, 254, 301, 480–7), not yet secured for themselves by his children but recovered after the killings, 965 ff.; or just 'prey such as a father might bring home from which to live'.

252 *I mean Electra*: strangely obtrusive in English, but the formality of Orestes' prayer to Zeus requires explicit naming of those who hope for his aid; cf. the Chorus at 789, 855 ff.

255–6 *the famous sacrifice*: the one at Aulis, 242. With the appeal to Zeus' self-interest compare the Chorus at 790–3, and the appeal to Agamemnon's interest at 483 ff. (n.).

261 *ox-sacrifice*: see n. to 483.

262 *raise . . . to greatness*: an echo of the image of 204.

268 *on fire in oozing pitch*: deliberately horrific: coated (while still alive: Aeschylus, *Fragment* 478) before burning. Compare the tortures in *Eum.* 186–90.

269 *Loxias*: Apollo. For the name's meaning see n. to *Ag.* 1074–5. *not betray*: *Eum.* 64 and n.

270–4: The first clear exposition in the play of Orestes' impossible future: his inescapable obligation to take revenge is simultaneously the certainty of inescapable punishment; cf. *Ag.* 1560–4.

275 *maddened like a bull . . . property*: the meaning is unclear. With 275 relocated here, after 277, the implication is that Orestes' madness from the Furies (for avenging his father by killing his mother, 1048 ff.) will be part of his punishment and continue the loss of his inheritance; some take the madness to be part of his punishment if he fails to avenge him—but that comes only at 288 'madness'. With the line positioned after 274 the meaning must be that Orestes'

anger at his lost inheritance (cf. 301) will be part of his mad desire to avenge. The line is sometimes transferred to follow 272 or 285.

278–85 Apollo's oracle is apparently presented first as individual to Orestes, then here as general to *men* (278–82, cf. 291); but it may be possible to translate as 'angry acts towards men from the earth's hostile powers'. In *59 seeing clearly . . . in darkness*, the noun to which this participle refers has been lost from the text. If the Greek participle is masculine it must point to Orestes; perhaps the idea is that in the dark underworld too his vision of the persecuting Furies will be no less clear. As an ancient paraphrase suggests, a reference would be more natural to the Furies themselves, or to other infernal powers, as if they had X-ray or infra-red vision or lit their way with torches (cf. n. to *Eum.* 1004–5); if the Greek participle is in the neuter gender, then this latter reference may indeed be possible, for at *Eum.* 644 Apollo uses a neuter plural noun to address the Furies, as 'brutish creatures'. [These lines are badly damaged and some text is lost after 284. In 279 *decreed* is a bold conjecture by West for senseless wording in the MS.]

290 *yoke of beaten bronze*: perhaps literal, a metal yoke, or allusive to the crushing blows of a metal flail, both symbolic of sin's burden; public scapegoats were flogged into outlawry from their city. The Greek word here for 'yoke' usually means the pendent scales of a balance (cf. Justice at 61); it is sometimes emended to 'lash'.

298 *Many desires*: or 'motives': vengeance, 2, 3a, 18, 435–7, etc., repeated at *Eum.* 464; repairing his absence from his father's funeral, 4–9, 300, 1014–15; anger at his own and Electra's deprivations 252–4, 275, 301–4, 407–8, cf. *Eum.* 755–6; desire to restore his house under Zeus, 260–3, 480, cf. *Eum.* 759–60.

303, 305 *their heart . . . at heart*: the same word in the Greek, either deliberately or unconsciously; but the first translates a little awkwardly.

304 *a pair of women*: Clytemnestra and Aegisthus; for his effeminate cowardice see *Ag.* 1224, 1625.

305 *he shall soon find out!*: i.e. I shall force him to the test, to prove that he is no coward. The threat is a colloquialism, used by the blustering Aegisthus himself at *Ag.* 1649; cf. n. to 838 below. [*if he is not* is doubted by editors, either as a hypothesis or as a question 'whether or not he is (a coward)'; some emend to 'whether I am (effeminate)'.]

306–475 The great *kommos* or lamentatory hymn (nn. to 22–31, 150) is sung by Orestes, Electra, and the Chorus over the tomb; it is climactic in ideas and passion as it evokes Agamemnon's murder and appeals for his aid from beyond the grave to avenge it (as

Clytemnestra tried to appease him with her libations). Introduced (306–14) and ended (466–75) by the Chorus, its sequence of metrically corresponding stanzas sung by all three voices (numbered from 1 to 11) and single separating stanzas chanted only by the Chorus (lettered from A to D) is the most complex surviving Greek lyric structure (331 *the lament . . . is roused in its full abundance may be* self-referential). The alternation of the voice-parts has been reconstructed by inference from the text and the ancient commentary; the MS lacks almost all indications. The first two groups of stanzas, each of three 'responding' pairs Strophe 1 to Antistrophe 3 and Str. 4 to Ant. 6, and the single separating stanzas A to D, have the same sequences of voices and responses; and the movement of the content and emotion is progressive (315–422). The third group of three pairs of corresponding stanzas, delimited in the text by Str. 7 to Ant. 8 (423–55), lacks single separating stanzas and has a different sequence of voices and responses (some editors move Str. 9 to follow Ant. 8 in order to regularize the sequence and to emphasize Orestes' moral outrage as he braces himself finally to his task). It is striking that Orestes has only one stanza in this third group, but Electra two—yet in this group an extra intensity is achieved and maintained. Then the polyphonic pair Str. 10 and Ant. 10 scale a new peak of recapitulatory appeal, and make both climax and end (456–65). Finally the purely choral Str. 11 and Ant. 11 (466–75) provide an impassioned general conclusion upon the miseries of the family. We lack the knowledge even to hypothesize, let alone reconstruct, any dance-movements of the parties during the *kommos*; but it is tempting to imagine them, and modern productions understandably attempt them (as in Sir Peter Hall's famous 1980s National Theatre production; cf. Ewans (Bibliography, §1), 172–3, and Wiles (Bibliography, §5, 1997), 82).

There is a similarly unusual but concentric order of stanzas in the purely choral ode 783–837, viz. 1, 2, 1=; 3, A, 3=; 4, 2=; 4=; its order is unrelated to the progression of ideas and emphasis.

306 *powers of Fate:* invoked to operate the retribution inevitable for injustice, 310–14; but the Furies themselves (283) are sometimes addressed with the name 'Fates' because their persecution is the inevitable fate of the polluted killer, e.g. *Eum.* 172. At *Eum.* 961 the Fates are their mother Night's sisters. On their names generally see n. to *Eum.* 1041.

309 *justice changes to the other side*: that is, leaves Clytemnestra and Aegisthus for Orestes and Electra. This is the apparent meaning (but the imagery may be that of 971, *Ag.* 774 ff., justice changing its dwelling, that is, into the house now Orestes has returned); there

seems no authority for an ancient interpretation 'as justice gives its approval'.

310–14 These lines, and 400–2, are the classic Greek exposition of the law 'an eye for an eye' (*Ag.* 1318, n. to *Ag.* 1429–30, Introduction, p. xl), bleaker than the derivative 'knowledge through suffering' of 314, *Ag.* 177 etc. Lines 310 and 312 have the style and rhythm of incantation; cf. e.g. n. to 327–8. *saying three times old*: and therefore authoritative; cf. *Ag.* 750.

315 *father in doom*: a specially coined compound word in the Greek, on the pattern of Paris 'fatal in marriage', *Ag.* 713; the implication is that Agamemnon passes to his son Orestes the dreadful doom inherited from his father Atreus.

317–22 Orestes in 320–2, the Chorus in 329–31, and Electra in 418 all hope that the power and value to the dead which the living conventionally attach to their laments will prove itself in securing assistance from Agamemnon (cf. Electra to the Chorus, 150–1 and n.); so the *lament . . . claims justice*, 330. In 322 the plural *Atreidae* is allusive merely; Agamemnon alone is meant. *waft . . . and reach to you*: a weak metaphor from a favouring wind which carries one to the destination; cf. 814, 821, *Eum.* 137. *sleep's bed*: death, a euphemism no less common in ancient Greece than now.

327–8 *The one meeting death . . . parents*: language, rhythm, and rhyme are sacral: Introduction, p. li. The present tenses in 327–8 and the plurals in 329 register timeless truth for the particular case, Agamemnon's; he is both *the one meeting death* and *the one doing harm*, as the visitor of vengeance on his killer; this was Clytemnestra's fear at 44, Electra's hope at 94–5.

337 *what without evil?*: cf. Agamemnon's words in his dilemma at Aulis, *Ag.* 211.

339 *ruin beyond reversal with three throws*: a wrestler needed three throws to win, *Ag.* 172 and n. At 498 and 866 the wrestling-image signals optimism for Orestes' success, at 692 Clytemnestra's pessimism against the Curse.

344 *bowl*: this noun is idiomatically omitted in the Greek, tempting the translation 'bring in our dear friend (Orestes welcomed in the palace) with newly-mixed bowl'—but it is final victory which is prayed for; Orestes is already home. For the *paean-hymn* see n. to 151.

345–54 A reflection of Homer, *Odyssey* 24.28–34, where Achilles in the Underworld tells Agamemnon he wishes Agamemnon had died at Troy and left glory for his children (*LB* 349).

347 *stripped you:* the Homeric practice: see n. to *Ag.* 1643.

350 *making eyes turn in the streets:* such celebrity is foreseen for herself by Electra at Sophocles, *Electra* 975 ff. if her own revenge-plan succeeds. Cf. 'palaces which fingers point out', *Ag.* 1333.

351 *overseas . . . your tomb:* an idea lamented at *Ag.* 453; a home-tomb is desired, *Ag.* 506.

354 *easy . . . to bear:* acceptable because a heroic death brings everlasting glory.

358 *minister . . . serving the kings:* great mortal kings have the same standing beneath the underworld kings ruled by Hades: Agamemnon at *Ag.* 1528, cf. *Persians* 691; Achilles at Homer, *Odyssey* 11.485.

361 [*holding* is a slight undertranslation of conjectural 'wielding, brandishing', to accommodate the verb's second object, *sceptre:* the MS has 'of (men) filling'.]

367 *his killers:* the change to third person from second in 364 is unexplained; a reverse difficulty at *Ag.* 1472.

369–71 *for someone far off to find out . . . troubles here!:* Electra appears to wish that her father's intending killers had fought and died far away, like the men at Troy, so that Agamemnon's family in Argos would have heard and been sure to escape the mischief which has occurred. [[*to enemies*] : others supply 'to family' or 'to his house'.]

374 *fortune outside this world:* literally 'from beyond the North', characteristic of the Hyperboreans, a mythical people imagined to live there and proverbially blessed by the gods.

375–9 The Chorus make the point that Orestes' and Electra's wishes in 345 ff. and 363 ff. are unreal; and that they must deal with their inheritance of sorrow, 379. *double lash:* perhaps the blows about to be dealt by Orestes and Electra (since Pylades is not mentioned as active until 562; but at 938 the 'double lion' appears to connote Orestes and Pylades jointly), or the double doom which looms for Clytemnestra and Aegisthus; but the reference may be to the two factors of 376–7, Agamemnon's aid and the usurpers' wickedness which condemns them to punishment sooner or later (383–5). [In 378 both the extent of the textual loss and its sense are uncertain.]

380 *sharply . . . through my ears:* this picture also at 452.

382–5 *Zeus . . . send up from below:* Zeus operative in the underworld, cf. 1–2, *Fragment 1* (n.). *ruin from later punishment:* *Ag.* 58 f. and n. to 59, Zeus' punishment of Troy. *parents:* an allusive plural common in the play (e.g. 329 and n., 385, 419). Only Agamemnon is meant, but some take the plural to include also Clytemnestra—but Orestes will not admit that she had any right to retribution; rather, she must pay.

Children will exact punishment for parents if they cannot for themselves.

386–7 *victory-cry*: see n. to *Ag.* 28. [*piercing* : a very doubtful word marked by West as corrupt; but it resembles one fairly confidently translated as 'piercing' (a sword) at 611. No conjecture satisfies.]

390–2 *hovers . . . at the front of my mind*: image as at *Ag.* 975 ff. *anger . . . blowing . . . from the prow*: this meaning is doubtful, since passions normally impel 'from the stern', that is, with a following wind and from where the ship is steered; it is a head-wind which blows from the prow, adverse; if this is the underlying meaning, then anger is frustrating any onset of confidence. [Text and meaning are extremely insecure throughout these three lines.]

395 The Greek has *strike* in the same place in the verse as 'striking' in the corresponding stanza at 381.

400–2 *bloodshed . . . demands . . . blood*: explicit repetition from 313 (see n., and n. to 66–7).

406 *Curses of the slain*: the Furies themselves, *Eum.* 417; cf. n. to *Eum.* 1041. [*of the slain* is implied by the MS reading, and good sense, but its anomalous form and metre cause West to mark it corrupt.]

409 *which way to turn?*: for vengeance. Orestes implores aid from Zeus and his father till the end, 456, 479–509; cf. the Chorus at 1051.

415–17 [The text is badly corrupt, in addition to actual loss; translation can be only approximation, here in line with West's own conjectures.]

418 *tell, for success?*: see n. to 317.

419 *a parent, yes, from her*: a slight overtranslation of a Greek 'allusive' plural (cf. e.g. 385).

421 *Fawn she may*: for Clytemnestra as fawning and deceitful bitch cf. *Ag.* 1228–9. Some editors take the fawning to be Electra's, and the sense overall to be 'though I may fawn, my misery from her is not soothed'; but Electra has been consistently hostile, 101.

423–8 *The beat of my grief . . . wretchedness*: theatrically self-referential; the Chorus recall their entry at 22 ff. In response to Electra's protest of her anger they burst into a frenzy of renewed lament, indicated by suddenly much freer rhythm and onomatopoeic words throughout 423–8; the repeated English participles try to create something of this effect. There are three freshly coined and unique polysyllabic adjectives, completely untranslatable, in 425–6 [they are (unsurprisingly) damaged in the MS and slightly different meanings may well be right.] The corresponding stanza 445–50 is much less colourful. *Arian . . . Cissian*: Middle Eastern, Medic and Persian respectively, and noisily demonstrative; cf. *Persians* 120 ff., 541 ff., 935 ff., 1054 ff. See n. to 159.

429–33 For Clytemnestra refusing Agamemnon an ordinary funeral see n. to 44–7.

436–7 *goth . . . my own hands*: Orestes' subsequent justification at 1027 ff.

439 *Mutilated:* literally 'arm-pitted', with ears, nose, hands, feet, and genitals severed and strung round the neck and beneath the armpits. The intention was to incapacitate the dead man from taking vengeance, by his own action or by begetting children; so Agamemnon is prayed to 'return' as he was before mutilation, 490 (n.). His insulting mutilation is told by Electra at Sophocles, *Electra* 445, where ancient commentators explain the act also as an attempt to placate the gods by 'sacrificing' important parts of the victim.

448 *tears . . . laughter*: see n. to 31 for the idea, 171 for the style of redundant antithesis.

450 *write in your mind*: the mind's recording tablet, *Eum.* 275 etc.

454 [*he is eager . . . himself*: text insecure; some editors write 'you (Orestes) must be eager yourself.']

456 The change to participatory stanzas may indicate that Orestes, Electra, and the Chorus markedly reposition themselves here; cf. n. to 308–475, at the end.

458 *Our side*: 114 and n.

459 *by coming into the light*: as Darius' ghost is invoked, *Persians* 630—where it indeed appears.

461 *War*: for the image of warfare see n. to *Ag.* 1511–12. *justice meet justice:* perhaps a semi-automatic rhythmic echo of *arms meet arms*, to create an incantatory effect (see n. to 310–14). Aeschylus may however be hinting Clytemnestra's claim to justice (e.g. *Ag.* 911–13, 1396), even if Orestes does not (*LB* 434, 930); cf. 120, *Eum.* 492 and n.

466 *troubles . . . born in it*: 379, 649–52, 806, *Ag.* 753, 1190, etc.. *discordant music*: this oxymoron is used of the Furies at *Ag.* 1187, cf. *Eum.* 308.

471 *stanch*: Greek medicine plugged wounds until their own discharge healed them from inside; so with the house of Atreus (cf. e.g. 967–8). Imagery as in 843; cf. n. to *Ag.* 1478–81.

474 *Strife*: as evil spirit in this house, *Ag.* 1461; *bloody* and operative in the Trojan background, 698 and n.

476 *blessed*: the term comprehends primarily the infernal gods, as a kind of precautionary euphemism (475), but is used also of the mortal dead, for the plural means only Agamemnon, who is invoked to aid his children (317 and n.). The term invokes the dead Darius, *Persians* 633.

478 *victory*: the hope variously of the Chorus at 868, Clytemnestra at 890, and Orestes at 584, 1017 (but Aeschylus may have established the motif for him already in the damaged prologue-speech). Compare the refrain at *Ag.* 121 etc. Orestes and Electra now continue their prayers, but in antiphonal dialogue 479–509, after which the Chorus turn him to action.

480 *I ask . . . house*: see 1–2 and n.

482 [*misery*: an attractive supplement, making Electra describe her own suffering with the same word as Apollo describes that of Orestes at *Eum.* 81–3 (n.).]

483 *banquets*: Orestes' return to power will ensure regular and special remembrance for his father, with the burnt animal sacrifices which were offered usually only during the mourning period; after mourning, liquids were usual (15, 92; *Ag.* 96 and n.).

487 *my complete inheritance*: when the deprivations of 132–7 are restored.

489 *to watch over the fight*: the prayer made through Hermes at 1–2 and 727–9, to Apollo at 583.

490 *Persephassa*: a variant name-form for Persephone, who was daughter of the goddess Demeter and abducted into the Underworld by Hades. *in all his handsomeness*: see n. to 439. The idea conventionally praises the warrior slain in his manly prime and beauty, *Ag.* 454.

491–2 *Remember . . . Remember*: stichomythic form adds intensity to this short sequence of appeals (489–96); cf. also 115, where the Chorus instruct Electra to 'Remember Orestes'. *bath . . . net to throw over you*: elaborated at 981 ff.; cf. *Ag.* 1115 ff., 1126 ff., etc.

492–4 *invented a net*: using Agamemnon's own robes, *Ag.* 1382–3. *shamefully*: an ignoble death for a warrior king, 479, 724, etc.

497–8 *Either . . . or*: a collateral pair rather than alternatives, since Orestes will claim Justice for any retaliation, including trickery like his mother's (556–7). *an equal hold*: the wrestling-image again: 339.

500–2 *this final cry*: Electra speaks for the last time. [Some editors however distribute 503–9 between her and Orestes to give approximate symmetry with 497–9, 500–2; see also n. to 691–9.]

503 *this seed-stock*: continuing the imagery of 204, 236. *Pelopidae*: Agamemnon's family line: see n. to *Ag.* 1600–2; the Family Tree.

506 *as corks do a net*: the simile is independent, rather than part of the
thematic imagery of nets ensnaring Troy, Agamemnon, and Clytemnestra (even though her trap for Agamemnon is metaphorically a
fish-net, 492, *Ag.* 1382).

511 *it is compensation . . . fortunes*: the Greek line too alliterates upon 't',
perhaps for emphasis.

514 *the course we run*: as on a race-track. Orestes is later pictured as a
charioteer speeding to victory (794–9, by the Chorus) and thrown off
his course (1022, by himself).

517 *cowardly grace*: like 44 (n.). *without senses*: but Orestes' whole
premiss is for his father to have both perception and reason, e.g.
315–18, 495 [the text is therefore suspect].

521 *work wasted*: the Greek has an alliteration. *the saying has it*: not
otherwise attested; an 'invented' axiom? Similar recourse to proverb-
like maxims 773, 919; cf. n. to *Ag.* 251–5.

529 *laid it up*: metaphor from beaching a ship and tying it firmly; see
n. to *Ag.* 985–6.

530 *monstrosity*: literally 'biting thing'; Aeschylus used the same noun
of Clytemnestra herself, *Ag.* 1232 (n.), cf. 1229; here, 'biting'
prepares for 531–4. With the baby snake-Orestes compare the
subsequently lethal suckling lion-cub (the loose analogue for
Helen) at *Ag.* 719.

534 [A convincing improvement by conjecture upon the insipid MS
'This is no empty vision of a man, I am certain.']

535 *shrieked . . . sleep*: 32 ff.

536 *like blinded eyes*: metaphor, not simile, in the Greek. The queen's
panic rekindles lights doused at full dark. The light relieving her
night-time terror ironically recalls the beacon-light releasing her joy
at the start of *Agamemnon*, e.g. 264–6; cf. Introduction, p. lviii.

539 *surgeon's cure:* literally 'cure by cutting'—but the 'cutting' which has
already come is Orestes' lock of hair (168), and the 'cure' (472) which
will come is from his sword ('severance', 1047). Cf. esp. *Ag.* 849 for
this particular medical image. *this dream may be fulfilled for me*: compare Clytemnestra's prayer for Agamemnon's fate, *Ag.* 973–4.

544 [*and was . . . swaddling*: the sense approximately required; the MS
is hopelessly damaged, only the word 'swaddling' being certain.]

549–50 *made into the snake*: as Clytemnestra is herself pictured, 249
and n., 994, etc. Orestes also assumes the snake's underworld

significance, as the embodiment of his dead father's power for revenge. *am to kill her*: 'prophetic' present tense, in the dream's interpretation: cf. the seer at *Ag.* 126.

552 *action for some, and for others to do nothing*: idiomatic but unnecessary antithesis; 171 and n

554 [West suggests for the missing line 'while you remain outside the outer doors'. Other editors simply emend 555 *I urge keeping* to 'while you are to keep'.]

556–7 *trickery . . . trickery too*: cf. Clytemnestra herself at 888. Apollo's command appears in this form also at Sophocles, *Electra* 35–7. *as Loxias declared*: 269 ff. *without falsity*: Orestes is reliant on that, 1029 ff., *Eum.* 64.

562–3 *Pylades . . . fighting-ally to the house*: coming from his father Strophius of Phocis (near whose territory was Parnassus, the mountain above Delphi: *Eum.* 11 and n.), already identified as such an ally at *Ag.* 880. The Greek contains an untranslatable play on Pylades' name, as if it meant 'Do(o)rman'; *pylē* is Greek for 'door'. His name may also allude to Pylae, the headquarters in Phocis of the league of local powers which guaranteed Delphi's special status. *both of us speak Parnassian*: Aeschylus allows this detail to be forgotten in the tension when Orestes knocks on the door, 653 ff. Orestes alone speaks there, and to Clytemnestra from 674, and in the 'same' Greek as here, although he does state that he is Phocian, 674.

569 *his door closed against the suppliant*: an inexcusable offence to Zeus the god of suppliants; cf. Apollo's protection of his suppliant Orestes at *Eum.* 91–3, 232–4, 576–8; below, 1034–9.

571–4 *if I get across the threshold . . . face to face*: it is the second alternative, Aegisthus' return, which happens, 838 ff. [*as soon as I get sight of him* is West's convincing correction of the awkward MS '(before he can) cast his eyes downward and (say) . . .']

576 *cover him with blows*: an echo of Agamemnon 'covered' with both nets and blows (494): *Ag.* 1126–8, 1382–4.

578 *to the third draught*: Zeus himself regularly gets the third libation, *Ag.* 246–7 and n.; cf. n. to 1074 below. The allusion here is however chiefly to the third blood-letting in the accursed house.

580 *fitting closely together*: as the dream 'fits', 542.

583 *him here*: Apollo (for his image see n. to 21), rather than the other god of street-doors, Hermes (1–3 n., invoked for similar aid at 727–9, cf. 812–13—in which case Orestes' appeal repeats his words upon

entry, 1–2); but some editors think of Agamemnon, invited *to watch over* the fight as at 489.

584 *s.d.*: The focus moves from Agamemnon's tomb to the palace-door; see nn. to opening Scene, *Eum.* 1, 234, and 490–565.

585–651 An evocation of the horrors of nature, which can be told (585–92), leads the Chorus to narrate the almost unspeakable crimes committed by mythical women against family members (593–622). These illustrations preface the still more monstrous but actual crime of Clytemnestra (623–30), an offence to gods and men (comparable with another mythical outrage, by wives against husbands, 631–8) which is now to be punished by resurgent Justice (639–48)—but also by an act which is one further pollution to the family and brought to it by the Fury (649–51); for emphasis the Fury's name is once more reserved to the end position (n. to *Ag.* 59). [Some editors believe that the stanza 623–30 has been displaced from its true position after 638; with this change all the mythical illustrations precede the present real case, its interpretation and its threat. The text of this ode is frequently insecure.]

585–92 [The ms text has been heavily corrected by editors.]

594 *too bold*: a prominent theme of the ode, 597, and an aspect of all the women destroying male family in 605–39, with Clytemnestra in particular at 630.

600 *selfishly*: insecure translation of a unique word explained by ancient lexicographers as 'not looking about out of concern, harsh'. [*subverting* is even more insecure as a translation; some editors emend it to 'overcoming' or 'disturbing'.]

605–12 *child of Thestius*: Althaea, who was told at the birth of her son, the famous hunter Meleager, that he would die when a branch then burning on the fire was consumed. She took it off and hid it, but returned it to a fire when Meleager killed her brothers in a quarrel.

608 *dark-red*: glowing, described as at the moment of removal.

614 *murderous daughter*: Scylla was bribed to betray her father Nisus' city to the Cretan Minos by cutting off his red hair on which his immortality depended; the mythical motif of the life-invested object is the same as that of Althaea. Scylla was punished by transformation into a sea-bird, the *keiris* (meaning 'shearer').

622 *Hermes came for him*: as his guide after death to Hades (n. to 1–2).

624–8 [*not inapposite too . . . his enemies'*: text very insecure and largely conjectural, and in 628 irrecoverable—where the translation *a man who had his enemies' respect* approximates to an ancient paraphrase.]

626 *the planned designs of a woman's mind*: cf. *Ag.* 11.

630 *women not emboldened to assume command*: 'with the spear' in the Greek: unlike Clytemnestra, *Ag.* 1237, cf. 483 there; see n. to 889 below.

631–2 *In evils   the Lemnian*. the women of Lemnos killed the men from anger at their taking concubines; similarly Clytemnestra, when confronted with Agamemnon and Cassandra, *Ag.* 1441–7 (and it is prospectively Clytemnestra's own fate for taking Aegisthus as lover, 906–7). [*unique* is West's conjecture amid a very corrupt text. Many editors write 'our suffering is lamented as abominable'.]

636–7 *perishes . . . has respect*: the present tenses accommodate both the mythical case (*a race of men*) and the immediate one.

638 *I collect those examples*: an echo of law-court language and technique.

639 *to go near my lungs*: near-fatal, affecting the heart deeply, 1024.

644 *men offending . . . lawful*: the abrupt and effective grammatical discontinuity is in the Greek.

646–7 *Justice . . . Fate*: an irresistible pair, *Ag.* 1535–7 (the same imagery), cf. 306 above; Introduction, §2.3, at start.

649–52 *The child . . . Fury*: the metaphor of murder and ruin breeding in the family: 466 and n., *Ag.* 754 ff. *The child of older bloody murders* is both figurative and also literally Orestes, after the acts involving his ancestors Atreus and Agamemnon (315 and n.). *famous . . . -scheming* is a play on Greek *Klutai-mestra*, 'famous-designer, -schemer'; for the *Fury* as such cf. 947.

656 *welcome strangers because of Aegisthus*: both politely hopeful and blackly ironic, the latter tone dominating much of the following scenes with Clytemnestra and Aegisthus. Cf. Orestes' expectation of Aegisthus at 569–70.

657 *What country's the stranger from?*: the Doorman is given Aegisthus' question, 575.

670 *hot baths*: as Clytemnestra arranged for Agamemnon, only to kill him there, 491.

672–3 *If there's need . . . communicate it to them*: 'men' will indeed be told—but at 770 ff. Aegisthus will get a message different from that intended by Clytemnestra at 716–18; and the man will be murdered who planned the murder of Agamemnon, *Ag.* 1609. *more deliberation*: reversing Clytemnestra's self-sufficiency remarked as early as *Ag.* 11, where she 'plans like a man'; but it also echoes Agamemnon's intention upon his return, *Ag.* 846–7—and the irony continues when Clytemnestra repeats the thought at 718.

674 *Daulian*: Daulis was the major city of Phocis (see the Map); Strophius (679) lived there.

690 *parent*: masculine serving as common gender in the Greek, but Orestes even as 'stranger' (674) knows that only one parent survives, and faces him now. *reasonable . . . to know*: that Orestes is now dead. The words can also mean 'it is reasonable to know his parent'—as Orestes indeed does.

691–9 [These lines are given to Electra by some editors, chiefly on the grounds that 695 conflicts with Clytemnestra's claim at 717 to have reliable friends, and that 698–9 must refer to the revenge about to be taken on her own *evil revelry* in the house. The scene nevertheless plays much more powerfully if it confronts only mother and son, and if Electra is indeed seen no more after she has been given the important sentry-post indoors, 554, 559. In 696–8 *but now this very hope . . . traitorous* the Greek syntax is broken, and there may be loss of text between 697 and 698. In 699 *you must write down as traitorous* corrects MS 'he (Orestes) records as present'.]

692 *so hard to wrestle down*: this metaphor again: 339 and n.

694 *With arrows well-sighted from afar*: possibly an allusion to Apollo the archer-god (*Ag.* 510 etc.) directing Orestes from distant Delphi, 269, 558, etc.

695 *my dear ones*: hypocritical if Orestes is meant, but the plural may suggest that she recalls Iphigenia's sacrifice, 242: cf. *Ag.* 1417.

696–9 Clytemnestra's syntax breaks down, indicating her turmoil. At *Ag.* 880 ff. she appeared to say that she had accepted a warning from Strophius, the house's ally (cf. 562 above), to put Orestes under his protection. *evil revelry*: imagery as *Ag.* 1189; cf. n. to 466 above. *write down*: the term for an official record or even prosecution.

700–3 *thanks to happy news*: Orestes uses the formal courtesies of a stranger; and a messenger could expect reward for good news, 707. *hosts . . . guest*: for their potent mutual obligations see Introduction, p. xli.

705–6, 708 *friends, friend*: the Greek word is that translated as 'dear ones' in 695 (cf. Introduction, p. xli). Here it is deliberately vague; the first 'friends' may allude to Strophius, or to Clytemnestra and Aegisthus, or even to Electra and the dead Agamemnon. The theatre audience relishes the irony in Clytemnestra's response. *I had agreed to*: with Strophius, 679, 688. *welcomed as their guest*: not unlike

Cassandra as a 'guest' in the house, *Ag.* 1320, bringing death as her message.

713 *followers and fellow-travellers.*: the plural is problematic [and often changed by editors to the singular], for the play-text names only Pylades as accompanying Orestes, 561, and they carry their own baggage, 560, 675. But Aeschylus may be making Clytemnestra in her preoccupation use an empty formula of welcome, or overstate it, perhaps to remind us of her fulsomeness in welcoming Agamemnon, *Ag.* 895 ff., 961 ff.

714 *what is appropriate to the house*: recalling 669 what is 'proper to the house' and repeating the irony of 'what is appropriate to them' in 711.

715–16 *I urge*: perhaps an ironic echo of Orestes' words when planning his entry to the palace, 555, 581. *shortage of friends*: she means only Aegisthus, *Ag.* 1435–7, 1654.

719–29 The Chorus briefly chant their anxious hopes after Orestes' entry to the palace, much as the Chorus of *Agamemnon* chanted their forebodings after Cassandra's entry immediately before Agamemnon's murder at *Ag.* 1331–42. For this kind of short lyric passage see the n. there.

720 *When . . . show the power of our tongues*: cf. Orestes' order to them at 581–2, to speak 'when opportune'.

723–5 *tomb our sovereign*: cf. the Chorus's respect for it at 106. *admiral*: fresh insistence on the status of the victim: 345–66, 431, 479, 556, 627–8, 1071; cf. *Ag.* 1227 and n. *listen . . . come to aid*: cf. the Chorus at 459–60, and the words of Orestes' appeals, 1–2, 456, 583–4.

726 *guileful Persuasion*: about to be voiced (720) to the Nurse as part of Orestes' scheme: 770 ff. For the goddess Persuasion see n. to *Ag.* 385.

728 *the moment is here* may be an ironic echo of Clytemnestra's 'it's well time' in 710 [wording from there has been convincingly restored in the Greek here, for the MS text is a garble]. *Hermes*: invoked here as the god who will conduct the revenge-victims to the *Underworld*, but also as the god able to help the revengers' deception, 815–16. *stand as reserve*: waiting to take on the winner of the previous bout (of wrestling: 339)—Clytemnestra; cf. 866.

730 *That man the stranger . . . trouble*: strangely unengaged in tone after the eagerness of 720, but Aeschylus may just be signalling the nature of the next scene to the audience. [Some editors nevertheless suppose that this tone explains a preceding line now lost, such as 'Listen, I can hear lamentation in the house.']

732 *Cilissa*: i.e. '(woman) from Cilicia' (modern south-east Turkey), a regular manner of naming slaves.

733 *Grief . . . takes no wages*: proverbially an involuntary companion; but the sense may be double, also '. . . gives no reward', as good news however may, 707–9.

734–82 The Nurse both interrupts the tension and is crucial to the deception's success; for her characterization see Introduction, p. xxii. Her syntax wanders, often quite violently, expressing her agitation— but some of this effect may be due to textual damage.

744 *mixture of . . . griefs*: as in a wine-bowl, *Ag.* 1397.

748 *wrung me dry*: a nautical metaphor, literally 'I bailed my troubles bilge-dry'.

751 [For the missing line (after *in the night* in the Greek, actually) West suggests approximately ('to hear) his (many) shrill commands . . . *in the night* (meant constant trouble), frequent . . .']

755 [*with due attention*: a mere guess at the meaning possibly intended in the Greek 'by a turn of mind', a very doubtful phrase usually condemned as corrupt.]

773 *to make bent words succeed*: that is, to have their deception believed as the truth. It is almost certainly a proverbial expression (otherwise unattested). [*bent* is conjectural, the MS having 'hidden'; and the line may not be authentic, for two ancient commentators on Homer cite it from Euripides.]

780 *the gods take care . . . care for*: euphemistic vagueness covering intense self-interest; similarly Clytemnestra at *Ag.* 974; cf. n. to 145 above. In 782 *May it turn out for the best* once more recalls *Ag.* 121.

783–837 The Chorus appeal to the gods supporting the justice of Orestes' cause, Zeus above all (783–93), but also the gods of his house (800–6) and especially Apollo (807–11) and Hermes (812– 18). These appeals support their confidence that Orestes is already moving steadily to his goal like a racer (794–9) and will set off their songs of celebration (819–25). The ode has however a calculatedly ominous ending. The Chorus's call to Orestes to reject his mother's cries for mercy out of hand (826–30) is belied by his later hesitation (899); and when he is urged to have the courage of Perseus slaying the Gorgon as he slays his Gorgon-like mother (831–7 and n.), Aeschylus is anticipating the courage he will need to face the Gorgon-like Furies (1048 ff.) who will persecute him for the matricide (Clytemnestra at 924). For the stanzaic structure see the end of the n. to 306–475. [This ode is one of the most pervasively damaged passages in the play.]

785–6 [These lines are almost entirely corrupt; the translation given approximates to an ancient commentator's paraphrase.]

790–1 *set . . . you raise . . . then he will*: the translation diminishes a sharp grammatical discontinuity, probably a device of emphatic association of ideas *regarding* for this argument towards Zeus' own satisfaction cf. 255–6 and n.

794–9 *orphan*: Orestes (and Electra) at 247, 249. *colt*: often a bare metaphor for a young person, but here apparently maintained in the image of a chariot running straight to its goal which develops the prayer in 789 ff. for Orestes' victory. [The MS text is however so damaged that the *steps* and *feet* of 796–9 may be those of a foot-runner, an individual 'colt'.]

800–1 *You gods . . . inside the house*: including prominently Zeus in his separate role as Zeus of Possessions (*Ag.* 1038 and n.), and Hestia, the Hearth-goddess herself (*Ag.* 1036–8 and n.). *wealth deep within*: *Ag.* 96.

803 [*Bring* : because a convincing supplement is hard to find, some editors delete this word, and the entire corresponding verse 815, so that 816 begins the sentence, 'Working his deception etc.'.]

805 *fresh justice*: 'fresh' may be an undertranslation of a word perhaps correctly interpreted in antiquity as 'freshly killed'. The prayer for fresh justice to expiate past bloodshed may seem false before 806 'I wish the old murder breeds no more in the house', but the Chorus are really praying that Orestes' imminent act of justice will be the last.

806 *murder breeds*: 466 and n.

807 *great . . . vault*: Apollo's temple at Delphi, sometimes described as his 'great hall'. *vault* translates literal 'mouth', i.e. the entry to a (large) interior; but the allusion may be to the 'cavern' or chasm believed to lie beneath the oracular shrine and to 'house' the god's power (modern archaeology has disproved its existence).

809–10 *he may see freedom's brilliant [light]*: for the metaphor see 961. [The text, which is insecure, may also be translated as '(the man's house) may see him as freedom's brilliant light'; for the latter image see 131.] *veil of darkness*: 52, *Eum.* 380.

812–16 *Maia's son*: Hermes is god of illusion and trickery (728); the Chorus hope for his continued aid with Orestes' disguise. *wafts any action best on its course*: the favouring-wind imagery of 317 (n.); again at 821, 823. [*Much . . . unseen*: text again extremely insecure throughout; *working his deception unseen* is West's conjecture for MS 'saying an (?) unintelligible word'.]

819–23 *a women's song*: their chant of victory, 386, 942 (n. to *Ag.* 28). *[high]-struck*: accompanied by a stringed instrument tuned high to suit women's voices. *magical*: literally 'of wizards', perhaps an allusion to the supposed power of ritual singing before and after success, like the *hammer* 306 475 and the 'binding-song' of the Furies, *Eum.* 329–33 = 342–6. [The text of these lines is once again most insecure.]

823–4 *voyage . . . gain*: the imagery of the favouring wind (821) is now linked to one from sea-trading.

827–30 *cry out over her appeal . . . censure*: Aeschylus has the Chorus anticipate precisely 908–9; cf. 896–8, 924–8. *a ruin which brings you no censure*: because it is Apollo's command, 270, 1031; see also 836–7 below. The idea is frequent in *Eumenides*, 84, 202, 465, 579, etc.

831–7 *Perseus . . . Gorgon inside the house*: suggesting Orestes as killer of the snake (Clytemnestra at 249, cf. 994); the Gorgon had hair of living snakes which turned all those who saw them to stone; Perseus killed the Gorgon by looking at their reflection in his shield. The analogy overrides the projection in the dream of Orestes as himself a snake; cf. n. to 549–50. *grace*: the word describing Clytemnestra's (insincere) funeral and libations for Agamemnon, *Ag.* 1545 and 44 above. [*a death which Apollo frees of guilt*: this is West's attractive conjecture (repeating and intensifying 830, the last line of the previous stanza) for the senseless and unmetrical MS 'destroying utterly the guilty death'.]

838 *I am not here unsummoned . . . message*: Aegisthus' first words betray his blustering weakness, cf. *Ag.* 1628–32 and n., Introduction, p. xxviii.

843 *open sores*: cf. 471, 'putrefaction' at 995, and the 'pus' at *Ag.* 1480.

845 *living fact*: literally 'seeing the light of day', a frequent expression for a person still living and of account; cf. *Eum.* 367–8 and n. Aeschylus perhaps hints at Aegisthus' subconscious fear that Orestes may somehow be still alive; cf. the Nurse at 778.

849–50 *nothing as strong in messengers*: the Chorus themselves manipulate Aegisthus' credulity, as they instructed the Nurse, 773. *one man . . . from another*: the Doorman at 665–6, Clytemnestra at 673.

854 *a mind that has good eyes*: for this half-proverbial concept of intelligent perception cf. *Eum.* 103–4 and n., 275, etc.

856–7 *begin . . . end*: the two words stand significantly first and last in the Greek order, enclosing both prayer and sentiment, but are a characteristic formula for a prayer's start (cf. n. to *Ag.* 160–83). The language is difficult, but we recall both the Chorus's goodwill to Orestes at 788 ff. and their constant doubt at 386 ff., 410 ff., 463 ff.

[*goodwill equal to the need*: only the sense possibly intended. West professes not to understand this line, but does not mark it as corrupt.]

861–2 *destruction . . . for all time*: if Clytemnestra survives retribution for her outrageous murder of man and husband, cf. the Chorus's mythical parallels at 596–638.

863–4 *or by kindling . . . Orestes*: deliberate change of subject from 'cutting-edge' in the first alternative, 859–62. *fire and light*: symbolic of success, and thematic in the trilogy: Introduction, §3.4, at end. Orestes is himself the light to be kindled at 131 (n.). [The missing words are usually supplied as 'and the riches of his house'.]

865 *his ancestors' great wealth*: cf. 480, 801.

866–7 *godlike Orestes*: this adjective was given to his father at *Ag.* 1548. *wrestling*: this imagery again: 339 etc. *adversary in waiting*: Hermes was invoked to be this, 728 and n.

868 *may it be for victory*: see n. to 478. For the register of the off-stage cry of grief (replaced in the translation by the stage-direction) see n. to *Ag.* 1072.

872 *Let us stand aside*: as women they would avoid violence, but we are meant to remember the dithering of the male Chorus while Agamemnon is killed, *Ag.* 1346 ff.

875 [*struck down*: this likely sense is restored from MS 'brought to fulfilment'.]

876 *three times I call*: the ritual number, but perhaps an echo of Orestes' three cries to the Doorman at 656; cf. Clytemnestra's three blows at *Ag.* 1386.

878 *the women's doors*: a cue for Clytemnestra's entry at 885; the single stage-door, representing the main door of the palace, no more leads directly from the women's quarters than to the men's (712). Some scholars have nevertheless suggested that this scene was played with two stage-doors: Introduction, §2.4, at n. 25.

881 *Ho there, ho!*: the Watchman's cry for celebratory action within the house, *Ag.* 25. The similarity but reversal of the stage-moments is effective.

884 *head*: 'neck' in the Greek, the death-stroke being through the throat like a sacrifical victim's (904 and n.). *the butcher's block*: Cassandra's forecast for herself, *Ag.* 1277.

886 *The dead are killing the living*: phrased like an enigmatic aphorism in the Greek, where the word-order encourages initial misunderstanding as the obvious but pointless 'the living man kills the dead

men'; hence Clytemnestra's 'riddle' in 887. There is remarkably little time for the actor playing the House-slave to exit and change mask (and costume?) if he is to re-enter as Pylades at 892; so some editors suppose the exceptional use of a fourth actor throughout the play for Pylades: see Introduction, §2.4, at n. 29.

888 *Trickery:* see n. to 556–7.

889 *an axe to slay a man*: the expression seems a little forced, but recalls Clytemnestra's unfeminine killing of Agamemnon (*Ag.* 1125–6; for the nature of her weapon see n. to 1149); and this last defiance before death is maintained in the vigour of her Ghost at *Eum.* 94 ff.

892 *has all he needed:* brutally colloquial. Some editors assume the exposure here of Aegisthus' corpse, but this would weaken the tableau of both bodies at 973.

896 *hold back, from respect for*: no single English verb adequately translates the Greek one (*aideisthai*) used here and in Orestes' agonized response in 899. It connotes any or all of deference, regard and reverence, or inhibition, compunction from pity or fear to act, shame or moral feeling. *this breast*: in the theatre the (male) actor would make only a gesture at this point, but such poetic appeals create vivid emotion, occurring first when Hecuba begs her son Hector not to offer himself to inevitable death at the hands of Achilles, Homer, *Iliad* 22.80.

900–1 *Then where's the future . . . the gods*: Pylades breaks the silence he has held throughout the play for just three decisive lines, and with a brusque near-colloquialism; compare the long silence of Cassandra between her entry at *Ag.* 810 and her outburst at 1071. *pledges sworn on oath*: by Orestes to the gods 244–5, 435–7, and to his father 540.

903 *I judge, you have the victory*: Pylades' reply hardens Orestes for his 'victory' over Clytemnestra: cf. n. to 868.

904 *slaughter*: the Greek word suggests 'sacrifice', a further such act in the sequence which began with Iphigenia, *Ag.* 224; Introduction, p. lvi. Clytemnestra's ghost describes her death with this word, *Eum.* 102.

908–30 Stichomythia is the natural and effective vehicle for the duel between victim and killer, as it was between Agamemnon and Clytemnestra at *Ag.* 931–44; cf. Introduction, p. l.

914 *fighting-ally*: Strophius, n. on 562. Clytemnestra here claims greater acknowledgement for preserving Orestes than at *Ag.* 880.

915 *sold away*: as Electra complained, 132.

916 *I got in exchange*: see n. to 132.

918 *Don't, unless . . . follies too*: tartly colloquial, adding to the sense of her defiance. *father's follies*: Cassandra and Chryseis, his concubines: cf. n. to 631–2, Clytemnestra at *Ag.* 1441.

919 *find fault with the worker*: half-proverbial, like 921. Aeschylus may be trying to suggest semi-automatic responses masking stress, as perhaps at 719 (n.). *sit about indoors*: compare Electra's outrage against Clytemnestra herself, 137. Orestes' sentiment reflects the normal contemporary attitude to married women, and to their husbands' sexual freedom.

924–5 *mother's fury-hounds*: the Furies (1054), who hunt like dogs, *Eum.* 131–2, 246. *how am I to escape my father's*: 283–4, cf. 273.

926 *dirge to my tomb . . . no effect*: this seems to be the meaning, with two definite points and perhaps a third allusion: (1) proverbial uselessness (like our 'talking to a brick wall'), (2) her dirge will not prevent the death it would uselessly mourn, her own (cf. Cassandra at *Ag.* 1322 f.), and (3) Agamemnon's tomb is still potent in the play; his death determines hers, 927.

927 *determines*: or (because metrical fusion of adjacent words gives the same Greek spelling) 'brings you (your death) on its course', the wind-metaphor of 317 (n.).

928–9 *the snake*: 526 ff.

930 *You killed*: the Greek verb-form is unusual and archaic, perhaps an attempt to add to the line's oracular tone ('prophetic', 929), which suggests Clytemnestra's imminent fate.

934 *eye of the house*: as its glory and saving guarantee, *Eum.* 1025. *fall . . . in destruction*: Orestes' own fear at 263, cf. 964.

935–71 The ode begins with an echo from *Agamemnon*: Zeus' justice for Troy's crime; so now, with the deaths of Aegisthus and Clytemnestra, just punishment has come to the house of Atreus (937–45) through the agency of Zeus and his daughter Justice (946–52) and of Apollo (953–60). Orestes' emergence from the house signals its own happy release from pollution (961–71), while he is himself now defiled by the matricide (n. to 965–71); but the ode ends without mention of his consequent danger from the Furies (Clytemnestra at 924), for this is about to be dramatized vividly in the final scene, at 1048 ff. [This choral ode too is extremely damaged in the MS.]

935 *There came*: the same expression stands in the corresponding verse 946 (and 936 = 947 share phrasing only partly reproducible); similar semi-sacral formulae with 'There . . .' in 937, 939, 948 are all marks of the hymnic style for victory, 942.

938 *double lion*: usually understood to mean Orestes and Pylades, although Orestes takes single responsibility, 866. There is no necessary allusion to the lion as the emblem of the house, 232 (n.), for 'two lions' is often used of two warriors after Homer, *Iliad* 5 554 [*double lion*: some editors change this to 'two-footed lion', i.e. Orestes alone, comparing *Ag.* 1258 'two-footed lioness', but *double warfare* must relate to two persons.]

939 *there drove . . . forward*: this verb, apparently intransitive here, describes Wrath driving disaster upon Troy, *Ag.* 701, where it also connotes oracular predestination. *the exile*: Orestes, 3 (n.), 254, etc. [*there drove . . . forward* is a certain correction of MS 'there got his inheritance'.]

946–7 The Fury is 'deep-scheming' at 651 (n.). The word *punishment* has the same place as in Strophe 1 at 936. [The text is insecure; some editors personify 'Punishment', one of the Furies' names (n. to *Eum.* 1041), others write the names of other gods.]

948 *her hand's touch*: a god's unmistakable aid, cf. Apollo at 1059, Fortune's at *Ag.* 662–4. Contrast Clytemnestra's poisonous 'touch', 995 below.

951 *with happy accuracy*: 'etymological' endorsement; cf. n. to *Ag.* 681. Here, Greek *Dike*, the *Justice* of 949, is apparently offered—but impossibly—as '*Di-*', a Greek stem of the name 'Zeus', coupled with *daughter*, Greek *k(or)e*; for the true etymology of Zeus' name see n. to *Ag.* 165. Justice is Zeus' daughter also at *Seven* 662.

953–6 *Parnassus*: 562 and n. *cried loud and clear*: Apollo's loud order to Orestes, 271–4; like all Apollo's words it was *without guile*—but Apollo commanded Orestes to repay Clytemnestra's guile with his own (557 and n.). *mature now with time*: a probably unconscious echo of *Ag.* 727, the instinctive violence of the lion-cub 'brought on by time'. [The text is insecure throughout these lines.]

958 [*in everything* is West's conjecture for some corrupt wording; note the same words in the same place in the corresponding verse 969.]

961–71 *The light is here . . . in the house*: delusive optimism, quickly undone by the Furies' appearance to Orestes, 1048 ff.

964 *lay . . . where you fell*: the same idea as in 934; cf. n. to 48.

965–71 Orestes (the house's *head*) is indeed about to *come* from a building now freed from pollution by the death of the killers (cf. Cassandra's greeting to it as polluted, *Ag.* 1085–1104 etc.); but he carries pollution in his own person, 1017, 1038, 1059–60. *expels . . . expel*: the repetition is in the Greek. *fortunes . . . move to live in the house*: as Justice was prayed to do, 309 and n. [Once more, much of the text in these lines is insecure.]

973 The display of the bodies of Clytemnestra and Aegisthus reproduces that of Agamemnon and Cassandra at *Ag.* 1372: see the n.

976 *dear to each other*; that is 'loving'; see 894, 906, ll. to *Ag.* 1445–7.

980 *see . . . the device . . . bonds*: the 'net', 492 above, etc. Orestes' extraordinary attempt to describe the net metaphorically at 997–1000 recalls Clytemnestra's own allusive words at *Ag.* 1382.

983 There is no clue in the Greek text whether the attendants do stretch the robing out, but some such gesture makes theatrical sense here. A producer would need to decide how to allow this moment not to prejudice the more important onset of Orestes' madness at 1048; probably the attendants held the robing motionless, or dropped it at the end of Orestes' speech, 1006.
[West suggests inserting Aeschylus, *Fragment* 375 after *stand round by it*, giving 'show the (irresistible contrivance and inescapable) thing which enveloped . . .' (the ancient author quoting this fragment refers it to the robe fatal to Agamemnon).]

984 *who watches over all this*: Zeus, e.g. *Eum.* 1045; cf. n. to 1–2. [Line 986 is rightly omitted by West: it destroys the pointed reference to supreme control by Zeus and gives instead the commonplace appeal '(but) the Sun who watches over all (these unholy deeds of my mother).']

987 *witness in justice one day*: Zeus' authorization is voiced by Apollo at Orestes' trial, *Eum.* 618 ff. *witness*: the legalistic tone now appearing in Orestes' language begins to prepare for his trial in *Eum.*; so too 987–90, 1010, 1027, 1029, 1038, 1041b, 1060.

990 *justice customary for an adulterer*: older Athenian law sanctioned such private vengeance; but by Aeschylus' time monetary compensation had become the usual penalty in law.

997–1004 [These lines are moved here because the crimes of Aegisthus otherwise interrupt the coherent denunciation of Clytemnestra in 991–1006. They best follow 990 *adulterer*, even though Orestes says in 989 that he sets no value on Aegisthus' death. Relocation after 982 or 1013 is less satisfactory. The lines are certainly Aeschylean; they contain some typically interlaced and daring images.]

997 *What would I be correct in calling it . . .?*: for this style of emphasis disguised in hesitation cf. Cassandra's doubt over how to describe the monstrous Clytemnestra at *Ag.* 1232–6.

999 The vivid image of 'tenting' returns at *Eum.* 634.

993 *a bad enemy, as she shows*: the unborn Orestes became the snake-child of her dream, 527. [*a bad enemy* is textually insecure; alternative punctuation gives (no more securely) 'but now her enemy, as the bad (outcome) shows.']

995 *more putrefaction . . . button*: 843 Ороton hypothesizes Clytemnestra's power to 'poison' existence; and textual insecurity makes his picture confusing. She was a viper lethal with coils rather than bite also at 248; but she slew Agamemnon with a weapon, *Ag.* 1149, which in Greek metaphor often 'bites' (n. to *Eum.* 802–3). While there is some evidence for a Greek belief that a snake's mere touch could be lethal, it is suggested that "touch" here connotes sexual contact (n. to 246–51); hence the feared 'mate' of 1005 (and 909).

1005–6 *no such mate*: a concise echo for the audience of the dangerous women cited by the Chorus in 585–651 (n.). *childless*: precisely the objective of the family Curse, *Ag.* 1600–2.

1007–8 *Sorrow . . . death!*: the Chorus repeat their (reluctant) feelings of 931.

1008–9 *You were done away*: Clytemnestra alone is meant. *suffering . . . for one who waits*: cf. *Ag.* 1564–5; again the theme of punishment inevitable even if delayed (61–5, 383), recurring in the corresponding line 1020. Orestes already senses his own inevitable punishment at 1017, 1021, 1026 ff.; he must await it no less than Agamemnon (*Ag.* 1563, cf. 153) and Clytemnestra (464 above). *flower*: paradoxical image of destruction springing up vigorously, *Ag.* 659 and n.

1011 *Aegisthus' sword*: presumably the one used by Clytemnestra.

1012–13 *ooze of blood . . . embroidery*: ageing bloodstains compound natural discoloration; both blood and thread-colours are here 'dyes'.

1015 *addressing*: as if in symbolic farewell to the corpse it once shrouded; cf. 8–9 and n.

1018–19 *with no price to pay*: translation insecure [and the verse has abnormal metre, often rectified without remedying the problem of meaning]. The axiom here has appeared at *Ag.* 1341–2.

1022 *like a charioteer*: as the Chorus in hope pictured him before the matricide, 794 ff.

1024–5 *Fear . . . song . . . dance . . . Rancour*: image as at 167, cf. *Ag.* 975 ff. *Fear* is personified like Sleep and Weariness at *Eum.* 127. For Rancour as the house's persistent persecutor see n. to 32–3.

1030 *I attribute mostly to*: terminology from the law-court; see n. to 987. *Loxias*: Apollo's command at 297 ff., 900.

1031 *without the evil of blame*: 830.

1033 *within a bowshot*: proverbial, like our 'within a shout, within a mile'. For the metaphor cf. *Suppliants* 473 and perhaps *Ag.* 1194. There may be a covert allusion to Apollo (Loxias, 1030) the Archer (694 and n.).

1035 *wreathed . . . branch*: with wool, a suppliant's emblem, *Eum.* 43–5 and n.

1036–7 *mid-earth's navel*: represented in a large circular stone consecrated at Delphi (*Eum.* 40, 167), iconic of the god Apollo in art since the earliest times. Delphi was imagined as the earth's centre, the place of central communication of Zeus' will (*Eum.* 2–19 and n.). *fire . . . undying*: a feature of many temples, not just that at Delphi.

1038 *flee pollution*: see n. to 965–71. The Greek wording however implies also 'as defendant on a charge of polluting bloodshed', anticipating Orestes' trial in *Eumenides*, especially 576–81; cf. n. to 980 above.

1040–3 The mention of *Menelaus* appears to anticipate his role in the satyr-play *Proteus* performed with the trilogy: see n. to *Ag.* 617 and Introduction, §2.4, at n. 23. Orestes' hope for protection by his uncle Menelaus is an element of Euripides' *Orestes*, lines 243 ff. [Probably two half-lines and after 1042 one whole line are missing; the translation supplies the sense wanted by most editors. In 1040 however *in later time* is suspect. After 1042, which repeats part of *Ag.* 1282, some editors supply e.g. 'I shall go as my father's avenger and as my mother's killer', on the model of *Ag.* 1281.]

1047 *clean*: the Greek word can mean both 'easy' and 'successful'. *severance* recalls Perseus cutting off the Gorgon's head, 831–7; but the idea here is immediately reversed in the frightening Furies' heads of 1049–50.

1048 [*grim*: a convincing conjecture for MS 'servants'; see the textual note to *Ag.* 639.]

1051–64 Distichomythia (Introduction, §3.2) carries a particularly significant and emotional exchange.

1051 *dearest of men to your father*: that is, he will protect you still; cf. Orestes at 456, 497, *Eum.* 598.

1054 *mother's rancorous fury-hounds*: repeated from 924.

1059–62 *purification . . . I'm being driven*: for Orestes the reversal of 967–8; cf. *Eum.* 421. *You don't see . . . but I can see*: T. S. Eliot, *The Family Reunion*, Part I, scene 1, of the Eumenides: 'Can't you see them? You don't see them, but I see them, | And they see me . . .'

1063 *watch over you*: full circle with 1, *Fragment 1*, the play's first line.

1064 *in critical times*: also possible is the translation 'with timely fortune', but Aeschylus is ending the play with strong pointers to Orestes' dangers; so too 1075–6.

1065 [*family-storm*: the Greek word, if it is not corrupt, has a final element typical of wind-names, but the sense is rather weak; so the more optimistic meaning 'generative storm, storm securing the family' is suggested, but the tone of anxiety in 1074–6 is against that. Some editors substitute e.g. 'bloody' or 'heavy' for *family*-.]

1067 *Children devoured*: by their father Thyestes, *Ag.* 1095 ff., 1593 ff.

1072 *the Achaeans' leader in war*: see n. to 723, 'admiral'.

1074 *a third . . . to bring safety*: Orestes the third (in the family line) like Zeus (third and) Saviour, *Ag.* 246–7 and n.; but Orestes is in peril of *death*. There is an allusion also to the third and final libation; Orestes' hope that the Furies will have drunk third and last (578 and n.) is now false.

1076 *Ruin*: the play's last word revives one of the trilogy's dominant concepts, whether abstract or personified, from *Ag.* 361 through to *Eum.* 1007: see Introduction, p. xxxiii and n. 16.

EUMENIDES

THE principal medieval manuscript preserves an ancient *hypothesis* ('introduction') to the play which goes back to Aristophanes of Byzantium, who edited Aeschylus at Alexandria in the third century BC. It summarizes the action concisely: 'Orestes is surrounded at Delphi by the Furies; by the design of Apollo he presented himself at Athens, at the temple of Athena. He was victorious by her design and returned from his exile to Argos. Athena mollified the Furies and named them the Eumenides. This version of the myth occurs in no other writer.' There follows a list of the play-characters.

s.d.: the action moves to Athens: see nn. to 234 and 490–565.

1 *the gods in this prayer*: compare the first line of *Ag.* and the second line of *LB*.

2–19 *Earth, the first prophet . . . Zeus' spokesman*: this history of the Delphic oracle relies both upon details found in earlier poets and upon Aeschylus' own apparent innovations. The possession of the immemorially sacred site first by Mother Earth and her daughter Themis is traditional (Themis' name means 'Right'; at *Prometheus* 209–11 she and Earth are 'one form with many names', and Themis makes prophecies to her son Prometheus). The succession of Apollo to Delphi as its permanent prophet by gift from Phoebe, another daughter of Earth, rather than by forcible conquest, is probably Aeschylean; in most accounts Apollo evicts Delphi's original occupants violently, including its guardian snake Pytho, his slaughter of it being commemorated in his cult-title 'Pythian' (e.g. *Ag.* 509).

The transition at Delphi narrated here, from dark, primeval Earth, who provides the Furies with their home (72), to Apollo, the brilliant, oracular voice of Zeus' supreme power (614–21), anticipates the whole progression of the play. Apollo's passage through Athens (10) before he arrives ceremoniously at Delphi by specially made road (11–15), his easy reception by the native mortals (16), and Zeus' support (17–20) all anticipate motifs of the action to come. Apollo and Zeus will save Orestes from the Furies (83, 93, cf. 616–21). As Apollo, a younger god immigrant to Delphi, finds a welcome and permanent abode there, so the Furies, older gods, will find this at Athens, as immigrants themselves (see especially 915 and n., 1018). Aeschylus begins the play on a note of settled confidence, only for it to be quickly imperilled (34 ff., cf. n. to 30–3).

7–9 *Phoebe . . . Phoebus, who has his name from hers*: an artifice of Aeschylus, perhaps inventing the name and role of Phoebe (see above). He relies upon the frequent association of names with their 'meanings', in terms of cause and effect (nn. to *Ag.* 681, *LB* 951). The Greek name-root '*Phoib-*' is of much-disputed meaning, 'Bright-', signifying Apollo's brilliance (cf. 744), or 'Fox-like' (cf. Lycean of 'wolf-like' Apollo, *Ag.* 1257 and n.), or possibly Indic in origin, 'bestower of fortune'.

9 *Delos*: Apollo's oldest cult-site, the Aegean island where he and his sister Artemis were born to Leto (323) as children of Zeus. The tiny island is nearly all barren rock, and its possession of a small *lake* (now dry) was therefore regularly celebrated as a divine miracle.

10 *Pallas' shore*: i.e. the goddess Athena's land, Athens, hospitable to Apollo on his way to Delphi as it is hospitable to Orestes and the Furies in the play.

11 *Parnassus*: the mountain above Delphi (*LB* 954).

13 *The sons of Hephaestus*: one of many kennings of the Athenians, from their ancient kings: king Erectheus (855) was the god Hephaestus' son.

16 *Delphos*: the eponymous king. *helmsman*: a frequent metaphor, of the ship of state: 765, *Ag.* 183, 1617–18.

19 *Loxias*: for his name see n. to *Ag.* 1074–5. *spokesman*: any 'prophet' is this, in that he speaks of what is destined; Apollo speaks uniquely the will of Zeus, so that he is infallible, 615–18, *LB* 559.

21 *Pallas Before the Temple*: a cult-title reflecting the position of her temple at Delphi, which met the ancient visitor to Apollo's precinct some way lower down on the access road. The prominent place given to Athena by the Prophetess helps emphasize the references to Athena throughout 10–13, in preparing for her major role in the play; cf. Introduction, pp. xix and xxxv.

24 *Corycus*: a cave high on Mt. Parnassus above Delphi, sacred to Pan god of wild things (*Ag.* 55) and the Nymphs; so its mountain is *welcoming to birds*: eagles were famous there. Euripides' *Ion*, set at Delphi, begins with its birds (106 ff., 155 ff.; eagles 158–60).

25–6 *Bromios*: 'Thunderer', a cult-name of Dionysus (or Bacchus) reflecting his father Zeus' insemination of his mother Semele in a flash of lightning. *led his Bacchants in an army*: as 'commander' of his cultic throng, an image prominent in Euripides' *Bacchae,* which dramatized his human opponent Pentheus' destruction; *death . . . like a hare's* alludes to the 'hunting' and physical dismemberment of Pentheus in the mountains, scene of Dionysus' wild worship (see Note on 499–502). Dionysus had a large role at Delphi alongside Apollo, his cult being particularly active during the winter months.

27 *Pleistus*: the river(-god) of the valley below Delphi.

28 *Zeus . . . the fulfiller*: an early hint that the play will confirm Zeus as the architect of peace in the family: cf. 974 and n.

30–3 *And now I wish . . . the god may lead me*: a conventional prayer to begin the day's routine; it is not an implication of past failures. The Prophetess gives no reason for anxiety, however, so that Aeschylus is hinting to the audience that her entrance will be unusual, as it proves, 34 ff.—for (*the Greek*) Orestes has already *come*, and is already within the temple, abnormally.

33 The short interval while the stage was empty was probably filled with the Prophetess's cries of horror from behind the door.

39–40 *garlands*: worn by consulters of the oracle, and left there. *navel-stone*: also 167; cf. n. to *LB* 1036–7.

41–5 *supplication*: Orestes as at the end of *Libation Bearers*, at 1034 ff. *new-drawn sword*: for theatrical continuity Orestes may still be costumed as he was when he drove his mother into the palace to kill her (*LB* 930); he reappears (973) with the bloody sword over the bodies of her and Aegisthus, from where he flees the Furies in madness; the sword remains as emblem of his bloody crime. *tall-grown branch*: big and symbolic of the supplication's importance; cf. *Suppliants* 346, 354; perhaps this explains also *much wool* ['very much' in the Greek, which some editors replace by conjecture].

white fleece: white symbolizes purity (353 and n.); Apollo has already purified Orestes, 237. *with these details my account . . . clear*: Aeschylus wishes to stress Orestes' special status as Apollo's protégé.

47 *chairs*: Aeschylus refers perhaps to seats available in his own day for those queuing to consult the oracle

48 *Gorgons*: as Orestes described them, *LB* 1048.

50–1 *women . . . carrying off Phineus' banquet*: the monstrous winged Harpies, in an incident much favoured by vase-painters and described if not dramatized in Aeschylus' *Phineus*, produced together with his *Persians* in 472 BC. *no wings to be seen*: cf. 250 and n.

54 *eyes . . . loathsome fluid*: repeating Orestes' description at *LB* 1058.

55–6 *Clothing of this form is not right . . . men's houses*: as black and death-laden, it is potentially polluting, 52, 190–5 etc., and therefore threatening; cf. the Furies at e.g. *LB* 1049. For the converse, the purity of white clothing, see 353 and n.

62–3 *doctor and diviner together*: one word in the Greek (as at *Ag.* 1622, but metaphorical there). *interpreter of portents*: in order to point to cleansing remedies; the 'amazing' Furies are themselves a portent, 46. *cleanser of others' houses*: of Orestes' house, 283, 578, *LB* 965 ff. (n.).

85–7, 64–117 The manner of staging this sequence and its successive entries is much disputed. With the transposition of 85–7 to precede 64 the stage-movements are much easier to imagine (I follow Taplin, *Stagecraft*, 363–74); the exchange between Orestes and Apollo has a start which is clearer to the audience, and a neater sequence and end; also, Orestes' opening appeal to Apollo at 85 matches his opening appeal to Athena at 235. [Some editors who retain the MSS order of lines think that the whole interior scene is disclosed after 63 in a tableau of Furies surrounding Orestes, either visibly through the open door, or by display on a moving platform which is rolled out (the *ekkyklêma*: see Introduction, p. xlv).] The entry of Clytemnestra at 94 and her exit at 139 seem more practical theatrically if made both by the one side, than through the door of the temple; there is no 'collision' between her and Apollo as he re-enters the temple at 93.

64 *I will not betray you*: echoing Orestes' confidence in Apollo at *LB* 269; cf. Orestes at 235 below.

69 *maidens in old age*: the Furies had a religious by-name 'The Aged (Women)' (for their names see n. to 1041). These ancient deities carry the name 'maidens, children' to convey their vigour unimpaired by longevity, cf. 416; similarly the monstrous female Phorcides at *Prometheus* 794. [Others punctuate to give 'the abominable maidens, ancient old women (that are) children'.]

78 *brooding*: *Ag.* 669 and n.

80 *her ancient statue*: made of olive-wood (the productive tree so valuable to Athens' subsistence and in Athena's protection). Believed to have fallen from the sky, it was carefully preserved on the Athenian Acropolis, even when Pheidias made the goddess's great gold and ivory statue for her new temple the Parthenon not long after Aeschylus' death. The formal clasping of a person (or god's image or altar) by a suppliant protected him from rejection and violence until his plea was at least heard. The mere presence of a suppliant also imposed obligation (*LB* 569 and n., cf. 232–4 below). Apollo has protected his suppliant Orestes (and himself ordered him to become one, 204, *LB* 1034–9): 92, 151.

81–3 *judges*: an intimation of the coming jury-trial at Athens, 483; cf. Apollo again at 224. *release you . . . from these miseries*: see *Ag.* 1 and n.

84, 88 *I did persuade you to kill your own mother*: Apollo at 203, 579–80; Orestes at 594, cf. *LB* 270, 297–8. *do not let fear . . . your mind*: see Orestes at *LB* 1023–4.

90 *Hermes . . . true to your name*: etymologically, Hermes is 'sender, escorter'; cf. n. to *LB* 1–2, *Fragment 1*. He carries the gods' messages, and so identifies with and protects human heralds, *Ag.* 515. *father we share*: Zeus: Hermes' mother was Maia (*LB* 813); Apollo's was Leto, 323 below.

92–3 *Zeus . . . escort*: for this role of Zeus see especially *Suppliants* 347. It correlates with his protection of all strangers and guests (*Ag.* 61 etc.). Apollo is criticizing the Furies' hostility to a suppliant's sanctuary (again at 232–4), which he expects Athens to respect in the normal way. [Text and punctuation are insecure; the translation represents a slight conjectural intervention into the markedly idiomatic MSS text kept by West.]

94–139 Clytemnestra's ghost: the text gives no hint of her costuming; probably she was dressed as in life, but her dress might have carried marks of her bloody death (*LB* 904). The ghost of King Darius at *Persians* 660–1 seems to wear the magnificent apparel of living royalty. Ghosts are not rare in Greek Tragedy (see Introduction, §2.4, at n. 27).

97–9 *the slain ceaselessly reproaching me*: those murdered, like Agamemnon, demand vengeful punishment; the Furies should defend her in Hades as well as persecute her killer on earth. *wander in shame*: unquiet like the ghost of the unburied Patroclus, Homer, *Iliad* 23.74.

103–4 *See these blows . . . by the eyes*: the meaning appears to be that the mind asleep nevertheless receives messages through the eyes from images seen in dreams (116, 132, 155; Clytemnestra's dream recounted at *LB* 527 ff.), and takes them 'to heart' (135); cf. (of men awake) 523 'in his heart's clear light' (n.) and *LB* 854 'a mind that has good eyes'. (Compare 'What hours, O what black hours we had spent / This night! What sights you heart, saw i . .', Gerard Manley Hopkins.)

105 [Omitted from the translation; it reads 'but by day men's fate is unforeseen', but editors believe it to have been imported from another play.]

106–9 *licked*: the Furies 'slurp' blood at 193, 264. *libations without wine, plain*: for such offerings to underworld deities and the dead cf. 860 and n. to *Ag.* 94–6. The description *plain* translates Greek 'sober', half-duplicating 'without wine': wine was omitted either because simple offerings were a ritual survival from ancient and conservative practice, or because nothing sharp was wanted in emollient offerings to powers whose potential ill-will was to be placated (see Clytemnestra's offerings at *LB* 15, 92). *Meals . . . by night . . . shared by no god*: 350–1—except by Hecate, a goddess of the underworld, the dark, and witchcraft. *altar-hearths*: 806, ground-level hearths, regular for offerings to the underworld, burned or not, and symbolically level with or even dug into the earth's surface.

112 *from your nets' midst*: repeating for Orestes the image of Agamemnon 'caught', most recently at *LB* 999–1000.

114 *existence*: literally 'life-spirit, soul', and ironic: she means her continued existence as a dead 'life' or 'spirit'. For the idea see *LB* 355–9.

117–29 *s.d.*: the MSS preserve apparently ancient stage-directions characterizing the Chorus's inarticulate sounds at 117, 120, 123, 126, and 129, which they make while asleep. Such surviving directions are extremely rare, and most are probably later editors' insertions. See Taplin, *Stagecraft*, 15.

119 *Suppliants are no friends of mine*: the Furies take up this hostility at 151–2, 176. Contrast Apollo at 92–3 (n.). [The MSS text is corrupt; most corrections give roughly this sense.]

125 *wreak evil*: cf. 71; see the catalogues of their brutality at 186–95, *LB* 276–90.

129 *serpent*: any individual Fury (cf. their snakes at *LB* 1050), but the image possibly recalls Clytemnestra herself as snake: *LB* 249, 995 and nn.

136 *goads to rightful minds*: a warning that the Furies may lose their privileged role if they fail to act energetically; cf. 143–6, 150, 219, 778–93.

138 *fire from your belly*: as if blasted out. The Furies wither their victims, 267, 339 = 916, *LB* 296.

142 *prelude*: the dream is prelude to what follows upon waking, the call to pursuit, 139, 231.

143 *Oh, the outrage!*: colloquial, in sudden and violent realization.

144 [*I laboured*: West's attractive replacement of a repeated 'suffered'.]

148–9 *Son of Zeus there*: Apollo. *turning to theft*: also 153. Theft was an occasional mythic act of Hermes (cf. his stealth at *LB* 816), Apollo's accomplice here in helping Orestes evade the Furies, 90.

150 *Young god*: (compare 162) . . . *ridden me down*: a complaint repeated both before the Furies' defeat in Orestes' trial (731) and after it (778 and 808); cf. 882.

152 *his parents*: only Clytemnestra is meant; for this allusive plural cf. *LB* 385, 419, etc.

154 *Which of these things . . . just?*: contrast Orestes' opinion of Apollo, 85–7.

155–61 = 162–8 These two stanzas show remarkable and sustained 'responsion' in the placing, the syllabic and rhythmic pattern and the grammatical function of words, especially in 157–61 and 164–8. Translation can hardly reproduce this insistent, sacral effect; cf. Introduction, §3.3, at n. 33.

157–8 *goad . . . core*: cf. the language of Clytemnestra, 135–6.

160–1 *scourging, brutal as a public hangman's . . . agony to have*: extreme violence familiar to the Athenian public, and appropriate rather to what the inhuman Furies themselves inflict (*LB* 290, cf. Apollo at 186–95 below). *frozen agony*: bodily movement only exacerbates it. *to have*: awkward in English, but corresponding with the end of 168 (the Greek has the same verb also at the end of 154, where it carries a different meaning).

164 *throne*: Apollo's prophetic seat, 18.

167 *earth's navel*: see n. to *LB* 1036–7.

170 *at his own urge, at his own call*: the Furies repeat this charge of harbouring Orestes at 200, 204; cf. Apollo at 84, 579–80.

173 *Fates*: almost certainly a self-reference here; for this title for the Furies see n. to *LB* 306. At 723 below, however, the ordinary Fates are meant.

175–7 *he flees below*: driven by the Furies, 139, 421–4. *never to be free*: 340. *another vengeful power*: see *Ag.* 1501 and n. The Furies pursue until death, when Hades will take over the everlasting persecution of the matricide (339–40). [The words *he is to go where* replace MSS 'for that one', meaning Orestes and imp̶o̶s̶s̶i̶b̶l̶y̶ d̶e̶s̶c̶r̶i̶b̶i̶n̶g̶ 'vengeful power'.]

179 *s.d.: Apollo . . . bow and arrows*: Apollo is an archer-god, 181–2, *Ag.* 510.

186–90 *decapitation . . . Do you hear?*: a collection of grisly punishments and tortures both barbarian and Greek (for stoning see e.g. n. to *Ag.* 1616).

192–3 *Every aspect of your form*: cf. the Prophetess at 55–6 (n.).

197 *no god's friendly favour*: i.e. no god would willingly act as your herdsman. Cf. the Furies' own words at 365.

198–234 The remainder of this scene, before the Furies leave Delphi and the action resumes at Athens in 235, anticipates and clarifies much of the argumentation there, especially about Apollo's role under Zeus in commanding Orestes to the matricide and then purifying him. With 199 (Apollo's joint responsibility with Orestes) cf. 465, 579–80; with 202 (the god's instruction to Orestes to kill his mother) cf. 467, 594–5, 623–4; with 204–5 and 233 (the god's protection of Orestes as his suppliant after the matricide) cf. 236–7, 281–7, 445–52, 473–4, 576–8; with 208–10 and 230–1 (the Furies' defence of their immemorial persecution of such killers) cf. 419 ff.; with 211–12 (the superiority of the father and king to the woman and mother, a particularly important argument) cf. 603–8, 622–66; with 213–21 (the Furies' offence against the gods as protectors of marriage) cf. 602, 627, 739–40.

The stichomythic form of 201–12 aptly regulates the antagonism of Apollo and Furies into a clear sequence of argument (and distichomythia between them has this function at 711–33), just as stichomythia shapes the recapitulatory argument of Orestes and Furies at 585–608.

202 *stranger*: Orestes is such as a suppliant at Delphi (41)—but was previously disguised as a treacherous stranger and guest in his mother's house, *LB* 657, 668, etc.

204 *give refuge to the murderer*: 163–70; *fresh*: 282.

206 *escorting him on his mission here*: grim humour: any mission to Delphi would go with a sanctified retinue. The Greek wording describes also the Furies' own escort by Athenians when they leave in ritual procession at 1005.

209 *Make a boast . . . privilege!*: both sardonic and contemptuous; cf. Apollo at 228.

214 *pledges . . . for a marriage's fulfilment*: Hera, as wife to the supreme god Zeus, was the particular god of marriage, e.g. *Suppliants* 1035; Zeus' power as 'fulfiller' at e.g. 28, 974 (n.).

216 *what is dearest to mankind*: not sexual pleasure alone (*Cypris*, i.e. Aphrodite, goddess of love, *Ag.* 419), but the generation of children and the ensuing closeness between them and their parents, e.g. 608, *LB* 234, 1051 (n.).

221 *driving Orestes into exile unjustly*: countering the Chorus's defence of their role at 210.

234 *betrayed*: Apollo's last words in this scene echo his first, 64–5 (see n.); and his last words to the Furies, on the sanctity of a suppliant, echo his last words after Orestes left Delphi, 92–3; cf. 270 and n. It is a variety of 'ring-composition', conveying importance (n. to *Ag.* 20).

    s.d.: There is speculation whether and how the *change of scene from Delphi to . . . Athens* was managed in performance. Some think that Athena's statue may have been brought on (Orestes approaches it at 242, but the language is allusive; but at 259 he seems indeed to be holding it; cf. n. to 80). Any opening of the stage-door to disclose it, as if in the interior of Athena's temple on the Acropolis, might have confused the spectators after the door had been so focal of the action in front of the Delphic temple. Furthermore, it is implicit in Athena's words at 685–90 that by 566 there is a further shift, for the jury-trial is set on the Areopagus, a hill opposite the Acropolis (n. to 490–565). It may be safest to think that the move to the Areopagus was left to the spectators' inference from the words: see Taplin, *Stagecraft*, 390 f.; Introduction, p. xliv.

235–43 These lines are in effect a brief 'second prologue', marking the start of the second 'action'; similarly Agamemnon's entry-speech at *Ag.* 810–54. Lines 235–6 are deliberately echoed in 240–2, to emphasize the imminent crisis: will Athena not save Apollo's agent? Orestes continues this argument in 276–99 and ignores the Furies although they have addressed him in 264–9.

235 *Queen Athena*: as again at 288 and 443, Orestes from Argos addresses the goddess as would a native Athenian to honour her supreme patronage of the democratic city. The Chorus of Furies use the same address at 892 as they move towards accepting her offer of a permanent place at Athens.

236 *one accursed*: i.e. possessed by the 'avenging demon' of the family, *Ag.* 1501 and n. *no polluted suppliant*: Orestes insists on this again, to Athena's face, at 445.

239 *other men's houses . . . journeyings*: Orestes has received such purification for kindred murder as heads of households could conventionally give to strangers, wherever he has visited during his exile (285, 451: contrast *LB* 291–5); see 92–3.

249 *Our flock has been ranging*: an echo for the audience of Apollo's jibe at 196, 'a flock like yours'.

250 *wingless*: the Prophetess so described them at 51. They pursued Orestes as he fled by ship, 240. The goddess Athena describes her own passage similarly at 403–4.

253 *blood smiles its greeting to me*: at Euripides, *Troades* 1176 blood smiles from a shattered skull. Cf. Introduction, §4, at n. 43, on the artist Francis Bacon's obsession with this line.

258 [*himself, with no defence*: the text is conjectural, the MSS giving no sense.]

260 *he wants to undergo trial*: Apollo told the Furies at 224 that this was Orestes' purpose.

261–3 *blood on the ground . . . is gone*: the message of *Ag.* 1018 ff. (n.).

264–5 *gruel . . . to slurp*: a coarsely vivid image, repeated from 193. The 'gruel' of blood perverts the regular ritual gruel of libations to the dead, for which see 106–9 and *Ag.* 96 and nn. The image also continues the principle of exact retaliation (*LB* 310–14 and n.); cf. the ritual described in 283 (n.).

270 *not reverencing . . . stranger*: Apollo had insisted on such reverence for a suppliant (92–3, 232–4), the Furies accusing him of harbouring a polluted one (169 ff., 205).

273 *auditor*: a term from the review conducted upon any Athenian magistrate leaving office.

275 *written tablets of his mind*: see n. to *LB* 450.

277 [*the moments for many things*: conjectural for MSS 'many purifications'.]

280 *The bloodshed . . . hand*: translation uncertain, because of the violent combination of images from sleep and medical 'pathology'; equally possible is 'the bloodshed on my hand drowses and wastes away'. *wasting away*: cf. 238.

283 *young pigs were killed*: piglets, as immature and therefore 'pure' creatures, were killed in a safe re-enactment of homicide and their blood poured over the hands of the murderer in symbolic cleansing of the polluted blood upon them; cf. 450.

286 [*time . . . as it ages*: many editors delete this line, obviously proverbial in character, as an anticlimax after Orestes' description of his purification in 280–5.]

289–91 *without warfare . . . faithful allies*: Apollo promises such an alliance before the verdict in the trial, 667–73; Orestes swears it after his acquittal, 762–74. See Introduction, p. xlx.

292–4 *marching . . . defensively*: a paraphrase; the literal meaning 'puts her foot straight forward or (has it) covered (by a shield)' shows an image from heavy infantry in battle. *Libyan places . . . Triton*: myth placed Athena's birth at the river Triton somewhere in North Africa ('Libya' is a general name for it). She was born fully armed from the head of her father Zeus (see 664–6); lines 294–6 appeal deliberately to her martial prowess, which she affirms herself at 913–15.

295 *Phlegra*: 'The Place of Burning', scene of the battle of the Gods and the Titans in which Athena helped her father Zeus incinerate them with lightning (*Prometheus* 205 ff., cf. *Eum.* 827–8). The mythical place was later identified with Pallene, a mountainous peninsula in northern Greece.

296 *manly captain bold in command*: in evoking Athena's possession of male attributes and powers, Orestes anticipates Apollo's appeal for her greater sympathy towards the murdered king, 625 ff.—which she confirms in acknowledging her greater affinity to the male, being herself motherless, 736 ff. and nn.

298 *set me free*: the wording appears deliberately vague; 'set me free' may refer to judicial acquittal (a synonymous term at 752), as well as freedom in general (cf. the Furies at 174–5). *what I have here*: a plural pronoun in the Greek; it can also be translated as 'these persons', i.e. the Furies.

300–1 *wandering exile . . . with happiness unknown*: cf. 423, *LB* 291–4.

302 *shadow drained of blood . . . powers*: their threat at 264–7, 333, cf. Clytemnestra at 138–9.

304–5 *nurtured and consecrated for me . . . altar*: the image once again of the 'sacrifice' of all the victims doomed by the family curse (again at 328 = 341 allusively to Orestes).

306 *song to bind you*: again at 332 = 345. The idea is from magic, and at once reverses Orestes' prayer to Athena to 'set him free', 298.

307–96 This long 'binding-song' of the Furies is sacral in shape and style: a chanted introduction (308–20) precedes pairs of responding sung stanzas pieced out by refrain-like sections; the first of these is duplicated (328–33 = 341–6), to convey the inflexible determination of the Furies, a device repeated at 778–93 = 808–23.

309 *our hateful music*: cf. 332 = 345, *Ag.* 1186–7 and n.

310 *our party*: the word used of their 'side' by Electra, Orestes, and Chorus at *LB* 114, 458.

323–4 *the blind and the seeing*: see n. to 388. *Leto's child*: Apollo.

335 *spun off*: the regular metaphor: fate is a length (of yarn), and so any fortune within it is 'spun off'; but the metaphor makes a violent paradox with *piercing blow*. This is an adjective in the Greek attached to *Fate*, meaning 'frontally right through', and used of blows struck by weapons, e.g. *LB* 184. The implication here is that Fate is penetrative, all-powerful, drastic.

340 *not too free*: sardonic understatement: death does not end their persecution; cf.175–7 and n.

351 *no god who shares . . . with us*: 109 and n.; repeated at 386.

353 *all-white clothing*: the garb both of those unpolluted by crime or purified from it (n. to 41–5), and of joyful celebration; it is the converse of the death-laden black worn by the Furies, 370, cf. 55–6 and n. [*no part in*: the Greek is faulty, but most conjectures keep this sense. The loss of a verse is suggested only by incomplete responsion with 366 in the antistrophe, for the sense is entire. Some editors have nevertheless transferred 368–71 to follow 380 as a separate stanza, so that 360–7 are followed immediately by 372–6 and make one stanza corresponding with 347–59.]

355–6 *Warfare reared tamely at home kills . . . friend*: perhaps a reminiscence of the lion-cub reared as a pet which later breaks out into innate violence, *Ag.* 717 ff. The War-god in the house: *Ag.* 1511 and n.

358–9 For the Furies *draining* human blood see 264–7 and n. [The text from *however* to *draining youth's blood* is badly damaged, and these last words are conjectural.]

360–4 *first interrogations*: a concept borrowed from Athenian judicial procedure. The Furies' justice is peremptory, and with no trial at all; now however they are themselves brought with similar abruptness to take part in a trial, 490 ff.; see n. to *Ag.* 813–14. [Both text and interpretation are insecure in these lines.]

367–8 *beneath a living sky*: 'living' is a slight over-translation of 'open sky', to give the full implication. [Some editors change *on earth* in 368 to 'under the earth', but it expresses the Furies' habitual view upward from the Underworld.]

375–6 *with pace in my legs . . . full stretch*: the athletic image recalls Orestes as chariot-racer or foot-runner also intent on vengeance, *LB* 794–9.

377 *the maiming* (359, 369–76) *takes his wits away*: earlier at 342–5.

380 *murk*: *LB* 52 and n.

382 *we bring to fulfilment*: the language commonly used of Zeus himself, 974 and n.

384 *awesome*: almost certainly an allusion to a cult-title of the Furies, 'The Awesome Ones', 1041 and n.

385 [*pursuit . . . dishonoured*: text and translation uncertain.]

387 [*on a path hard and rocky* translates one remarkable compound word in the Greek; possibly not corrupt, although West marks it so; it seems to contradict *slime* in 386.]

388 *seeing and sightless eyes*: both literal (even eyes cannot aid escape from the Furies, and darkness is their strength, e.g. 378 ff., *LB* 285–9; and they blind their victims, 186) and allusive, of the living and the dead alike, as 322.

394 *and I meet with no dishonour*: although the Furies are 'objects of hate' (73), men pay them full respect, unlike the Olympian gods who reject them, 350–1, 365–6, 385. Athena promises them special honour once they settle in Athens, 992, 1029.

397 *s.d.*: *Athena enters . . . from the side*: there is dispute, whether Athena entered by walking on or riding in a chariot, or by appearing on top of the stage-building, or aerially and more theatrically on the 'crane' or 'machine'.

The details of 404, *wingless and with the fold of my aegis flapping*, imply miraculous solo flight and seem to conflict with 405, 'yoking this chariot with its superb horses', so that most editors delete the latter verse (it is omitted from the translation); but neither is absolutely incompatible with entry at ground level or on high, since the words 'this chariot' could be aided by a gesture towards one notionally just off-stage. Because Athena leaves at 488 to gather some of her citizens to form a jury, it is easiest to think of both entry here and exit there as on one level, the ground. She is magnificently clad in full armour, fresh from a role in war (398–402, cf. 292–6) and wears her identifying *aegis* (404). The name apparently means 'goat-skin' (but in a discrepant myth at Euripides, *Ion* 996 it is made from the skin of the Gorgon which the goddess helped Perseus kill: cf. *LB* 835); another ancient etymology derived it from the verb *aisso*, 'dart', as if it gave Athena supernatural speed. Art represents it as a loose half-garment or cloak-like thing, rough-textured and tasselled—sometimes with snakes, terrifying appendages like the Gorgons' snake-hair, *LB* 1049–50. One might compare the Scottish tartan worn over the shoulder.

397–402 *From far away I heard*: as Orestes was confident she would, 297. These few lines may be more than mere colour; they go with evocation later in the play (864–6, 913–15 and n.) of Athens' prowess in war and conquest; and some take them to allude to contemporary Athenian reassertion of rights over Sigeum near Troy (Scamander, its river, *Ag.* 511 etc.), where there was a temple to Athena. *Theseus' sons*: one of many proud kennings for the Athenians, honouring their greatest hero-king; cf. 13, 683 and nn., 1026.

404 *unwearied*: the Greek adjective <u>atrutos</u> probably yielded Athena's cult-name Atrytone (not to be confused with her birth-place Triton, 293 and n.). *wingless*: crossing the sea nevertheless like the Furies, 250.

410 *you who are like no kind of begotten things*: Athena is at a loss to describe the Furies, as was the Prophetess at 57–8. [The suggestion of a line missing is West's, e.g. '. . . *statue* (and you; I count him among strangers), *and you who etc.*'. Other editors change the Greek syntax in 410–11 to give roughly the same sense.]

411 *neither belonging to goddesses seen by gods*: kept apart from the whole divine company by Zeus, 365–7; the expression seems rather flat, but may echo a cultic by-name for the Furies.

414 *to assume a right*: a small amplification of just 'a right' in the Greek, for the implication seems to be 'to make this a right'. [Many editors read 'is far from justice, and right is at a distance'.]

415–35 Stichomythia carries the measured interrogation of the Furies by Athena. She is polite (413–14) until her remark in 430 briefly creates a tension swiftly resolved when the Furies accept her jurisdiction, 432–4—as Orestes has already done (243, cf. 468–9) and as Apollo both proposed (81–3, 224) and later confirms (580–1). For this style of 'acceptance'-stichomythia cf. 892–902 (n. to 778–1047).

416–18 *eternal children*: 69 and n. *Curses*: for the Furies' roles and names see n. to 1041. *names in their meaning*: for this idea see n. to *Ag.* 681.

426–7 Athena tries to establish whether Orestes' act was entirely his own, or due to so great a fear that it may be pardonable on that ground (compare fear as a factor in Agamemnon's behaviour at *Ag.* 933–4). *goad*: for this common image see 157 and n., 466. [*When no necessity overcame him*: West's correction of a linguistically faulty phrase usually emended to 'from necessity'.]

429 *He would not accept an oath . . . give one*: a reference to 303, although Orestes' refusal to swear his innocence is not there explicit.

431 *not poor in cleverness*: the Chorus hear Athena's 430 as an equivocation. She is goddess of wisdom, born from Zeus' head (663–6) and therefore possessed of his intellect (850).

441 *a solemn suppliant like Ixion*: only a broad comparison; Athena is registering the gravity of Orestes' plight. Ixion shed his father-in-law's blood, to avoid paying him a bride-price; he supplicated Zeus himself for purification, and succeeded; but his ungrateful attempt to seduce Zeus' wife Hera led to his famous torment on the wheel in Hades. Orestes has stressed that he has already been purified by Apollo, 283.

450–2 *suckling beast . . . cleanse from bloodshed*: 283 and n. *at other men's houses*: 239.

456–7 *with whom you yourself . . . a city no more*: at *Ag.* 810 ff. Agamemnon seemed to equate his own part in taking Troy with that of the unnamed gods who were his partners. Athena's role at Troy in Homer was her support for the Greeks, in particular helping Achilles kill the Trojan champion Hector (*Iliad* 22.177–299), and as the inspiration of the Trojan Horse (*Odyssey* 8.493).

458 *He did not die well*: 625–7, *LB* 479; but possibly a point is being made to reinforce 'well' in 455.

460–1 *trapping him . . . his sight*: literally 'hiding him in cunningly worked traps', the fatal robes against which Agamemnon was blindly helpless *in his bath*, 634–5 and n.

466 *warned me of pains . . . like goads*: *LB* 271–96.

472 [*to custom*: text conjectural for MSS 'nevertheless'.]

475 *giving the city . . . no cause for blame*: cf. Athena's circumspection towards the Furies at 413.

481 *no wrath against me*: from the Furies (478–9), from either of Athena's difficult choices, to allow Orestes to stay in her protection or to send him safely away. The anger is however unspecific in the Greek, so that potential anger by Apollo may be hinted, if Orestes is surrendered to the Furies. This is why Athena devolves the matter upon a human jury-court over which she will preside in her godhead, so that a joint decision by god and man may cause no angry resentment from the Furies (see Introduction, p. xxxv). [The MSS are unmetrical in *bring harsh pain*, but a small change gives the same sense. Further, the MSS have 'impossibly (harsh)', which runs against an ancient interpretation of the line, 'it is difficult for me to send the Furies away without their anger', and editors emend accordingly.]

482–9 [Not just a verb like *I shall appoint* is missing, but a whole line
containing it, and editors usually locate it after 484; 489 is variously
moved, so that 487–8 may stand out as crisp exit-lines for Athena.]

490–565 While Athena is absent assembling her jurors, the Furies
again sing powerfully of their age-old role (earlier at 311–16, 299–
390, especially their 'binding-song' 321–96): they fear a collapse of
moral and social order if they are defeated, 490–516, and they
advocate moderation in all human conduct as the only way to
prosperity, 517–65 (a theme repeated when they are reconciled to
Athena, 955–1020). Their moralizing upon Justice recalls Aeschylus' sermons through the Chorus at *Ag.* 750–82, 1001–33.

The scene is notionally reset during this ode (see also n. to 234).
Both Orestes and the Furies have remained visible since their arrival
at the Athenian Acropolis, yet 685–90, 'this hill . . . Ares' rocky hill',
locates the trial-scene from 566 and the remainder of the play upon
the Areopagus. Taplin, *Stagecraft*, 390 ff., speaks of a 'refocussing' of
the action, without explicit stage-directions; comparable is the shift
from Agamemnon's tomb to the palace-door at *LB* 584 (n.). If
Athena's statue is brought on before 234, stage-hands must now
remove it when they here bring on seats for the jurors (629) during
the trial-scene, and two urns for the votes to condemn or acquit (675,
709, etc.), as in Athenian judicial practice.

490–1 *Catastrophe . . . from new ordinances*: destruction for the Furies'
ancient prerogatives from Athena's new court, as they assert when
Orestes is acquitted, 778–9 and 808–9, cf. 150. The translation of
these two lines is however hotly disputed. [Some editors secure this
meaning by changing the text to 'The overthrow of established
ordinances is coming'; the alternative translation 'catastrophe to the
new ordinances' implies a power for the Furies which they do not
have, and contradicts 491–2.]

492 *justice which is harm to justice*: a dilemma of the *Oresteia*'s moral
theology: cf. *Ag.* 1560 ff., *LB* 461; Introduction, p. xxxiii.

499–502 The argument of these lines appears to be 'if licence brings
all manner of crime (490–8), and the threat of our anger is
insufficient consequence, we shall cause indiscriminate death'.
madness-driven translates the Greek word describing women possessed by the god Dionysus, who were imagined to celebrate him
by running free in nature's wild, by ecstatic dancing and by the
hunting down and ingestion of living animal prey (cf. n. to 25–6)—
the activities of the Furies themselves: pursuit 131, 251; dancing
371; hunting 131–9, 147, 246–7, *LB* 287 ff.; ingestion of living
blood 184, 263–7.

499 *neither . . .*: answered not by 'nor' but by a positively worded (if still adverse) idea in 503.

503–7 [*and all men . . . comfort*: West's text includes many emendations.]

518 *when Justice's house falls*: the Furies mean here the collapse of their own justice against parent-killers.

518–19 *a watch on minds by fear*: the imagery of *Ag.* 975–7, cf. 696–9 below. *seated above*: among the Olympian gods, *Ag.* 183 etc.; Zeus terrifying to men, *Suppliants* 479.

520–1 *wisdom through grief*: recalling *Ag.* 180–1 and 1425 once more and varying the maxim 'learning through suffering', *Ag.* 177 etc.

522–3 *in his heart's clear light*: perhaps while asleep: so West, comparing 103–4 (see n.), *Ag.* 179, cf. 14. [The text of these two lines is particularly insecure.]

524–5 *city . . . revere Justice*: civic morality as precondition for prosperity (537) here enters the thinking of the play; it is at once developed in 526 ff., and features in the play's resolution, e.g. 976–95; n. to 490–565 above.

528–9 *anarchic . . . despots*: the same antithesis at 696.

534 *insolence is child to irreverence*: the sermon of the Chorus at *Ag.* 750 ff.; cf. n. on 757 there.

539 *the altar of Justice*: *Ag.* 381–4, where the imagery of kicking it over also occurs; *godless feet*: cf. 110 above and *LB* 643.

544 *an end is appointed and waits*: the doctrine of inevitable if delayed punishment occurs first at *Ag.* 58–9 (see n.; Introduction, §2.3, at start); in this context of insolence punished cf. especially *Ag.* 782.

547–8 *attentiveness to . . . guests*: a reverse-echo of Paris' crime against his host, *Ag.* 61, 401 and of Atreus' against his (unwanted) guest (and brother) Thyestes 1590—and recalling Orestes as guest at *LB* 700 ff.

554–7 *cargo . . . shatters*: life's material success and disaster as voyage and shipwreck. The image continues through the Antistrophe 558–65, and the whole sequence recalls *Ag.* 1005–13.

559 *hard to struggle with*: the image from wrestling again, cf. *LB* 692, of the house's Curse.

566 *s.d.: The scene is now the Areopagus*: see nn. to 234 and 490–565; for the Areopagus itself see n. to 685–90.

567 *Etruscan trumpet*: although Etruria (a neighbour of Rome) was credited with the instrument's invention, the adjective has almost lost its literal meaning, rather as in 'French horn'. When does the

trumpet sound—at once, or only when Athena formally institutes the court at 681? [*to the heaven* is an almost certain supplement.]

571–3 *it helps for the whole city . . . well judged*: directed almost at the contemporary audience, to strengthen their belief in the divine antiquity of the Council of the Areopagus; see Introduction p. xiv

Some editors transfer 681–710, Athena's long speech 'instituting' the Court, to follow 573, so as to remove the apparent awkwardness implicit in the MSS order: the new court does some of its work (the jurors are addressed by the parties at e.g. 601, 613) before it is inaugurated (681–4). But Apollo enters unannounced at this very place, 573, so that, it is argued, Aeschylus may show Athena taken by surprise and needing at once to assert her supremacy in her own city, 574. Orestes has however told her of Apollo's order to come to Athens (241) and his shared responsibility (465). Apollo accordingly acts as defence witness but also as advocate for Orestes (576–80), accepting the goddess's presidency (580–1) exactly as the Furies had done (435). [*as well as these parties* translates a conjecture in 573 which West himself does not put into his text; but the MSS have 'as well as Orestes', which excludes the Furies. I can make no sense of the ancient commentator's reading 'as well as of these persons', which West accepts, without supposing the loss of a line after *for all time* in 572.]

579 *to support his case myself*: Apollo's next words show even more clearly that his actions are as much on trial as those of Orestes; cf. Orestes at 465, and the Furies' accusation of Apollo's total responsibility at 200.

585–608 This carefully formed exchange shows stichomythia at its most appropriate, in a probing, relentless interrogation; the final couplet, 607–8, presents Orestes with a question which he must appeal to Apollo to answer, 609 ff.

589–90 *three throws*: the number needed for victory in wrestling: *Ag.* 172 and n. *one who is not yet down* is also a wrestling-image.

592 *cut into her throat*: once more, bloodshed like a sacrificial killing; cf. 328.

597 *gets you caught*: literally 'snatches, seizes', further language from hunting.

598 *I have my trust*: in Apollo: see Orestes at *LB* 296–7. *my father . . . from the grave*: see especially *LB* 142–4, 456–60, 479–509, 1051.

603 *So you have your life, and she is now free through her murder?*: i.e. if she was guilty (the Furies weaken their case by seeming to admit this

possibility), her death was the just penalty and gave her 'freedom'; why then should not your death be equally just?

604 *why didn't you drive her . . . alive*: cf. Clytemnestra herself at *Ag.* 1412 ff., asking why Agamemnon had not been exiled for killing their daughter Iphigenia.

605 *She was no blood-kin . . . killed*: the answer the Furies gave Apollo at 212.

606 *And am I blood-kin of my mother?*: Orestes has now to forget his statement that he shared his mother's blood, *LB* 1038.

607–8 *How else did she nurture you . . . a mother's blood*: except by giving you her blood, something more precious than the milk which Clytemnestra herself used as a plea, *LB* 896–8. *nearest and dearest*: Orestes (464) and Apollo (216 and n.) had argued that the father had this supreme value to the child.

612–13 *you are now to give your judgement . . . justly shed or not*: approximately the wording which Orestes used at 468 to Athena, to whom an appeal for 'judgement' is better directed; Apollo can and will confirm only the 'justice' of his instruction to Orestes, 615. But Apollo's role as advocate becomes rather the communication of Zeus' justice (618–19), which is to prevail over everything (620–1). *so I may tell them here*: it sounds as if Orestes will conduct his own defence, despite Apollo's promise to share it (579); but when Apollo's evidence (614–21, cf. 609) is directed at the jurors, it is taken up by the Furies and their argument continues with him alone; Orestes speaks again only after the votes are cast, 744.

621 *an oath is in no way stronger than Zeus*: at 218 Apollo argued that any oath was weaker than the just allegiance of husband and wife, and at *LB* 901 Pylades claimed supremacy for the oath sworn to avenge Agamemnon. Here, Apollo asks the jurors to set greater value on the power of Zeus and its implicit conformity with justice than on anything sworn—although at 486 Athena invited both parties to bring their evidence on oath.

628 *like an Amazon's*: Clytemnestra's treacherous murder of the kingly Agamemnon was even more monstrous than would have been his killing in war by an Amazon, one of the mythical women-warriors (685 and n.); but for Clytemnestra's unfeminine resort to weapons see nn. to *Ag.* 1149 and 1232–6, *LB* 630.

632 *trafficking*: warfare treated as commerce, because of the booty in prospect, 400, *Ag.* 342; at *Seven* 545 war is 'petty trading'. *mostly for the better*: possibly an allusion to the misery from Agamemnon's war

(*Ag.* 432 ff.), but hardly to his killing of Iphigenia, which goes unmentioned in this play, even by Clytemnestra's Ghost.

632 [For the missing line West suggests '. . . *loyal* (words, stood by him) *when he was completing his* (soothing wash in the silver) *bath*'.]

634–5 *threw a cloak over him like a tent* , , , *cut him down*: a last rehearsal of the killing, *Ag.* 1126 ff. etc. and 460–1 above, repeating many of the images. *cunning*: the Greek word is ambiguous, meaning both 'ingeniously contrived' and 'artfully worked, variegated'.

637–8 *absolute in his majesty*: Apollo repeats the insistence on Agamemnon's majesty (456, 625–6) which was so dominant in *Ag.* and *LB* (n. to *LB* 723–5). *now told to you*: the wording echoes a law-court formula of conclusion (used by Athena at 710 'My speech is said'), and Aeschylus' intention is explicit in *it is the ending of my speech*.

641 *his old father Cronus in bonds*: *Ag.* 171–2 (see n. to 168–9).

647–9 *dust . . . no raising him up*: 261–3 and n. *no spells*: *Ag.* 1021.

652 [*acquittal*: a conjecture replacing MSS 'Now (*see how you are pleading for his*) being on trial'.]

654 *then to live in his father's house*: the converse of Orestes' argument against Clytemnestra, *LB* 909.

655–6 *altars . . . public ones . . . brotherhood . . . sprinkled water*: the Furies see Orestes as polluted still, and an unpurified man would be barred from any public ceremony as officiator (as 'owner' of his father's house), and from admission to any smaller religious group: *brotherhood* translates Greek 'phratry', a clan-based group. Exclusion from a phratry in historical Athens would threaten loss of citizen's rights. Again, compare Apollo's threats at *LB* 291–4.

660–1 *the one who mounts her*: an astonishingly intrusive image, its animal violence (the Greek verb is literally 'leaps on') suggesting the crude unreason of Apollo's assault on motherhood. *not thwarted by god*: when the woman fails to conceive.

664–6 [The missing line probably contained the idea 'neither begotten in any union'. *goddess* is an emendation for MSS 'god', a slip by a Greek copyist which destroys the point. Some editors emend more drastically, or supplement the text, e.g. West himself with '*but the kind of child a god* (himself makes grow, but which without a father) *no* (woman) *could give birth to*'.]

667–73 *Pallas . . . the pledges sworn*: Apollo abandons defensive argument against the Furies for inducement of Athenian goddess and jurors; Orestes made the same promise to Athena upon Apollo's instruction when he reached Athens, 289–91, and confirms it at 762 ff.

676–80 [The MSS attribution of 676–7 to the Furies and 679–80 to Apollo is reversed by many editors; and the best arguments for this change are that 676 then associates the metaphor of archery with the archer-god (n. to 179), and that the Furies remind the jurors of their oath (680) which Apollo had told them to override in obedience to Zeus, 620–1.]

679 *You have heard what you have heard*: imitating a closing formula of law-court speeches; cf. 710.

680 *strangers*: the form of address seems a little unnatural, since Apollo has just offered the Athenians everlasting alliance with Argos; but Apollo is perhaps maintaining a slight detachment; he uses the same address immediately before the votes are counted, 748.

683 *Aegeus*: mythical king of Athens, named here because his son Theseus (686) was regarded as the ultimate founder of Athenian democracy; cf. n. to 397–402.

685–90 The Areopagus (*Ares' rocky hill*): Aeschylus has apparently invented this origin for the hill's name (the usual version had the War-god Ares tried there by the other gods for murdering a son of Poseidon who had raped his daughter; Poseidon was another divine protector of Athens). To confirm Apollo's premonition that Orestes will escape the female Furies who persecute his murder of a man-killing mother, Aeschylus draws on the place's long mythic association with an unsuccessful attack by the female warrior Amazons, man-haters and man-killers. The Amazons were angry with Athenian Theseus because he helped Heracles take Ares' belt from them, and had himself taken away the Amazon princess Hippolyte; the Amazons would naturally sacrifice to Ares for success in the war. Aeschylus deliberately postpones the hill's name, although it was in long-standing and everyday use by his contemporaries, to sentence-end, to help emphasize the new significance of its homicide-court; for this technique of postponement see n. to *Ag.* 59. [*it shall have its seat* replaces an invasive gloss 'belonging to Ares', which was perhaps intended to help the reader grasp at once the sentence's direction.]

690–4 The allusions and apparent political message in these lines are much debated (see Introduction, p. xxxvii, cf. p. xix), but the overall intention is plain: Aeschylus identifies the essential power of the Areopagus Council as an inviolable and deterrent sanction against kindred feuding and murder, the severest risks to communal well-being (Athena at 857–63, the Furies at 976–83). *through evil infusions*: literally 'influxes', a metaphor for spoiling clauses 'flooding in'. [In 693 the MSS text is insecure at *make no innovation*, but the sense is almost certainly right.]

698–9 *all fear . . . if he fears nothing*: Aeschylus makes Athena praise deterrence, as the Furies had done at 517–25, just as in 696 she echoes their deprecation (526–30) of anarchy and despotism in favour of moderation. In this way Aeschylus begins to prepare for the accommodation of the terrifying Furies to Athenian self-discipline 700 ff. *see* Athena again at 881 ff., 956 ff.

701 *bulwark*: see n. to *LB* 152–6.

703 *Pelops' regions*: those in the eponymous Peloponnese ruled by the mythical Pelops, and especially Sparta, a Greek city as famous for its strict laws as were the barbarian and nomadic *Scythians* (c.g. Aeschylus, *Fragment* 198). Aeschylus may have forgotten that at *Ag.* 1600 and *LB* 503 he referred to Orestes' own family-line as the Pelopidae.

709 *take your votes for casting*: each juror had a single pebble, to cast either for condemnation or for acquittal.

711–33 In this tense exchange it seems likely that each of the eleven couplets accompanied successive voting by eleven jurors; see n. to 735.

715–16 *you concern yourself . . . pure of taint*: the Furies again taunt Apollo with polluting his own Delphi through his reception of the killer Orestes; cf. 162–71, 204–5.

717–18 *Ixion*: for his story see 441 and n. Aeschylus has the Furies mark the weakness of this precedent for Apollo's own purification of Orestes only with the laconic 719 'You say not'; the precedent would justify mercy towards Clytemnestra as much as Orestes.

723 *Pheres*: his son Admetus spared Apollo hardship when the god was in penitential 'human' servitude to him, and was rewarded when Apollo secured prolongation of his life if another person would die for him. Admetus' wife Alcestis volunteered, only to be rescued miraculously from Death by Heracles (this is the plot of Euripides' *Alcestis*). The Furies' accusation *make men immortal* is a tactical exaggeration, therefore; their point is that Apollo is again attempting to reverse the fated way of things (172).

728 *distracted . . . with wine*: Euripides at *Alcestis* 12 and 33–4 has just 'tricked'.

730 *vomiting . . . poison*: clotted blood, see n. to 802–3. *no heavy harm*: Apollo dismisses the Furies' word at 711 and 720, but Athena herself fears their threat to poison the land as 'heavy', 478, 800–1, cf. 830, 858–9.

731 *riding me down*: 150 and n.

735 *this vote of mine*: 'this' shows that Athena casts a vote into one of the urns before both are emptied (742) and counted; so her vote

makes the totals 'truly equal' (795) and she need not vote again to acquit Orestes (752–3)—although 'one vote' in 751 has been taken to imply this. In this interpretation Athena's vote in favour of Orestes is the twelfth cast after eleven citizen jurors vote individually during the eleven couplets (the last of them is actually a triplet) exchanged between Apollo and the Furies in 711–33; when the tallied votes prove equal at 753, Orestes goes free as Athena announced at 741 that he should. Many interpreters have taken Athena's vote here as her 'casting vote' as president, when an evenly divided number of jurors has produced a tie. For a full review of the question see Sommerstein, *Eumenides* (1989), 222–6; it seems unlikely that scholars will agree upon an answer.

737 *except for union with it*: it is hard to know the tone of this qualification, artfully placed by Aeschylus between *in everything* and *with all my heart*. Athena's antipathy to sex or marriage matches her sexless conception and birth (n. to 664–6); the phrase may be a simple allusion to the virginity of Athens' patron goddess, or an oblique one to her failed rape by the god Hephaestus; it may be intended as tactful moderation in front of the female Furies.

738 *I am very much my father's*: deliberately wide in meaning. Athena implicitly accepts Apollo's contention that only the father is the parent (658 ff.), predicated on her own birth (previous note); as Zeus' child she shares his blood therefore (cf. Orestes' argument at 606); she is on her father's side as a male (737) and as head of his house, as the murdered Agamemnon was head (740, cf. *Ag.* 1452; Orestes at *LB* 965); she is Zeus' adherent and supporter (826 ff., cf. 295–6 and n., 797); she shares his lightning (827–8) and his wisdom (850).

746 *noose:* suicide, the final victory for the Furies: 338, *LB* 295–6.

749 *with reverent care*: conformably with their 'respect' for their oath, 710.

750–1 *When good judgement's gone away, great harm happens*: another utterance in the informal style of a proverb, perhaps expressing Apollo's anxiety: see n. to *Ag.* 251–5. *a single vote*: see n. to 735. [*comes in*: the best conjecture available for MSS 'strikes (a house)', for it makes a neat contrast with *gone away* in 750 and also preserves MSS *house*, marked by West as corrupt.]

759–61 *the third, the Saviour*: Zeus, always third in libations (*Ag.* 246–7 and n.); *who accomplishes everything*: 974 and n. *from proper regard for a father's death*: reversing the context of *LB* 899, when Orestes falters in face of the matricide; cf. also *LB* 1 and n. *on seeing*: a surprisingly weak motive for Zeus' opposition to the Furies, unless it is meant to recall his ancient disgust with them (365–6, cf. 411 and n.). *advocates for my mother*: recalling 210, 268, etc. The words are a bitter coda from an Orestes at last free from the Furies' long persecution (cf. 238–40, 298).

762–74 Orestes fulfils on oath his promise of future alliance between his own and Athena's city, 289–91 (n.).

765 *helmsman*: 16 and n.

769–70 *in our tomb*: Aeschylus alludes to an age-old practice of burying great heroes, or siting memorials to them, close by potential invasion-routes or outside city-gates, to deter aggression. *bring . . . ill omens to their passage*: literally 'make their passage ill-birded'—the reverse of the eagle-omen afforded Agamemnon and Menelaus 'destined' on their road at Aulis, *Ag.* 104 ff.

774 *we are to be*: apparently a 'prophetic' present tense; cf. Calchas the seer at *Ag.* 126.

776 *your grip in wrestling:* a further such image; cf. Orestes at *LB* 498.

777 *s.d.: Orestes and Apollo leave*: some editors wonder whether a final speech from Apollo is lost here, since he otherwise makes no response to Orestes' acquittal; we have to infer his departure together with Orestes.

778–1047 (the end of the trilogy). This long and passion-filled sequence begins with an alternation between lyric stanzas of protest and threat from the Chorus of Furies and measured persuasion from Athena in short speeches (778–880; a comparable sequence in *Ag.* 1072–1177: Introduction, p. liii). The Furies' two stanzas are twice repeated exactly (778–93 = 808–23; 837–46 = 870–80), in order to convey unalterable resentment; for similar devices see n. to 307–96. Then comes a brief dialogue-scene (881–915); at 892–902 it includes brisk stichomythia when the Furies accept Athena's assurances, just as stichomythia carried their earlier acceptance of her jurisdiction (415–36). The acceptance given (916), both parties look to the Furies' future beneficent role at Athens; the Furies' lyric stanzas alternate now with Athena's chanted encouragement to her citizens (916–1020; see n. to 951–5). Then a short oration by Athena introduces the play's joyful lyric end, a singing procession which escorts the Furies from the theatre (1032–47).

778 = 808 *younger . . . ancient*: the Furies' charge against Apollo at 150; cf. also 731, 882. They now link Athena with Apollo: see Athena at 882–3.

785–7 = 815–17 *canker . . . blight*: destroying all fertility; the language recalls the bodily lesions inflicted by the Furies at *LB* 280–2, and the castration at *Eum.* 187–8 above.

789–91 = 819–21 [*what I suffer . . . is great*: this is only the probable sense of a badly corrupt text, much subject to conjecture.]

798 *the giver of the oracle himself . . . giver of the evidence*: the symmetry of expression and rhythm in this line gives distinct solemnity to Athena's persuasion; the style resembles that of ritual insistence, e.g. *Ag.* 1541 (n.).

802–3 *droplets . . . from your lungs*: the 'poison' of 730 and 783; it is blood, 137, 183–4. *spears which devour*: a violent (and textually suspect) metaphor for the imagined corrosive effect of spattered blood. Spear-points like sword-edges have mouths and 'bite', e.g. Homer, *Iliad* 15.389 etc.: *LB* 995.

806 *gleaming thrones*: anointed with oil, a common ritual tribute to sanctified stones ('thrones'). At 164 Apollo's Delphic altar drips not with oil but with the blood Orestes brings there. *altar-hearths*: 108 and n.

826 *I too have my trust—in Zeus*: Athena counters the Furies' appeal to 'Justice', 815. *and what need I say?*: Zeus is all-mighty (cf. Apollo at 621, Orestes at 759)—as the Furies come to admit, 918.

828 *keys . . . sealed*: the master of the house's goods secured from undetected theft, *Ag.* 610. Athena both stresses her unique closeness to Zeus (n. to 738) and threatens the Furies with destruction by him.

832 *your black anger in its bitter force*: their gall, cf. *LB* 183–4.

833 *you are to be honoured with awe*: her repeated assurance, 796, 807, 824, later e.g. 854, 868. *sharer of my home*: see n. to 1010.

835 *sacrifices made for children and for marriage's fulfilment*: wording reflecting the Athenian marriage-oath; cf. *Ag.* 1207.

849 [*Yet while . . . wiser than I*: the line in the MSS is deficient by a syllable, but this meaning was likely.]

855 *the temple of Erectheus*: the cult-site of the Furies as 'The Awesome Ones' was below the Areopagus; but here Aeschylus rather freely moves it to the northern side of the Athenian Acropolis, near this temple—that is, closer to the great protective deities of Athens; for Erectheus see n. to 13.

857 [*more than*: only a tiny correction to the MSS gives this sense, but some editors suppose the loss of at least one line.]

859–60 *whetstones for bloodshed*: an image of Fate's potential to destroy, *Ag.* 1536, *LB* 648. *rage unhelped by wine*: not the madness to kill born of simple drunkenness, but conceived against kin (cf. 863). The words may also imply 'rage which no wine (as poured to mark a truce) can still', or allude to the libations not compounded with wine which are offered to the Furies, 107 and n.

861 [*to excite*: an ancient commentator's paraphrase points to this ᴠᴀʀɪᴀᴛɪᴏɴ ᴏf ᴍᴏᴏ 'ᴛᴏ ʀᴇᴍᴏᴠᴇ'.]

866 *a bird's battling in its own home*: the petty squabbling of a vainglorious cockerel on its own dung-hill, the taunt hurled at Aegisthus at *Ag.* 1671. This second use of the cockerel-image in so few lines (see 861) is striking, and emphatically deprecates the Furies' threats of angry violence at 840–1.

869 *this land which the gods love most*: words endorsed by the Furies when they have accepted Athena's offer of sharing her home, 916–20.

885–6 *Persuasion*: an echo of Athena's 829; at 970 she will thank the goddess for her aid. For persuasion in the trilogy see Introduction, p. xxxvii. *winning way*: cf. 900, like those 'winning words' which Apollo promised Orestes during his trial, 81–2.

888 *weigh down*: like a balance-scale, n. to *Ag.* 250.

890 *settled holding*: Athena uses the technical term for land-ownership by full citizens—but see n. to 1010.

892 *Queen Athena*: the Furies' new and deferential address heralds Athena's victory over them. Contrast their initial plain 'Daughter of Zeus', 415, and compare Orestes' hopeful 'Queen Athena' of 235 (n.), 443.

899 *I may not say anything which I shall not fulfil*: reminiscent of Apollo's voicing only Zeus' commands, 616–17.

902 *invoke for this land*: the beneficent promises of which the Furies sing at 916 ff., to which Athena adds her solemn chant at 927 ff., 949 ff., etc.

904–5 *earth . . . sea . . . heaven . . . winds*: the elements of nature's world, hostile to the Greeks at Troy, *Ag.* 558–66, and dangerous to mankind generally, *LB* 585–93.

910 [*May you bring more to birth who are reverent*: this conjectural text and translation suit both 911–12, and the Furies' positive role as fosterers of fertility (924–6 and n.), better than the questionable tone of MSS 'bring more funerals of those who are irreverent'.]

913–15 *for this city and its people's victories*: compare Orestes' parting wish for Athens, 777.

918–20 *Ares*: named here because of the future importance of the Areopagus Council; cf. n. to 685–90.

922 *with kind intent*: the Furies now signal their change from hostility to favour; 939 also. See n. to 1041.

924–6 *good fortune . . . gleam*: the order of ideas is artful; general good fortune suddenly narrows into rich harvests, which the Furies can ensure no less than blight: 938–48, cf. 785–7.

928 *hard to placate*: they will retain their deterrent power, 951–5 and n., 990–5; cf. 518–19. Their integrity (cf. 312) will make them valuable allies for virtuous Athenians, 963–8, 984–8, 994–5.

930 *all that men do allotted them to manage*: cf. the Furies' own descriptions, 310, 334, 349.

931 [*have sinned overmuch* gives the sense generally agreed to be missing.]

935 *sins beginning with his ancestors*: the idea first expressed in the trilogy at *Ag.* 760 ff., cf. 1338, *LB* 329; Introduction, pp. xxxix f.

936 *Silent destruction*: in the lonely death of the polluted criminal, a social outcast hounded by the Furies *LB* 291–6. The goddess Ruin has soft footsteps in Homer, *Iliad* 19.91 ff.

944–5 *Pan . . . twin young*: the language recalls the opposite image of the vultures' young and the pregnant hare destroyed, at which the gods intervene, *Ag.* 55 ff., 119–44. *twin young* have always been a farmer's hope from his animals.

946–8 *the gods' gift of rain*: Zeus' bounty, *Ag.* 1014–17, 1391–2. [West's text is particularly adventurous in these lines, but gives the stanza a convincing end with the Furies' promise of fertility from rain for the field-crops. Most editors retain the different benefit offered by the MSS, unconfidently translated either as 'may the produce of the rich earth (or 'enriching the land') do honour to the gods' lucky (or 'profitable') gift' or as 'may generations in the rich land do honour to the gods' lucky gift', a supposed allusion to Athens' important silver-mines (*Persians* 238).]

950 *you guardians of the city*: addressed to the jurors as members of the Areopagus Council; cf. Athena at 700–6.

951–5 *The sovereign Furies . . . tears*: Athena's evocation of the Furies' powers increasingly emphasizes their capacity for benefit as well as harm (cf. nn. to 922, 924–6 above): she moves from deprecation of their vindictive anger 800 ff., 830 f., 858 ff., 888 ff. through promises of their new honour at Athens 833 ff., 854 f., 867 ff., 890 ff., 929 f., 1020 ff. to invitations of their blessing 903 ff., 989 ff., 1012—but she insists on their undiminished if differently directed power, 894 ff., 928 (see n.), 930 ff., 989 ff. The Furies carry the courteous title *sovereign* at *Seven* 887 and in other authors. *fulfilment*: see the Furies themselves at 320. *cause for singing*: a slight expansion, for clarity, of bare 'songs' in the Greek.

961–2 *the Fates, my mother's sisters*: sisters of Night, 322, 745, etc.

967 *to your lawful visitations*: the translation 'to lawful assemblies' is tempting; but this stanza evokes only family life, in which the Furies here claim a lawful role for their deterrence of kindred murder. It is the corresponding stanza 976–87 which deals with political life ('assemblies').

970 *Persuasion and her eye*: see n. to 885–6. A deity's watch is benevolent *Ag.* 520; more often it is stern, e.g. 220, 275, *Ag.* 947, *LB* 126.

974–5 *The power . . . was with Zeus*: Athens' reception of the Furies is also the resolution of the family feud which brought Orestes' presence in the city: this is the message of Zeus' total wisdom and providence heard first at *Ag.* 175–8; cf. Apollo at 616–21 above, the Furies at 918, 1046: Introduction, p. xxx. *Zeus the god of assemblies*: watching over debate in the communal interest; unspecified gods do this, *Ag.* 90, cf. 844–6. *our struggle for good wins out* recalls the refrain of the opening chorus of the *Agamemnon*, 121, 139, and 159, immediately before the 'Hymn to Zeus' at 160 ff.

980 *dust drinks . . . blood*: 647, recalling the irremediable life-taking of the family feud (262, 647–8, 653, *Ag.* 1018–21 and n.) but also reversing the Furies' own blood-thirst (264–6, *LB* 578, etc.); *black*: congealed after shedding, in the same image as *Ag.* 1020, *LB* 67.

981–3 [*from counter-killings . . . ruin*: the text is insecure in detail but the thought is clear.]

992 *goodwill towards goodwill*: a mild echo of the Furies' own recognition that Athena respects them, 435; cf. 1012.

996–7, 1014 *Greetings . . . people of Athens*: this first direct salutation to Athens' people marks the Furies' final acceptance of their new home and role; so Athena formally returns their greeting on behalf of her city at 1003. Some translate the salutation as 'Farewell, farewell!', as if the Furies are already moving away; but this will not suit Athena's matching response in 1003 (where she is to precede them as they leave the scene).

999–1000 *hard by*: evocatively archaic phrasing; see n. to *Ag.* 115–16. *wise amid surfeit*: unlike those who abuse such surfeit of riches, and doom themselves; this is another echo from *Ag.* 381–4, cf. 750–6. [*amid surfeit* is West's bold replacement of MSS 'in time', weak in this context.]

1002 *due respect from her father*: Zeus and daughter together inaugurate the system of justice at Athens which links god and man (1015–19, cf. 795–8) and wins the city divine respect (1045–6 in confirmation of 917–20). Cf. also *LB* 949–51 for Justice as Zeus' daughter.

1004–6 *these escorts*: apparently the jurors are to escort the Furies, 1010. When they entered at 566, they were not then holding torches (which are first mentioned here, *holy flame-light*), so that either 'light' here is allusive and prospective (cf. Athena at 1022, 1029) or, less probably, torches are brought on by extras together with sacrificial animals (the strict meaning of the word translated *sacrifices*) in order to augment the procession. Torches are however carried by the secondary Chorus which now begins entering: see 1042, 1044.

Torches are to accompany the Furies for a number of reasons: they are appropriate to a human procession about to enter an underground holy place (1036); they are regular in ritual, by day or night, in symbolizing light, hope, and joy, but particularly in the ritual which honours underworld powers; the future ceremonial honouring the Furies there will constantly employ them (1044); torches are themselves emblematic of the Furies, one of their weapons being fire (138).

1010 *settlers in our home*: the Furies seen as 'metics', coming to share (Greek *met-*) house and home (Greek *-oik*) in Athens; again at 1018, cf. 833 (Athena) and 916 'I will accept a home with Pallas'; the word also at *Ag.* 57, *LB* 684. In real life such immigrants acquired no full rights as citizens and could not own land; but the Furies acquire not only a permanent home but also permanent and special tokens of worship, 1028–9, 1032 ff. Metics needed also a citizen sponsor: Athena acts as a surrogate sponsor for the Furies (804 ff., 854–5, etc.) before she urges the citizen jurors to accept them, 992–5. Like the Furies in Athena's hopes, metics brought benefits to their hosts, at Athens chiefly through manufacturing and trade.

1011 *children of Cranaos*: another early king of Athens; his name means 'rocky', an obvious name-formation for a ruler of the craggy Acropolis.

1012 *goodness to answer their goodness*: Athena pointedly repeats her wish of 992; cf. also her 868, 1030.

1025 *eye*: for this metaphor for someone important and precious cf. *LB* 934, Orestes as the eye of his house, the guarantor of its future as the children and wives here are to be for that of Athens (cf. 958–60, 1030–1).

1028–9 *red-dyed clothing*: a ritual and ceremonial colour. [Some text is missing; some editors suppose the loss to be before 1028, so that the clothing belongs rather to the Furies; and indeed it would be effective and appropriate for the black-clad Furies to change to red either on stage or prospectively, since this was the colour worn at ceremonies by metics (as the Furies are, 1010 and n.). Others suggest that the missing lines contained a reference to the renaming of the Furies as 'The Kindly Ones': see n. to 1041]

1030–1 *this company for the land . . . its goodwill*: a pointed reversal of the Furies' self-description 'company heavy on this land', 711 (cf. Athena at 406); their presence becomes beneficially 'weighty', 965. *fortune of noble manhood*: 958–60, 1031.

1032–47 [West accepts a hint in the ancient commentary that this concluding secondary chorus comprised Athena's ritual women attendants mentioned in 1024. The MSS name the members simply as 'chorus', while the List of Characters has them as 'processional escorts'.]

1033 *children—not children!*: the allusion is that of 68–9 'maidens in old age, ancient children'.

1037 *may you receive high respect*: cf. 1032 'honour-loving'; one last reassurance for the Furies of their future status; see n. to 951–5.

1040 *straight intentions*: the Furies claimed to be 'straight in their justice', 312.

1041 *Awesome Ones*: a title alluded to by the Furies in self-reference at 383. This euphemistic title at the trilogy's end registers their new beneficent role as the Eumenides ('The Kindly Ones') and is as near as the play comes to giving them the name which it bears itself (the *hypothesis* by Aristophanes of Byzantium, translated at the start of the Explanatory Notes on the play, implies that Athena renamed the Furies during it; some editors think that this may have been done in the passage missing after 1028: n.). Athena calls them 'sovereign Furies' at 951. They appear in the *Oresteia* first as punishers of any wrong-doing (*Ag.* 59 and n.; Introduction, §2.3, n. 17) and then as spirits avenging the dead: they are 'Curses' *LB* 406, *Eum.* 417, cf. *LB* 692; 'Retributions' *LB* 947, *Eum.* 323; 'Fates' *LB* 306 and n., cf. nn. to 173, 961–2 above. Cf. also n. to 69 above.

1046 *Zeus the all-seeing and Fate . . . together*: a last emphasis on the combination of powers directing the whole story: Zeus *Ag.* 62, 160 ff., etc., Fate 129 etc; cf. n. to 974–5. *come down . . . to support*: to fight on their side, as allies: the image is that of *LB* 727.

   s.d.: those given are only one possible way of performing the end of the trilogy. The spectacular massing of persons for a final exit is unusual in surviving Tragedy, but Aeschylus fills the scene with a secondary chorus also at the end of *Suppliants*, 1034 ff.

Textual Appendix

A list of conjectural readings taken from West's *apparatus* to replace words which he retains in his edited text but marks as corrupt, and of other differences.

AGAMEMNON

7 'I mark them closely', τηρῶν Campbell for †ἄστερας†

50–1 'extreme' ἐκπάγλοις Blomfield for ἐκπατίοις; 'high above their nests' †ὕπατοι† λεχέων hesitantly retained.

70 after 'libation' the words οὔτε †δακρύων† 'nor of tears' are omitted (Bamberger)

304 'no delay in', μὴ χρονίζεσθαι Casaubon for †μὴ χαρίζεσθαι†

374–5 'destruction is shown exacting its price for their audacity', πέφανται δ' ἐκτίνουσα τόλμαν τῶν ἀρή Hartung, West for πέφανται δ' †ἐγγόνους ἀτολμήτων ἄρη†

433 '[The land]', γαῖα δ', supplemented by West

478 'it is really', ἐστι δὴ Karsten for †ἐστιν μὴ†

539 'my death', τὸ τεθνάναι Schneidewin for †τεθνάναι†

597 'lulling', †κοιμῶντες†, retained

665 'to prevent mooring', ἄνορμον Bothe for †ἐν ὅρμωι†

913 'done', εἰργασμένα Karsten for †εἰμαρμένα†

985 'the sand flying upward', ψάμμος ἄμπτα Wecklein, Wilamowitz for †ψαμμίας ἀκάτα†

1001 'great health as a condition is truly insatiable' seems to be the approximate sense underlying †τᾶς πολλᾶς ὑγιείας ἀκόρεστον†

1091 'carving like meat', κρεατόμα Weil for †κἀρτάναι†

1092 'floor sprinkled with blood' is the sense approximately suggested by †πεδορραντήριον† (πέδον ῥαντήριον a correcting hand in the principal MS)

1216 'stormy', δυσχειμέροις Campbell for †ἐφημένους† duplicated from the end of 1217

1343 both 'deep', †ἔσωτ, and 'blow', †πληγὴντ, retained; but the translation is insecure

1377–8 'long ago', †πάλαιτ, retained, with 'victory (has come) in fulfilment', νίκη τέλειος Wilamowitz for †νίκης παλαιᾶςτ

1388 'after his fall', †πεσόντ, retained

1447 ηὐνή West for †εὐνῆςτ

1479 'afflicts it . . . fostered . . .', τείρει (followed by a stop) τρέφεται Margoliouth for †νείρειτ τρέφεται (followed by a stop).

1481 'for this house' translates literally †οἴκοις τοῖσδετ, which is unmetrical

1526–7 '. . . Iphigenia, [her father sacrificed]', Ἰφιγένειαν ἔθυσε πατήρ Wilamowitz for †τ' Ἰφιγένειαντ

1595–6 'at a distance', ἄπωθεν Fuhr for †ἄνωθεν (ἀνδρακὰς καθημένος ἄσημα)τ. A line of text may be lost before the word, and the translation gives only the general sense.

1658 the word καιρόν, '(?) right moment', directly after '*(words missing)*' is not translated

LIBATION BEARERS

129 'to the dead', φθιτοῖς Herwerden for †βροτοῖςτ

145 'before those whose concern it may be', τοῖσπερ ἂν μέληι Mazon for †τῆς κακῆς ἀρᾶςτ, a doubling of the end of 146

206 'the feet equally like mine' translates a little freely ποδῶν [δ'] Turnebus ὁμοίως Weil τοῖς γ' Scholiast for †ποδῶν δ' ὁμοῖοιτ τοῖς τ'

361 'holding', πιπάλλων Wilamowitz for †πιμπλάντωντ

386 'piercing' †πευκήεντ'τ hesitantly retained, in this apparent sense

406 'you . . . (Curses) of the slain', ⟨ὦ⟩ φθιμένων (Ἀραί) Wellauer for (Ἀραί) †φθειμένωντ

417 'to give expectation', προσδοκᾶν τι West for †πρὸς τὸ φανεῖσθαιτ

544 'and was wrapped in my own swaddling', ἐμοῖσι σπαργάνοις Turnebus/Porson εἱλίσσετο Faehse for †ἐπᾶσασπαργανηπλείζετοτ

628 'a man who had his enemies' respect' is freely based upon the Scholiast's paraphrase ἐπ' ἀνδρὶ φοβερῶι καὶ σεβαστῶι καὶ παρὰ τοῖς πολεμίοις for †ἐπ' ἀνδρὶ δηΐοισ ἐπικότω σέβαστ

664 'in charge', γ' ἄπαρχος Ahrens for †ταπαρχοςτ

785 'grant good fortune and success lasting and sure for this house' is loosely based upon the Scholiast's paraphrase δός μοι εὐτυχίαν

εὐτυχῆσαι βεβαίως, and the separate suggestions δόμου Bothe κυρίους Musgrave, for δὸς †τύχας τυχεῖν δὲ μου κυρίως τὰ σωφροσυνευ†

799 'his feet . . . straight' approximates to εὐθὺ ποδῶν West for †βημάτων†

875 'struck down' πεπληγμένου Schütz for †τελουμένου†

958 'in everything, refusing', παρὰ ⟨πᾶν⟩, τὸ μή θ' West for †παρὰ τὸ μή†

969–70 'seen in everything . . . in glory', κατὰ πάντ' ἰδεῖν, κλυταί, West for †κοίται τὸ πᾶν ἰδεῖν ἀκοῦσαι†

EUMENIDES

92–3 'when they are sped', ὁρμωμένων Blaydes for ὁρμώμενον.

119 'no friends of mine', φίλοι . . . οὐκ ἐμοὶ Schütz for †φίλοις . . . οὐκ ἐμοῖς†

177 'he is to go where', εἶσιν οὗ Kirchhoff for †ἐκείνου†

258 'himself . . . no,' αὐτὸς οὐκ Auratus for †ταῦτε γοῦν†

277 'the moments for many things' is based upon πολλῶν τε καιρὸς Blass and others for †πολλοὺς καθαρμούς,† and upon the Scholiast's paraphrase of 277–8

352 'no part in, no share', ἄκληρος, ἄμοιρος Drake for †ἄμοιρος† ἄκληρος

358 'however (strong he is) and enfeeble him, draining youth's blood' gives the sense apparently underlying κράτερον ὄνθ' †ὁμοίως μαυροῦμεν ὑφ' αἵματος νέου† (in which the metre too is not recoverable)

387 'on a path hard and rocky' "translates" †δυσοδοπαίπαλα†

481 'bring harsh pain', δυσπήμαντ' Scaliger for †δυσπήματ'†

567 'And . . . the Etruscan trumpet which pierces [to the heaven]', ἥ τ' (West: εἶτ') οὐρανόνδε διάτορος Τυρσηνικὴ Tournier for ἥ τ' †οὖν† διάτορος Τυρσηνικὴ

573 'as well as these parties', τοῦσδ' Hermann for τῶνδ'

638 'it is the ending', ταύτην τελευτὴν Butler for †ταύτην τοιαύτην†

652 'for . . . acquittal', τἀποφεύγειν Dittenberger for †γὰρ τὸ φεύγειν†

685 'it shall have its seat', ἑδεῖται Wecklein for † Ἄρειον†

693 'make no innovation', μὴ 'πικαινούντων Stephanus for μὴ †'πικαινόντων†

751 'comes in . . . house', μολοῦσα δ'(Portus) οἶκον Blass for †βαλοῦσά τ' οἶκον†

789–91 = 819–21 'what I suffer from the citizens is hard to bear. Oh, your ruin is great' may be the approximate sense underlying †δύσοιστα πολίταις ἔπαθον. ἰὼ μεγάλατοι†

849 'Yet while there are things in which', καίτοι ⟨τὰ⟩ μὲν Hermann for †καίτοι μὲν†

857 ὅσ' ἂν Ahrens, general in sense, 'more (things)' for †οσην† 'more (Feminine, but without a noun)'

861 'excite . . . like (fighting-cocks)', ἐξάγουσ' ὡς Burges for †ἐξελοῦσ' ὡς†

1033 'go to your house', βᾶτε δόμον Hermann for βᾶτ' †ἐν δόμωι†

The Oxford World's Classics Website

www.worldsclassics.co.uk

- Information about new titles
- Explore the full range of Oxford World's Classics
- Links to other literary sites and the main OUP webpage
- Imaginative competitions, with bookish prizes
- Peruse the Oxford World's Classics Magazine
- Articles by editors
- Extracts from Introductions
- A forum for discussion and feedback on the series
- Special information for teachers and lecturers

www.worldsclassics.co.uk

American Literature

British and Irish Literature

Children's Literature

Classics and Ancient Literature

Colonial Literature

Eastern Literature

European Literature

History

Medieval Literature

Oxford English Drama

Poetry

Philosophy

Politics

Religion

The Oxford Shakespeare

A complete list of Oxford Paperbacks, including Oxford World's Classics, Oxford Shakespeare, Oxford Drama, and Oxford Paperback Reference, is available in the UK from the Academic Division Publicity Department, Oxford University Press, Great Clarendon Street, Oxford OX2 6DP.

In the USA, complete lists are available from the Paperbacks Marketing Manager, Oxford University Press, 198 Madison Avenue, New York, NY 10016.

Oxford Paperbacks are available from all good bookshops. In case of difficulty, customers in the UK can order direct from Oxford University Press Bookshop, Freepost, 116 High Street, Oxford OX1 4BR, enclosing full payment. Please add 10 per cent of published price for postage and packing.